America's TOP MILITARY CAREERS

Fourth Edition

Official Guide to Occupations in the Armed Forces

- ★ **Official career information resource for the military world of work**
- ★ **Detailed coverage of opportunities with the nation's largest employer**
- ★ **Complete reprint of *Military Careers: A Guide to Military Occupations* as produced by the U.S. Department of Defense**

Part of America's Top Jobs® Series

Works
America's Career Publisher

U.S. Department of Defense

America's Top Military Careers, *Fourth Edition*
Official Guide to Occupations in the Armed Forces

© 2004 by JIST Publishing, Inc.

Published by JIST Works, an imprint of JIST Publishing, Inc.
8902 Otis Avenue
Indianapolis, IN 46216-1033

Phone: 1-800-648-JIST   Fax: 1-800-JIST-FAX
E-mail: info@jist.com   Web site: www.jist.com

Visit our Web site at www.jist.com for information on JIST, free job search information, book excerpts, and ordering information on our many products. For free information on 14,000 job titles, visit www.careeroink.com.

Other Books in JIST's America's Top Jobs® Series

America's Top 300 Jobs
America's 101 Fastest Growing Jobs
America's Top 101 Jobs for People Without a Four-Year Degree
America's Top 101 Jobs for College Graduates

America's Top 101 Computer and Technical Jobs
Career Guide to America's Top Industries
America's Top Resumes for America's Top Jobs

Quantity discounts are available for JIST books. Please call our sales department at 1-800-648-JIST for a free catalog and more information.

Printed in Canada

08 07 06 05 04 03   9 8 7 6 5 4 3 2 1

ISBN 1-59357-001-5

About This Book

America's Top Military Careers is an ideal starting point for learning more about the types of jobs available in the military. This resource by the U.S. Department of Defense covers 140 enlisted and officer occupations for five service branches—the Army, Navy, Air Force, Marine Corps, and Coast Guard.

Enlisted members serve in diverse roles, from computer systems specialists to medical care technicians to infantry. They carry out and maintain the basic operations of the military. Officers lead and manage activities in every occupational specialty in the military.

America's Top Military Careers describes the type of work performed, training, employment, and advancement opportunities. See pages 6–7 for details on how to read the job descriptions.

Getting Started Is Easy

A good way to become familiar with the book is to browse through the Table of Contents. Identify job groups that interest you. Then go to those sections and determine whether the corresponding jobs appeal to you.

You may also want to look at the indices, which give occupational listings using job titles from civilian career exploration resources.

Foreword

The Department of Defense recruits and trains approximately 200,000 enlisted members and officers each year, making it one of the largest employers in the U.S. This book has been developed to help educators and youth learn about the many career opportunities the military has to offer. The book is a compendium of military occupational, training, and career information and is designed for use by students desiring to explore the military world of work. The document is an important career information resource that is part of the Armed Services Vocational Aptitude Battery (ASVAB) Career Exploration Program. This program assists individuals in understanding their aptitudes, interests, and personal preferences and matching these characteristics to civilian and military occupations.

This book is a single reference source for educators and students to use for learning about the diverse opportunities available to young people in the military. This publication contains descriptions of 140 enlisted and officer occupations. Students who have taken the ASVAB can use their scores to estimate their chances of qualifying for enlisted occupations based on their aptitudes.

Many individuals contributed to the development and production of this book. Specifically, we wish to thank Ms. Denise Lawson, Dr. Jan Bayer, Ms. Signe George, Mr. Stephen Reardon, Ms. Andrea Sharples, Mr. Michael Tedeschi, Mr. Kent Willard, and Ms. Dana Pao of Booz Allen and Hamilton Inc. Their contributions are most appreciated.

Various members of the Department of Defense have contributed to this publication, particularly members of the Defense Manpower Data Center (DMDC) in Seaside, California. Dr. Harley Baker conducted the analyses supporting the new Military Careers Score and the resulting graphs for the enlisted occupations, and edited the final document. Mr. Randy Marks designed the original cover and assisted in preparing the document for publication. Members of the Manpower Accession Policy Working Group helped to gather service-specific information and reviewed the contents for accuracy and currency. The Directorate for Accession Policy, Office of the Assistant Secretary for Defense (Force Management Policy), headed by Dr. W. S. Selman, provided policy oversight for the program.

Finally, the project was directed by Dr. John Welsh, DMDC, Testing Division, Seaside, CA. His guidance and leadership were instrumental in the quality, accuracy, and utility of this book.

Alphonso Maldon, Jr.
Assistant Secretary of Defense
(Force Management Policy)

Table of Contents

Introduction to
Military Careers

Introduction to Military Careers

Your future. It's coming just ahead. One of the important decisions you will need to make concerning your future is what type of career you want to enter. In today's world, where there are hundreds of occupations to choose from, it is important to spend some time investigating different occupations that you might be interested in pursuing. Career information resources are a good place to start because they contain detailed descriptions of occupations, including the type of duties performed, amount of education/training required, career advancement opportunities, and working conditions.

Military Careers is the leading career information resource for the military. It contains information about the type of work performed, as well as employment, training, and career advancement opportunities for Army, Navy, Air Force, Marine Corps, and Coast Guard occupations. Moreover, it provides information about similarities between military and civilian jobs. Many occupations that exist in the civilian job market are also available in the military. In addition to the combat oriented jobs that may come to mind when someone mentions the military, the services offer opportunities in many fields such as aircraft maintenance, health care, and transportation. *Military Careers* is a good starting point for learning more about the types of jobs available in the military and an important part of the career exploration process.

Military Careers is organized into two main sections:

• Enlisted Occupations

• Officer Occupations

The enlisted occupations section on pages 11–190 provides general information and descriptions of 81 enlisted occupations. Enlisted personnel carry out the fundamental operations of the military. They are people like finance and accounting specialists, infantry, avionics technicians, computer systems specialists, medical laboratory technicians, photographic specialists, and transportation specialists. Enlisted personnel are usually high school graduates and are required to meet established physical and aptitude standards before enlisting.

The officer occupations section on pages 191–329 provides general information and descriptions of 59 officer occupations. Officers are the leaders of the military and usually are college graduates. Their roles are like those of corporate managers or executives. Officers develop plans, set goals, and direct the efforts of other military personnel in meeting established objectives. Young men and women hoping to become officers must meet the minimum entrance requirements set by each military service.

Both the enlisted and officer sections of the book are organized so that similar occupations are grouped together in job families. Within the job families of each section, you will also find career paths and profiles for selected occupations. The sample paths show an example of the progression of a 20-year career in that particular occupation. The profiles summarize the career experience of actual servicemembers.

EXPLORING CAREERS

"What do I want to do for a living?" Choosing a career can be very confusing, especially for someone just coming out of high school. You have your whole life ahead of you. After you graduate from high school, you can get a job immediately, or you can seek additional training and education to help prepare you for the world of work. Your friends or relatives may have suggested vocational or on-the-job training, or you may want to attend college. Although making this first decision is a major step in the lifelong process of developing a career, it will not be the last.

Some people believe that once they have decided which occupation to enter, they will follow it for the rest of their lives. That is not necessarily true. People and jobs change over time. For example, people reevaluate their careers because their interests and values change, because new technology alters the skills necessary for a certain career, or because of changing economic factors.

You may now be asking yourself, "But how do I go about exploring what careers might be best for me?" There are two basic steps to career exploration:

• Learning about yourself

• Learning about careers

The following paragraphs explain how to go about career exploration using this two-step process.

LEARNING ABOUT YOURSELF

The first step is to spend some time finding out about yourself. Your interests, values, and abilities are important in making career plans. They help you think about what you might want in a career and what you are likely to enjoy. Your counselor can help you begin to clarify your interests, values, and abilities and may also be able to give you tests that measure interests and abilities.

An important resource for learning more about yourself is *Exploring Careers: The ASVAB Workbook.* Copies of this book are available to all students who have taken the Armed Services Vocational Aptitude Battery (ASVAB). Ask your counselor for details on the ASVAB and on obtaining a copy of the Workbook. Below are some things for you to consider when learning about yourself.

Interests

What do you enjoy doing or would you like to do? Do you like to work on car engines? Perhaps you enjoy writing stories or drawing pictures. Do you prefer to work by yourself or as part of a team? Exploring your interests is helpful at the beginning of the career planning process; knowing your interests will help you identify careers to investigate.

Your interests are also important to your career development and enjoyment of life. Working in an occupation that interests you makes it easier to work harder and advance in a career. One way to learn more about your interests is to take an "interest inventory" which measures interest in the following types of activities:

- **Realistic:** Activities that allow you to work with your hands and involve using machines, tools, and equipment.

- **Investigative:** Activities that involve learning about a new subject area or allow you to use your knowledge to solve problems or create things or ideas.

- **Artistic:** Activities that allow you to write, paint, play a musical instrument, or use your imagination to do original work.

- **Social:** Activities that allow you to use your skills to interact effectively with others and involve working with and helping others.

- **Enterprising:** Activities that allow you to take a leadership role or speak in front of groups, such as those that require that you take on a lot of responsibility.

- **Conventional:** Activities that allow you to use organizational, clerical, and arithmetic skills and require attention to detail or accuracy.

Knowing your primary interest areas can help you determine a career field or occupation that is best suited for you. *Exploring Careers: The ASVAB Workbook* contains such an inventory, the *Interest-Finder*™. [1]

---

[1] The *Interest-Finder*™ is a trademark of the U.S. Department of Defense.

Values

What do you consider most important or desirable in life? We all place a high value on having food to eat and a place to sleep. We also have values that affect what we want from our jobs. Some people want careers that pay high salaries almost immediately, even if the work is not very interesting. Others are willing to accept careers with lower wages if the work is challenging and exciting. Many consider having flexible hours or opportunities to travel very important. Some people value having time to pursue non-work-related interests such as being with their families. Understanding what you value is important in planning your future.

The following list provides some specific values that may be important to you:

- Challenge
- Creativity
- Helping Others
- Income
- Independence
- Outdoor Work
- Prestige
- Public Contact
- Security
- Variety
- Working in a Group
- Little Physical Activity
- Physically Challenging Activity

An occupation may satisfy one or several of these work values. *Exploring Careers: The ASVAB Workbook* has several exercises that further explain these work values and can help you clarify them.

Abilities

Abilities are those things that you are able to do, or have a natural talent for, even if you have never had any training in those areas. What do you do well? Are there school subjects in which you get particularly good grades? Are you physically strong and well-coordinated? Can you communicate well with others? Your abilities can help you find occupations in which you may have a successful career. But, just because you do not have the abilities for a certain occupation now does not mean that you cannot acquire them. Additional courses and training may help you to develop your abilities.

Also, it is possible that your interests and abilities may not always match. People are usually interested in things they do well, but this is not always the case. For example, you may be interested in becoming an electronics technician but may not have the manual dexterity to make the precise adjustments needed to keep electronic equipment functioning. However, with additional training, you may acquire the skills needed to become an electrical engineer or a computer programmer who helps to design electronic equipment.

Each year, many high school students take the ASVAB. The ASVAB is a test that measures a person's academic and occupational abilities. ASVAB scores, combined with information about your interests, achievements, values, and other test results, may help you select appropriate areas for career exploration in the military.

Exploring Careers: The ASVAB Workbook will help you develop the necessary skills for learning more about yourself. It can help you identify your interests, clarify what is important to you, and better understand your abilities. You can use these skills again and again as you explore different career opportunities.

LEARNING ABOUT CAREERS

Next, you will need to take the information you have learned about yourself and compare it to information about different occupations.

While learning about various careers, you need to be constantly asking yourself, "How well does this career match my current interests, values, and abilities?" and "Will this career lead to a lifestyle I want?" Other questions you might want to ask are:

- What do people do in this career?

- In what type of environment do people in this career work?

- What kind and how much training is needed to enter this career?

- What are the opportunities for obtaining work in this career?

Chances for a rewarding career are improved if you select a career field that matches your interests, values, and aptitudes.

Before reading about opportunities in *Military Careers*, make sure you read the next section, "How to Read the Occupational Descriptions."

How to Read the Occupational Descriptions

Each of the occupational descriptions in this book gives a summary of similar jobs across two or more of the military services. Therefore, individual job specialties across the services will differ somewhat from the general occupations described in this book. If you are interested in learning more about a particular service or occupation, you should contact a recruiter for details.

① Occupational Title: Contains the name of the military occupation.

② Military Service Representation: Lists service branches that offer employment and training opportunities in the occupation. Not all services offer every occupation described in *Military Careers.*

③ Summary: Provides background information about the military occupation.

④ What They Do: Describes the major work activities performed by workers in the occupation.

⑤ Physical Demands: Identifies certain physical abilities, such as strength, swimming, climbing, and acute vision or hearing which are required in the occupation.

⑥ Special Requirements: Lists special abilities required for the occupation, such as fluency in a foreign language. This section also identifies certain combat occupations from which women are excluded by law at the time of this publication.

⑦ Training Provided: Lists the preparation that is given for people training in the occupation.

⑧ Work Environment: Describes typical work settings and conditions, such as indoors or outdoors, on land, aboard ships, or in aircraft.

⑨ Helpful Attributes: Includes interests, experience, school subjects taken, and other personal characteristics that may be helpful for working in this occupation.

⑩ Civilian Counterparts: Lists similar occupations that are found in the civilian world of work.

⑪ Opportunities: Provides information on the total number of personnel across all services working in the occupation in 1998 and a summary of military career advancement.

---

① INFANTRY ② Army / Marine Corps

③ The infantry is the main land combat force of the military. In peacetime, the infantry's role is to stay ready to defend our country. In combat, the role of the infantry is to capture or destroy enemy ground forces and repel enemy attacks. The infantry operate weapons and equipment to engage and destroy enemy ground forces.

④ What They Do

Infantry perform some or all of the following duties:

- Set up camouflage and other protective barriers
- Operate, clean, and store automatic weapons, such as rifles and machine guns
- Parachute from troop transport airplanes while carrying weapons and supplies
- Carry out scouting missions to spot enemy troop movements and gun locations
- Operate communications and signal equipment to receive and relay battle orders
- Drive vehicles mounted with machine guns or small missiles
- Perform hand-to-hand combat drills that involve martial arts tactics
- Dig foxholes, trenches, and bunkers for protection against attacks

⑤ Physical Demands

The infantry has very demanding physical requirements. Infantry personnel must perform strenuous physical activities, such as marching while carrying equipment, digging foxholes, and climbing over obstacles. They also need good hearing and clear speech to use two-way radios, and good night vision and depth perception to see targets and signals.

⑥ Special Requirements

This occupation is open only to men.

⑦ Training Provided

Infantry training starts with basic training of about 7 or 8 weeks. Advanced training in infantry skills lasts for another 8 weeks. While some of the training is in the classroom, most is in the field under simulated combat conditions. In reality, training for an infantry soldier never stops. Infantry soldiers keep their skills sharp through frequent squad maneuvers, target practice, and war games. War games conducted without live ammunition allow soldiers to practice scouting, troop movement, surprise attack, and capturing techniques.

⑧ Work Environment

Because the infantry must be prepared to go anywhere in the world they are needed, they work and train in all climates and weather conditions. During training exercises, as in real combat, troops work, eat, and sleep outdoors. Most of the time, however, they work on military bases.

⑨ Helpful Attributes

Helpful attributes include:

- Readiness to accept a challenge and face danger
- Ability to stay in top physical condition
- Interest in working as a member of a team

⑩ Civilian Counterparts

Although the job of infantrymen has no equivalent in civilian life, the close teamwork, discipline, and leadership experiences it provides are helpful in many civilian jobs.

⑪ Opportunities

The military has about 68,000 personnel in infantry positions. Each year, the services need new infantrymen due to changes in personnel and the demands of the field. Leadership ability and job performance are the main factors for advancement in the infantry. Those who have the ability to motivate, train, and supervise others assume greater responsibility.

---

⑫ MILITARY CAREERS SCORE

The circled score shows the typical Military Careers Score of servicemembers in this occupation.

1　2　**③**　4　5　6　7

Compare this score to your Military Career Score to see how well your aptitudes, skills, and abilities match those of personnel currently in these positions. See your recruiter for more information about qualification requirements.

⑬ INTEREST CODE

This occupation generally appeals to people whose primary Interest Code is *Realistic. Realistic* jobs:

- Allow you to work with your hands
- Let you see the results of your work
- Involve using machines, tools, and equipment

Pages 8 and 9 explain the Military Careers Score and the Interest Codes

70

12 **Military Careers Score:** Shows the typical Military Careers Scores of servicemembers in this occupation. The Military Careers Score is explained on pages 8 and 9. These scores are shown for enlisted occupations only. They do not apply to officer occupations.

13 **Interest Code:** Shows the interest code most often associated with this occupation – Realistic, Investigative, Artistic, Social, Enterprising, or Conventional. The Interest Code is explained on page 9.

Career Paths and Profiles

Some of the occupational descriptions in *Military Careers* are accompanied by a *profile* and a *sample career path*.

14 The profile describes the duties and assignments of an actual servicemember during his or her career. Because each individual's career path is unique and spans many years, some assignments will not be typical or representative of current policy or circumstances. However, these profiles portray an example of what your career could look like if you chose that particular military occupation. Some names in the profiles have been changed for privacy or security reasons.

15 The sample career paths outline the career progression or advancement for that occupation, from entry level to supervisor. A description of the typical duties is provided for each level. Because job specialties may differ among the services, some of the job titles and duties listed may not apply to all services.

The years shown next to each level indicate the average number of years a servicemember spends in the military before advancing to that level. The time for each individual career will differ according to that person's performance and the needs of the specific military service. It is important to remember that only qualified individuals are promoted to each level.

SAMPLE CAREER PATH **15**

Company/Battalion Sergeant   17–20 years

Company/battalion sergeants direct the several platoons that make up an infantry company or battalion. They help decide how and when troops and equipment will be used. Company/battalion sergeants supervise the operation of the unit command post and prepare situation briefings, combat orders, and other reports. They also plan and conduct training programs.

Platoon Sergeant   7–8 years

Platoon sergeants supervise platoons, which consist of several squads. They receive and give combat or training exercise orders and help develop battle plans. Sergeants also coordinate the movement of troops, supplies, and weapons.

Squad or Fire Team Leader   3–4 years

Squad or fire team leaders command small groups of soldiers in combat or training exercises. They coordinate the collection of information about the enemy and read maps and photographs taken from aircraft to locate enemy forces. Squad leaders also motivate and give on-the-job training to new troops.

Infantryman

Infantry personnel train and take part in all aspects of combat exercises. They fire and maintain rifles, machine guns, and other weapons. They also drive trucks to transport troops, weapons, and supplies.

The years shown represent typical time-in-service before advancement to that level. Actual career advancement depends on individual experience and performance.

14 **Profile: Justin Glymph**

Justin Glymph grew up in inner city New York where he successfully avoided gang involvement and excelled in academics. Justin knew that he wanted more out of life than what he saw in his own neighborhood. While in his second year of high school, Justin passed the high school equivalency exam and went to work at a nearby electronics assembly plant where he quickly rose to a plant supervisory position. However, Justin did not see the future that he wanted in that role. On a career research trip to the local military recruiting office, he found what he was searching for. On that particular day, he witnessed an incident that served to focus his determination and direction. An obviously intoxicated individual stormed into the recruiting office making demands and threats. Justin was very impressed with the way a Marine sergeant resolved the situation with confidence and professionalism. At that moment, Justin decided that he wanted to join the Marine Corps. Initially, he was not accepted because of a hernia. In his determination to become a Marine, Justin endured a hernia operation and a 6 month recovery period, after which, the Marine Corps accepted him.

After completing the rigorous recruit training at Camp Pendleton in California, Justin performed security duties at a munitions storage site in Earle, New Jersey. Subsequently, he accompanied his battalion to the island of Grenada in the Caribbean. Their mission was to rescue a group of American students who were being held by an armed force and help to restore democracy to the island nation. Justin came away from that operation with a great sense of accomplishment. Of that experience, he says "I felt so honored when people lined the streets and cheered after we helped them regain democratic freedoms…we made a difference." The battalion then immediately departed for Beirut, Lebanon to perform peace keeping duties in a time of political unrest. Since Beirut, Justin has been an anti-terrorist response instructor, a drill instructor, a platoon sergeant, a company gunnery sergeant, and an assistant military officer instructor at Carnegie Mellon University.

Over the years, Justin's infantry career has taken him to many different locations throughout the world. With each new assignment, he received more training, more experience, and ultimately, more opportunities to "help his fellow Marines." Gunnery Sergeant Glymph is presently responsible for assigning the infantry unit leaders throughout the Marine Corps. He intends to continue "making a difference" as long a the Marine Corps needs him.

Military Careers Score

If you have taken the Armed Services Vocational Aptitude Battery (ASVAB) you will have received a Military Careers Score. You can use this score to see how well your aptitudes, skills, and abilities match those of personnel currently in each enlisted occupation.

What is the ASVAB?

The ASVAB is a test that can help you with your educational and career planning. Because the ASVAB assesses your aptitudes across a number of relevant educational and occupational areas, you can use ASVAB scores to help you explore occupations that might interest you.

The officer occupational descriptions do not include Military Careers Scores because the ASVAB is not used in the selection process for officers.

If you have not taken the ASVAB and would like to, ask your school counselor for information on how to do so.

Which ASVAB Score Should I Use?

On your Student Results Sheet, you will find a section marked ASVAB Scores. At the bottom of that section is your Military Careers Score. This is the score that you should use when exploring enlisted occupations in *Military Careers*.

What Is My Military Careers Score?

For each of the 81 enlisted occupational descriptions listed in this edition of *Military Careers*, we have included Military Careers Score information. By comparing the information shown with your Military Careers Score, you can determine how well your aptitudes, skills, and abilities match those required in the occupation. The closer the match between your Military Careers Score and the score listed for the occupation, the better the fit between the skills required for the job and the skills you bring to the job.

The Military Careers Score is a composite of several ASVAB tests that combines your scores on the verbal, math, mechanical and electronic portions of the ASVAB. This score reflects your current skills and aptitudes in these areas. The score itself ranges from 1 to 7, with higher scores indicating higher levels of proficiency. Like many other scores, there is no "passing" or "failing" score. The score simply reflects where you stand right now on these areas when compared with the military personnel currently employed in these occupations.[1] Like other scores, it may increase as you complete more math, English, electronic or mechanical shop courses. As such, it is wise to remain in school and complete more courses in these areas. If you take the ASVAB again after completing more courses, the knowledge that you gained should be reflected in a higher Military Careers Score.

MILITARY CAREERS/SCORE	INTEREST CODE
The circled score shows the typical Military Careers Score of servicemembers in this occupation. 1 2 3 4 **(5)** 6 7 Compare this score to your Military Career Score to see how well your aptitudes, skills, and abilities match those of personnel currently in these positions. See your recruiter for more information about qualification requirements.	This occupation generally appeals to people whose primary Interest Code is *Realistic*. *Realistic* jobs: • Allow you to work with your hands • Let you see the results of your work • Involve using machines, tools, and equipment
Pages 8 and 9 explain the Military Careers Score and the Interest Codes	

---

[1] The Military Careers Score was derived through a complex set of statistical procedures. First, the ASVAB scores for all those who entered any of these enlisted occupations in the Services between 1993 and 1997 were examined. In particular, their Military Career Scores were calculated. Statistical procedures were then employed to determine (a) how similar the scores were within each occupational group, and (b) how the average scores differed among the occupations. With this information, it was possible to determine the best formula to use to calculate the Military Careers Score so that the score would provide the best way to characterize the skills and abilities needed for success in that occupation. This formula then was validated. Your Military Careers Score is calculated according to the same formula used to derive the scores of the military personnel currently engaged in these occupations. That is why when there is a good match between your Military Careers Score and the occupation's Military Careers Score, it suggests that you have the aptitude necessary to be successful at that job.

*How Do I Use My Military Careers
Score?*

Using your Military Careers Score is a
fairly simple and straightforward process.
To help you learn this process, let's assume you are interested in an enlisted
occupation which indicates a Military
Careers Score of 5, as shown in the example on the previous page.

On your Student Results Sheet, locate
your Military Careers Score. For example,
let's assume you have obtained a Military Careers Score of 4. (If your Military
Careers Score is a three-digit number,
the conversion chart below will help you
convert your score to the new scores
used in this book.)

Determine how closely your score
matches the score for the occupation. In
this example, they differ by one. This is a
pretty good match. In general, when the
scores differ by no more than two, the
match is considered to be good. Finding
occupations for which you have a good
match is important because it indicates
that your skills and aptitudes are similar
to the skills and aptitudes held by those
actually doing those jobs. That can give
you confidence that you can do the job if
called on to do so.

Interest Code

If you have taken the *Interest-Finder*™
test using *Exploring Careers: The ASVAB
Workbook* or the ASVAB Career Exploration System (ACES), you will have Summary Code results. Your Summary Code
consists of your primary interest code and
your next two highest scoring codes.
Each of the enlisted and officer job descriptions in this book has an interest
code assigned to it, indicating that the
duties required for that particular occupation might appeal to someone with that
interest code. If you have not taken an
interest inventory or you cannot remember your interest codes, look at the interest code types on page 4 and try to
determine which one is most suited for
you.

To search for jobs by interest code, go
to the Interest Code Index on page 342 to
see a list of occupations that match your
interest codes and the page numbers
where you can find their descriptions in
this book. Keep in mind that although
only one interest code is shown for each
occupation, most occupations involve
activities that may appeal to more than
one interest type.

Old MC Score		New MC Score
140 - 166	=	1
167 - 193	=	2
194 - 211	=	3
212 - 214	=	4
215 - 217	=	5
218 - 230	=	6
231 - 240	=	7

SEARCHING FOR CAREERS

There are different ways to use *Military Careers* to search for jobs depending on where you are in the career exploration process. A good way to familiarize yourself with the occupations in the book is to browse through the Table of Contents and identify the job families or groupings that interest you. Go to those sections in the book and determine whether the corresponding occupations appeal to you. You may also want to look at the different indices in the back of the book which provide occupational listings using many alternative job titles from civilian career exploration resources. If you have taken the ASVAB and the *Interest-Finder*™, you can use your Military Careers Score and interest codes to help you in the career exploration process.

ADDITIONAL RESOURCES

After exploring Military Careers, you may want to consult some additional resources:

- Talk to a recruiter if you have additional questions (Air Force, 1-800-423-8723; Army, 1-800-USA-ARMY; Coast Guard, 1-800-424-8883; Marines, 1-800-MA-RINES; and Navy, 1-800-372-NAVY)

- Talk to people in occupations which interest you

- Attend career fairs

- Explore career shadowing, mentoring, internships, and cooperative education programs

- See your school guidance counselor.

Your counselor or librarian can direct you to these and other career exploration resources:

- http://www.myfuture.com
- http://www.militarycareers.com

- ASVAB Career Exploration System (ACES) computer software

- The *Occupational Outlook Handbook (OOH)*

The ASVAB Career Exploration System (ACES) is a computer software program designed to supplement *Exploring Careers: The ASVAB Workbook* by giving the user the capability to print a list of occupations that best match his or her interests, values, and abilities. This system currently automates Chapter 2: What are your Interests? and Chapter 5: The OCCU-FIND, of the ASVAB Workbook.

The *Occupational Outlook Handbook (OOH)* provides occupational descriptions for about 250 civilian occupations. In addition, many schools have a computerized system that provides local, state, and national occupational information for individuals exploring the world-of-work. Your counselor, teachers, or librarians can direct you to these and other resources.

Military Enlisted Occupations

General Information on Enlisted Occupations

For the latter half of the 20th century, the potential for global war with the former Soviet Union and its allies shaped the military's personnel requirements and overall strategies. In response to continuing changes in areas such as Eastern Europe, Africa, and the former Soviet Union, the military services have refocused their strategies to address smaller regional conflicts and the growing need for peacekeeping and humanitarian aid missions. As the military moves into the 21st century, it will need a multidimensional workforce that will be able to take advantage of new technologies and adapt quickly to new requirements.

Enlisted members are the supervisors and workers who carry out and maintain the basic operations of the military. Their roles are like those of company employees and supervisors. Enlisted members serve in occupations as diverse as computer systems specialists, automotive and heavy equipment mechanics, medical care technicians, and personnel specialists. As supervisors, enlisted members are responsible for the well-being of other enlisted members and for the care of equipment and property under their control. Overall, the services have available a broad range of enlisted occupations that require personnel with various types of knowledge, skills, and abilities.

MILITARY ENLISTED OCCUPATIONS

Besides being the single largest employer in the nation, the military offers the widest choice of career opportunities. Together, the five services offer training and employment in over 2,000 enlisted job specialties. To help you explore the enlisted world-of-work, these specialties are grouped into 81 enlisted occupations in this book. These 81 occupations are organized into 13 broad groups:

- Administrative
- Combat Specialty
- Construction
- Electronic and Electrical Equipment Repair
- Engineering, Science, and Technical
- Health Care
- Human Resource Development
- Machine Operator and Production
- Media and Public Affairs
- Protective Service
- Support Service
- Transportation and Material Handling
- Vehicle and Machinery Mechanic

Figure 1 shows the distribution of enlisted members across the 13 occupational groups.

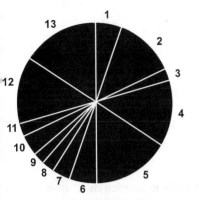

Figure 1
Distribution of Enlisted Personnel by Occupational Group

1. Administrative
2. Combat Specialty
3. Construction
4. Electronic and Electrical Equipment Repair
5. Engineering, Science, and Technical
6. Health Care
7. Human Resource Development
8. Machine Operator and Production
9. Media and Public Affairs
10. Protective Service
11. Support Service
12. Transportation and Material Handling
13. Vehicle and Machinery Mechanic

Table 1 – General Enlisted Qualifications*

Age: Must be between 17 and 35 years. Consent of legal parent or legal guardian required if 17.

Citizenship Status: Must be either (1) U.S. citizen, or (2) an immigrant alien legally admitted to the U.S. for permanent residence and possessing immigration and naturalization documents.

Physical Condition: Must meet minimum physical standards listed below. Some occupations have additional physical standards.

Height –		Maximum	Minimum
	For males:	6'5"/190.5 cm	5'0"/152.4 cm
	For females:	6'5"/190.5 cm	4'10"/147.3 cm

Weight – There are minimum and maximum weights for the various services according to height, wrist size, and/or percentage of body fat.

		Maximum	Minimum
	For males:	243 lb/110.4 kg	100 lb/45.35 kg
	For females:	205 lb/93.18 kg	90 lb/40.82 kg

Vision – The requirements are specific for each service and are determined by job specialty. In general, servicemembers must have at least 20/400 or 20/200 vision that can be corrected to 20/20 with eyeglasses or contacts lenses. The vision requirements are also based on depth perception as well as color blindness.

Overall Health – Must be in good health and pass a medical exam. Certain diseases or conditions may exclude persons from enlistment, such as diabetes, severe allergies, epilepsy, alcoholism, and drug addiction.

Education: High school graduation is desired by all services and is a requirement under most enlisted options.

Aptitude: Must achieve the minimum entry score on the Armed Services Vocational Aptitude Battery (ASVAB). Minimum entry scores vary by service and occupation.

Moral Character: Must meet standards designed to screen out persons likely to become disciplinary problems. Standards cover court convictions, juvenile delinquency, arrests, and drug use.

Marital Status and Dependents: May be either single or married; however, single persons with one or more minor dependents are not eligible for enlistment into military service.

Waivers: On a case-by-case basis, exceptions (waivers) are granted by individual services for some of the above qualification requirements.

* Each service sets its own enlistment qualification requirements. If you are interested in a specific service's enlistment requirements, see the "Service Information on Enlisted Occupations" section beginning on page 31, or contact a military recruiter.

In order to function as a self-sufficient community, the military must employ individuals with many different skills and abilities. The services need auto, ship, and aircraft mechanics to keep their many forms of transportation moving; food service specialists to provide meals for thousands of soldiers; and computer systems specialists to maintain information and communication systems. Therefore, the military has a wide spectrum of occupations.

Over 75 percent of all military occupations have counterparts in the civilian world-of-work. For example, dental hygienist, air traffic controller, computer systems specialist, and aircraft mechanic exist in both the military and civilian work forces.

The services offer training and an opportunity to progress in each occupation. No matter which occupation newly enlisted personnel enter, they will find a well-defined career path leading to higher pay and increased responsibility.

ENLISTMENT

Enlisted personnel are usually high school graduates and must meet minimum standards such as physical and aptitude requirements before enlisting. The general qualifications required for enlistment are shown in Table 1. If you are interested in a specific service's enlistment requirements or programs, see the "Service Information on Enlisted Occupations" section beginning on page 31.

Service Obligation

Joining the military involves entering into a legal contract called an enlistment agreement. The service agrees to provide a job, pay, benefits, and occupational training. In return, the enlisted member agrees to serve for a certain period of time, which is called the service obligation. The standard service obligation is eight years, which is divided between active military duty and reserve duty. Depending on the enlistment program selected, enlisted members spend two to six years on active duty with the balance of the eight-year obligation period spent in reserve status.

Enlistment Programs

Enlistment programs vary by service. The services adjust the programs they offer to meet changing recruiting needs. Major enlistment options include cash bonuses for enlisting in certain occupations and guaranteed choice of job training and assignments. Currently, all services also offer a Delayed Entry Program (DEP), an option that is used by many high school students who wish to enlist now but wait a short while before entering into active duty. By enlisting under the DEP option, an applicant delays entry into active duty for up to one year. High school students often enlist under the DEP during their senior year and enter a service after graduation. Other qualified applicants choose the DEP because the job training they desire is not currently available but will be within the next year.

Enlistment Contracts

The enlistment contract specifies the enlistment program selected by the applicant. It contains the enlistment date, term of enlistment, and other options, such as a training program guarantee or a cash bonus. If, for any reason, the service cannot meet its part of the agreement (for example, to provide a specific type of job training), then the applicant is no longer bound by the contract. If the applicant accepts another enlistment program, a new contract is written.

High School Graduates

The military encourages young people to stay in high school and graduate. Research has shown that high school graduates are more likely to adjust to military life and complete an initial tour of duty. Therefore, the services accept very few non-high school graduates.

ENLISTING IN THE MILITARY

Enlisting in the military involves a four-step process.

Step 1: Talking with a Recruiter

If you are interested in applying for one of the military services, you must talk with a recruiter from that service. Recruiters can provide detailed information about the employment and training opportunities in their service, as well as answer specific questions about service life, enlistment options, and other topics. They can also provide details about their service's enlistment qualification requirements.

If you decide to apply for entry into the service, and the recruiter identifies no problems (such as a severe health problem), the recruiter will examine your educational credentials. The recruiter will then schedule you for enlistment processing.

Step 2: Qualifying for Enlistment

Full enlistment processing occurs at one of the more than 60 Military Entrance Processing Stations (MEPS) located around the country. At the MEPS, applicants take the ASVAB, if they have not already done so, and receive medical examinations to determine if they are qualified to enter the service. The ASVAB may also be administered at Mobile Examining Team (MET) sites.

ASVAB results are used to determine if an applicant qualifies for entry into a service, and if the applicant has the specific aptitude level required to enter job specialty training programs. If you have taken the ASVAB at your school, you can use your scores to determine if you qualify for entry into the military services, provided the scores are not more than two years old. Applicants with current ASVAB scores are not required to take the ASVAB a second time.

Step 3: Meeting with a Service Classifier

A service classifier is a military career information specialist who helps applicants select military occupations. For example, if you are applying for entry, the classifier would inform you of service job training openings that match your aptitudes and interests. Specifically, the classifier would enter your ASVAB scores into a computerized reservation system. Based on your scores, the system would show the career fields and training programs for which you qualify and when job training would be available.

After discussing job training options with the classifier, you would select an occupation and schedule an enlistment date. Enlistment dates may be scheduled up to one year in the future to coincide with job training openings. This option is called the Delayed Entry Program (DEP) as described on the previous page.

Following selection of a military training program, you would sign an enlistment contract and take the oath of enlistment. If you chose the DEP option, you would return home until your enlistment date.

Step 4: Enlisting in the Service

After completing enlistment processing, applicants who select the immediate enlistment option receive their travel papers and proceed to a military base for basic training. Applicants who select the DEP option return to the MEPS on their scheduled enlistment date. At that time, applicants officially become "enlistees" (also known as "recruits") and proceed to a military base.

In the uncommon event that your guaranteed training program, through no fault of your own, is not available on the reserved date, you have three options:

*   Make another reservation for the same training and return at a later date to enter the service

*   Select another occupation and job training option

*   Decide not to join the service and be free from any obligation.

MILITARY TRAINING

The military operates one of the largest training systems in the world. The five services sponsor nearly 300 technical training schools offering more than 10,000 separate courses of instruction.

Education and training provided by the services offer servicemembers valuable opportunities for career development. The services spend billions of dollars each year training servicemembers for jobs ranging from air traffic controller to medical service technician. The main purpose of training is to prepare individuals to perform jobs in the service. Training also helps individuals meet personal goals and prepares them to assume greater responsibility in the service work force.

The military generally provides four kinds of training for its personnel:

- Recruit training
- Job training
- Advanced training
- Leadership training.

Recruit Training

Recruit training, popularly called basic training, is a rigorous orientation to the military. Depending on the service, recruit training lasts from six to ten weeks and provides a transition from civilian to military life. The services train recruits at selected military bases across the country. Where an enlistee trains depends on the service and the job training to be received. Through basic training, recruits gain the pride, knowledge, discipline, and physical conditioning necessary to serve as members of the Army, Navy, Air Force, Marine Corps, and Coast Guard.

Upon reporting for basic training, recruits are divided into training groups of 40 to 80 people. They then meet their drill instructor, receive uniforms and equipment, and move into assigned quarters.

During basic training, recruits receive instruction in health, first aid, and military skills. They also improve their fitness and stamina by participating in rigorous daily exercises and conditioning. To measure their conditioning progress, recruits are tested on sit-ups, push-ups, running, and body weight.

Recruits follow a demanding schedule throughout basic training; every day is carefully structured with time for classes, meals, physical conditioning, and field instruction. Some free time (including time to attend religious services) is available to recruits during basic training. After completing basic training, recruits normally proceed to job training.

Job Training

Through job training, also called technical or skill training, recruits learn the skills they will need to perform their job specialties. The military provides its personnel with high-quality training because lives and mission success depend on how well people perform their duties. Military training produces highly qualified workers, and for this reason many civilian employers consider military training excellent preparation for civilian occupations.

The type of job specialty determines the length of training. Most training lasts from 10 to 20 weeks, although some specialties require over one year of training.

Military training occurs both in the classroom and on the job. Classroom training emphasizes hands-on activities and practical experience, as well as textbook learning. For example, recruits who will be working with electronic equipment practice operating and repairing the equipment, in addition to studying the principles of electronics.

At their first assignments, enlisted members continue to learn on the job. Experienced enlisted members and supervisors help service men and women further develop their skills. In addition, the military offers refresher courses and advanced training to help military personnel maintain and increase their skills. As personnel advance in rank, they continue their training with leadership and management courses.

Three services, the Army, Navy, and Marine Corps, offer apprenticeship programs for some job specialties. These programs consist of classroom and on-the-job training that meet U.S. Department of Labor apprenticeship standards. After completing an apprenticeship program, personnel receive a Department of Labor apprenticeship certificate. To military commanders and civilian employers, these certificates demonstrate that the worker has acquired specific skills and qualifications.

For each of the 81 enlisted occupations described in this book, a summary of the typical training content and length is provided.

Advanced Training

Hundreds of advanced training courses have been developed by the services to improve the technical skills of the enlisted work force. These courses offer instruction in skills not covered in initial training. An automobile mechanic, for example, may take advanced instruction in troubleshooting (identifying engine problems) or preventive maintenance techniques. Advanced training also includes courses covering new or additional job-related equipment. An auto mechanic may go to school to learn how to repair a new type of vehicle, or a radiological technician may take instruction in the use of ultrasound equipment. Advanced training is especially important in high technology areas where military technicians are constantly being exposed to newer and more sophisticated equipment. Other advanced courses provide instruction in supervising and managing the daily operations of military units, such as repair shops or medical facilities.

Some advanced training involves classroom training, but the services also provide enlisted members with a wide choice of self-study correspondence courses. Some of these are general courses and address most duties of a job. Other courses are designed to cover highly complex tasks or job-related skills. Self-study courses are particularly important to individual career advancement. Completing a self-study course can provide a servicemember with the job skills and knowledge to perform more advanced job duties. Self-study courses also include material that prepares enlisted personnel to take the competitive examinations required to advance through the noncommissioned officer (NCO) ranks.

Leadership Training

Each service has schools and courses to help supervisors be more effective in managing the day-to-day operations of their units. These classes are designed primarily for noncommissioned officers. Courses include instruction in leadership skills, service regulations, and management techniques needed to train and lead other servicemembers.

CAREER DEVELOPMENT, GUIDANCE AND COUNSELING

Almost every military base has an education center. At these centers, counselors are available with information about education and training (military and civilian) and requirements for career advancement. They can also provide information about retraining for other military occupations.

Counselors coordinate the services' education programs and help service men and women set educational goals. They can explain the many opportunities available and help servicemembers enroll in programs or courses. The counselors help enlisted personnel tailor their educational programs to meet their career goals.

Continuing Education

The services recognize the value of education, both military and civilian. Military training helps enlisted personnel perform their job duties and develop leadership and supervisory skills. Continuing civilian education, regardless of the subject, also helps an enlisted person to become a more well-rounded individual, better prepared to deal with the challenges of service life. The services offer many programs to help and encourage enlisted men and women to continue their civilian education. Enlisted personnel may enroll in courses to earn college degrees, improve work skills, or simply for personal enjoyment. Each service's training department offers self-study courses on many different topics in which any enlisted person can enroll. If you are interested in a specific service's continuing education program, see the "Service Information on Enlisted Occupations" section beginning on page 31.

Defense Activity for Nontraditional Education Support (DANTES)

DANTES is an organization within the Department of Defense designed to support education in all of the services. It helps develop and administer education programs. In addition to supporting individual service programs, DANTES also offers many different programs for active-duty servicemembers. The College Level Examination Program (CLEP) allows servicemembers to obtain college credits through examination without attending courses. The Independent Study Program allows enlisted personnel to take high school through graduate-level self-study courses offered by accredited colleges and universities.

Servicemembers Opportunity Colleges (SOCs)

The Servicemembers Opportunity Colleges are a consortium of colleges and universities that help enlisted personnel satisfy the requirements for college degrees. SOCs began in the early 1970s to help expand and improve postsecondary educational opportunities for military personnel and veterans. This civilian/military partnership consists of more than 1,000 colleges and universities, the Department of Defense, the military services, and is supported by 12 national higher education associations. Because enlisted personnel are frequently reassigned, they can find it difficult to complete their coursework for a degree at one college or university. In this program, participating colleges and universities accept credits earned at other schools and award credit for some military training courses. Through SOCs, enlisted personnel can more easily complete the requirements for a college degree. For additional information on SOCs, call 800-368-5622 or 202-667-0079.

Other College Programs

The services offer tuition assistance programs that pay from 75 to 100 percent of the fees for off-duty study in most courses at accredited schools, depending upon the availability of funds. Enlisted personnel can use these courses to pursue bachelor's or advanced degrees. The services also have agreements with many colleges and universities that allow the schools to hold classes on the base. Similar programs also offer courses at overseas locations and aboard ships.

ENLISTED CAREER ADVANCEMENT

A military career is more than just a job. The military offers the opportunity to advance in exciting careers. Motivated men and women advance by improving their job skills and taking on greater responsibility. Advancement means recognition for a job well done, a promotion to more responsible duties, and increased military rank and pay grade. Pay grade and length of service determine a servicemember's pay. Figure 2 shows the insignias for the ranks of each service. It also depicts the relationship between rank and pay grade.

Figure 2
Enlisted Insignia of the United States Armed Forces

SERVICE / PAY GRADE	ARMY	NAVY	AIR FORCE	MARINE CORPS	COAST GUARD
E-9	COMMAND SERGEANT MAJOR / SERGEANT MAJOR	MASTER CHIEF PETTY OFFICER	CHIEF MASTER SERGEANT	SERGEANT MAJOR / MASTER GUNNERY SERGEANT	MASTER CHIEF PETTY OFFICER
E-8	FIRST SERGEANT / MASTER SERGEANT	SENIOR CHIEF PETTY OFFICER	SENIOR MASTER SERGEANT	FIRST SERGEANT / MASTER SERGEANT	SENIOR CHIEF PETTY OFFICER
E-7	SERGEANT FIRST CLASS	CHIEF PETTY OFFICER	MASTER SERGEANT	GUNNERY SERGEANT	CHIEF PETTY OFFICER
E-6	STAFF SERGEANT	PETTY OFFICER FIRST CLASS	TECHNICAL SERGEANT	STAFF SERGEANT	PETTY OFFICER FIRST CLASS
E-5	SERGEANT	PETTY OFFICER SECOND CLASS	STAFF SERGEANT	SERGEANT	PETTY OFFICER SECOND CLASS
E-4	CORPORAL / SPECIALIST	PETTY OFFICER THIRD CLASS	SENIOR AIRMAN	CORPORAL	PETTY OFFICER THIRD CLASS
E-3	PRIVATE FIRST CLASS	SEAMAN	AIRMAN FIRST CLASS	LANCE CORPORAL	FIREMAN / SEAMAN
E-2	PRIVATE	SEAMAN APPRENTICE	AIRMAN	PRIVATE FIRST CLASS	FIREMAN APPRENTICE / SEAMAN APPRENTICE
E-1	No Insignia PRIVATE	No Insignia SEAMAN RECRUIT	No Insignia AIRMAN BASIC	No Insignia PRIVATE	No Insignia SECOND RECRUIT

Enlisted Promotion

Men and women in the lower pay grades (E-1 to E-3) usually advance to the next grade based on their length of service and time in their present pay grade. They must also receive their commanding officer's approval and be satisfactorily progressing in their training and job performance. Only individuals who show superior performance may be promoted to E-4.

All enlisted personnel are led, supervised, and evaluated by senior enlisted personnel and officers. Factors that qualify an enlisted person for promotion include:

- Length of service
- Time in present pay grade
- Job performance
- Leadership ability
- Awards or commendations
- Job specialty
- Educational achievement through technical, on-the-job, or civilian instruction.

Each service sets minimum standards for the length of service and time in current pay grade that must be met before a person can compete for promotion to the next higher pay grade.

Figure 3 shows the average time an enlisted member has been in the military (time-in-service) when he or she is promoted to each pay grade. For example, it takes an average of one year to reach pay grade E-3 and nine years to reach E-6. The time-in-service and advancement information shown is developed from data provided by each of the services.

Good performance reports are essential to continue along a career path. Although a good performance report does not automatically qualify an individual for promotion, a less than satisfactory rating severely limits chances for promotion. By selecting from among qualified individuals for promotion to each rank, the services try to ensure that the most qualified personnel are promoted. Because the number of enlisted positions is limited by Congress, the competition for promotion at the senior levels is intense. Changes in the number of personnel in a particular specialty, or in the armed services as a whole, can also affect promotion.

Enlisted Commissioning Programs

Officers and enlisted personnel advance along separate career paths. However, each service has programs that enable selected enlisted personnel to become commissioned officers. The entrance standards for these programs are high, and the competition is strong.

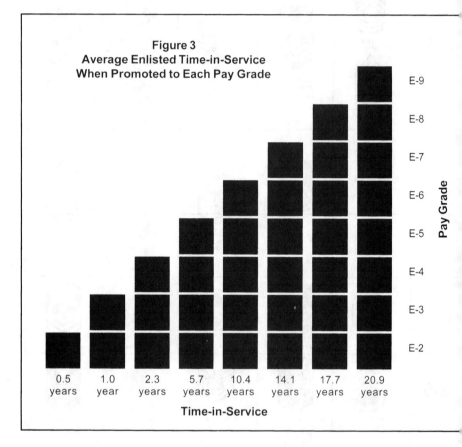

Figure 3
Average Enlisted Time-in-Service
When Promoted to Each Pay Grade

Pay Grade

E-9 · E-8 · E-7 · E-6 · E-5 · E-4 · E-3 · E-2

0.5 years · 1.0 year · 2.3 years · 5.7 years · 10.4 years · 14.1 years · 17.7 years · 20.9 years

Time-in-Service

Typically, there are two ways for enlisted personnel to earn commissions: through direct appointment and acceptance to officer training and through service programs that send enlisted personnel to college full-time to obtain a degree. Direct appointment programs usually require an outstanding performance record and a college degree. Individuals selected for these programs go to officer training schools operated by their service. Enlisted personnel selected to complete their college degree attend college through a Reserve Officers' Training Corps (ROTC) program or one of the service academies. After completing officer training, these individuals are awarded commissions as officers in their respective services.

DUTY ASSIGNMENT

The five services have similar systems for assigning personnel to jobs. Each system is designed to satisfy the staffing needs of the particular service. For example, if the service needs a machinist at a remote location, a servicemember trained as a machinist is assigned there. However, at the same time, the services also attempt to meet the desires of the individual servicemember and provide opportunities for career development. The duty assignment process determines where enlisted personnel work, how often they move, and the opportunities open to them.

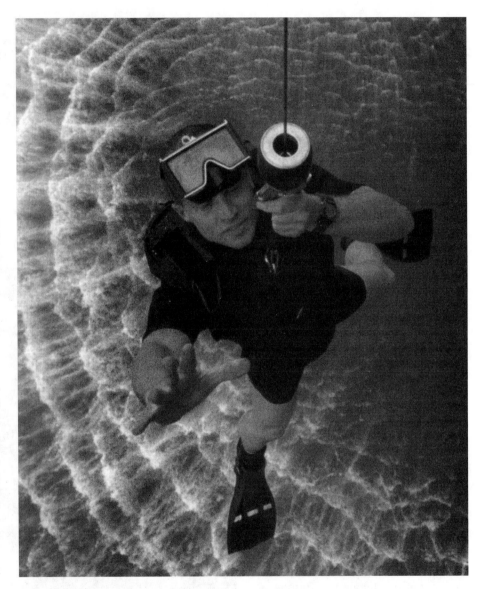

Assignment Decisions

The services use noncommissioned officers who are familiar with a particular occupation to manage assignments for people in that job. Although they cannot always meet each person's needs or desires, these noncommissioned officers try to make duty assignments that will enhance each servicemember's career.

Each service tries to give enlisted members job assignments in different types of organizations. Gaining a range of experience is more important to people at supervisory levels, because with each assignment, servicemembers learn more about their jobs and gain confidence in their abilities to react effectively to unexpected events or to assume greater responsibility.

Possible Location

All services require their members to travel. Enlisted personnel are stationed in each of the 50 states and in countries all over the world. They are routinely reassigned after two-, three-, or four-year tours of duty. To many people, this is one of the attractive parts of service life and, in fact, many men and women join for the opportunity to travel, live in foreign countries, and see different parts of the U.S.

Nearly three-quarters of all service personnel are assigned to duty in the United States. Each service also has personnel stationed overseas; many personnel are located in Europe, in countries such as Great Britain, Italy, and Germany. Enlisted personnel are also assigned to the Pacific and Far East, in countries such as Japan, South Korea, and Australia. During their careers, many servicemembers will serve at least one overseas assignment. Several of the

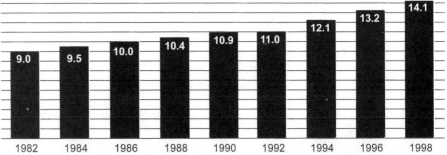

**Figure 4
Percentage of Active Duty
Enlisted Women
1982 – 1998**

1982	1984	1986	1988	1990	1992	1994	1996	1998
9.0	9.5	10.0	10.4	10.9	11.0	12.1	13.2	14.1

services have programs that allow enlisted personnel returning from overseas to select the location in the United States where they will be stationed.

Length of Tours

The time an enlisted person spends at a particular duty assignment is called a "tour." The length of a tour varies by service and geographic location. Typically, a tour lasts from three to four years, although there are many exceptions.

WOMEN IN THE MILITARY

Military women make important contributions to national defense. As shown in Figure 4, military women have increased in numbers to 14.1 percent of active duty personnel.

Although there are still laws and policies that do not allow the assignment of women to direct ground combat duties, opportunities for women in the military continue to expand. Women are currently eligible to enter almost 90 percent of all military job specialties. Examples of the many enlisted occupations women occupy include radio intelligence operator, computer systems specialist, environmental health and safety specialist, and power plant operator.

In 1994, the Department of Defense decided to open more than 80,000 additional positions to women. The outlook for women in the military suggests that the future will provide even greater opportunities.

RESERVE FORCES

Seven different forces make up the Reserves—the Army, Navy, Air Force, Marine Corps, and Coast Guard Reserves and the Army and Air National Guard. Currently, approximately 900,000 Americans serve as Reservists. Each year, the military needs about 160,000 new Reservists.

The Reserves are important to our overall national defense. In a national emergency, Reservists can be called up immediately to serve on active duty, because they are highly trained by the services and drill regularly.

During peacetime, the Reserves perform many functions to support active-duty forces in our country's defense, such as reconnaissance, rescue missions, air defense for the continental U.S., installation and repair of communications equipment, and transport of troops, material, and medical support.

Enlistment

To enlist in the Reserves, applicants must meet physical, aptitude, citizenship, educational, and moral requirements similar to those that active-duty applicants must meet. They must also be between 17 and 35 years of age. Parental consent is required for 17-year-olds. Specific age standards vary by service.

Reservists normally enlist for eight years. They serve an initial period on active duty while completing basic training and receiving job training. After the training period, which usually lasts several months, Reservists return to civilian life. For the remainder of their service obligation, they attend training sessions and perform work in their job specialty one or two days per month (usually on weekends or in the evening) with their local unit. Once a year (often during the summer), Reservists participate in an active-duty training session of 10 to 14 days.

Pay and Promotions

Reservists are paid at the same rate as active-duty members for the time they spend working or training. Pay grade and length of service determine their rate of pay.

The Reserves have promotion systems similar to, but separate from, the regular services. Reservists compete only with other Reservists for promotion; advancement is based on performance and length of service.

Training

The military generally offers the same basic and initial job training to Reservists as it does to active-duty members. Reservists may attend the same schools and complete similar training programs. Besides basic training and initial job training, Reservists may enroll in advanced training courses by correspondence or may attend regular service training classes.

PAY AND BENEFITS

Military personnel in all five services are paid according to the same pay scale and receive the same basic benefits. Military pay and benefits are set by Congress, which normally grants a cost-of-living pay increase once each year. In addition to pay, the military provides many of life's necessities, such as food, clothing, and housing, or pays monthly allowances for them. The following sections describe military pay, allowances, and benefits in more detail.

Enlisted Pay Grades

Enlisted members can progress through nine enlisted pay grades during their career. Pay grade and length of service determine a servicemember's pay. Figure 2, on page 21, shows the relationship between pay grade and rank in each service and also illustrates the insignia for the ranks.

GI Bill Benefits

Individuals who have entered active duty since June 30, 1985, have been automatically enrolled in the Montgomery GI Bill Program unless they have chosen not to participate. Those enrolled in the program have their basic pay reduced by $100 per month for their first 12 months of service. Upon completion of three years of continuous active duty, individuals are eligible for $536 per month for 36 months, for a maximum of $19,296 in basic benefits for full-time schooling (individuals who complete a two-year obligation will receive $436 per month for 36 months).

Basic Pay

The major part of an enlisted member's paycheck is basic pay. Pay grade and total years of service determine an enlisted member's basic pay. Table 2 contains information on annual basic pay as of 2000. Cost-of-living increases generally occur once a year.

Incentives and Special Pay

The military offers incentives and special pay (in addition to basic pay) for certain types of duty. For example, incentives are paid for submarine and flight duty. Other types of hazardous duty with monthly incentives include parachute jumping, flight deck duty, and explosives demolition. In addition, the military gives special pay for sea duty, diving duty, special assignments, duty in certain foreign places, and duty in areas subject to hostile fire. Depending on the service, bonuses are also paid for entering certain occupations.

Table 2 – 2000 Basic Pay for Enlisted Members (Annual Figures)

	Under 2 yrs	2	3	4	6	8	10	...	26
				Years of Service					
E-9	*	*	*	*	*	*	$36,184	...	$46,591
E-8	*	*	*	*	*	*	31,219	...	41,605
E-7	*	*	*	*	$25,387	$26,191	27,032	...	37,433
E-6	$18,227	$19,868	$20,693	$21,571	22,385	23,191	24,041	...	*
E-5	15,991	17,406	18,252	19,048	20,300	21,132	21,960	...	*
E-4	14,915	15,754	16,682	17,968	18,680	*	*	...	*
E-3	14,058	14,828	15,414	16,031	*	*	*	...	*
E-2	13,529	*	*	*	*	*	*	...	*
E-1	12,067	*	*	*	*	*	*	...	*
Less than 4 months	11,164	*	*	*	*	*	*	...	*

E-1 Basic Pay for the first four months is about $790 per month ($9,482 on an annual basis).

* Military Personnel with this many years of service will probably not be in this pay grade. (Pay scale between 10 and 26 years not shown.)

Allowances

Most enlisted members, especially in the first year of service, live in military housing and eat in military dining facilities free of charge. Those living off base receive quarters (housing) and subsistence (food) allowances in addition to their basic pay. As of 2000, the monthly housing allowance ranges from $222 to $724, depending on pay grade and number of dependents. The food allowance ranges from $210 to $350 per month, depending on living circumstances. Because allowances are not taxed as income, they provide a significant tax savings in addition to their cash value.

When added up, housing and food allowances, together with their tax savings, are substantial additions to basic pay. Table 3 contains information on the total value of basic pay, allowances, and tax savings, called Regular Military Compensation. The table represents the amount of pay a civilian worker would need to earn to realize the same "take home" pay as a servicemember. These figures provide a more realistic basis of comparison between military and civilian wages than do the figures in Table 2.

Table 3 – 2000 Regular Military Compensation (Annual Figures)

	Years of Service								
	Under 2 yrs	2	3	4	6	8	10	...	26
E-9	*	*	*	*	*	*	*	...	$60,484
E-8	*	*	*	*	*	*	$44,449	...	54,402
E-7	*	*	*	$37,117	$37,933	$38,716	39,528	...	49,567
E-6	$30,196	$31,692	$32,444	33,313	34,104	34,883	35,717	...	*
E-5	26,830	28,233	29,098	29,896	31,037	31,784	32,586	...	*
E-4	24,271	25,119	26,027	27,249	27,935	*	*	...	*
E-3	22,991	23,744	24,319	24,921	*	*	*	...	*
E-2	22,325	*	*	*	*	*	*	...	*
E-1	20,863	*	*	*	*	*	*	...	*
Less than 4 months	19,736	*	*	*	*	*	*	...	*

E-1 Regular Military Compensation reflects basic pay, allowances, and the value of the tax advantage for allowances.

* Military Personnel with this many years of service will probably not be in this pay grade. (Pay scale between 10 and 26 years not shown.)

Employment Benefits

Military personnel receive substantial benefits in addition to their pay and allowances. While they are in the service, enlisted members' benefits include health care, vacation, legal assistance, recreational programs, educational assistance, and commissary/exchange (military store) privileges. Families of servicemembers also receive some of these benefits. Table 4 contains a summary of these employment benefits.

Retirement Benefits

The military offers one of the best retirement programs in the country. After 20 years of active duty, personnel may retire and receive a monthly payment equal to 40 percent of their average basic pay for their last five years of active duty. Persons who retire with more than 20 years of service receive higher pay. Other retirement benefits include medical care and commissary/exchange privileges.

Veterans' Benefits

Veterans of military service are entitled to certain veterans' benefits set by Congress and provided by the Veterans Administration. In most cases, these include guarantees for home loans, hospitalization, survivor benefits, educational benefits, disability benefits, and assistance in finding civilian employment.

Table 4 – Summary of Employment Benefits for Enlisted Members

Vacation	Leave time of 30 days per year.
Medical, Dental and Eye Care	Full medical, hospitalization, dental, and eye care services for enlistees and most health care costs for family members.
Continuing Education	Voluntary educational programs for undergraduate and graduate degrees or for single courses, including tuition assistance for programs at colleges and universities.
Recreational Programs	Programs include athletics, entertainment, and hobbies:
	Softball, basketball, football, swimming, tennis, golf, weight training, and other sports
	Parties, dances, and entertainment
	Club facilities, snack bars, game rooms, movie theaters, and lounges
	Active hobby and craft clubs, book and music libraries.
Exchange and Commissary Privileges	Food, goods, and services are available at military stores, generally at lower costs than at regular retail stores.
Legal Assistance	Many free legal services are available to assist with personal matters.

Service Information on Enlisted Occupations

Army

OVERVIEW

Today's "Army of Excellence" is a modern and powerful military force redesigning to a goal of 69,000 officers, 11,500 warrant officers, and 450,000 enlisted soldiers. Army men and women work in many types of jobs, ranging from general administration to the operation and maintenance of the Army's many thousands of weapons, vehicles, aircraft, and highly technical electronic systems.

Soldiers, working as a team, perform the Army's mission of protecting the security of the United States and its vital resources. The Army stands constantly ready to defend American interests and the interests of our allies through land-based operations anywhere in the world.

The Army needs approximately 80,000 to 90,000 new enlistees each year. Those who enlist into the Army will find hundreds of challenging career opportunities that can offer a lifetime of security and excitement to them and their families.

ENLISTMENT

Enlistment in the Army may be for two, three, four, five, or six years. Applicants must be from 17 to 35 years old, American citizens or registered aliens, and in good health and physical condition. To determine what careers they are best suited for, all applicants must take the Armed Services Vocational Aptitude Battery (ASVAB). The ASVAB is offered at most high schools and at military enlistment processing sites.

In most cases, qualified applicants can be guaranteed their choice of training or duty assignment. There are often combinations of guarantees that are particularly attractive to those who are qualified. For those who wish to be guaranteed a specific school, a particular area of assignment, or both, the Army offers the Delayed Entry Program (DEP). An applicant for the DEP can reserve a school or an assignment choice as much as one year in advance of entry into active duty. Other enlistment programs include the Army Civilian Acquired Skills Program, which gives recognition to those skills acquired through civilian training or experience. This program allows enlisted members with previously acquired training to be promoted more quickly than they ordinarily would be. In some cases, the Army also offers enlistment bonuses.

Enlistment programs and options vary from time to time. Local Army recruiters always have the latest information and are ready to answer inquiries without obligation.

TRAINING

Initial Army training is provided in two phases: basic training and Advanced Individual Training (job training).

Basic Training

Basic training is a rigorous eight-week orientation for men and women entering the Army. Basic training transforms new enlistees from civilians into soldiers. During basic training, new soldiers gain the discipline, spirit, pride, knowledge, and physical conditioning necessary to perform Army duties.

Army basic training is given in several locations throughout the country, including training centers in South Carolina, Georgia, Kentucky, Alabama, Oklahoma, and Missouri.

Upon reporting for basic training, new soldiers are assigned to a training company and are issued uniforms and equipment. They are introduced to their training leaders, otherwise known as drill sergeants. Drill sergeants are experienced noncommissioned officers who direct soldiers' training to ensure that they are successful.

Army basic training stresses teamwork. Soldiers are trained in groups known as squads or platoons. These groups range from nine to approximately 80 soldiers; they are small enough that each soldier can be recognized for his or her special abilities. Such groups tend to become closely knit teams and develop group pride and camaraderie during the eight weeks of rigorous training they experience together.

Basic training is conducted on a demanding schedule, but each soldier progresses at the rate he or she can handle best. Soldiers attend a variety of classes and field instruction that include military training, weapons familiarization, physical conditioning, and military drills. All training emphasizes team work and therefore includes classes in human relations. These classes help trainees from different backgrounds learn to work closely together. Only limited personal time is available during basic training, but there is plenty of time for receiving and answering mail, for personal care, and for attending religious services.

Job Training (Advanced Individual Training)

After basic training, Army soldiers go directly to Advanced Individual Training in the occupational field that they have chosen and qualified for, where they learn a specific Army job. Advanced Individual Training schools are located at many Army bases throughout the country.

The Army offers skills training in a wide range of career fields that include programs maintenance, administration, electronics, health care, construction, and combat specialty occupations, to name a few.

Advanced Individual Training students generally attend traditional classes very similar to those in a high school or college. These classes are supplemented with demonstrations by highly qualified instructors and by practical exercises that use "hands-on" training, Army equipment, or Army procedures in a way that prepares students for their jobs. Many soldiers also receive on-the-job training, learning job skills by working at a job with other soldiers under the guidance of qualified instructors.

Some Advanced Individual Training courses are registered with the U.S. Department of Labor as certified apprenticeship training programs. Generally, this training qualifies participants for both federal and state apprenticeship programs and helps secure future civilian employment in their chosen trade.

ADVANCEMENT

Every job in the Army has a career path leading to increased pay and responsibility with well-defined promotion criteria. After six months of service, new soldiers advance to Private (E-2). The next step in the promotion ladder is Private First Class (E-3), which occurs after the 12th month. Promotion to Corporal or Specialist (E-4) occurs after established time-in-grade and time-in-service requirements are met. These times vary, but every soldier can ordinarily expect to become a corporal within his or her first three years of service. Starting with grade E-5, promotions to Sergeant through Sergeant Major are accomplished on a competitive basis. At each grade, there are minimum periods of time in service and time in grade that must be met before a soldier can be considered for promotion. In some cases, there also are educational requirements that must be met for promotion.

The Army offers a number of ways to advance beyond enlisted status as either a warrant officer or commissioned officer. These programs usually are reserved for only the best qualified soldiers. Warrant officers perform duties similar to commissioned Army officers. Many warrant officers are directly appointed from the enlisted grades as vacancies occur. These opportunities usually exist in the technical fields, especially those involving maintenance of equipment. Other opportunities are available in Army administration, intelligence, and law enforcement. Unique among the Armed Forces is the Army's Warrant Officer Aviator Program. Qualified personnel may enlist for Warrant Officer Candidate School and, upon completion, receive flight training and appointment as Army warrant officer aviators.

Enlisted soldiers may also compete for a limited number of selections to attend Officer Candidate School (OCS) or the United States Military Academy. Upon graduating from OCS or the academy, soldiers receive officer commissions. For soldiers with college degrees, there are opportunities for direct commissioning.

EDUCATION PROGRAMS

For enlisted personnel, the Army has a well-defined system for progressive service school training. Soldiers are often able to volunteer for this schooling or, in some cases, they are selected on a competitive basis.

As a soldier progresses in his or her career, advanced technical training opportunities are offered. These courses include, but are not limited to, advanced noncommissioned officer courses at the staff sergeant grade level and the Sergeants Major Academy at the E-8 and E-9 levels.

Civilian education is stressed as a means to improve both the soldier's work performance and preparedness for life in a technical and competitive society. The Army Continuing Education System provides counseling, academic services, and vocational-technical services at little or no cost. In a few cases, the Army sends its soldiers to college, but generally they are encouraged to pursue college training during off-duty time.

Army personnel are also eligible to participate in educational assistance programs with the government, such as the Montgomery GI Bill, which can provide approximately $19,000 for future educational needs. Additionally, the Army College Fund may add additional monetary incentives to qualified soldiers' accounts to total $50,000 for education.

FOR FURTHER INFORMATION

Students who wish to learn more about specific military jobs and careers are encouraged to use this manual to its fullest. In addition, many career information systems found in high schools and libraries have information about Army careers. The most up-to-date information about Army programs or careers is always available from an Army recruiter. For the Army recruiter nearest you, check the Yellow Pages or call 1-800-USA-ARMY for details. There is no obligation.

Navy

OVERVIEW

The Navy plays an important role in helping to maintain the freedom of the seas. It defends the right of our country and its allies to travel and trade freely on the world's oceans and helps protect our country and national interests overseas during times of international conflict through power projection ashore. Navy sea and air power make it possible for our country to use the oceans when and where our national interests require it.

The Navy is a large and diverse organization. It is made up of about 371,000 officers and enlisted people. Navy personnel operate and repair more than 320 ships and over 4,000 aircraft; they serve in such diverse fields as radio operators, network systems administrators, dental specialists, seamen, computer programmers, photographers, ship electricians, and gas turbine systems technicians and work in many other exciting careers. Navy people serve on ships at sea, on submarines under the sea, in aviation positions on land and sea, and at shore bases around the world.

The Navy recruits over 50,000 officers and enlisted people each year to fill openings in Navy career fields.

ENLISTMENT

To qualify for enlistment in Navy programs, men and women must be between the ages of 17 and 34. Parental consent is required for all 17-year-olds. In the nuclear field, the maximum enlistment age is 23, due to extensive training requirements. Since most Navy programs require enlistees to be high school graduates, the Navy prefers young people to graduate first before entering the Navy.

Enlistees must be citizens of the United States or immigrant aliens with immigration and naturalization papers. A physical examination and the Armed Services Vocational Aptitude Battery (ASVAB) test must be completed.

Initial enlistment in the Navy usually is for four years. However, two-, three-, or six-year enlistments are also available for men and women, depending on the programs they select.

After going through the enlistment process at a Military Entrance Processing Station, Navy people usually are placed in the Delayed Enlistment Program (DEP). Recruits in the DEP are guaranteed training assignments. The DEP allows enlistees to finish high school, take care of personal business, or just relax before reporting for duty. There is even an opportunity to earn advancement in the DEP which translates into a higher paygrade when entering basic training.

There is extra pay in the Navy for sea duty, submarine duty, demolition duty, diving duty, work as a crew member of an aviation team, or jobs that require special training. Signing bonuses are available for those who enter the nuclear field or other highly technical fields in the Navy. Because the nuclear field is such a critical and unique area of the Navy, quicker promotions are earned and bonuses are available when the training in this field is completed and also when sailors with nuclear training reenlist.

TRAINING

The Navy is known for the excellent training it provides. The Navy provides both recruit training and job training.

Recruit Training

The first assignment for every Navy enlistee is recruit training. It is a challenging nine-week period of transition from civilian to Navy life. It provides the discipline, knowledge, and physical conditioning necessary to continue serving in the Navy.

The Navy's recruit training command is located in Great Lakes, Illinois. After reporting, recruits are placed into training divisions, issued uniforms and equipment, and assigned living quarters.

The recruit's day starts at 0530 (5:30 a.m.). Taps (lights out) is at 2200 (10:00 p.m.). During weekdays, the daily schedule varies and includes periods of physical fitness, classroom training, and hands-on instruction.

Physical fitness training includes push-ups, sit-ups, sit-reach, distance running, water survival, and swimming instruction. Recruits are tested for physical fitness at the beginning and end of recruit training. The test requirements differ slightly for men and women.

Recruits are given classroom and hands-on training covering more than 30 subjects, including aircraft and ship familiarization, basic deck seamanship, firefighting, career incentives, decision-making, time management, military drill, Navy mission and organization, military customs and courtesies, and the chain of command.

Job Training

After recruit training, most Navy people go directly to the technical school (called class A school) they signed up for at the Military Entrance Processing Station.

The Navy has more than 60 job fields from which enlistees may choose. They are grouped in occupational categories similar to the occupations described in *Military Careers*.

Navy class A schools are located on military bases throughout the United States, including Great Lakes, Illinois; San Diego, California; Newport, Rhode Island; and Pensacola, Florida. They range in length from a few weeks to many months, depending on the complexity of the subject.

Those who complete recruit training and are still undecided about what career path they want to take in the Navy can begin an on-the-job apprenticeship training program. One such program for men is the Subfarer Program, which trains men to serve aboard submarines. The Divefarer Program trains personnel in diving specialties, and the Aircrew Program trains enlistees in inflight maintenance and tactical crew duties in naval aircraft.

When apprentices finish on-the-job training, they should have an idea of what type of job (rating) they want to pursue during the rest of their Navy service. They may then apply to class A school for training in that rating. Advanced training in most job fields is available later in a Navy person's career.

The Office of Education Credit of the American Council on Education regularly reviews and evaluates Navy training and experience. It has recommended that colleges and universities award credits for nearly all Navy courses.

ADVANCEMENT

Like other branches of the service, the Navy has nine enlisted pay grades, from E-1 to E-9. A new enlistee entering the Navy is an E-1 (Seaman Recruit). After about six months in the Navy, the E-1 normally is eligible for advancement to E-2 (Seaman Apprentice).

Navy promotions are based on: 1) job performance, 2) competitive examination grades, 3) recommendations of supervisors, 4) length of service, and 5) time in present level of work. It is impossible to predict exactly when promotions will occur; however, every job in the Navy has a defined career path leading to supervisory positions.

People with highly developed skills in certain critical occupations may enter the Navy at advanced pay grades. Some people qualify for one of the specialized technical training programs in the electronics or nuclear fields, where advancement is often rapid.

Enlisted petty officer ratings (E-4 through E-9) are not to be confused with Navy commissioned officer rankings. Most Navy enlisted personnel are not college graduates, while most Navy commissioned officers have college degrees. However, the Navy does offer several programs that allow enlisted personnel to advance to officer status.

Two Navy programs, Limited Duty Officer (LDO) and Warrant Officer (WO), permit career enlisted Navy people to advance to commissioned officer status without a college education. Enlisted Navy people interested in officer commissions through these two programs should start planning for them early in their careers. These commissions are limited to successful career petty officers. The competition is keen and the standards are high.

The Enlisted Commissioning Program enables an eligible enlisted man or woman with previous college credits and between 4 and 11 years of active service to earn a bachelor's degree in 30-36 months while assigned to a Naval Reserve Officers' Training Corps (NROTC) college. The summer prior to beginning their academic program, ECP Selectees attend the Naval Science Institute in Newport Rhode Island. This is a six-and-one-half-week course which provides the first two years of NROTC Naval Science Courses. Once the ECP Selectee reports to an NROTC Unit, he/she becomes an officer candidate and completes the last two years of their Naval Science Courses. Upon graduation the ECP Officer Candidate is commissioned at the NROTC Unit.

EDUCATION PROGRAMS

The Navy believes that the more education people receive, the better equipped they are to perform their jobs and fulfill personal goals. A program called Navy Campus provides opportunities for enlisted members to take continuing education classes throughout their Navy careers. Through Navy Campus, enlisted members can pursue all levels of education and training, from high school equivalency to vocational certificate to college degree, wherever they are stationed. Navy Campus offers on-duty and off-duty study to provide a complete package of educational benefits to Navy people. They can enroll in any combination of Navy Campus programs and keep adding credits toward a civilian college degree or vocational certificate of their choice.

The Navy offers enlisted members two officer preparatory programs to improve their academic status so they may compete for a commissioning program such as the NROTC or the United States Naval Academy in Annapolis, Maryland. These preparatory programs are the Broadened Opportunity for Officer Selection and Training (BOOST) and the Naval Academy Preparatory School (NAPS).

The United States Naval Academy offers a fully subsidized 4-year college education—plus a monthly salary. About 1,300 people are selected for the Naval Academy each year from nominations by Senators, Representatives, the President and Vice President of the United States, and the Secretary of the Navy.

Candidates must be U.S. citizens, aged 17 to 22, and single with no children. Enlisted Navy men and women applying to the academy must have served at least one year of active duty by the date of entrance. Graduates receive a bachelor of science degree and a commission.

The NROTC program offers a fully subsidized tuition scholarship plus a monthly stipend. Approximately 1,100 people are selected for the NROTC Program each year.

FOR FURTHER INFORMATION

The occupational information provided in *Military Careers* can be useful in exploring career opportunities in the Navy. Many career information systems found in high schools and libraries have similar information about military careers. However, to learn more detailed information about the latest training and enlistment programs, contact your local Navy recruiter. There is no obligation. The Navy toll free number for recruiting information is 1-800-USA-NAVY. Another good source for information is the Navy's recruiting website: www.navyjobs.com.

Air Force

OVERVIEW

The mission of the Air Force is to defend the United States through control and exploitation of air and space. The Air Force flies and maintains aircraft, such as long-range bombers, supersonic fighters, Airborne Warning and Control System (AWACS) aircraft, and many others, whenever and wherever necessary, to protect the interests of America and American allies. Almost 400,000 highly trained officers and airmen make up today's Air Force. Some pilot aircraft – everything from helicopters to the Space Shuttle. Many others do the jobs that support the Air Force's flying mission; they may work as firefighters, aircraft mechanics, security police, or air traffic controllers, or in many other Air Force career fields. The Air Force currently recruits about 30,000 to 40,000 men and women each year to fill openings in hundreds of challenging Air Force careers.

ENLISTMENT

Applicants for enlistment in the Air Force must be in good health, possess good moral character, and make the minimum scores on the Armed Services Vocational Aptitude Battery (ASVAB) required for Air Force enlistment. They must also be at least 18 years of age. (Individuals who are 17 years of age may enlist if they are married, have parental consent to enlist, or have been emancipated by the courts.)

Prior to taking the oath of enlistment, qualified applicants may be guaranteed either to receive training in a specific skill or to be assigned within a selected aptitude area. The Guaranteed Training Enlistment Program guarantees training and initial assignment in a specific job skill. The Aptitude Area Program guarantees classification into one of four aptitude areas (mechanical, administrative, general, or electronic); specific skills within these aptitude areas are selected during basic training.

After choosing one of these programs, applicants will enter the Delayed Entry Program (DEP). DEP enlistees become members of the Air Force Inactive Reserve with a delayed date for active-duty enlistment. They do not participate in any military activities or earn pay or benefits while in the DEP. The individual agrees to enter active duty on a certain date, and the Air Force agrees to accept him or her (if still qualified) and provide training and initial assignment in the aptitude area or job specified.

TRAINING

The Air Force provides two kinds of training to all enlistees: basic training and job training. Select candidates can also pursue a Management Training program explained below.

Basic Training

All Air Force Basic Military Training (BMT) is conducted at Lackland Air Force Base (AFB) in San Antonio, Texas. BMT teaches enlistees how to adjust to military life, both physically and mentally, and promotes pride in being a member of the Air Force. It lasts approximately six weeks and consists of academic instruction, confidence courses, physical conditioning, and marksmanship training. Trainees who enlist with an aptitude-area guarantee receive orientation and individual counseling to help choose a job specialty compatible with Air Force needs and with their aptitudes, education, civilian experience, and desires. After graduation from BMT, recruits receive job training in their assigned specialty.

Job Training

All BMT graduates go directly to one of the Technical Training Centers (DoD or another Service) for formal, in-residence training. In-residence job training is conducted at Keesler AFB, Biloxi, Mississippi; Lackland AFB, San Antonio, Texas; Sheppard AFB, Wichita Falls, Texas; Goodfellow AFB, San Angelo, Texas; and several other locations nationwide. In formal classes and practice sessions, airmen learn the basic skills needed for the first assignment in their specialty.

Air Force training does not end with graduation from basic training and technical training school. After three months at their first permanent duty station, airmen begin on-the-job training (OJT). OJT is a two-part program consisting of self-study and supervised job performance. Airmen enroll in skill-related correspondence courses to gain broad knowledge of their Air Force job, and they study technical orders and directives to learn specific tasks they must perform. They also work daily with their trainers and supervisors who coach them during hands-on task performance. Through OJT, they develop the job skills needed to progress from apprentice airmen to skilled noncommissioned officers (NCOs). Airmen also complete advanced training and supplemental formal courses throughout their careers to increase their skills in using specific equipment or techniques.

Management Training

In addition to becoming skilled in their specialties, Air Force airmen and NCOs are also leaders and supervisors. Schools in the professional military education (PME) system teach airmen and NCOs to be more effective in the operation of the Air Force. PME is a progressive system consisting of leadership schools for airmen, NCO academies for intermediate NCOs, and the Senior NCO Academy for selected Master Sergeants and Senior Master Sergeants. Through PME, airmen and NCOs develop management abilities that are valuable in any chosen career, military or civilian.

ADVANCEMENT

Typically, Airman Basic (pay grade E-1) is the initial enlisted grade. However, there are several programs available that may qualify individuals for enlistment at a higher initial grade. These programs include: successful completion of a Civil Air Patrol program and receipt of the Billy Mitchell, Amelia Earhart, or Carl Spaatz Award; successful completion of at least three years of a Junior Reserve Officer Training Corps (JROTC) program (any service); receipt of a Boy Scout Eagle Scout or Girl Scout Gold Award; or completion of certain levels of course work at accredited colleges or universities.

Every job in the Air Force has a defined career path leading to supervisory positions. Airman Basic enlistees are normally promoted to Airman (E-2) upon completion of six months of service and to Airman First Class (E-3) after 16 months of service. Promotion to Senior Airman (E-4) usually occurs at the three-year point of service. However, some airmen qualify for accelerated promotion. Local Air Force recruiters have all the details on qualifications for accelerated promotions and advanced enlistment grades.

Promotions to the higher enlisted grades of Staff Sergeant (E-5), Technical Sergeant (E-6), Master Sergeant (E-7), and Senior and Chief Master Sergeant (E-8 and E-9) are competitive. Eligible airmen compete with others worldwide in the same grade and skill, based on test scores, performance ratings, decorations, and time in service and grade. All airmen receive a promotion score that shows how they stand in relation to others in their specialty and where improvement may be needed. Additionally, E-8 and E-9 candidates are reviewed by an evaluation board.

Chief Master Sergeants occupy the top enlisted grade, and they have great responsibility and prestige in the Air Force. They have the management ability to head several enlisted specialties related to their own skill, or they may be the top enlisted expert in a highly technical field.

Normally, enlisted airmen and commissioned officers advance along separate career fields. However, the Air Force offers three programs through which airmen can receive commissions: the Air Force ROTC Scholarship Commissioning Program, the Airman Education and Commissioning Program, and the Air Force Academy. The Air Force ROTC Scholarship Commissioning Program allows airmen to complete their college degrees and earn officer commissions through Air Force ROTC scholarships. If selected for the program, the individual is transferred from active duty into the Air Force Reserve, then attends college (at the same time enrolling in the college's Air Force ROTC program) for completion of degree requirements. This highly competitive program pays tuition, fees, and a monthly allowance.

Airmen can also apply for a commission as an Air Force officer under the Airman Education and Commissioning Program (AECP) or by acceptance to the United States Air Force Academy. Under AECP, enlisted personnel attend school full time and draw full pay and allowances. Enlisted personnel who possess bachelor's degrees or who complete degree requirements under AECP in areas of critical need may be accepted into the Officer Training School. They are commissioned upon graduation.

Each year, airmen on active duty and airmen serving in the Air Force Reserve and Air National Guard receive appointments to the Air Force Academy. There are 85 appointments available for active duty airmen and another 85 for those in the Air Force Reserve or Air National Guard. All candidates are considered for admission on a competitive basis. Examination results and previous performance determine selection. Graduates from the Air Force Academy receive bachelor of science degrees and are commissioned as Second Lieutenants in the active duty Air Force.

EDUCATION PROGRAMS

The Air Force has many education programs to help men and women pursue their educational goals while serving in the Air Force. These programs are in addition to veterans' educational benefits set up by the Federal Government for members of all services. All Air Force bases have education service centers, where trained counselors help airmen decide on a program or combination of programs and help them enroll. Some of these programs are:

Community College of the Air Force

The Community College of the Air Force (CCAF) offers education programs directly related to Air Force specialties; graduates are awarded an associate degree. The college works with Air Force training schools, regional accrediting agencies, and hundreds of cooperating civilian colleges and universities. Since the technical nature of most Air Force courses places them on a level with college study, airmen earn fully recognized college credits for most of what they learn in job training and on-the-job training. They can combine those credits with attendance at off-duty courses from civilian colleges to earn a two-year accredited associate degree in applied sciences from CCAF. The college offers more than 80 fields of study, ranging from police science to environmental services technology. Registration is free, and CCAF establishes a special study program for each student. Professional, industrial, and governmental organizations that issue licenses and certifications and set standards for civilian work recognize Air Force training and education through CCAF.

The College Level Examination Program (CLEP)

This program allows airmen to receive credit for selected college courses by examination. The program is free, and education services centers maintain a current list of college tests available.

The Extension Course Institute

The Extension Course Institute (ECI) is the Air Force's correspondence school. It offers, free of charge, nearly 400 courses to some 250,000 students who register for ECI each year. These courses include everything from fundamentals of solid state devices to apprentice carpentry. Air Force personnel may voluntarily enroll in courses such as auto mechanics, plumbing, carpentry, or electrical wiring simply for background knowledge.

Tuition Assistance

The Air Force will pay up to 75 percent of the tuition costs of most college courses. College programs are offered on all Air Force bases, with local college professors coming to the base at most installations.

FOR FURTHER INFORMATION

Local Air Force recruiters have the latest information on enlistment programs, and career opportunities; contact them if you have any questions. High school guidance counselors can also give you advice on Air Force ROTC programs and the USAF Academy.

Marine Corps

OVERVIEW

The Marine Corps has become one of the most elite fighting forces in the world. Since its creation on November 10, 1775, the U.S. Marine Corps has allowed America to project power far from its shores. Against the Barbary pirates off the coast of Tripoli, Libya, the Marines, from 1801 through 1805, launched a series of punitive raids in retaliation for attacks on U.S. ships. The attacks ceased. Almost 200 years later, when Saddam Hussein sent his forces into Kuwait in August 1990, the Marines rushed to the region, arriving just seven days after President Bush ordered U.S. forces to respond. The Marines brought the first heavy tanks and artillery to prevent Hussein's advance into Saudi Arabia.

The Marines are a part of the Department of the Navy and operate in close cooperation with U.S. naval forces at sea. The Marine Corps' mission is unique among the services. Marines serve on U.S. Navy ships, protect naval bases, guard U.S. embassies, and provide a quick, ever-ready strike force to protect U.S. interest anywhere in the world. All Marines can move on short notice to match up with equipment stored on floating bases on the world's oceans. In the post-Cold War world, this remains an essential capability for the U.S.

To perform the many duties of the Marine Corps, approximately 174,000 officers and enlisted Marines fly planes and helicopters; operate radar equipment; drive armored vehicles; gather intelligence; survey and map territory; maintain and repair radios, computers, jeeps, trucks, tanks, and aircraft; and perform hundreds of other challenging jobs. Each year, the Marine Corps recruits approximately 41,000 enlisted men and women to fill openings in its numerous career fields. The Marine Corps training programs offer practical, challenging, and progressive skill development. The Marine Corps stresses professional education for all ranks and emphasizes the development of mental strength as well as traditional physical prowess. In this way, the Marine Corps provides the Nation with a modern well-armed force that is both "tough" and "smart."

ENLISTMENT

Marine Corps enlistment terms are for three, four, or five years, depending on the type of enlistment program. Young men and women enlisting in the Marine Corps must meet exacting physical, mental, and moral standards. Applicants must be between the ages of 17 and 29, American citizens or registered aliens, and in good health to ensure that they can meet the rigorous physical training demands. The Armed Services Vocational Aptitude Battery (ASVAB), described in this guide, is used by the Marine Corps to assess each person's vocational aptitudes and academic abilities. Some

applicants for enlistment may have taken the ASVAB while still in high school. For those applicants who have not previously taken the ASVAB, a Marine recruiter can arrange for them to do so.

Applicants for enlistment can be guaranteed training and duty assignment with a wide variety of options, depending upon the degree of education and the qualifications they possess. Women are eligible to enlist in all occupational fields, with the exception of combat arms—infantry, artillery, and tank and amphibian tractor crew members.

In addition to regular enlistment, the Marine Corps offers special enlistment programs.

Delayed Entry Program

Students who wish to complete the Marine Corps enlistment process before graduating from high school or a community college may enlist in the Marine Corps Delayed Entry Program (DEP). Enlistment in the DEP allows applicants to postpone their initial active-duty training for up to a full year. Enlisting in the DEP has two principal benefits: the student can finish high school or community college, and the highly desirable enlistment programs that are available in limited numbers, such as all computer specialties and many aviation specialties, can be reserved early.

Musician Enlistment Option Program

The Musician Enlistment Option Program gives graduates with musical talent an opportunity to serve in Marine Corps bands or the Marine Corps Drum and Bugle Corps. The program's incentives include formal school training, accelerated promotions, and duty station choices.

Enlistment Options Program

The Enlistment Options Program guarantees well-qualified applicants, before they enlist, assignment to one of over 30 occupational fields. The occupational fields contain every job available in the Marine Corps, ranging from combat arms to motor transport to high technology avionics, electronics, and computer science. Some enlistment options feature cash bonuses as well as formal training programs.

Quality Enlistment Program

The Quality Enlistment Program is for highly qualified young men and women for enlistment and assignment primarily to technical occupational fields. The program provides incentives, including choice of geographic assignment, to qualified high school graduates or seniors who enlist.

TRAINING

Marine Corps training occurs in two sections: recruit training and job training.

Recruit Training

Upon completing the enlistment process, all applicants enter Marine Corps recruit training. Young men undergo recruit training either at Parris Island, South Carolina, or in San Diego, California. All young women attend recruit training at Parris Island. Recruit training is rigorous, demanding, and challenging. The overall goal of recruit training is to instill in the recruits the military skills, knowledge, discipline, pride, and self-confidence necessary to perform as United States Marines.

In the first several days at the recruit depot, a recruit is assigned to a platoon, receives a basic issue of uniforms and equipment, is given an additional physical, and takes further assignment classification tests. Each platoon is led by a team of three Marine drill instructors. A typical training day for recruits begins with reveille at 0500 (5:00 a.m.), continues with drill, physical training, and several classes in weapons and conduct, and ends with taps at 2100 (9:00 p.m.).

Job Training

Upon graduation from recruit training, each Marine takes a short vacation, then reports to the School of Infantry for combat skills training. Upon graduation from the School of Infantry, Marines then report either to a new command for formal school training or to the on-the-job training to which he or she has been assigned. The Marine Corps sends students to over 200 basic formal schools and to over 300 advanced formal schools. The length of formal school varies from four weeks to over a year, depending on the level of technical expertise and knowledge required to become proficient in certain job skills. For example, different military occupational specialties (MOSs) within the electrical and electronic repair occupational field require from 10 to 50 weeks to complete; different MOSs in the vehicle and machinery mechanic occupational field require from six to 18 weeks to complete.

Marines assigned to an MOS within the combat specialty occupational field conduct most of their training outdoors. Marines receiving training in highly technical MOSs receive most of their training in a classroom. The main thrust of Marine Corps training is toward "hands-on" training and practical application of newly acquired skills. As soon as possible after classroom instruction is completed, students are placed in an actual work environment to obtain practical experience and to develop confidence. After completing entry-level MOS training, most Marines are assigned to operational units of the Fleet Marine Forces to apply their skills.

Marines assigned to the more technical MOSs may require more advanced training prior to their first operational duty assignment.

Job performance requirements in a number of MOSs are comparable to requirements needed for journeyman certification in civilian occupations. A Marine assigned to these MOSs may apply for status as a registered apprentice.

ADVANCEMENT

Advancement is directly linked to an individual's performance in an MOS and development as a Marine. Each Marine is evaluated based on job performance, experience, and ability to apply newly learned skills. While promotion criteria rely heavily upon individual job performance, Marines are also in competition with others of the same rank in the same MOS. Promotion becomes increasingly competitive as Marines advance in rank. The normal time-in-grade requirements for promotion are as follows: Private to Private First Class, six months; Private First Class to Lance Corporal, eight months; Lance Corporal to Corporal, eight months; and Corporal to Sergeant, 24 months. Promotions above Sergeant to the staff noncommissioned officer (SNCO) ranks are determined by promotion boards.

The Meritorious Promotion System is used to recognize Marines who demonstrate outstanding job performance and professional competence. Marines recommended for meritorious promotion are carefully screened for accelerated advancement. Qualified enlisted Marines can compete for and be accepted into the officer corps through several different programs. Competition is keen, and only the best qualified Marines are accepted.

The Enlisted Commissioning Program

This program provides the opportunity for enlisted Marines with two years of college to apply for assignment to the Officer Candidates School and subsequent appointment as unrestricted commissioned officers.

Enlisted Commissioning Education Program

The Marine Corps Enlisted Commissioning Education Program provides to selected enlisted Marines (who have had no college experience) the opportunity to earn baccalaureate degrees by attending a college or university as full-time students. Marines in this program who obtain their baccalaureate degrees and subsequently complete officer candidate training are commissioned as Second Lieutenants.

The Warrant Officer Program

Warrant officers are technical specialists who are assigned to duties only in their area of expertise. All other officers are said to be "unrestricted" and are assigned to a wide variety of assignments during their career. The Warrant Officer Program provides for the selection and appointment to permanent warrant officer those qualified applicants who are in the grade of Sergeant or above at the time of application.

EDUCATION PROGRAMS

All Marines on active duty are encouraged to continue their education by taking advantage of service schools and Marine Corps funded off-duty courses at local civilian colleges. Three educational assistance programs are available to enlisted Marines.

The Marine Corps has developed an extensive professional military education program to provide Marine leaders with the skill, knowledge, understanding, and confidence that will better enable Marines to make sound military decisions.

Tuition Assistance Program

The Marine Corps Tuition Assistance Program provides Marines with financial assistance to pursue educational programs at civilian secondary and postsecondary institutions during off-duty time. Tuition assistance may only be used to fund courses at a higher academic level than the degree or diploma currently held by the Marine.

Servicemembers' Opportunity Colleges

The Servicemembers' Opportunity Colleges (SOC) is a consortium of colleges and universities that have agreed to help military personnel gain access to higher education by minimizing residency requirements, recognizing nontraditional education attainment, such as the College Level Examination Program (CLEP) tests, easing the transfer of college credit of similarly accredited institutions, and granting credit for formal military training.

College After the Corps

Marines are also eligible to participate in educational assistance programs with the Government, such as the Montgomery G.I. Bill, which can provide approximately $19,000 for future educational needs. The Marine Corps College Fund may add monetary incentives to qualified Marines' accounts to total no more than $50,000 for education.

FOR FURTHER INFORMATION

The above information provides the general scope of enlistment policies, recruit training, follow-on training, and educational opportunities found in the Marine Corps today. Young men and women who are interested in joining the Marine Corps can contact a Marine recruiter by calling 1-800-MARINES or logging onto our website at MARINES.COM.

Coast Guard

OVERVIEW

The Coast Guard constantly performs its mission of protecting America's coastlines and inland waterways by enforcing customs and fishing laws, combating drug smuggling, conducting search and rescue missions, maintaining lighthouses, and promoting boating safety. The Coast Guard is part of the Department of Transportation; in time of war it may be placed in the Department of Defense under the command of the Navy. A vital part of the Armed Services, the Coast Guard has participated in every major American military campaign. With a work force of about 5,580 commissioned officers, 1,490 warrant officers, and 27,130 enlisted members, Coast Guard personnel perform in many different occupations to support the missions of the Coast Guard. Each year, the Coast Guard has openings for about 4,000 new enlistees in a wide range of challenging careers.

ENLISTMENT

Applicants for enlistment in the Coast Guard must be physically qualified, possess high moral character, and make at least the minimum required scores on the Armed Services Vocational Aptitude Battery (ASVAB). Coast Guard regular enlistments are for two, three, four or six years of active duty. Provided openings are available, qualified enlistees may be guaranteed an assignment to a geographical region (not an individual unit). Guaranteed geographic assignments cannot be used in conjunction with a guaranteed school. Qualified applicants may also enlist up to 12 months prior to beginning active duty. Coast Guard recruits must be at least 17 years old and must not have reached their 28th birthday on the day of enlistment.

COAST GUARD RESERVE

There are approximately 8,000 Coast Guard Reservists. For those without prior service, enlistment into the Coast Guard Reserve is for a period of eight years. The Coast Guard has four programs for individuals with no prior service experience. Three of the programs are for individuals who are at least 17 and who have not reached their 28th birthday. The other program is for individuals who are at least 26 but have not reached their 36th birthday. The programs all include a period of basic training and Class A school or on-the-job training and then release from initial active duty for training. Upon completion, these reservists return to their home and drill with their Reserve units monthly. One of the four programs is a direct petty officer program for persons who possess specialized civilian skills and can convert these skills to the various ratings in the Coast Guard Reserve. Reservists augment the regular Coast Guard component on a regular basis, keeping the spirit of the "One Coast Guard Family."

TRAINING

Two types of training are provided to Coast Guard recruits: recruit training and job training.

Recruit Training

After completing the enlistment process, all Coast Guard recruits attend recruit training, or "boot camp," at Cape May, New Jersey. Boot camp lasts approximately eight weeks; it is designed to provide a transition from civilian life to that of service with the Coast Guard. The course is demanding, both physically and mentally. Coast Guard recruit training instills in each trainee a sense of teamwork and discipline. Coast Guard history, missions, customs, and basic discipline are all part of the training course. Boot camp includes physical training, classroom work, and practical application of the subjects studied.

Job Training

The Coast Guard maintains basic petty officer (Class A) schools for formal training in specific occupational specialties. Courses of study in these Class A schools vary from 8 to 42 weeks, depending on the rating or specialty area taught. Each school provides a course of study that leads to advancement to the Petty Officer Third Class level. Specialty schools in the other services can be used by Coast Guard personnel in addition to, or in place of, Coast Guard schools for training in certain ratings. Upon successful completion of Class A school, the graduate becomes a qualified specialist and can expect assignment to a field unit for duty and further on-the-job training in his or her specialty.

Opportunities for additional professional training are available to qualified, career-oriented personnel in the form of advanced petty officer (class B) and special (class C) schools. These advanced schools range in length from a few weeks to several months, depending on the skills taught. Senior enlisted personnel in certain ratings are also eligible to compete for assignment to special degree programs within their occupational specialty areas.

ADVANCEMENT

The Coast Guard enlisted rating structure consists of paths of advancement from pay grade E-1 through E-9. Two general apprenticeships are available within pay grades E-1 through E-3: Fireman (FN) and Seaman (SN). Approximately 25 occupational fields, called ratings, exist in pay grades E-4 through E-9.

Every job in the Coast Guard has a career path leading to increased pay and responsibility—with well-defined promotion criteria. A Coast Guard Seaman Recruit (E-1) is promoted to Seaman Apprentice (E-2) upon completion of basic training. Eligibility for promotion to Seaman or Fireman (E-3) is based on four requirements: adequate time-in-grade, successful demonstration of military and professional qualifications, recommendation of the commanding officer, and completion of correspondence courses.

To earn petty officer ratings (E-4 through E-9), an individual must, in addition to the requirements above, pass the Coast Guard-wide competitive examination for the rating.

A Coast Guard enlisted member can expect to spend the majority of his or her career within the 48 contiguous states, primarily on the East, West, or Gulf Coast. The Coast Guard also has a number of units on the Great Lakes and along the Midwest's river system. At some point in his or her career, a Coast Guard member should expect to serve one or more tours of duty in an overseas assignment. Tour lengths vary from one to four years, depending upon the location of the assignment and the nature of the duty. The amount of sea duty varies according to the individual's rating and might range from a slight majority to a small fraction of the career. The Coast Guard, the smallest of the military forces, prides itself on its ability to give personal consideration to the needs of its members in the personnel assignment process.

EDUCATION PROGRAMS

The Coast Guard believes strongly in the continued education of its members. The Coast Guard offers several education assistance programs, including a Tuition Assistance Program, the Physician's Assistant Program, and the Pre-Commissioning Program for Enlisted Personnel (PPEP).

Tuition Assistance Program

The Coast Guard sponsors a tuition assistance program for off-duty education within the limits of available funds. This program allows Coast Guard members, both officer and enlisted, to enroll in off-duty courses at accredited colleges, universities, junior colleges, high schools, and commercial schools. Seventy-five percent of the tuition is paid by the Coast Guard for all courses not in excess of six credits per semester (or quarter) or for any course not extending beyond one semester or a maximum of 17 weeks, whichever is longer.

Physician's Assistant Program

The Physician's Assistant Program is a two-year, full-time course of study at Sheppard AFB, Wichita Falls, Texas, offered to warrant officers in the medical specialty. The program includes 12 months of study and 12 months of clinical rotation at an Air Force hospital. Upon successful completion, Coast Guard graduates receive their certificates as physician's assistants and promotion to lieutenant (O-3). Completion of the program results in a bachelor's degree in Health Science.

Pre-commissioning Program for Enlisted Personnel (PPEP)

The Pre-commissioning Program for Enlisted Personnel enables selected enlisted personnel to attend college on a full-time basis for up to two years, receive a bachelor's degree, attend Officer Candidate School (OCS), and upon graduation from OCS, receive a commission. The program provides an upward mobility mechanism for qualified enlisted personnel to become commissioned officers. The number of PPEP selections made annually will be determined at the time of selection.

FOR FURTHER INFORMATION

Although the preceding section gives a general overview of the Coast Guard and its programs, it by no means covers the wide range of opportunities available in the Coast Guard. Use *Military Careers* to begin exploring career possibilities in the Coast Guard. Your local Coast Guard recruiter would be pleased to supply you with current, more detailed career information. There is no obligation. The Coast Guard toll-free information number is 1-877-NOW-USCG, Ext. 1704.

Enlisted Occupational Descriptions

Administrative Occupations

Administrative careers include a wide variety of career fields and positions. The military must keep accurate information for planning and managing its operations. Paper and electronic records are kept on equipment, funds, personnel, supplies, and all other aspects of the military. Enlisted administrative personnel record information, type reports, and maintain files to assist in the operation of military offices. Personnel may work in a specialized area such as finance, accounting, legal, maintenance, or supply.

- Administrative Support Specialists
  Profile: Ray Kanakis
- Finance and Accounting Specialists
- Flight Operations Specialists
- Legal Specialists and Court Reporters
- Preventive Maintenance Analysts
- Sales and Stock Specialists

ADMINISTRATIVE SUPPORT SPECIALISTS

Army
Navy
Air Force
Marine Corps
Coast Guard

The military must keep accurate information for planning and managing its operations. Paper and electronic records are kept on equipment, funds, personnel, supplies, and all other aspects of the military. Administrative support specialists record information, fill out reports, and maintain files to assist in the operation of military offices.

What They Do

Administrative support specialists in the military perform some or all of the following duties:

- Use a computer to type and prepare letters, reports, and other kinds of documents

- Proofread written material for spelling, punctuation, and grammatical errors

- Organize and maintain electronic and paper files and publications

- Order office supplies

- Greet and direct office visitors

- Sort and deliver mail to office workers

- Use office equipment such as fax machines, copiers, and computers

- Schedule training and leave for unit personnel

- Answer phones and provide general information

- Take meeting notes

Helpful Attributes

Helpful school subjects include English, math, and business administration. Helpful attributes include:

- Interest in keeping organized and accurate records

- Preference for office work

- Interest in operating computers and other office machines

- Ability to organize and plan

Training Provided

Job training consists of 6 to 10 weeks of classroom instruction, including practice in various office functions. Course content typically includes:

- English grammar, spelling and punctuation

- Keyboard and clerical skills

- Setting up and maintaining filing and publication systems

- Preparing forms and correspondence in military style

Further training occurs on the job.

Work Environment

Administrative support specialists work in office settings, both on land and aboard ships.

Civilian Counterparts

Civilian administrative support specialists work in most business, government, and legal offices. They perform duties similar to military administrative support specialists and are called secretaries, general office clerks, administrative assistants, or office managers.

Opportunities

The military has about 23,000 administrative support specialists. Each year, the services need new specialists due to changes in personnel and the demands of the field. After job training, administrative support specialists develop their skills under close supervision. As they gain experience, specialists are assigned more difficult tasks and work more independently. In time, they may supervise and eventually manage an office.

MILITARY CAREERS/SCORE	INTEREST CODE
The circled score shows the typical Military Careers Score of servicemembers in this occupation.	This occupation generally appeals to people whose primary Interest Code is *Conventional. Conventional* jobs:
1 **②** 3 4 5 6 7	• Require attention to detail
Compare this score to your Military Career Score to see how well your aptitudes, skills, and abilities match those of personnel currently in these positions. See your recruiter for more information about qualification requirements.	• Require attention to accuracy
Pages 8 and 9 explain the Military Careers Score and the Interest Codes	

Profile: Ray Kanakis

Ray Kanakis joined the Coast Guard on the recommendation of an older brother who had already joined. After boot camp, he was sent for his general duty assignment to the United States Coast Guard (USCG) Yard, Baltimore, MD. As a seaman apprentice, he worked on vessels at the Yard and learned basic seamanship. He was also selected to be in the color guard representing the Coast Guard in parades and other ceremonies.

While in Baltimore, Ray took a Coast Guard correspondence course in administrative support and became a trainee in this field. This is when his career really began. He started out in a personnel office, typing correspondence, maintaining service records, preparing forms, and operating computers and word processors. He liked his new career. "I enjoy working with people and I like a desk job," he explains.

After 2 years at the Yard, Ray was assigned to USCG Headquarters, Washington, DC, in the legal administration division, where he worked processing and preparing legal documents. He was selected for a 16-week course at the Defense Race Relations Institute, Patrick Air Force Base, FL, where he trained to be an equal opportunity specialist and military civil rights counselor/facilitator. Ray says, "I enjoy providing a service to people when I help someone or solve a problem." After 5 1/2 years at Headquarters, Ray was assigned to shipboard duty.

To prepare for his new assignment, Ray was given advanced training in the computerized systems used on board Coast Guard ships. He was then assigned to the USCG cutter *Hamilton*. As the cutter's yeoman, he handled 180 service records and maintained and updated all publications for the cutter. Ray was on board when the cutter went on search and rescue, pollution cleanup, and law enforcement missions.

After 2 years on the cutter, Ray was again assigned to USCG Headquarters, this time in the command post exercise division. Working with classified information, he helped coordinate and plan wargames for 2 years. He was then personally selected by the Master Chief Petty Officer of the Coast Guard to be his aide. Since he works for the top enlisted person of the Coast Guard, he feels he must know everything. "I have to be ready to carry on when he's not there," says Ray.

SAMPLE CAREER PATH

Office Manager · **17–19 years**

Office managers supervise consolidated office facilities or serve as senior supervisors at command or staff headquarters. They plan and control administrative support activities and may recommend and implement new office procedures. Managers also develop operating budgets and track expenses.

Clerical Supervisor · **9–12 years**

Clerical supervisors oversee one or more administrative support sections. They prepare directives, job descriptions, and standard operating procedures. Supervisors divide the work load among personnel and train new clerks. They also handle and safeguard classified documents.

Administrative Technician · **4–6 years**

Administrative technicians perform clerical duties and give technical assistance to administrative clerks. Technicians maintain different types of records and files, compose correspondence, and handle dictation needs. They also proofread documents and make necessary corrections.

Administrative Clerk

Administrative clerks perform a variety of clerical duties in support of office operations. They may perform receptionist duties, handle mail, and generate documents and correspondence. They perform other office support functions under the direction of administrative technicians and clerical supervisors.

The years shown represent typical time-in-service before advancement to that level. Actual career advancement depends on individual experience and performance.

FINANCE AND ACCOUNTING SPECIALISTS

Army
Navy
Air Force
Marine Corps
Coast Guard

Millions of paychecks are issued and large amounts of materials are purchased by the services each year. To account for military spending, exact financial records must be kept of these transactions. Finance and accounting specialists organize and keep track of financial records. They also compute payrolls and other allowances, audit accounting records, and prepare payments for military personnel.

What They Do

Finance and accounting specialists in the military perform some or all of the following duties:

- Use computers to perform calculations, record details of financial transactions, and maintain accounting records

- Review or audit financial records to check the accuracy of figures and calculations

- Prepare paychecks, earnings statements, bills, and financial accounts and reports

- Disburse cash, checks, advance pay, and bonds

- Organize information on past expenses to help plan budgets for future expenses

Training Provided

Job training consists of 6 to 12 weeks of classroom instruction, including practice in accounting techniques. Course content typically includes:

- Accounting principles and procedures

- Preparation and maintenance of financial reports and budgets

- Statistical analyses to interpret financial data

- Computation of pay and deductions

Special Qualifications

Depending on the specialty, entry into this occupation may require courses in mathematics, bookkeeping, or accounting.

Helpful Attributes

Helpful school subjects include mathematics, statistics, bookkeeping, and accounting. Helpful attributes include:

- Ability to work with numbers

- Interest in using office machines such as computers, and calculators

- Interest in work requiring accuracy and attention to detail

Work Environment

Finance and accounting specialists work in offices on land or aboard ships.

Civilian Counterparts

Civilian finance and accounting specialists work for all types of businesses and government agencies. They perform duties similar to military finance and accounting specialists. Civilian finance and accounting specialists are also called accounting clerks, audit clerks, bookkeepers, or payroll clerks.

Opportunities

The services have over 10,000 finance and accounting specialists. Each year, they need new specialists due to changes in personnel and the demands of the field. After job training, finance and accounting specialists typically perform routine financial recording activities under the direction of supervisors. With experience, they are given more difficult tasks, such as auditing, and may become responsible for checking the work of others. In time, finance and accounting specialists may become supervisors or managers of accounting units or pay and finance centers.

MILITARY CAREERS/SCORE	INTEREST CODE
The circled score shows the typical Military Careers Score of servicemembers in this occupation. 1 2 3 **(4)** 5 6 7 Compare this score to your Military Career Score to see how well your aptitudes, skills, and abilities match those of personnel currently in these positions. See your recruiter for more information about qualification requirements.	This occupation generally appeals to people whose primary Interest Code is **Conventional. Conventional** jobs: • Require attention to detail • Require attention to accuracy
Pages 8 and 9 explain the Military Careers Score and the Interest Codes	

FLIGHT OPERATIONS SPECIALISTS

Army
Navy
Air Force
Marine Corps
Coast Guard

The services operate one of the largest fleets of aircraft in the world. Hundreds of transport, passenger, and combat airplanes and helicopters fly missions every day. Accurate flight information keeps operations safe and efficient. Flight operations specialists prepare and provide flight information for air and ground crews.

What They Do

Flight operations specialists in the military perform some or all of the following duties:

- Help plan flight schedules and air crew assignments
- Keep flight logs on incoming and outgoing flights
- Keep air crew flying records and flight operations records
- Receive and post weather information and flight plan data
- Coordinate air crew needs, such as ground transportation
- Plan aircraft equipment needs for air evacuation and dangerous cargo flights
- Check military flight plans with civilian agencies

Work Environment

Flight operations specialists work indoors in flight control centers or air terminals.

Physical Demands

The ability to speak clearly and distinctly is required.

Helpful Attributes

Helpful school subjects include general math and typing. Helpful attributes include:

- Interest in work involving computers
- Interest in work that helps others
- Ability to keep accurate records

Training Provided

Job training consists of 7 to 14 weeks of classroom instruction. Training length varies depending on specialty. Course content typically includes:

- Introduction to aviation operations
- Procedures for scheduling aircraft and assigning air crews
- Flight planning and airfield operations
- Preparing flight operations reports and records

Further training occurs on the job and through advanced courses.

Civilian Counterparts

Civilian flight operations specialists work for commercial and private airlines and air transport companies. They perform duties similar to military flight operations specialists.

Opportunities

The services have about 8,000 flight operations specialists. Each year, they need new specialists due to changes in personnel and the demands of the field. After training, new specialists keep logs and type schedules. With experience, they schedule air crews. In time, they may plan flight operations and supervise others.

MILITARY CAREERS/SCORE	INTEREST CODE
The circled score shows the typical Military Careers Score of servicemembers in this occupation. 1 2 ③ 4 5 6 7 Compare this score to your Military Career Score to see how well your aptitudes, skills, and abilities match those of personnel currently in these positions. See your recruiter for more information about qualification requirements.	This occupation generally appeals to people whose primary Interest Code is **Conventional. Conventional** jobs: • Require attention to detail • Require attention to accuracy
Pages 8 and 9 explain the Military Careers Score and the Interest Codes	

LEGAL SPECIALISTS AND COURT REPORTERS

The military has its own judicial system for prosecuting lawbreakers and handling disputes. Legal specialists and court reporters assist military lawyers and judges in the performance of legal and judicial work. They perform legal research, prepare legal documents, and record legal proceedings.

What They Do

Legal specialists and court reporters in the military perform some or all of the following duties:

- Research court decisions and military regulations
- Process legal claims and appeals
- Interview clients and take statements
- Prepare trial requests and make arrangements for courtrooms
- Maintain law libraries and trial case files
- Use a variety of methods and equipment to record and transcribe court proceedings
- Prepare records of hearings, investigations, court-martials, and courts of inquiry

Training Provided

Job training consists of 6 to 10 weeks of instruction. Course content typically includes:

- Legal terminology and research techniques
- How to prepare legal documents
- High speed transcription
- Military judicial processes

Special Requirements

Some specialties require the ability to type at a rate of 25–50 words per minute.

Helpful Attributes

Helpful school subjects include business mathematics, typing, speech, and shorthand. Helpful attributes include:

- Interest in the law and legal proceedings
- Ability to keep organized and accurate records
- Ability to listen carefully

Work Environment

Legal specialists and court reporters work in military law offices and courtrooms.

Physical Demands

Good hearing and clear speech are needed to record and read aloud court proceedings. A clear speaking ability is necessary to interview clients.

Civilian Counterparts

Civilian legal specialists and court reporters work for private law firms, banks, insurance companies, government agencies, and local, state, and federal courts. They perform duties similar to military legal specialists and court reporters. Civilian legal specialists and court reporters may also be called legal assistants, law clerks, paralegals, and court reporters.

Opportunities

The services have about 3,000 legal specialists and court reporters. Each year, they need new specialists and court reporters due to changes in personnel and the demands of the field. After training, they normally work under an attorney or in a legal office. With experience, legal specialists and court reporters perform more demanding activities and may supervise other specialists.

MILITARY CAREERS/SCORE	INTEREST CODE
The circled score shows the typical Military Careers Score of servicemembers in this occupation. 1 2 3 **(4)** 5 6 7 Compare this score to your Military Career Score to see how well your aptitudes, skills, and abilities match those of personnel currently in these positions. See your recruiter for more information about qualification requirements.	This occupation generally appeals to people whose primary Interest Code is **Conventional. Conventional** jobs: • Require attention to detail • Require attention to accuracy
Pages 8 and 9 explain the Military Careers Score and the Interest Codes	

PREVENTATIVE MAINTENANCE ANALYSTS

**Army
Navy
Air Force
Marine Corps
Coast Guard**

Regular maintenance extends the time aircraft, vehicles, and machinery can be used. To make sure military equipment is well maintained, the services prepare detailed maintenance schedules. Preventive maintenance analysts promote equipment maintenance. They watch schedules and notify mechanics about upcoming maintenance needs.

What They Do

Preventive maintenance analysts in the military perform some or all of the following duties:

- Review maintenance schedules and notify mechanics about the types of service needed

- Compare schedules to records of maintenance work actually performed

- Prepare charts and reports on maintenance activities

- Calculate how many mechanics and spare parts are needed to maintain equipment

- Operate computers and calculators to enter or retrieve maintenance data

Helpful Attributes

Helpful school subjects include general mathematics and algebra. Helpful attributes include:

- Interest in working with numbers and statistics

- Preference for work requiring attention to detail

- Ability to use mathematical formulas

- Interest in working with computers

Physical Demands

Normal color vision is required to read and interpret maintenance charts and graphs in some specialties.

Some specialties require the ability to speak clearly.

Work Environment

Preventive maintenance analysts usually work in office settings.

Training Provided

Job training consists of 4 to 15 weeks of classroom instruction. Training length varies depending on specialty. Course content typically includes:

- Equipment maintenance management concepts

- Accounting procedures

- Statistical reporting methods

- Parts and supply inventory control procedures

Civilian Counterparts

Civilian preventive maintenance analysts work for government agencies, airlines, and large transportation firms. They also work for firms with large numbers of machines. They perform duties similar to military preventive maintenance analysts.

Opportunities

The services have about 9,000 preventive maintenance analysts. Each year, they need new analysts due to changes in personnel and the demands of the field. After job training, new analysts work under close supervision. As they gain experience, they are given more responsibility and more difficult work assignments. Eventually, they may become supervisors of maintenance control units.

MILITARY CAREERS/SCORE	INTEREST CODE
The circled score shows the typical Military Careers Score of servicemembers in this occupation. 1 2 3 **(4)** 5 6 7 Compare this score to your Military Career Score to see how well your aptitudes, skills, and abilities match those of personnel currently in these positions. See your recruiter for more information about qualification requirements.	This occupation generally appeals to people whose primary Interest Code is **Conventional. Conventional** jobs: • Require attention to detail • Require attention to accuracy
Pages 8 and 9 explain the Military Careers Score and the Interest Codes	

SALES AND STOCK SPECIALISTS

Navy
Air Force
Marine Corps
Coast Guard

The military operates retail stores that sell food and merchandise to make it easier for personnel to obtain whatever they need where they are stationed. Sales and stock specialists perform a variety of duties to support the operation of these stores whether working aboard a ship or overseas in a remote location.

What They Do

Sales and stock specialists in the military perform some or all of the following duties:

- Order and receive merchandise and food for retail sales

- Inspect food and merchandise for spoilage or damage

- Price retail sales items, using stamping machines

- Stock shelves and racks for the display of products

- Count merchandise and supplies during inventory checks

- Operate cash registers

- Record money received and prepare bank deposits

Helpful Attributes

Helpful school subjects include bookkeeping, and mathematics. Helpful attributes include:

- Ability to use cash registers, and calculators

- Interest in working with people

Training Provided

Job training consists of 6 to 7 weeks of classroom instruction for some specialties. For others, training occurs on the job. Course content includes:

- Stock procedures

- Record keeping and bookkeeping procedures

Further training occurs on the job.

Physical Demands

The ability to speak clearly is required. Sales and stock specialists may have to lift and carry heavy objects.

Civilian Counterparts

Civilian sales and stock specialists work in many kinds of retail businesses, such as grocery stores and department stores. They perform duties similar to military sales and stock specialists. They may also be called sales clerks or stock clerks.

Work Environment

Sales and stock specialists work on land and aboard ships in retail stores, and storerooms.

Opportunities

The services have over 1,500 sales and stock specialists. Each year, they need new specialists due to changes in personnel and the demands of the field. After job training, sales and stock specialists are assigned to retail stores and storerooms. Initially, they work under close supervision. With experience, they work more independently, train new workers, and assume more responsibility for sales and stock activities.

MILITARY CAREERS/SCORE	INTEREST CODE
The circled score shows the typical Military Careers Score of servicemembers in this occupation. 1 **②** 3 4 5 6 7 Compare this score to your Military Career Score to see how well your aptitudes, skills, and abilities match those of personnel currently in these positions. See your recruiter for more information about qualification requirements.	This occupation generally appeals to people whose primary Interest Code is *Conventional. Conventional* jobs: • Require attention to detail • Require attention to accuracy
Pages 8 and 9 explain the Military Careers Score and the Interest Codes	

Combat Specialty Occupations

Combat specialty occupations refer to those enlisted specialties, such as infanty, artillery, and special forces, that operate weapons or execute special missions during combat situations. They normally specialize by the type of weapon system or combat operation. These personnel maneuver against enemy forces, and position and fire artillery, guns, and missiles to destroy enemy positions. They may also operate tanks and amphibious assault vehicles in combat or scouting missions. When the military has difficult and dangerous missions to perform, they call upon special forces teams. These elite combat forces stay in a constant state of readiness to strike anywhere in the world on a moment's notice. Special forces team members conduct offensive raids, demolitions, intelligence, search and rescue, and other missions from aboard aircraft, helicopters, ships, or submarines.

- Armored Assault Vehicle Crew Members
- Artillery and Missile Crew Members
- Infantry
  Profile: Justin Glymph
- Special Forces
  Profile: Thomas Wilson

ARMORED ASSAULT VEHICLE CREW MEMBERS

In peacetime, the role of armored units is to stay ready to defend our country anywhere in the world. In combat, their role is to operate tanks, amphibious assault vehicles, and other types of armored assault vehicles to engage and destroy the enemy. Armored units also conduct scouting missions and support infantry units during combat. Crew members work as a team to operate armored equipment and fire weapons to destroy enemy positions. They normally specialize by type of armor, such as tanks, light armor (cavalry), or amphibious assault vehicles.

What They Do

Armored assault vehicle crew members in the military perform some or all of the following duties:

- Drive armored land or amphibious assault vehicles in combat formations
- Operate target sighting equipment to aim guns
- Load and fire guns
- Operate communications and signaling equipment to receive and relay battle orders
- Gather and report information about enemy strength and target location
- Perform preventive maintenance on armored vehicles and mounted guns
- Read maps and battle plans

Physical Demands

Armored assault vehicle crew members must be in good physical condition and have exceptional stamina. They must be able to work inside a confined area for long periods of time. Good vision and normal color vision are required in order to read maps, drive vehicles around obstacles, and locate targets.

Special Requirements

This occupation is open only to men.

Helpful Attributes

Helpful attributes include:

- Ability to work as a member of a team
- Readiness to accept a challenge and face danger
- Ability to follow directions and execute orders quickly and accurately
- Ability to work well under stress

Training Provided

Job training consists of 6 to 9 weeks of classroom and field training under simulated combat conditions. Course content typically includes:

- Vehicle operations
- Armor offensive and defensive tactics
- Map reading
- Scouting and reconnaissance techniques

Further training occurs on the job and through training exercises.

Work Environment

Armored assault vehicle crew members, like other combat troops, work in all climates and weather conditions. During training exercises, as in real combat conditions, crew members work, eat, and sleep outdoors and in vehicles.

Civilian Counterparts

Although the job of armor crew member has no equivalent in civilian life, the close teamwork, discipline, and leadership experiences it provides are helpful in many civilian jobs.

Opportunities

The services have about 23,000 armor crew members. Each year, they need new crew members due to changes in personnel and the demands of the field. After job training, new crew members help operate weapons and control their armored vehicles. Leadership potential and job performance are the most important factors for advancement in this field.

MILITARY CAREERS/SCORE	INTEREST CODE
The circled score shows the typical Military Careers Score of servicemembers in this occupation. **1 2 ③ 4 5 6 7** Compare this score to your Military Career Score to see how well your aptitudes, skills, and abilities match those of personnel currently in these positions. See your recruiter for more information about qualification requirements.	This occupation generally appeals to people whose primary Interest Code is ***Realistic***. *Realistic* jobs: • Allow you to work with your hands • Let you see the results of your work • Involve using machines, tools, and equipment
Pages 8 and 9 explain the Military Careers Score and the Interest Codes	

ARTILLERY AND MISSILE CREW MEMBERS

The military uses artillery and missiles to protect infantry and tank units, as well as to secure and protect land and sea positions from enemy attack. The personnel who operate these systems will usually specialize by type of weapon system such as cannons, howitzers, missiles, or rockets. Artillery and missile crew members position, direct, and fire these weapons to destroy enemy positions and aircraft.

What They Do

Artillery and missile crew members in the military perform some or all of the following duties:

- Operate computerized equipment to determine target locations

- Prepare ammunition for firing

- Set up and load weapons

- Fire artillery and missile systems at enemy targets

- Clean and maintain weapons

Physical Demands

Artillery and missile crew members must have physical stamina to perform strenuous activities for long periods without rest. They are also required to have normal color vision to identify color-coded ammunition and to read maps and charts.

Helpful Attributes

Helpful attributes include:

- Ability to think and remain calm in stressful situations

- ability to work as part of a team

- Interest in cannon and rocket operations

- Willingness to face danger

Special Requirements

Some specialties in this area are closed to women.

Training Provided

Job training consists of between 10 to 14 weeks of classroom instruction and field training under simulated combat situations. Training length varies depending upon specialty. Course content typically includes:

- Methods of computing target locations

- Ammunition-handling techniques

- Gun, missile, and rocket system operations

- Artillery tactics

Further training occurs on the job and through advanced courses.

Civilian Counterparts

Although the job of artillery and missile crew member has no equivalent in civilian life, the close teamwork, discipline, and leadership experiences it provides are helpful in many civilian jobs.

Opportunities

The services have over 38,000 artillery and missile crew members. Each year, they need new crew members due to changes in personnel and the demands of the field. After job training, new crew members work as part of an artillery or missile team. Leadership ability and job performance are the most important factors for advancement in this field. Those with leadership potential may assume supervisory positions. In time, they may lead artillery or missile crews.

MILITARY CAREERS/SCORE	INTEREST CODE
The circled score shows the typical Military Careers Score of servicemembers in this occupation. 1 2 **(3)** 4 5 6 7 Compare this score to your Military Career Score to see how well your aptitudes, skills, and abilities match those of personnel currently in these positions. See your recruiter for more information about qualification requirements.	This occupation generally appeals to people whose primary Interest Code is **_Realistic. Realistic_** jobs: • Allow you to work with your hands • Let you see the results of your work • Involve using machines, tools, and equipment
Pages 8 and 9 explain the Military Careers Score and the Interest Codes	

INFANTRY

The infantry is the main land combat force of the military. In peacetime, the infantry's role is to stay ready to defend our country. In combat, the role of the infantry is to capture or destroy enemy ground forces and repel enemy attacks. The infantry operate weapons and equipment to engage and destroy enemy ground forces.

What They Do

Infantry perform some or all of the following duties:

- Set up camouflage and other protective barriers

- Operate, clean, and store automatic weapons, such as rifles and machine guns

- Parachute from troop transport airplanes while carrying weapons and supplies

- Carry out scouting missions to spot enemy troop movements and gun locations

- Operate communications and signal equipment to receive and relay battle orders

- Drive vehicles mounted with machine guns or small missiles

- Perform hand-to-hand combat drills that involve martial arts tactics

- Dig foxholes, trenches, and bunkers for protection against attacks

Physical Demands

The infantry has very demanding physical requirements. Infantry personnel must perform strenuous physical activities, such as marching while carrying equipment, digging foxholes, and climbing over obstacles. They also need good hearing and clear speech to use two-way radios, and good night vision and depth perception to see targets and signals.

Special Requirements

This occupation is open only to men.

Training Provided

Infantry training starts with basic training of about 7 or 8 weeks. Advanced training in infantry skills lasts for another 8 weeks. While some of the training is in the classroom, most is in the field under simulated combat conditions. In reality, training for an infantry soldier never stops. Infantry soldiers keep their skills sharp through frequent squad maneuvers, target practice, and war games. War games conducted without live ammunition allow soldiers to practice scouting, troop movement, surprise attack, and capturing techniques.

Work Environment

Because the infantry must be prepared to go anywhere in the world they are needed, they work and train in all climates and weather conditions. During training exercises, as in real combat, troops work, eat, and sleep outdoors. Most of the time, however, they work on military bases.

Helpful Attributes

Helpful attributes include:

- Readiness to accept a challenge and face danger

- Ability to stay in top physical condition

- Interest in working as a member of a team

Civilian Counterparts

Although the job of infantry has no equivalent in civilian life, the close teamwork, discipline, and leadership experiences it provides are helpful in many civilian jobs.

Opportunities

The military has about 68,000 personnel in infantry positions. Each year, the services need new infantry soldiers due to changes in personnel and the demands of the field. Leadership ability and job performance are the main factors for advancement in the infantry. Those who have the ability to motivate, train, and supervise others assume greater responsibility.

MILITARY CAREERS/SCORE	INTEREST CODE
The circled score shows the typical Military Careers Score of servicemembers in this occupation. 1 2 **③** 4 5 6 7 Compare this score to your Military Career Score to see how well your aptitudes, skills, and abilities match those of personnel currently in these positions. See your recruiter for more information about qualification requirements.	This occupation generally appeals to people whose primary Interest Code is *Realistic*. *Realistic* jobs: • Allow you to work with your hands • Let you see the results of your work • Involve using machines, tools, and equipment
Pages 8 and 9 explain the Military Careers Score and the Interest Codes	

Profile: Justin Glymph

Justin Glymph grew up in inner city New York where he successfully avoided gang involvement and excelled in academics. Justin knew that he wanted more out of life than what he saw in his own neighborhood. While in his second year of high school, Justin passed the high school equivalency exam and went to work at a nearby electronics assembly plant where he quickly rose to a plant supervisory position. However, Justin did not see the future that he wanted in that role. On a career research trip to the local military recruiting office, he found what he was searching for. On that particular day, he witnessed an incident that served to focus his determination and direction. An obviously intoxicated individual stormed into the recruiting office making demands and threats. Justin was very impressed with the way a Marine sergeant resolved the situation with confidence and professionalism. At that moment, Justin decided that he wanted to join the Marine Corps. Initially, he was not accepted because of a hernia. In his determination to become a Marine, Justin endured a hernia operation and a 6 month recovery period, after which, the Marine Corps accepted him.

After completing the rigorous recruit training at Camp Pendleton in California, Justin performed security duties at a munitions storage site in Earle, New Jersey. Subsequently, he accompanied his battalion to the island of Grenada in the Caribbean. Their mission was to rescue a group of American students who were being held by an armed force and help to restore democracy to the island nation. Justin came away from that operation with a great sense of accomplishment. Of that experience, he says "I felt so honored when people lined the streets and cheered after we helped them regain democratic freedoms...we made a difference." The battalion then immediately departed for Beirut, Lebanon to perform peace keeping duties in a time of political unrest. Since Beirut, Justin has been an anti-terrorist response instructor, a drill instructor, a platoon sergeant, a company gunnery sergeant, and an assistant military officer instructor at Carnegie Mellon University.

Over the years, Justin's infantry career has taken him to many different locations throughout the world. With each new assignment, he received more training, more experience, and ultimately, more opportunities to "help his fellow Marines." Gunnery Sergeant Glymph is presently responsible for assigning the infantry unit leaders throughout the Marine Corps. He intends to continue "making a difference" as long as the Marine Corps needs him.

SAMPLE CAREER PATH

Company/Battalion Sergeant   17–20 years

Company/battalion sergeants direct the several platoons that make up an infantry company or battalion. They help decide how and when troops and equipment will be used. Company/battalion sergeants supervise the operation of the unit command post and prepare situation briefings, combat orders, and other reports. They also plan and conduct training programs.

Platoon Sergeant   7–8 years

Platoon sergeants supervise platoons, which consist of several squads. They receive and give combat or training exercise orders and help develop battle plans. Sergeants also coordinate the movement of troops, supplies, and weapons.

Squad or Fire Team Leader   3–4 years

Squad or fire team leaders command small groups of soldiers in combat or training exercises. They coordinate the collection of information about the enemy and read maps and photographs taken from aircraft to locate enemy forces. Squad leaders also motivate and give on-the-job training to new troops.

Infantryman

Infantry personnel train and take part in all aspects of combat exercises. They fire and maintain rifles, machine guns, and other weapons. They also drive trucks to transport troops, weapons, and supplies.

The years shown represent typical time-in-service before advancement to that level. Actual career advancement depends on individual experience and performance.

SPECIAL FORCES

When the military has difficult and dangerous missions to perform, they call upon special forces teams. These elite combat forces stay in a constant state of readiness to strike anywhere in the world on a moment's notice. Special forces team members conduct offensive raids, demolitions, intelligence, search and rescue, and other missions from aboard aircraft, helicopters, ships, or submarines. Due to the wide variety of missions, special forces team members are trained swimmers, parachutists, and survival experts, in addition to being combat trained.

What They Do

Special forces team members in the military perform some or all of the following duties:

- Carry out demolition raids against enemy military targets, such as bridges, railroads, and fuel depots
- Clear mine fields, both underwater and on land
- Conduct missions to gather intelligence information on enemy military forces
- Conduct offensive raids or invasions of enemy territories
- Destroy enemy ships in coastal areas, using underwater explosives

Physical Demands

The special forces have very demanding physical requirements. Good eyesight, night vision, and physical conditioning are required to reach mission objectives by parachute, overland, or underwater. In most instances, special forces team members are required to be qualified divers, parachutists, and endurance runners.

Helpful Attributes

Helpful attributes include:

- Ability to work as a team member
- Readiness to accept a challenge and face danger
- Ability to remain calm in stressful situations

Training Provided

Job training consists of up to 72 weeks of formal classroom training and practice exercises. Course content typically includes:

- Physical conditioning, parachuting, swimming, and scuba diving
- Using land warfare weapons and communications devices
- Explosives handling and disposal

Additional training occurs on the job. Basic skills are kept sharp through frequent practice exercises under simulated mission conditions.

Special Requirements

This occupation is open only to men.

Work Environment

Because special forces team members must be prepared to go anywhere in the world, they train and work in all climates, weather conditions, and settings. They may dive from submarines or small underwater craft. Special forces team members may also be exposed to harsh temperatures, often without protection, during missions in enemy-controlled areas. Most of the time, however, they work and train on military bases, ships, or submarines.

Civilian Counterparts

Although the job of special forces team members has no equivalent in civilian life, training in explosives, bomb disposal, scuba diving, and swimming may be helpful in such civilian jobs as blaster, police bomb disposal specialist, diver, or swimming instructor. The discipline and dependability of special forces are assets in many civilian occupations.

Opportunities

The services have about 5,500 special forces team members. Each year, they need new team members due to changes in personnel and the demands of the field. After training, they practice their skills under close supervision. With experience, they may supervise and train other team members. They may also work alone on certain missions. Eventually, they may become team leaders.

MILITARY CAREERS/SCORE	INTEREST CODE
The circled score shows the typical Military Careers Score of servicemembers in this occupation. 1 2 **3** 4 5 6 7 Compare this score to your Military Career Score to see how well your aptitudes, skills, and abilities match those of personnel currently in these positions. See your recruiter for more information about qualification requirements.	This occupation generally appeals to people whose primary Interest Code is *Realistic. Realistic* jobs: • Allow you to work with your hands • Let you see the results of your work • Involve using machines, tools, and equipment
Pages 8 and 9 explain the Military Careers Score and the Interest Codes	

Profile: Thomas Wilson

When Thomas (Tom) Wilson received his draft notice, he could have easily received a student deferment. "But I wanted to do my part," he says, "so I decided to join the Army." Because he was small, his family and friends teased him about enlisting. To prove himself, he decided to enlist for what he thought was the toughest training available – airborne. Then, while he was at Fort Gordon training to be a heavy weapons specialist, he heard about the special forces. He applied because it was an even bigger challenge. "By the time I finished airborne and special forces training," Tom says, "I felt there wasn't anything I couldn't do."

For the next 6 years, Tom was a member of a special forces team with assignments in Fort Bragg, NC; Vietnam; and Fort Devins, MA. He started as a junior demolition man and advanced to team engineer. Tom describes his assignments as continuous training. He went on field exercises all over the world, learning jungle operations in Panama and northern warfare in Alaska. He even went to school to learn French and Spanish. Vietnam, Tom says, was the time he was finally able to put his training to work, a modest statement from a Green Beret with a Purple Heart and two Bronze Stars. Throughout his career, Tom has had further training in operations and intelligence, advanced engineering, and leadership, but he feels that he learned the most during his years as a member of a special forces team.

Tom spent the next 3 years as an engineering sergeant for Army battalions on Okinawa and at Fort Bragg, NC. He coordinated with other Army units to supply equipment and support for battalion activities. At Fort Bragg, Tom was promoted to First Sergeant and assigned as operations sergeant for a special forces team. He was then assigned as a first sergeant at the Headquarters of a battalion in Korea. In this job, Tom supervised over 200 people providing administrative support to the battalion. He returned to the States as battalion intelligence sergeant for the 82nd Airborne.

In his current job as a combat development project noncommissioned officer (NCO), Tom evaluates new techniques, equipment, and methods for the special forces. He was recently promoted to Sergeant Major – a goal he set for himself after returning from Vietnam.

SAMPLE CAREER PATH

Special Forces Coordinator   **15–20 years**

Special operations coordinators plan and coordinate multi-team operations and training courses. They advise special forces commanders on planning missions and assign missions to specific teams. Coordinators also develop and evaluate new procedures and techniques.

Team Leader   **6–8 years**

Special forces team leaders plan and lead sabotage and combat raids, air rescue, air delivery, and other operations. They train team members in communications, combat tactics, and intelligence gathering. Team leaders collect, interpret, and distribute intelligence information and assign specific mission tasks to team members.

Team Member

Special forces team members are assigned to small elite units where they continually train to improve their special skills. They go on reconnaissance (scouting) missions to identify terrain features and spot enemy troop and gun positions. Special forces teams also carry out rescue and recovery operations for stranded or trapped service personnel. They give regular and emergency medical treatment in the field.

The years shown represent typical time-in-service before advancement to that level. Actual career advancement depends on individual experience and performance.

Construction Occupations

Construction occupations in the military include personnel who build and/or repair buildings, airfields, bridges, foundations, dams, bunkers, and the electrical and plumbing components of these structures. Enlisted personnel in construction occupations operate bulldozers, cranes, graders, and other heavy equipment. Construction specialists may also work with engineers and other building specialists as part of military construction teams. Some personnel specialize in areas such as plumbing or electrical wiring. Plumbers and pipe fitters install and repair the plumbing and pipe systems needed in buildings, on aircraft, and ships. Building electricians install and repair electrical wiring systems in offices, airplane hangars, and other buildings on military bases.

- Building Electricians
- Construction Equipment Operators
- Construction Specialists
    Profile: Frank Dalton
- Plumbers and Pipe Fitters

BUILDING ELECTRICIANS

The military uses electricity to do many jobs, including lighting hospitals, running power tools, and operating computers. Building electricians install and repair electrical wiring systems in offices, repair shops, airplane hangars, and other buildings on military bases.

What They Do

Building electricians in the military perform some or all of the following duties:

- Install and wire transformers, junction boxes, and circuit breakers, using wire cutters, insulation strippers, and other hand tools

- Read blueprints, wiring plans, and repair orders to determine wiring layouts or repair needs

- Cut, bend, and string wires and conduits (pipe or tubing)

- Inspect power distribution systems, shorts in wires, and faulty equipment using test meters

- Repair and replace faulty wiring and lighting fixtures

- Install lightning rods to protect electrical systems

Helpful Attributes

Helpful school subjects include science and math. Helpful attributes include:

- Ability to use hand tools

- Preference for doing physical work

- Interest in electricity

Work Environment

Building electricians usually work indoors while installing wiring systems. They work outdoors while installing transformers and lightning rods.

Physical Demands

Normal color vision is required for working with color-coded wiring and circuits.

Training Provided

Job training consists of 8 to 12 weeks of classroom instruction, including practice in the installation and repair of electrical wiring systems. Course content typically includes:

- Fundamentals of electricity

- Electrical circuit troubleshooting

- Safety procedures

- Techniques for wiring switches, outlets, and junction boxes

Further training occurs on the job and through advanced courses.

Civilian Counterparts

Civilian building electricians usually work for building and electrical contracting firms. Some work as self-employed electrical contractors. They perform duties similar to military building electricians.

Opportunities

The military has about 3,000 building electricians. Each year, the services need new electricians due to changes in personnel and the demands of the field. After job training, building electricians work under close supervision. As they gain experience, building electricians work more independently. In time, they may be promoted to supervisors of one or more work crews. Eventually, they may become construction superintendents.

MILITARY CAREERS/SCORE	INTEREST CODE
The circled score shows the typical Military Careers Score of servicemembers in this occupation. 1 2 **③** 4 5 6 7 Compare this score to your Military Career Score to see how well your aptitudes, skills, and abilities match those of personnel currently in these positions. See your recruiter for more information about qualification requirements.	This occupation generally appeals to people whose primary Interest Code is *Realistic. Realistic* jobs: • Allow you to work with your hands • Let you see the results of your work • Involve using machines, tools, and equipment
Pages 8 and 9 explain the Military Careers Score and the Interest Codes	

CONSTRUCTION EQUIPMENT OPERATORS

Army
Navy
Air Force
Marine Corps
Coast Guard

Each year the military completes hundreds of construction projects. Tons of earth and building materials must be moved to build airfields, roads, dams, and buildings. Construction equipment operators use bulldozers, cranes, graders, and other heavy equipment in military construction.

What They Do

Construction equipment operators in the military perform some or all of the following duties:

- Drive bulldozers, roadgraders, and other heavy equipment to cut and level earth for runways and roadbeds

- Lift and move steel and other heavy building materials using winches, cranes, and hoists

- Dig holes and trenches using power shovels

- Remove ice and snow from runways, roads, and other areas using scrapers and snow blowers

- Operate mixing plants to make concrete and asphalt

- Spread asphalt and concrete with paving machines

- Drill wells using drilling rigs

- Place and detonate explosives

Helpful Attributes

Helpful school subjects include shop mechanics. Helpful attributes include:

- Interest in operating heavy construction equipment

- Preference for working outdoors

Work Environment

Construction equipment operators work outdoors in all kinds of weather conditions. They often sit for long periods and are subject to loud noise and vibrations. They may work indoors while repairing equipment.

Training Provided

Job training consists of 4 to 12 weeks of classroom instruction, including practice operating construction equipment. Course content typically includes:

- Operation of different types of construction equipment

- Maintenance and repair of equipment

Further training occurs on the job and through advanced courses.

Physical Demands

Some specialties require normal hearing, color vision, and heavy lifting.

Civilian Counterparts

Civilian construction equipment operators work for building contractors, state highway agencies, rock quarries, well drillers, and construction firms. Civilian construction equipment operators may also be known as operating engineers, heavy equipment operators, well drillers, or riggers.

Opportunities

The services have about 10,000 construction equipment operators. Each year, they need new equipment operators due to changes in personnel and the demands of the field. With time, they have the opportunity to become construction supervisors or construction superintendents.

MILITARY CAREERS/SCORE	INTEREST CODE
The circled score shows the typical Military Careers Score of servicemembers in this occupation. **1 ②3 4 5 6 7** Compare this score to your Military Career Score to see how well your aptitudes, skills, and abilities match those of personnel currently in these positions. See your recruiter for more information about qualification requirements.	This occupation generally appeals to people whose primary Interest Code is ***Realistic. Realistic*** jobs: • Allow you to work with your hands • Let you see the results of your work • Involve using machines, tools, and equipment
Pages 8 and 9 explain the Military Careers Score and the Interest Codes	

Military Careers   77

CONSTRUCTION SPECIALISTS

The military builds many temporary and permanent structures each year. Lumber, plywood, plasterboard, and concrete and masonry (bricks, stone, and concrete blocks) are the basic building materials for many of these projects. Construction specialists build and repair buildings, bridges, foundations, dams, and bunkers. They work with engineers and other building specialists as part of military construction teams.

What They Do

Construction specialists in the military perform some or all of the following duties:

- Build foundations, floor slabs, and walls with brick, cement block, mortar, or stone

- Erect wood framing for buildings using hand and power tools, such as hammers, saws, levels, and drills

- Lay roofing materials, such as asphalt, tile, and wooden shingles

- Install plasterboard, plaster, and paneling to form interior walls and ceilings

- Lay wood and ceramic tile floors and build steps, staircases, and porches

- Build temporary shelters for storing supplies and equipment while on training maneuvers

Physical Demands

Construction specialists may have to lift and carry heavy building materials, such as lumber, plasterboard, and concrete. Sometimes, they climb and work from ladders and scaffolding.

Helpful Attributes

Helpful school subjects include math, woodworking, and industrial arts. Helpful attributes include:

- Preference for physical work

- Ability to work with blueprints

- Interest in using power tools

Work Environment

Construction specialists work indoors and outdoors on construction sites.

Civilian Counterparts

Civilian construction specialists usually work for construction or remodeling contractors, government agencies, utility companies, or manufacturing firms. They perform duties similar to military construction specialists. They may also be called bricklayers, stonemasons, cement masons, cement finishers, carpenters, or cabinetmakers.

Training Provided

Job training consists of 5 to 8 weeks of instruction, including practice with carpentry and masonry tools. Course content typically includes:

- Building construction

- Masonry construction methods

- Types and uses of construction joints and braces

- Interpretation of blueprints and drawings

- How to mix and set concrete, mortar, and plaster

Further training occurs on the job and through advanced courses.

Opportunities

The military has about 5,000 construction specialists. Each year, the services need new specialists due to changes in personnel and the demands of the field. After job training, construction specialists work in teams under close supervision. Initially, they perform simple work, such as form building and rough framing. With experience, they perform more difficult tasks. In time, they may supervise and train other specialists. They may become construction superintendents.

MILITARY CAREERS/SCORE	INTEREST CODE
The circled score shows the typical Military Careers Score of servicemembers in this occupation. 1 2 **③** 4 5 6 7 Compare this score to your Military Career Score to see how well your aptitudes, skills, and abilities match those of personnel currently in these positions. See your recruiter for more information about qualification requirements.	This occupation generally appeals to people whose primary Interest Code is ***Realistic. Realistic*** jobs: • Allow you to work with your hands • Let you see the results of your work • Involve using machines, tools, and equipment
Pages 8 and 9 explain the Military Careers Score and the Interest Codes	

Profile: Frank Dalton

Frank Dalton worked in construction during his summer breaks from school. He found that he liked working with his hands. So when he joined the Air Force, he asked to sign on as a structural technician. Because of his previous experience, he was able to take a test that allowed him to bypass initial training and go directly to his first duty assignment after basic training.

Frank started as a carpenter's apprentice at Maxwell Air Force Base (AFB), AL. From there, he was sent to Korea, where he renovated buildings and built roads, shelters, and maintenance hangars. Looking back, he feels that this was one of his most interesting experiences in the military. "I really got to see how the people there lived." Back in the States at Seymour Johnson AFB, NC, he performed minor construction and maintenance, such as paneling, patching roofs, and replacing floor tiles. With this experience behind him, Frank then transferred to the planning section where he learned to plan and construct buildings.

Frank's next assignments placed him as crew leader. At Keesler AFB, MS, he was promoted to Staff Sergeant and led a crew of carpenters who carried out maintenance for the base. At Rhein Mein AB, Germany, he was in charge of a crew that built a hobby shop, a squadron compound, a recreation center, and a communications facility. He then became the noncommissioned officer in charge (NCOIC) of a 3-person shop at the North Charleston Air Force Station, SC. "We did everything – roofing, plumbing, painting, maintenance, and renovation."

Promoted to Technical Sergeant, Frank became the NCOIC of carpentry shops, first at Homestead AFB and then at Hurlburt Field in Florida. At Homestead, his shop renovated the officers' open mess and the headquarters building, an improvement that won the base an award as the "Best Base in Tactical Air Command of the Air Force." At Hurlburt Field, his crew constructed 11 buildings, renovated the base marina, and rebuilt a Boy Scout camp as a community relations project. Frank is now on temporary duty assignment at Myrtle Beach AFB, SC, where his crew is moving and reconstructing an old hangar.

SAMPLE CAREER PATH

Trades Superintendent   19–20 years

Trades superintendents supervise large construction and maintenance units. They plan personnel and equipment needs for construction and repair jobs. Superintendents set work priorities and timetables and direct inspections of completed structures and facilities. They also develop training programs for construction workers and equipment operators

Trades Supervisor   8–12 years

Trades supervisors oversee the work of several construction trades. They coordinate construction and support unit operations. Supervisors help plan construction projects and prepare technical, work progress, and cost reports. They also carry out training programs and assign trainers for new workers.

Crew Leader   4–6 years

Crew leaders oversee teams of construction specialists. They interpret drawings and blueprints to plan and lay out work. Leaders assign jobs to specialists and keep records of the time and materials spent on projects. They also train new construction specialists.

Construction Specialist

Construction specialists work under close supervision in construction and maintenance units. They repair or build structures. They also repair and install indoor fixtures such as doors, windows, cabinets, locks and doorknobs.

The years shown represent typical time-in-service before advancement to that level. Actual career advancement depends on individual experience and performance.

PLUMBERS AND PIPEFITTERS

Army
Navy
Marine Corps
Coast Guard

Military buildings and equipment require pipe systems for water, steam, gas, and waste. Pipe systems are also needed on aircraft, missiles, and ships for hydraulic (fluid pressure) and pneumatic (air pressure) systems. Plumbers and pipe fitters install and repair plumbing and pipe systems.

What They Do

Plumbers and pipe fitters in the military perform some or all of the following duties:

- Plan layouts of pipe systems using blueprints and drawings

- Bend, cut, and thread pipes made of lead, copper, and plastic

- Install connectors, fittings, and joints

- Solder or braze pipe and tubing to join them

- Install sinks, toilets, and other plumbing fixtures

- Troubleshoot, test, and calibrate hydraulic and pneumatic systems

Training Provided

Job training consists of 8 to 12 weeks of classroom instruction, including practice in repairing plumbing systems. Course content typically includes:

- Installation, operation, and repair of pipe systems

- Installation and repair of plumbing fixtures and boiler controls

- Maintenance and repair of hydraulic and pneumatic systems

- Methods of soldering, welding, silver brazing, and cutting

Physical Demands

Plumbers and pipe fitters have to lift and carry heavy pipes and tubes.

Helpful Attributes

Helpful school subjects include math and shop mechanics. Helpful attributes include:

- Preference for doing physical work

- Ability to work with detailed plans

Civilian Counterparts

Civilian plumbers and pipe fitters usually work for mechanical or plumbing contractors or as self-employed contractors. Some plumbers and pipe fitters work for public utilities. Civilian plumbers and pipe fitters perform duties similar to those performed in the military.

Work Environment

Plumbers and pipe fitters work both indoors and outdoors on land and aboard ships.

Opportunities

The military has over 1,000 plumbers and pipe fitters. Each year, the services need new plumbers and pipe fitters due to changes in personnel and the demands of the field. After job training, plumbers and pipe fitters work under close supervision. With experience, they work more independently and may supervise others. Eventually, they may advance to become managers of utilities departments, construction units, or missile maintenance units.

MILITARY CAREERS/SCORE	INTEREST CODE
The circled score shows the typical Military Careers Score of servicemembers in this occupation. 1 2 **③** 4 5 6 7 Compare this score to your Military Career Score to see how well your aptitudes, skills, and abilities match those of personnel currently in these positions. See your recruiter for more information about qualification requirements.	This occupation generally appeals to people whose primary Interest Code is **_Realistic. Realistic_** jobs: • Allow you to work with your hands • Let you see the results of your work • Involve using machines, tools, and equipment
Pages 8 and 9 explain the Military Careers Score and the Interest Codes	

Military Careers

Electronic and Electrical Equipment Repair Occupations

Electronic and electrical equipment repair personnel repair and maintain electronic and electrical equipment used in the military today. Repairers normally specialize by type of equipment being repaired, such as avionics, computer, communications, or weapons systems. For example, avionics technicians install, test, maintain, and repair a wide variety of electronic systems including navigational and communications equipment on aircraft. Weapons maintenance technicians maintain and repair weapons used by combat forces, most of which have electronic components and systems that assist in locating targets, aiming weapons, and firing them.

- Avionics Technicians
- Electrical Products Repairers
- Electronic Instrument and Equipment Repairers
    Profile: Kim Fry
- Power Plant Electricians
- Precision Instrument and Equipment Repairers
- Ship Electricians
- Weapons Maintenance Technicians
    Profile: Reginald Barnes

AVIONICS TECHNICIANS

Airplanes and helicopters have complex electrical and electronic systems for communication, navigation, and radar. Instruments, lights, weapons, landing gear, sensors and many other aircraft parts are also controlled by electronics. Avionics technicians install, maintain and repair electronic and electrical systems on all types of aircraft.

What They Do

Avionics technicians in the military perform some or all of the following duties:

- Troubleshoot aircraft electronics and electrical systems using test equipment

- Repair or replace defective components

- Inspect and maintain electronics and electrical systems

- Replace faulty wiring

- Install electronic components

- Repair or replace instruments, such as tachometers, temperature gauges, and altimeters

- Read electronic and electrical diagrams

Helpful Attributes

Helpful school courses include math and shop mechanics. Helpful attributes include:

- Interest in solving problems

- Interest in electronics and electrical equipment

- Ability to work with tools

Work Environment

Avionics technicians usually work indoors, in aircraft hangars, airplanes, and repair shops. They may also work on aircraft parked outdoors.

Training Provided

Job training consists of 18 to 25 weeks of classroom instruction, including practice in repairing avionics systems. Training length varies depending on specialty. Course content typically includes:

- Electronics and electrical theory

- Troubleshooting procedures

- Installation techniques

- Avionics and electrical system maintenance

Further training occurs on the job and through advanced courses.

Physical Demands

Normal color vision is required to work with color-coded wiring.

Civilian Counterparts

Civilian avionics technicians work mainly for airlines and aircraft maintenance firms. They may also work for aircraft manufacturers and other organizations that have fleets of airplanes or helicopters. Their duties are similar to those of military aircraft electricians. They may also be called aircraft electricians.

Opportunities

The military has over 25,000 avionics technicians. Each year, the services need new technicians due to changes in personnel and the demands of the field. After job training, avionics technicians perform maintenance and routine repairs under close supervision. With experience, they are assigned more complicated troubleshooting and repairs and may supervise other technicians. In time, they may become supervisors of aircraft maintenance shops.

MILITARY CAREERS/SCORE	INTEREST CODE
The circled score shows the typical Military Careers Score of servicemembers in this occupation. 1 2 3 4 5 **(6)** 7 Compare this score to your Military Career Score to see how well your aptitudes, skills, and abilities match those of personnel currently in these positions. See your recruiter for more information about qualification requirements.	This occupation generally appeals to people whose primary Interest Code is **Realistic. Realistic** jobs: • Allow you to work with your hands • Let you see the results of your work • Involve using machines, tools, and equipment

Pages 8 and 9 explain the Military Careers Score and the Interest Codes

ELECTRICAL PRODUCTS REPAIRERS

Army
Navy
Air Force
Marine Corps
Coast Guard

Much of the military's equipment is electrically powered. Electric motors, electric tools, and medical equipment require careful maintenance and repair. Electrical products repairers maintain and repair electrical equipment. They specialize by type of equipment.

What They Do

Electrical products repairers in the military perform some or all of the following duties:

- Maintain, test, and repair electric motors in many kinds of machines, such as lathes, pumps, office machines, and appliances

- Inspect and repair electrical, medical, and dental equipment

- Inspect and repair electric instruments, such as voltmeters

- Maintain and repair portable electric tools, such as saws and drills

Training Provided

Job training consists of 4 to 22 weeks of classroom instruction, including practice in repairing electrical products. Training length varies depending on specialty. Course content typically includes:

- Maintenance and repair procedures

- Use of electrical test equipment

Further training occurs on the job and through advanced courses.

Helpful Attributes

Helpful school subjects include math, electricity, and shop mechanics. Helpful attributes include:

- Ability to use tools

- Interest in electric motors and appliances

- Interest in solving problems

Work Environment

Electrical products repairers usually work in repair shops on land or aboard ships.

Civilian Counterparts

Civilian electrical products repairers work in many industries, including hospitals, manufacturing firms, and governmental agencies. They also work in independent repair shops. They perform duties similar to military electrical products repairers. They may be called electric tool repairers, electrical instrument repairers, electromedical equipment repairers, or electric motor repairers.

Physical Demands

Normal color vision is required to work with color-coded wiring.

Opportunities

The military has about 4,000 electrical products repairers. Each year, the services need new repairers due to changes in personnel and the demands of the field. After job training, they normally make simple repairs under the direction of more experienced workers. With experience, they perform more complicated repairs. In time, repairers may become electrical repair shop supervisors.

MILITARY CAREERS/SCORE	INTEREST CODE
The circled score shows the typical Military Careers Score of servicemembers in this occupation.	This occupation generally appeals to people whose primary Interest Code is *Realistic. Realistic* jobs:
1 2 3 4 5 **6** 7	• Allow you to work with your hands • Let you see the results of your work
Compare this score to your Military Career Score to see how well your aptitudes, skills, and abilities match those of personnel currently in these positions. See your recruiter for more information about qualification requirements.	• Involve using machines, tools, and equipment
Pages 8 and 9 explain the Military Careers Score and the Interest Codes	

ELECTRONIC INSTRUMENT AND EQUIPMENT REPAIRERS

Army
Navy
Air Force
Marine Corps
Coast Guard

The military uses electronic instruments and equipment in many different areas, including health care, weather forecasting, and combat, to name a few. Electronics repairers maintain and repair instruments and equipment, such as computers, communications equipment, radar and sonar systems, precision measuring equipment, and biomedical instruments. Electronic instrument and equipment repairers normally specialize by type of equipment or instrument being repaired.

What They Do

Electronic instrument and equipment repairers in the military perform some or all of the following duties:

- Maintain, test, adjust, and repair electronic equipment using frequency meters, circuit analyzers, and other specialized test equipment.

- Install and repair circuits and wiring using soldering iron and hand tools

- Install computers and other data processing equipment

- Use technical guides and diagrams to locate defective parts and components of equipment

- String overhead communications and electric cables between utility polls

- Monitor the operation of air traffic control, missile tracking, air defense, and other radar systems to make sure there are no problems

Helpful Attributes

Helpful school subjects include math, electricity or electronic repair, shop mechanics, and or physics. Helpful attributes include:

- Interest working with electrical, electronic, and electrochemical equipment

- Interest in solving problems

- Ability to apply electronic principles and concepts

Physical Demands

Normal color vision is required to work with color-coded wires. Some repairers may work from ladders or tall utility polls.

Training Provided

Job training varies between 8 to 40 weeks of classroom instruction, including practice in repairing electronic instruments and equipment. Training length varies depending on specialty. Course content typically includes:

- Mechanical, electronic, and electrical principles

- Maintenance and repair procedures

- Line installation and wiring techniques

- Use of test equipment

Work Environment

Electronic instrument and equipment repairers usually work in repair shops and laboratories on land or aboard ships.

Civilian Counterparts

Civilian electronic instrument and equipment repairers work for a variety of organizations, such as manufacturing firms, communications firms, commercial airlines, and government agencies. They perform the same kind of duties as military electronic instrument and equipment repairers. Depending on their specialty, they may be called electronics mechanics, telecommunications equipment installers and repairers, radio mechanics, or computer technicians.

Opportunities

The services have about 58,000 electronic instrument and equipment repairers. Each year, they need new repairers due to changes in personnel and the demands of the field. After job training, they are assigned to an operations or equipment maintenance unit where they perform routine repair jobs. In time, they may perform more difficult repairs and supervise other repair personnel. Eventually, they may become supervisors or managers of electronic equipment maintenance units.

MILITARY CAREERS/SCORE	INTEREST CODE
The circled score shows the typical Military Careers Score of servicemembers in this occupation.	This occupation generally appeals to people whose primary Interest Code is **Realistic. Realistic** jobs:
1 2 3 4 5 **6** 7	• Allow you to work with your hands • Let you see the results of your work • Involve using machines, tools, and equipment
Compare this score to your Military Career Score to see how well your aptitudes, skills, and abilities match those of personnel currently in these positions. See your recruiter for more information about qualification requirements.	
Pages 8 and 9 explain the Military Careers Score and the Interest Codes	

Profile: Kim Fry

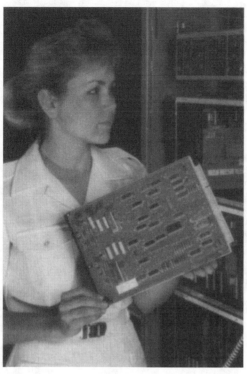

When Kim Fry graduated from high school in Massachusetts, she had never considered entering the military. She wanted to get out of the house, get a job, and go to college. After struggling to pay rent and school expenses for two years, Kim decided to talk to a Navy recruiter to explore employment opportunities in the military. She scored well on the entrance exams and decided to enter the Navy in a technical field because she knew those skills would be in demand when she decided to leave the military. She also liked the education options that went along with the enlistment.

After some initial training, Kim had the opportunity to specialize in the electronics field. She says, "I decided to become an electronics technician because the big companies are always looking for those people." Kim completed technical training in Norfolk, Virginia where she was impressed by the amount of preparation she received for her first assignment aboard the USS Puget Sound. Kim departed on the USS Puget Sound for a six month tour in the Mediterranean Sea. She was responsible for repairing calibration and test equipment used to analyze electronic components and systems, such as communications equipment, radar and sonar units, navigation systems, and electronic warfare systems. Aboard ship everybody must become a jack of all trades, so Kim was also trained to be a fire and security investigator in addition to performing her main duties as an electronics repair technician. Her Mediterranean tour was, she says, "an unbelievable experience." Not only did she visit places such as Spain, Greece, Turkey, Italy, and Monaco, but she also completed 12 semester hours of college.

Kim's experience on the USS Puget Sound prepared her for a later assignment to the USS Wasp for pre-cruise testing. On the USS Wasp, she was responsible for insuring that the electronic systems were operating properly before the ship went on an extended cruise.

Kim is currently stationed at the Norfolk Naval Shipyard (NSY). Although she initially planned to use the skills she gained in the military to help her find a good job in the civilian sector, Kim has decided to stay in the Navy so she can keep the lifestyle and benefits that she has grown to love. Higher education is still a priority in Kim's life, and she plans to finish her college degree by using tuition assistance programs. Her long term career plan is to become an officer.

SAMPLE CAREER PATH

Electronic Maintenance Superintendent   19–21 years

Electronic maintenance superintendents direct an entire repair facility. They plan for needed personnel, equipment, parts, and supplies. They set up quality control standards and conduct inspections to ensure that guidelines are met. They also write technical and administrative reports and develop training programs.

Shop Supervisor   10–13 years

Shop supervisors oversee an entire repair shop. They coordinate repair and support activities to meet deadlines and develop work assignments. Supervisors give technical guidance to repairers and inspect completed repairs. They also conduct training programs and assign trainers for new repairers.

Senior Repairer   4–8 years

Senior repairers take on the most complex repair jobs. They set up and run electronic testing equipment and machines, align and calibrate (adjust) equipment, and use troubleshooting techniques to find faulty parts or wiring. They also assist repairers with less experience.

Electronic Instrument and Equipment Repairer

Electronic instrument and equipment repairers perform routine maintenance and simple repairs on various types of electronic equipment. They work under close supervision to find, test, and repair faulty parts. Repairers also clean and maintain electronic testing equipment.

The years shown represent typical time-in-service before advancement to that level. Actual career advancement depends on individual experience and performance.

POWER PLANT ELECTRICIANS

Each military base – anywhere in the world – must have its own electricity. Power plant electricians maintain and repair electricity generating equipment in mobile and stationary power plants.

What They Do

Power plant electricians perform some or all of the following duties:

- Maintain and repair motors, generators, switchboards, and control equipment

- Maintain and repair power and lighting circuits, electrical fixtures, and other electrical equipment

- Detect and locate grounds, open circuits, and short circuits in power distribution cables

- Read technical guides and diagrams to locate damaged parts of generators and control equipment

Helpful Attributes

Helpful school subjects include electrical and electronic theory, math, and technical drawing. Helpful attributes include:

- Ability to use hand and power tools

- Interest in working with machinery

- Interest in electricity

Physical Demands

Normal color vision is required to work with color-coded wiring.

Work Environment

Power plant electricians work in repair shops on land, aboard ships, or wherever generating equipment needing repair is located.

Training Provided

Job training consists of 4 to 17 weeks of classroom instruction, including practice in maintaining electrical power systems. Course length varies depending on specialty. Course content typically includes:

- Generator and power plant operations

- Electrical generation and distribution

- Diesel generator operation, disassembly, inspection, and maintenance

- Principles of electrical and electronic circuitry

Further training occurs on the job and through advanced courses.

Civilian Counterparts

Civilian power plant electricians often work for construction companies, manufacturers, and utility companies. They perform duties similar to military power plant electricians.

Opportunities

The services have about 3,000 power plant electricians. Each year, they need new electricians due to changes in personnel and the demands of the field. After job training, power plant electricians perform routine maintenance and repairs under supervision. In time, they perform more complex tasks and may help train others. Eventually, they may become supervisors of power plant operations.

MILITARY CAREERS/SCORE	INTEREST CODE
The circled score shows the typical Military Careers Score of servicemembers in this occupation. 1 2 3 **(4)** 5 6 7 Compare this score to your Military Career Score to see how well your aptitudes, skills, and abilities match those of personnel currently in these positions. See your recruiter for more information about qualification requirements.	This occupation generally appeals to people whose primary Interest Code is *Realistic. Realistic* jobs: • Allow you to work with your hands • Let you see the results of your work • Involve using machines, tools, and equipment
Pages 8 and 9 explain the Military Careers Score and the Interest Codes	

The military uses precision instruments and equipment to perform a variety of functions. Some precision instruments are used to measure distance, pressure, altitude, temperature, underwater depth, and other physical properties. Other types of precision equipment include photographic and imaging equipment such as cameras, projectors, and film processing equipment. All of these items have many sensitive mechanisms which require regular attention to stay in good working order. Precision instrument and equipment repairers maintain and adjust these delicate items. They may specialize by the type of equipment that they work on.

What They Do

Precision instrument and equipment repairers in the military perform some or all of the following duties:

- Calibrate and repair instruments used in aircraft
- Calibrate measuring instruments such as, barometers, thermometers, and telemeters
- Adjust and repair weapon aiming devices such as range finders, telescopes, and periscopes
- Diagnose and repair problems in all types of cameras and photo processing equipment
- Repair watches, clocks, and timers
- Calibrate electrical test instruments

Helpful Attributes

Helpful school subjects include math, science, electronics, and shop mechanics. Helpful attributes include:

- Ability to use repair tools
- Ability to solve mechanical problems

Work Environment

Precision instrument and equipment repairers usually work in repair shops on land or aboard ships.

Civilian Counterparts

Civilian precision instrument and equipment repairers work in a variety of industries that use precision instruments and equipment. They may work for manufacturing firms, airlines, machinery repair shops, photographic labs, or engineering firms. Civilian precision instrument and equipment repairers perform duties similar to military repairers. Depending on their specialty, they may also be called instrument mechanics, calibration specialists, camera repairers, or photographic equipment technicians.

Physical Demands

Normal color vision is required to work with color-coded wiring.

Training Provided

Job training varies between 9 and 34 weeks of classroom instruction, including practice in repairing precision instruments and equipment. Training length varies depending upon specialty. Course content typically includes:

- Calibration and repair of precision measuring instruments
- Use of blueprints and schematics
- Test and repair of cameras and darkroom equipment
- Test and repair of aerial sensor equipment

Further training occurs on the job and through advanced courses.

Opportunities

The services have about 7,000 precision instrument and equipment repairers. Each year, they need new repairers due to changes in personnel and the demands of the field. After job training, precision instrument and equipment repairers make routine adjustments and simple repairs under close supervision. With experience, they perform more complicated repairs and may supervise others. They may eventually become managers of repair shops.

MILITARY CAREERS/SCORE	INTEREST CODE
The circled score shows the typical Military Careers Score of servicemembers in this occupation. 1 2 3 4 5 6 **7** Compare this score to your Military Career Score to see how well your aptitudes, skills, and abilities match those of personnel currently in these positions. See your recruiter for more information about qualification requirements.	This occupation generally appeals to people whose primary Interest Code is ***Realistic***. *Realistic* jobs: • Allow you to work with your hands • Let you see the results of your work • Involve using machines, tools, and equipment
Pages 8 and 9 explain the Military Careers Score and the Interest Codes	

SHIP ELECTRICIANS

Electrical systems supply power to operate ships and submarines. Lights, radar, weapons, and machinery all need electricity. Ship electricians operate and repair electrical systems on ships. They keep electrical power plants, wiring, and machinery in working order.

What They Do

Ship electricians in the military perform some or all of the following duties:

- Install wiring for lights and equipment

- Troubleshoot electrical wiring and equipment using test meters

- Inspect and maintain devices that distribute electricity throughout ships, such as circuits, transformers, and regulators

- Monitor and maintain electrical devices connected to the ship's main engines or nuclear reactors

Helpful Attributes

Helpful school courses include math and shop mechanics. Helpful attributes include:

- Interest in electricity and how electrical machines work

- Interest in solving problems

- Ability to use tools

Training Provided

Job training consists of 18 to 25 weeks of classroom instruction, including practice repairing electrical systems. Course content typically includes:

- Electrical theory

- Troubleshooting procedures

- Maintenance and repair procedures

- Reading diagrams and calculating amperage, voltage, and resistance levels

Further training occurs on the job and through advanced courses.

Physical Demands

Normal color vision is required to work with color-coded wiring.

Civilian Counterparts

Civilian ship electricians work for shipbuilding and drydock firms and shipping lines. They perform duties similar to military ship electricians. Other civilian electricians, such as building electricians and electrical products repairers, also perform similar work.

Work Environment

Ship electricians usually work indoors, aboard ships or submarines. They also work in ship repair shops on land.

Opportunities

The military has over 2,000 ship electricians. Each year, the services need new ship electricians due to changes in personnel and the demands of the field. After job training, ship electricians perform maintenance work and repair electrical problems. Eventually, they may become superintendents of electrical repair shops or of ship electrical systems.

MILITARY CAREERS/SCORE	INTEREST CODE
The circled score shows the typical Military Careers Score of servicemembers in this occupation.	This occupation generally appeals to people whose primary Interest Code is *Realistic*. *Realistic* jobs:
1 2 3 4 5 (6) 7	• Allow you to work with your hands • Let you see the results of your work • Involve using machines, tools, and equipment
Compare this score to your Military Career Score to see how well your aptitudes, skills, and abilities match those of personnel currently in these positions. See your recruiter for more information about qualification requirements.	
Pages 8 and 9 explain the Military Careers Score and the Interest Codes	

WEAPONS MAINTENANCE TECHNICIANS

Army
Navy
Air Force
Marine Corps
Coast Guard

Combat forces use many different types of weapons from small field artillery to large ballistic missiles. Weapons may be fired from ships, planes, and ground stations. Most modern weapons have electronic components and systems that assist in locating targets, aiming weapons, and firing them. Weapons maintenance technicians maintain and repair weapons used by combat forces.

What They Do

Weapons maintenance technicians in the military perform some or all of the following duties:

- Repair and maintain artillery, naval gun systems, and infantry weapons
- Clean and lubricate gyroscopes, sights, and other electro-optical fire control components
- Repair and maintain missile mounts, platforms, and launch mechanisms
- Test and adjust weapons firing, guidance, and launch systems

Training Provided

Job training consists of 15 to 30 weeks of classroom instruction and practical experience. Training length varies depending on specialty. Course content typically includes:

- Electronic and mechanical principles and concepts
- Use of schematics, drawings, blueprints, and wiring diagrams
- Operation, testing, and maintenance of weapons systems and fire control systems

Further training occurs on the job and through advanced courses.

Work Environment

Weapons maintenance technicians work in workshops when testing and repairing electronic components. They may work outdoors while inspecting and repairing combat vehicles, ships, artillery, aircraft, and missile silos.

Helpful Attributes

Helpful school subjects include science and math. Helpful attributes include:

- Interest in working with electronic or electrical equipment
- Ability to do work requiring accuracy and attention to detail
- Interest in working with weapons

Civilian Counterparts

Civilian weapons maintenance technicians work for firms that design, build, and test weapons systems for the military. They perform duties similar to military weapons maintenance technicians. They may also be called avionics technicians, electronic mechanics, or missile facilities repairers.

Physical Demands

Some specialties involve moderate to heavy lifting. Normal color vision is required to read color-coded charts and diagrams.

Opportunities

The services have about 34,000 weapons maintenance technicians. Each year, they need new technicians due to changes in personnel and the demands of the field. After job training, they are assigned to weapons operations or maintenance units. They perform routine maintenance and work under close supervision. With experience, they may work more independently and train new personnel. Eventually, they may become managers of missile facilities, avionics, or electronics maintenance units or shops.

MILITARY CAREERS/SCORE	INTEREST CODE
The circled score shows the typical Military Careers Score of servicemembers in this occupation. 1 2 3 4 5 **6** 7 Compare this score to your Military Career Score to see how well your aptitudes, skills, and abilities match those of personnel currently in these positions. See your recruiter for more information about qualification requirements.	This occupation generally appeals to people whose primary Interest Code is **Realistic**. *Realistic* jobs: • Allow you to work with your hands • Let you see the results of your work • Involve using machines, tools, and equipment

Pages 8 and 9 explain the Military Careers Score and the Interest Codes

Profile: Reginald Barnes

Master Sergeant Reginald Barnes sees himself and the other airborne weapons maintenance technicians as a "special breed." They like to work independently, and they enjoy a challenge. Even though they may work on only a few systems in their careers, they are constantly learning. As Reginald says, "We never see the same problem twice."

For his first 11 years in the Army, Reginald worked mainly on one weapon system: the Chaparral. His training on this system began soon after he joined the military. During a series of assignments in the United States and Germany, he advanced from technician to assistant Chaparral system mechanic to senior mechanic. He was also promoted through the ranks to staff sergeant. As senior mechanic, he reported to the Commander on weapon status and supervised training in maintenance and troubleshooting. He also monitored the stock of weapons and made sure that forms and the log book were kept up-to-date. In one assignment, he was the noncommissioned officer-in-charge (NCOIC) of projects to prepare a directory for training and to develop a mechanic's manual for the Chaparral system.

At this point in his career, Reginald felt that he needed to get experience in another system, so he requested training in the Vulcan weapon system. He also requested parachute training – something he had always wanted to do. Both requests were granted. Reginald is proud of the "wings" on his uniform that show that he is parachute qualified. He earned them when he was 32 years old, 12 years after he joined the military.

Reginald spent the next several years as a senior Vulcan mechanic. Now, with several years of Army experience behind him, he is at Fort Bragg, NC, with the 82nd Airborne, a rapid deployment force. He is maintenance control NCOIC and yard master in charge of all missile support for the division. He supervises over 130 men and controls the work flow of jobs on several weapons systems. Since the division must be ready to deploy at a moment's notice, he and his crew ensure that the weapons are always ready to go.

SAMPLE CAREER PATH

Maintenance Superintendent　　　18–20 years

Maintenance superintendents manage weapons systems maintenance units. They help officers plan maintenance personnel and material needs. They also set work priorities, develop quality control and training programs, and conduct maintenance inspections.

Shop Supervisor　　　9–12 years

Shop supervisors oversee maintenance units. They give technical assistance to shop personnel who work on complex weapons systems and inspect repaired electronic weapons systems. Supervisors also give work and training assignments.

Senior Repairer　　　4–7 years

Senior repairers perform more difficult and complex repairs. They install and calibrate (adjust) electronic guidance and fire control systems. Senior repairers use troubleshooting techniques to find faulty parts and causes for system breakdowns. They also test repaired systems and subsystems. They are responsible for training new technicians.

Weapons Maintenance Technician

Weapons maintenance technicians perform simple repairs and routine maintenance on all types of weapons systems. They read maintenance manuals and wiring diagrams to find system parts, and they use electronic equipment to check systems.

The years shown represent typical time-in-service before advancement to that level. Actual career advancement depends on individual experience and performance.

Engineering, Science, and Technical Occupations

The military has many engineering, science, and technical occupations that require knowledge in a specific area to operate technical equipment, solve complex problems or to provide and interpret information. Enlisted personnel normally specialize in a particular area such as information technology, space operations, environmental health and safety, or intelligence. Information technology specialists, for example, develop software programs and operate computer systems. Space operations specialists use and repair spacecraft ground control command equipment, including electronic systems that track spacecraft location and operation. Environmental health and safety specialists inspect military facilities and food supplies for the presence of disease, germs, or other conditions hazardous to health and the environment. Intelligence specialists gather and study information using aerial photographs, and various types of radar and surveillance systems.

- Communications Equipment Operators
- Computer Systems Specialists
  Profile: Dorothy Hartsfield
- Divers
- Environmental Health and Safety Specialists
- Intelligence Specialists
- Meteorological Specialists
- Non-Destructive Testers
- Ordnance Specialists
- Radar and Sonar Operators
  Profile: Juan Delgado
- Space Operations Specialists
- Surveying, Mapping, and Drafting Technicians
- Unmanned Vehicle Operations Specialists

COMMUNICATIONS EQUIPMENT OPERATORS

The ability to relay information between air, sea, and ground forces is critical in the military. The military has sophisticated communications systems that use a variety of technologies and telecommunications equipment such as radios, telephones, antennas, satellites, and complex security and network devices. Communications equipment operators use these systems to transmit, receive, and decode messages at military locations throughout the world.

What They Do

Communications equipment operators in the military perform some or all of the following duties:

- Transmit, receive, and log messages according to military procedures
- Encode and decode classified messages
- Operate different types of telephone switchboards, satellite communications terminals, and network switches
- Set up and operate communications equipment and security equipment
- Monitor and respond to emergency calls

Training Provided

Job training consists of 9 to 22 weeks of instruction, including practice with equipment. Course content typically includes:

- Installation and usage of various types of communications equipment
- Communications security
- Message encoding and decoding

Further training occurs on the job and through advanced courses.

Physical Demands

Normal color vision, normal hearing, and the ability to speak clearly and distinctly are required to enter some specialties in this occupation. Operators must often sit for long periods.

Work Environment

Communications equipment operators may work either indoors or outdoors, depending on the specialty. They may be assigned to ships, aircraft, land bases, or mobile field units.

Civilian Counterparts

Civilian communications equipment operators work in airports, harbors, police stations, fire stations, telephone companies, telegraph companies, and many businesses. They may also work aboard ships. Their duties are similar to those of military communications equipment operators. They may be called radio operators, telephone operators, communication center operators, or switchboard operators, depending on their specialty.

Helpful Attributes

Helpful school subjects include English and speech. Helpful attributes include:

- Interest in working with communications equipment
- Interest in working with codes
- Ability to remain calm in an emergency

Opportunities

The military has about 40,000 communications equipment operators. Each year, the services need new operators due to changes in personnel and the demands of the field. After job training, they prepare and send messages under supervision. With experience, they work more independently. In time, they may become supervisors of communications centers.

MILITARY CAREERS/SCORE	INTEREST CODE
The circled score shows the typical Military Careers Score of servicemembers in this occupation. 1 2 3 **(4)** 5 6 7 Compare this score to your Military Career Score to see how well your aptitudes, skills, and abilities match those of personnel currently in these positions. See your recruiter for more information about qualification requirements.	This occupation generally appeals to people whose primary Interest Code is ***Realistic. Realistic*** jobs: • Allow you to work with your hands • Let you see the results of your work • Involve using machines, tools, and equipment
Pages 8 and 9 explain the Military Careers Score and the Interest Codes	

COMPUTER SYSTEMS SPECIALISTS

The military uses computers to store and process data on personnel, weather, finances, and many other areas, as well as to operate sophisticated equipment during combat and peace time maneuvers.

What They Do

Computer systems specialists in the military perform some or all of the following duties:

- Install, configure, and monitor local and wide area networks, hardware, and software

- Collect, enter, and process information using computers

- Provide customer and network administration services, such as electronic mail accounts, security, virus protection, and troubleshooting

- Use computer programs to solve problems

- Determine and analyze computer systems requirements

- Program information into languages that computers can read

- Develop, test, and debug computer programs

Helpful Attributes

Helpful school subjects include computer science, math, and typing. Helpful attributes include:

- Interest in work requiring accuracy and attention to detail

- Ability to communicate effectively

- Interest in solving problems

- Ability to understand and apply math concepts

Physical Demands

Some computer systems specialists may sit at a computer for long periods of time.

Training Provided

Job training varies between 7 and 13 weeks of classroom instruction, depending upon the specialty area. Course content typically includes:

- Use of computers and peripheral equipment

- Computer systems concepts

- Planning, designing, and testing computer systems

- Program structuring, coding, and debugging

- Use of current programming languages

- Computer security issues

- Network management

Further training occurs on the job and through advanced courses in specific computer systems and languages.

Civilian Counterparts

Civilian computer systems specialists work anywhere that computer systems are used. They may be employed as network support technicians for large companies or as data processing technicians in local banks or school. Those who specialize in computer programming may work as programmers for software developers. The skills learned as a computer systems specialist are highly transferable to the civilian workforce.

Opportunities

The services have about 24,000 computer systems specialists. Each year, they need new specialists to meet the changing demands in the field. After training, computer systems specialists work under the direction of experienced computer systems officers. With experience they may manage other computer systems specialists.

MILITARY CAREERS/SCORE	INTEREST CODE
The circled score shows the typical Military Careers Score of servicemembers in this occupation. 1 2 3 4 ⑤ 6 7 Compare this score to your Military Career Score to see how well your aptitudes, skills, and abilities match those of personnel currently in these positions. See your recruiter for more information about qualification requirements.	This occupation generally appeals to people whose primary Interest Code is *Investigative. Investigative* jobs: • Involve learning about a new subject area • Allow you to use your knowledge to solve problems or create things or ideas
Pages 8 and 9 explain the Military Careers Score and the Interest Codes	

Profile: Dorothy Hartsfield

Dorothy Hartsfield decided to specialize in computers after six years as an administrative staff member in the Army. Dorothy switched specialty areas because she saw a great deal of opportunity both in the military and the civilian world for people with computer expertise. In the computer field, "there is so much to learn, you can learn something new every day" she notes. Over the last 12 years, Dorothy received frequent training to keep her skills up to date in the latest technologies. During her military career, she also took the time to pursue a degree in business administration, one of her personal goals.

After her initial training at Fort Benjamin Harrison in Indianapolis, Dorothy went to Germany where she performed systems analysis and troubleshooting duties for a financial system at the Army's Information Systems Command. She was then posted to Fort Lee in Virginia where she installed a complex contracting system that would be used at bases all over the world. After 3 years in Virginia, Dorothy had the opportunity to go to Hawaii where she worked on a team installing and maintaining a global command and control system. It was an exciting and hectic time for Dorothy because, "our mission was to do whatever it took to get the system on-line." On this assignment, Dorothy gained a lot of experience and developed great teamwork skills as the project enabled her to work with personnel from all branches of the armed forces.

Dorothy recently returned to Virginia, this time to the Army's Information Systems Command at Fort Belvoir near Washington, DC. She is now the Non-Commissioned Officer-In-Charge of the Army's Computer Emergency Response Team, which responds to computer failures due to everything from natural disasters to intrusions by hackers. In this role, she is responsible for maintaining team readiness and ensuring that the staff is well trained on the latest technologies.

Dorothy has enjoyed her military career and says, "The Army is close knit and supportive. I have had the opportunity for a lot of cutting edge training." She has been able to learn and develop her career in high technology in the military more than she would have been able to in the civilian world. When her military service is completed, she looks forward to bringing the skills and confidence she has developed in the Army to the civilian computer industry.

SAMPLE CAREER PATH

Computer Systems Operations Supervisor   **18–21 years**

Computer systems operations supervisors manage entire computer centers. They plan and direct computer network operations and software programming. Operations supervisors develop budgets, track expenses, and predict equipment requirements. They also implement staff training programs.

Computer Systems Supervisor   **9–12 years**

Computer systems supervisors oversee a team of specialists. They help programming staff with technical problems and review proposed software programs and hardware configurations. Supervisors assign work to staff, organize teams for major projects and train new specialists.

Senior Computer Systems Specialist   **4–6 years**

Senior computer specialists design and implement complex hardware and software configurations for military organizations. They meet with supervisors and system users to determine system objectives and needs, and define specifications for proposed systems. Senior computer specialists also write software programs, and test and debug systems.

Computer Systems Specialist

Computer systems specialists work with more experienced staff on routine hardware and software installation and maintenance. They write basic programs and prepare documentation on software and hardware capabilities.

The years shown represent typical time-in-service before advancement to that level. Actual career advancement depends on individual experience and performance.

DIVERS

Sometimes, military tasks such as search and rescue, ship repair, construction, and patrolling must be done under water. Divers in the military perform this work. They usually specialize either as scuba divers, who work just below the surface, or as deep sea divers, who may work for long periods of time in depths up to 300 feet.

What They Do

Divers in the military perform some or all of the following duties:

- Perform search and rescue activities

- Recover sunken equipment

- Patrol the waters below ships at anchor

- Inspect, clean, and repair ship propellers and hulls

- Assist with underwater construction of piers and harbor facilities

- Survey rivers, beaches, and harbors for underwater obstacles

- Use explosives to clear underwater obstacles

- Conduct underwater research

Physical Demands

Divers must be good swimmers and physically strong.

Helpful Attributes

Helpful school subjects include shop mechanics and building trades. Helpful attributes include:

- Interest in underwater diving

- Ability to stay calm under stress

- A high degree of self-reliance

Work Environment

Divers work under water. However, they plan and prepare for work on land or aboard ships. Because diving is not usually a full-time job, divers often have another job specialty in which they work.

Training Provided

Job training consists of 5 to 13 weeks of classroom instruction, including practice in diving and repair work. Training length varies depending on specialty. Course content typically includes:

- Principles of scuba diving

- Underwater welding and cutting

- Maintenance of diving equipment

Further training occurs on the job and through advanced courses.

Civilian Counterparts

Civilian divers work for oil companies, salvage companies, underwater construction firms, and police or fire rescue units. They perform duties similar to divers in the military.

Opportunities

The services have over 1,500 divers. Each year, they need new divers due to changes in personnel and the demands of the field. After job training, divers work in teams headed by experienced divers. Eventually, they may become master divers and supervise diving operations.

MILITARY CAREERS/SCORE	INTEREST CODE
The circled score shows the typical Military Careers Score of servicemembers in this occupation.	This occupation generally appeals to people whose primary Interest Code is *Realistic. Realistic* jobs:
1 2 3 **4** 5 6 7	• Allow you to work with your hands • Let you see the results of your work
Compare this score to your Military Career Score to see how well your aptitudes, skills, and abilities match those of personnel currently in these positions. See your recruiter for more information about qualification requirements.	• Involve using machines, tools, and equipment

Pages 8 and 9 explain the Military Careers Score and the Interest Codes

ENVIRONMENTAL HEALTH AND SAFETY SPECIALISTS

Each military base is a small community. The health and well-being of the residents and surrounding land is a major concern of the services. Keeping military work places and living areas sanitary helps to prevent illness. Environmental health and safety specialists inspect military facilities and food supplies for the presence of disease, germs, or other conditions hazardous to health and the environment.

What They Do

Environmental health and safety specialists in the military perform some or all of the following duties:

- Monitor storage, transportation, and disposal of hazardous waste

- Analyze food and water samples to ensure quality

- Conduct health and safety investigations of living quarters and base facilities

- Provide training on industrial hygiene, environmental health, and occupational health issues

- Monitor noise and radiation levels at job sites

Training Provided

Job training consists of 11 to 19 weeks of classroom instruction, including practice in making health and sanitation inspections. Training length varies depending on specialty. Course content typically includes:

- Identification of health hazards

- Inspection of food products and food service operations

- Inspection of wastewater and waste disposal facilities

Further training occurs on the job and through advanced courses.

Helpful Attributes

Helpful school subjects include algebra, biology, chemistry, and general science. Helpful attributes include:

- Interest in gathering information

- Preference for work requiring attention to detail

- Interest in protecting the environment

Physical Demands

Normal color vision is required to inspect foods for quality and freshness.

Work Environment

Environmental health specialists work indoors while inspecting food facilities and buildings. They work outdoors while inspecting waste disposal facilities and field camps.

Civilian Counterparts

Most civilian environmental health and safety specialists work for local, state, and federal government agencies. Their duties are similar to the duties of military environmental health specialists. They may be called food and drug inspectors, public health inspectors, health and safety inspectors, or industrial hygienists.

Opportunities

The services have about 5,500 environmental health and safety specialists. Each year, they need new specialists due to changes in personnel and the demands of the field. After job training, environmental health and safety specialists help to make inspections. With experience, they work more independently and may supervise other environmental health and safety specialists. Eventually, they may become superintendents of environmental health programs at large military bases.

MILITARY CAREERS/SCORE	INTEREST CODE
The circled score shows the typical Military Careers Score of servicemembers in this occupation. **1 2 ③ 4 5 6 7** Compare this score to your Military Career Score to see how well your aptitudes, skills, and abilities match those of personnel currently in these positions. See your recruiter for more information about qualification requirements.	This occupation generally appeals to people whose primary Interest Code is *Investigative. Investigative* jobs: • Involve learning about a new subject area • Allow you to use your knowledge to solve problems or create things or ideas
Pages 8 and 9 explain the Military Careers Score and the Interest Codes	

INTELLIGENCE SPECIALISTS

Army
Navy
Air Force
Marine Corps
Coast Guard

Military intelligence is information needed to plan for our national defense. Knowledge of the number, location, and tactics of enemy forces and potential battle areas is needed to develop military plans. To gather information, the services rely on aerial photographs, electronic monitoring using radar and sensitive radios, and human observation. Intelligence specialists gather and study the information required to design defense plans and tactics.

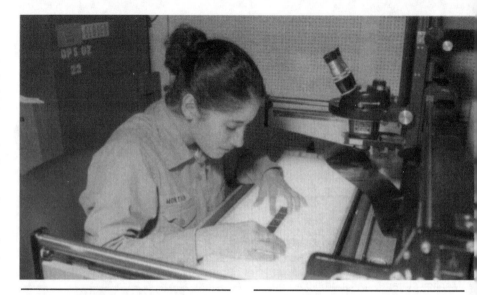

What They Do

Intelligence specialists in the military perform some or all of the following duties:

- Study aerial photographs of foreign ships, bases, and missile sites
- Study foreign troop movements
- Operate sensitive radios to intercept foreign military communications
- Study land and sea areas that could become battlegrounds in time of war
- Store and retrieve intelligence data using computers
- Study foreign military codes
- Prepare intelligence reports, maps, and charts

Helpful Attributes

Helpful school subjects include algebra, geometry, trigonometry, and geography. Helpful attributes include:

- Interest in reading maps and charts
- Interest in gathering information and studying its meaning
- Ability to organize information
- Ability to think and write clearly

Physical Demands

Normal color vision is required for some specialties in order to work with color-coded maps.

Training Provided

Job training consists of 9 to 24 weeks of classroom instruction, including practice in intelligence gathering. Training length varies depending on specialty. Course content typically includes:

- Planning aerial and satellite observations
- Preparing intelligence reports, maps, and charts
- Analyzing aerial photographs
- Using computer systems

Further training occurs on the job and through advanced courses.

Work Environment

Intelligence specialists work in offices on land and aboard ships, and in tents when in the field.

Civilian Counterparts

Civilian intelligence specialists generally work for federal government agencies such as the Central Intelligence Agency or the National Security Agency. Their duties are similar to those performed by military intelligence specialists. The analytical skills of intelligence specialists are also useful in other fields, such as research or business planning.

Opportunities

The services have over 26,000 intelligence specialists. Each year, they need new specialists due to changes in personnel and the demands of the field. After job training, they collect information and prepare maps and charts under close supervision. With experience, they are given more responsibility for organizing intelligence data. Eventually, they may become chiefs of intelligence units.

MILITARY CAREERS/SCORE	INTEREST CODE
The circled score shows the typical Military Careers Score of servicemembers in this occupation. 1 2 3 4 5 ⑥ 7 Compare this score to your Military Career Score to see how well your aptitudes, skills, and abilities match those of personnel currently in these positions. See your recruiter for more information about qualification requirements.	This occupation generally appeals to people whose primary Interest Code is ***Investigative. Investigative*** jobs: • Involve learning about a new subject area • Allow you to use your knowledge to solve problems or create things or ideas
Pages 8 and 9 explain the Military Careers Score and the Interest Codes	

METEOROLOGICAL SPECIALISTS

Weather information is important for planning military operations. Accurate weather forecasts are needed to plan troop movements, airplane flights, and ship traffic. Meteorological specialists collect information about weather and sea conditions for use by meteorologists. They make visual observations and take readings from weather equipment, radar scans, and satellite photographs.

What They Do

Meteorological specialists in the military perform some or all of the following duties:

- Launch weather balloons to record wind speed and direction

- Identify the types of clouds present and estimate cloud height and amount of cloud cover

- Take readings of barometric pressure, temperature, humidity, and sea conditions

- Operate radio equipment to receive information from satellites

- Plot weather information on maps and charts

- Forecast weather based on readings and observations

Helpful Attributes

Helpful school subjects include geography, mathematics, and physical science. Helpful attributes include:

- Interest in working with formulas, tables, and graphs

- Ability to communicate effectively

- Interest in learning how weather changes

- Interest in gathering and organizing information

Physical Demands

Normal color vision is required to use color-coded maps and weather charts. Some specialties may involve heavy lifting.

Training Provided

Job training consists of 7 to 18 weeks of classroom instruction. Training length varies depending on specialty. Course content typically includes:

- Basic meteorology (study of weather) and oceanography (study of the ocean)

- Methods for plotting weather data

- Analyzing radar and satellite weather information

- Preparation of weather reports

Advanced training in weather forecasting is available for some specialties.

Work Environment

Meteorological specialists usually work in offices either on land or aboard ships. They work outdoors when making visual weather observations and launching weather balloons.

Civilian Counterparts

Civilian meteorological specialists work for government agencies (such as the U.S. Weather Service), commercial airlines, radio and television stations, and private weather forecasting firms. They perform duties similar to military meteorological specialists. Civilian meteorological specialists may also be called oceanographer assistants and weather clerks.

Opportunities

The services have over 4,000 meteorological specialists. Each year, they need new specialists due to changes in personnel and the demands of the field. After job training, new specialists collect weather information under the supervision of experienced workers. With experience, they perform more complex collection and analysis tasks and may become weather forecasters. Eventually, they may become managers of weather observation units.

MILITARY CAREERS/SCORE	INTEREST CODE
The circled score shows the typical Military Careers Score of servicemembers in this occupation. 1 2 3 4 5 **6** 7 Compare this score to your Military Career Score to see how well your aptitudes, skills, and abilities match those of personnel currently in these positions. See your recruiter for more information about qualification requirements.	This occupation generally appeals to people whose primary Interest Code is *Realistic. Realistic* jobs: • Allow you to work with your hands • Let you see the results of your work • Involve using machines, tools, and equipment
Pages 8 and 9 explain the Military Careers Score and the Interest Codes	

NON-DESTRUCTIVE TESTERS

Military equipment is often placed under heavy stress. An airplane's landing gear absorbs heavy runway impact. Submarine hulls withstand tremendous pressure in the ocean depths. In time, stress may cause structural weakening or damage. Non-destructive testers examine metal parts for stress damage. They use X-rays, ultrasonics, and other testing methods that do not damage (are non-destructive to) the parts tested.

What They Do

Non-destructive testers in the military perform some or all of the following duties:

- Inspect metal parts and joints for wear and damage
- Take X-rays of aircraft and ship parts
- Examine X-ray film to detect cracks and flaws in metal parts and welds
- Operate ultrasonic, atomic absorption, and other kinds of test equipment
- Conduct oil analysis and heat damage tests to detect engine wear
- Prepare inspection reports

Helpful Attributes

Helpful school subjects include math and metal shop. Helpful attributes include:

- Thoroughness and dependability
- Interest in operating test equipment
- Interest in machines and how they work

Work Environment

Non-destructive testers work indoors in laboratories and aircraft hangars. They also work outdoors in shipyards and in the field.

Physical Demands

Normal color vision is required to read color-coded diagrams.

Training Provided

Job training consists of 9 to 13 weeks of classroom instruction, including practice in testing metal parts. Course content typically includes:

- Methods for inspecting parts and welds
- Operation of X-ray and film processing equipment
- Operation of ultrasonic test equipment
- Preparation of test reports

Civilian Counterparts

Civilian non-destructive testers work for commercial testing laboratories, airlines, aircraft maintenance companies, and industrial plants. They perform duties similar to military non-destructive testers and may be called radiographers.

Opportunities

The military has about 1,500 non-destructive testers. Each year, the services need new testers due to changes in personnel and the demands of the field. After job training, testers are assigned to testing units, where they perform tests under supervision. With experience, they work more independently. In time, non-destructive testers may become supervisors of testing laboratories or maintenance units.

MILITARY CAREERS/SCORE	INTEREST CODE
The circled score shows the typical Military Careers Score of servicemembers in this occupation. 1 2 **(3)** 4 5 6 7 Compare this score to your Military Career Score to see how well your aptitudes, skills, and abilities match those of personnel currently in these positions. See your recruiter for more information about qualification requirements.	This occupation generally appeals to people whose primary Interest Code is *Realistic*. *Realistic* jobs: • Allow you to work with your hands • Let you see the results of your work • Involve using machines, tools, and equipment
Pages 8 and 9 explain the Military Careers Score and the Interest Codes	

ORDNANCE SPECIALISTS

Ordnance is a military term for ammunition and weapons. Ordnance includes all types of ammunition, missiles, toxic chemicals, and nuclear weapons. Ammunition and weapons must be handled carefully and stored properly. Ordnance specialists transport, store, inspect, prepare, and dispose of weapons and ammunition.

What They Do

Ordnance specialists in the military perform some or all of the following duties:

- Load nuclear and conventional explosives and ammunition on aircraft, ships, and submarines
- Inspect mounted guns, bomb release systems, and missile launchers
- Assemble and load explosives
- Defuse unexploded bombs
- Locate, identify, and dispose of chemical munitions

Training Provided

Job training consists of 15 to 25 weeks of classroom instruction, including practice in ordnance maintenance. Training length varies depending on specialty. Course content typically includes:

- Maintenance of nuclear weapons
- Handling, testing, and maintenance of missiles and rockets

Further training occurs on the job and through advanced courses.

Helpful Attributes

Helpful school subjects include general science and shop mechanics. Helpful attributes include:

- Interest in working with guns and explosives
- Ability to remain calm under stress

Physical Demands

Ordnance specialists may have to lift and carry artillery shells and other heavy ordnance.

Civilian Counterparts

There are no direct civilian counterparts for many of the military ordnance specialties. However, there are many occupations that are related. For example, civilians work for government agencies and private industry doing research and development. Others work for police or fire departments as bomb-disposal experts. Some also work for munitions manufacturers and firearms makers. Ordnance specialists may also be called bomb disposal experts.

Work Environment

Ordnance specialists work indoors and outdoors. They work in repair shops while assembling explosives and repairing weapons. They work outdoors while repairing equipment in the field and loading weapons on tanks, ships, or aircraft.

Opportunities

The services have about 16,000 ordnance specialists. Each year, they need new ordnance specialists due to changes in personnel and the demands of the field. After job training, ordnance specialists work under close supervision. With experience, they perform more complex duties. In time, they may become trainers or supervisors. Eventually, they may become managers of weapons maintenance units.

MILITARY CAREERS/SCORE	INTEREST CODE
The circled score shows the typical Military Careers Score of servicemembers in this occupation. 1 2 3 **4** 5 6 7 Compare this score to your Military Career Score to see how well your aptitudes, skills, and abilities match those of personnel currently in these positions. See your recruiter for more information about qualification requirements.	This occupation generally appeals to people whose primary Interest Code is *Realistic. Realistic* jobs: • Allow you to work with your hands • Let you see the results of your work • Involve using machines, tools, and equipment
Pages 8 and 9 explain the Military Careers Score and the Interest Codes	

RADAR AND SONAR OPERATORS

Army
Navy
Air Force
Marine Corps
Coast Guard

Radar and sonar devices work by bouncing radio or sound waves off objects to determine their location and measure distance. They have many uses, such as tracking aircraft and missiles, determining positions of ships and submarines, directing artillery fire, forecasting weather, and aiding navigation. Radar and sonar operators monitor sophisticated equipment. They normally specialize in either radar or sonar.

What They Do

Radar and sonar operators in the military perform some or all of the following duties:

- Detect and track position, direction, and speed of aircraft, ships, submarines, and missiles
- Plot and record data on status charts and plotting boards
- Set up and operate radar equipment to direct artillery fire
- Monitor early warning air defense systems
- Send and receive messages using electronic communication systems

Helpful Attributes

Helpful school subjects include geometry, algebra, and science. Helpful attributes include:

- Ability to concentrate for long periods
- Interest in working with electronic equipment

Work Environment

Radar and sonar operators in the military primarily work indoors in security-controlled areas. They work in operations centers and command posts either on land or aboard aircraft, ships, or submarines. Some may work in a mobile field radar unit.

Physical Demands

Normal color vision is required to enter this occupation. Specialties involving flying require passing a special physical exam.

Training Provided

Job training consists of 7 to 12 weeks of classroom instruction and practice operating radar or sonar equipment. Training length varies by specialty. Course content typically includes:

- Operation and maintenance of radar and sonar equipment
- Identification of ships, submarines, aircraft, and missiles
- Computation of aircraft or missile speed, direction, and altitude

Further training occurs on the job and through advanced courses.

Civilian Counterparts

There are no direct civilian counterparts to military radar and sonar operators. However, workers in civilian occupations that use radar and sonar equipment in their jobs include weather service technicians, air traffic controllers, ship navigators, and ocean salvage specialists.

Opportunities

The services have over 11,000 radar and sonar operators. Each year, they need new operators due to changes in personnel and the demands of the field. After job training, new operators use radar or sonar equipment under close supervision. With experience, they work more independently and may eventually become supervisors of ground, airborne, or shipboard radar or sonar units.

MILITARY CAREERS/SCORE	INTEREST CODE
The circled score shows the typical Military Careers Score of servicemembers in this occupation. 1 2 3 4 **5** 6 7 Compare this score to your Military Career Score to see how well your aptitudes, skills, and abilities match those of personnel currently in these positions. See your recruiter for more information about qualification requirements.	This occupation generally appeals to people whose primary Interest Code is *Realistic*. *Realistic* jobs: • Allow you to work with your hands • Let you see the results of your work • Involve using machines, tools, and equipment

Pages 8 and 9 explain the Military Careers Score and the Interest Codes

Profile: Juan Delgado

Juan Delgado had always been fascinated by submarines. So after enlisting in the Navy in advanced electronics, he volunteered for submarine duty. "After 16 years," Juan says, "I'm still glad I made that decision."

Juan's trip to boot camp was his first airplane ride and his first trip away from home. After this, things began to happen fast. By the time he left boot camp, he had been promoted to seaman. He then went to submarine school for training in electricity, electronics, sonar, and a specific sonar system. On leaving, he was selected class leader and became a petty officer third class.

Juan's first assignment was on the USS *Wahoo,* operating and maintaining the sonar system. Life aboard the submarine was all Juan hoped it would be. He liked the camaraderie among the men, and he enjoyed learning to stand all the different watches. During his second year on the *Wahoo,* he was promoted to petty officer second class and soon after became sonar supervisor. After his tour on the *Wahoo,* Juan went back to school in San Diego for 6 months of training on a new sonar system. He made petty officer first class soon after he arrived and did so well in the course that he was asked to stay on as an instructor.

Juan went back to sea on the USS *William H. Bates*, a nuclear submarine, as the Leading Petty Officer of a 12-man division. Since he had never operated the ship's particular sonar system, he had to qualify to operate it through on-the-job training. He then became sonar supervisor. When the sonar system was replaced during a ship refit, Juan monitored the installation of the new system and conducted training for other operators. He was able to use this experience on his next assignment – monitoring the installation of sonar equipment on the new PCU *Houston*. He also wrote the training plan for the equipment and trained the entire sonar division. Two years later, he made chief petty officer and remained on board as the chief sonar technician.

Juan likes his career in sonar. "The new technology keeps me challenged," he says. He is also proud to see the success of people he has trained. Juan says he has one last ambition for his Navy career – to be the Chief of the Boat, the top enlisted person aboard a submarine.

SAMPLE CAREER PATH

Operations Superintendent   18–21 years

Radar and sonar operations superintendents oversee both the administrative and technical aspects of their units. They inform and advise superiors on the use and capabilities of personnel, equipment, and material. They also assign duty positions and develop and schedule training programs. Superintendents prepare reports, correspondence and technical instructions.

Radar or Sonar Supervisor   8–11 years

Radar or sonar supervisors oversee the operations of ground, airborne, or shipboard radar or sonar units. They also supervise training of personnel who operate, maintain, and repair radar or sonar equipment. Supervisors give technical advice and assistance to operators when needed.

Radar or Sonar Operator   4–6 years

Radar or sonar operators operate radar and sonar computer equipment during complex operations and exercises. They ensure that radar or sonar stations are monitored during watch and rest periods. They also train new operators.

Apprentice Radar or Sonar Operator

Apprentice radar or sonar operators find, classify, and track the movement of airborne, surface, and underwater objects. They also relay information to pilots, gunners, and navigators by internal communications or radio equipment. Apprentice operators keep records on objects identified and perform preventive maintenance on equipment.

The years shown represent typical time-in-service before advancement to that level. Actual career advancement depends on individual experience and performance.

SPACE OPERATIONS SPECIALISTS

Orbiting satellites and other space vehicles are used for communications, weather forecasting, and collecting intelligence data. In the future, more and more military operations will involve space systems. Space operations specialists use and repair spacecraft ground control command equipment, including electronic systems that track spacecraft location and operation.

What They Do

Space operations specialists in the military perform some or all of the following duties:

- Transmit and verify spacecraft commands using aerospace ground equipment
- Monitor computers and telemetry display systems
- Analyze data to determine spacecraft operational status
- Repair ground and spacecraft communication equipment
- Assist in preparing spacecraft commands to meet mission objectives
- Operate data-handling equipment to track spacecraft

Training Provided

Job training consists of 17 to 30 weeks of classroom instruction, including practice in spacecraft command and control operations. Course content typically includes:

- Operation of electronic transmitting, receiving, and computing equipment
- Analysis of data that indicate spacecraft operational status
- Application of electronic and satellite system principles
- Alignment of ground and spacecraft communication systems
- Space command and control system operational procedures

Physical Demands

Normal color vision is required to enter this occupation.

Helpful Attributes

Helpful school subjects include physics, geometry, algebra, and trigonometry. Helpful attributes include:

- Interest in operating electronic equipment and systems
- Interest in working as part of a team
- Ability to work with formulas to solve math problems
- Interest in space exploration

Civilian Counterparts

Civilian space operations specialists work for the National Aeronautics and Space Administration, the U.S. Weather Service, and private satellite communications firms. They perform duties similar to military space operations specialists.

Work Environment

Space operations specialists work in space operations centers.

Opportunities

The military has over 1,000 space operations specialists. Each year, the services need new specialists due to changes in personnel and the demands of the field. After job training, space operations specialists are assigned to space operations centers, where they use and repair equipment under close supervision. After gaining experience, they work more independently and may help train new workers. Eventually, space operations specialists may become supervisors of space operations centers.

MILITARY CAREERS/SCORE	INTEREST CODE
The circled score shows the typical Military Careers Score of servicemembers in this occupation. **1 2 3 4 5 6 (7)** Compare this score to your Military Career Score to see how well your aptitudes, skills, and abilities match those of personnel currently in these positions. See your recruiter for more information about qualification requirements.	This occupation generally appeals to people whose primary Interest Code is **_Realistic. Realistic_** jobs: • Allow you to work with your hands • Let you see the results of your work • Involve using machines, tools, and equipment
Pages 8 and 9 explain the Military Careers Score and the Interest Codes	

SURVEYING, MAPPING, AND DRAFTING TECHNICIANS

The military builds and repairs many airstrips, docks, barracks, roads, and other projects each year. Surveying, mapping, and drafting technicians conduct land surveys, make maps, and prepare detailed plans and drawings for construction projects. Surveys and maps are also used to locate military targets and plot troop movements.

What They Do

Surveying, mapping, and drafting technicians in the military perform some or all of the following duties:

- Draw maps and charts using drafting tools and computers

- Make scale drawings of roads, airfields, buildings, and other military projects

- Conduct land surveys and compute survey results

- Draw diagrams for wiring and plumbing of structures

- Build scale models of land areas that show hills, lakes, roads, and buildings

- Piece together aerial photographs to form large photomaps

- Use global positioning systems to collect location information from satellites

Work Environment

Surveying, mapping, and drafting technicians work both indoors and outdoors in all climates and weather conditions. Those assigned to engineering units sometimes work outdoors with survey teams. Those assigned to intelligence units may work on ships as well as on land.

Physical Demands

Good depth perception is required to study aerial photos through stereoscopes. Normal color vision is required to work with color-coded maps and drawings.

Training Provided

Job training consists of 9 to 31 weeks of classroom instruction, depending on specialty. Course content typically includes:

- Surveying and drafting techniques

- Aerial photo interpretation

- Architectural and structural drawing

Further training occurs on the job and through advanced courses.

Helpful Attributes

Helpful school subjects include algebra, geometry, and trigonometry. Helpful attributes include:

- Ability to convert ideas into drawings

- Interest in maps and charts

- Interest in working with drafting equipment and computers

Civilian Counterparts

Civilian surveying, mapping, and drafting technicians work for construction, engineering, and architectural firms and government agencies such as the highway department. Their work is used for planning construction projects such as highways, airport runways, dams, and drainage systems. They are also called cartographic technicians, and photogrammetrists.

Opportunities

The military has about 3,000 surveying, mapping, and drafting technicians. Each year, the services need new technicians due to changes in personnel and the demands of the field. After job training, technicians make simple drawings, trace photos, perform basic survey duties, or help make maps under close supervision. With experience, they work more independently. Eventually, they may supervise mapmaking facilities, surveying teams, or construction units.

MILITARY CAREERS/SCORE	INTEREST CODE
The circled score shows the typical Military Careers Score of servicemembers in this occupation.	This occupation generally appeals to people whose primary Interest Code is *Realistic*. *Realistic* jobs:
1 2 3 4 5 **6** 7	• Allow you to work with your hands
Compare this score to your Military Career Score to see how well your aptitudes, skills, and abilities match those of personnel currently in these positions. See your recruiter for more information about qualification requirements.	• Let you see the results of your work • Involve using machines, tools, and equipment
Pages 8 and 9 explain the Military Careers Score and the Interest Codes	

UNMANNED VEHICLE (UV) OPERATIONS SPECIALISTS

Army
Navy
Air Force
Marine Corps

The military uses remotely piloted unmanned vehicles for a variety of purposes, such as deep sea exploration, intelligence gathering, remote surveillance, and target applications. These vehicles are used in the air, on land, and at sea in operations or missions that could be dangerous for human operators onboard the vehicle. The military requires skilled operators and technicians to maintain and control these vehicles. Personnel normally specialize by the type of vehicle they operate, such as unmanned aerial vehicles, ground vehicles, surface vehicles, and undersea vehicles.

What They Do

Unmanned vehicle operations specialists in the military perform some or all of the following duties:

- Prepare and install equipment on or within the unmanned vehicle
- Operate, navigate, launch, track, and recover unmanned vehicles
- Operate equipment in remote receiving stations and ground control stations
- Coordinate with other personnel to complete the designated mission
- Inspect and maintain components in unmanned vehicles

Helpful Attributes

Helpful attributes include:

- Superior adaptability to three dimensional spatial relationships
- Enjoy working with tools
- Knowledge of electronic theory and schematic drawing

Work Environment

Unmanned vehicle operations specialists work under a variety of conditions depending upon the type of vehicle and mission. Some specialists work in control stations or receiving stations on land, while others work aboard ships.

Physical Demands

Normal color vision is required for some specialties.

Training Provided

Job training varies from 3 to 30 weeks depending on the position. Course content typically includes:

- Unmanned vehicle concepts and capabilities
- Operation of unmanned vehicles
- Basic preventative maintenance

Civilian Counterparts

Unmanned vehicles are used in several civilian areas, such as mining, petroleum exploration, environmental research, and manufacturing. Civilian unmanned vehicle operations specialists perform duties similar to those of their military counterparts.

Opportunities

The services have over 500 unmanned vehicle operations specialists. Each year, they need new specialists due to changes in personnel and the growing use of this kind of technology. After job training, new unmanned vehicle operations specialists normally work under close supervision to prepare unmanned vehicles for their missions. With experience, they may perform more difficult duties, such as piloting, navigating, and recovering unmanned vehicles. In time, some operations specialists may plan and oversee unmanned vehicle missions.

MILITARY CAREERS/SCORE	INTEREST CODE
The circled score shows the typical Military Careers Score of servicemembers in this occupation. 1 2 3 4 5 **6** 7 Compare this score to your Military Career Score to see how well your aptitudes, skills, and abilities match those of personnel currently in these positions. See your recruiter for more information about qualification requirements.	This occupation generally appeals to people whose primary Interest Code is *Realistic. Realistic* jobs: • Allow you to work with your hands • Let you see the results of your work • Involve using machines, tools, and equipment
Pages 8 and 9 explain the Military Careers Score and the Interest Codes	

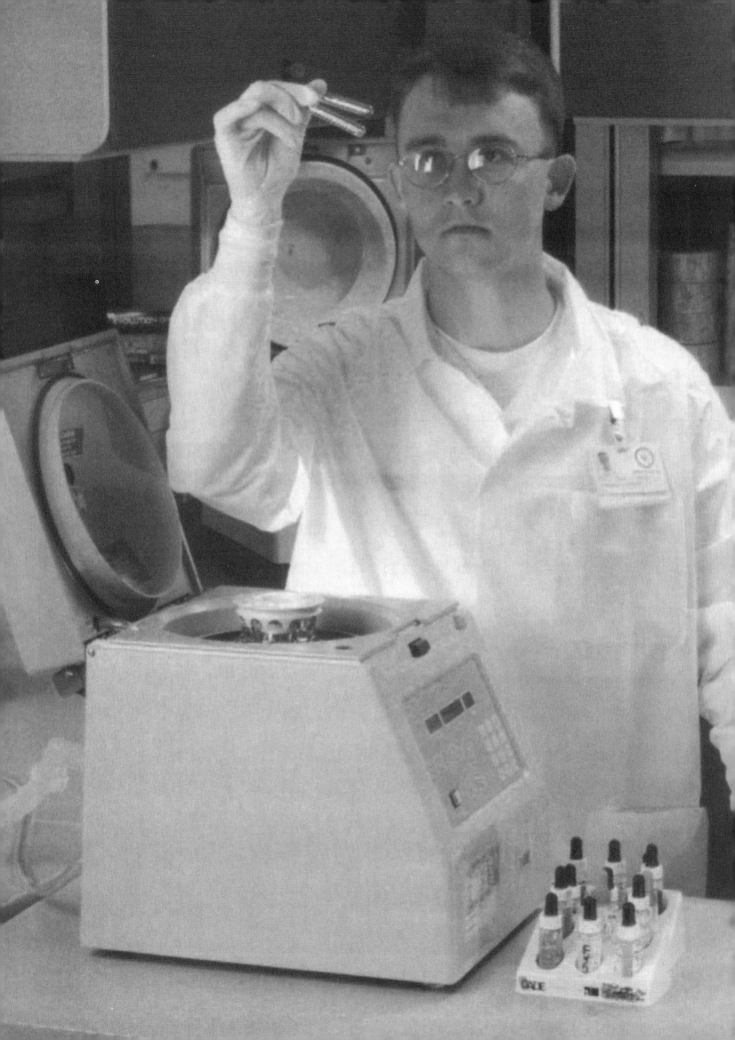

Health Care Occupations

Health care personnel assist medical professionals in treating and providing services for patients. They may work as part of a patient service team in close contact with doctors, dentists, nurses, and physical therapists to provide the necessary support functions within a hospital or clinic. Health care specialists normally specialize in a particular area. They may provide emergency medical treatment, operate diagnostic equipment such as X-ray and ultrasound equipment, conduct laboratory tests on tissue and blood samples, maintain pharmacy supplies, or maintain patient records.

- Cardiopulmonary and EEG Technicians
- Dental and Optical Laboratory Technicians
- Dental Specialists
- Medical Care Technicians
- Medical Laboratory Technicians
- Medical Record Technicians
- Medical Service Technicians
    Profile: Larry Roberts
- Optometric Technicians
- Pharmacy Technicians
- Physical and Occupational Therapy Specialists
- Radiologic (X-Ray) Technicians
    Profile: Ernie Hughes

CARDIOPULMONARY AND EEG TECHNICIANS

Army
Navy
Air Force
Coast Guard

Military health care includes medical treatment for heart, lung, and brain disorders. Physicians need sophisticated tests to help diagnose and treat these problems. Cardiopulmonary and EEG (electroencephalograph) technicians administer a variety of diagnostic tests of the heart, lungs, blood, and brain using complex electronic testing equipment.

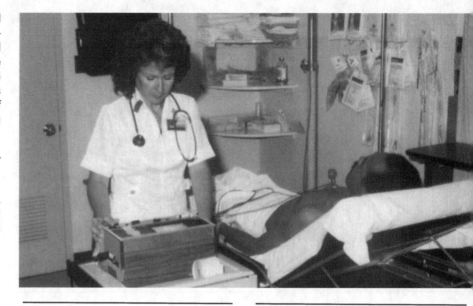

What They Do

Cardiopulmonary and EEG technicians in the military perform some or all of the following duties:

- Take patients' blood pressure readings
- Attach electrodes or other test equipment to patients' bodies
- Help physicians revive heart attack victims
- Adjust settings and operate test equipment
- Monitor graphs and screens during tests
- Talk to physicians to learn what tests or treatments are needed
- Keep records of test results and discuss them with medical staff
- Operate electrocardiographs and other test equipment

Training Provided

Job training consists of 26 to 30 weeks of classroom instruction. Course content typically includes:

- Diagnostic procedures
- Operation and maintenance of diagnostic equipment
- Preparation of patients for testing
- Methods of resuscitation

Further training occurs on the job and through advanced courses.

Physical Demands

Normal color vision is required for some specialties in order to set up and monitor equipment.

Helpful Attributes

Helpful school subjects include algebra, chemistry, biology, or related courses. Helpful attributes include:

- Interest in electronic equipment
- Ability to follow strict standards and procedures
- Interest in learning how the heart, lungs, and blood work together
- Ability to keep accurate records

Work Environment

Cardiopulmonary and EEG technicians usually work in hospitals and clinics. In combat situations, they may work in mobile field hospitals.

Civilian Counterparts

Civilian cardiopulmonary and EEG technicians work in hospitals, clinics, and physicians' offices. Their duties are similar to those performed in the military. They may specialize in either cardiovascular (heart), pulmonary (lungs), or electroencephalographic (brain) testing.

Opportunities

The services have about 6,000 cardiopulmonary and EEG technicians. Each year, they need new technicians due to changes in personnel and the demands of the field. After job training, new technicians are assigned to hospitals and clinics, where they work under the supervision of physicians and senior technicians. With experience, they may supervise others and assist in managing clinics.

MILITARY CAREERS/SCORE	INTEREST CODE
The circled score shows the typical Military Careers Score of servicemembers in this occupation. 1 2 3 **(4)** 5 6 7 Compare this score to your Military Career Score to see how well your aptitudes, skills, and abilities match those of personnel currently in these positions. See your recruiter for more information about qualification requirements.	This occupation generally appeals to people whose primary Interest Code is ***Realistic. Realistic*** jobs: • Allow you to work with your hands • Let you see the results of your work • Involve using machines, tools, and equipment
Pages 8 and 9 explain the Military Careers Score and the Interest Codes	

DENTAL AND OPTICAL LABORATORY TECHNICIANS

Army
Navy
Air Force
Coast Guard

The military provides dental and optical care as part of its comprehensive health service program. Dental and optical laboratory technicians make and repair dental devices and eyeglasses that are provided for military personnel.

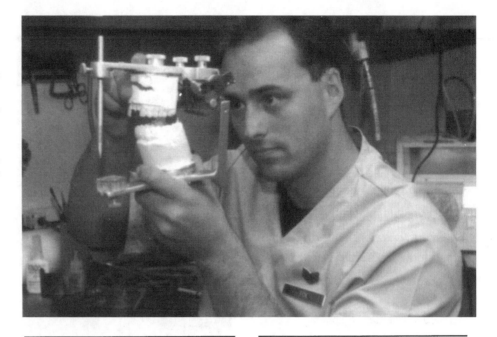

What They Do

Dental and optical laboratory technicians perform some or all of the following duties:

- Make dentures, braces, and other dental or optical devices

- Construct, assemble, repair, and align dental and optical devices (metal braces and retainers, eyeglass frames and lenses)

- Harden and cure dentures or lenses using high temperature ovens or other heat-treating equipment

- Grind, polish, and smooth dentures or lenses using hand or power tools

Training Provided

Job training consists of 21 to 26 weeks of classroom instruction, including practice in making and repairing dental and optical devices. Course content varies depending on specialty, but typically includes laboratory operating procedures (for dental or optical specialty). Further training occurs on the job and through advanced courses.

Helpful Attributes

Helpful school subjects include biology, chemistry, and industrial arts. Helpful attributes include:

- Ability to use precision tools and instruments

- Interest in work requiring attention to detail

- Ability to follow detailed instructions and work procedures

- Interest in working with one's hands

Special Requirements

Successful completion of high school algebra is required to enter some specialties in this occupation.

Physical Demands

Normal color vision for some specialties is required to match color of artificial teeth with natural tooth color.

Civilian Counterparts

Civilian dental laboratory technicians normally work for small dental laboratories or large dental offices. Optical laboratory technicians work in optical laboratories or for retail opticians. They perform duties similar to military technicians. Civilian optical laboratory technicians may also be called opticians or ophthalmic laboratory technicians.

Work Environment

Dental and optical laboratory technicians normally work in dental or optical laboratories and occasionally in examination and dispensing offices.

Opportunities

The services have about 1,500 dental and optical laboratory technicians. Each year, they need new technicians due to changes in personnel and the demands of the field. After job training, technicians work under very close supervision. With experience, they work more independently and perform more challenging tasks. Eventually, they may become supervisors or managers of dental or optical laboratories.

MILITARY CAREERS/SCORE	INTEREST CODE
The circled score shows the typical Military Careers Score of servicemembers in this occupation.	This occupation generally appeals to people whose primary Interest Code is ***Realistic***. *Realistic* jobs:
1 2 3 4 5 **6** 7	• Allow you to work with your hands • Let you see the results of your work • Involve using machines, tools, and equipment
Compare this score to your Military Career Score to see how well your aptitudes, skills, and abilities match those of personnel currently in these positions. See your recruiter for more information about qualification requirements.	
Pages 8 and 9 explain the Military Careers Score and the Interest Codes	

DENTAL SPECIALISTS

Army
Navy
Air Force
Coast Guard

Dental care is one of the health services provided to all military personnel. It is available in military dental clinics all over the world. Dental specialists assist military dentists in examining and treating patients. They also help manage dental offices.

What They Do

Dental specialists in the military perform some or all of the following duties:

- Help dentists perform oral surgery

- Prepare for patient examinations by selecting and arranging instruments and medications

- Help dentists during examinations by preparing dental compounds and operating dental equipment

- Clean patients' teeth using scaling and polishing instruments and equipment

- Operate dental X-ray equipment and process X-rays of patients' teeth, gums, and jaws

- Provide guidance to patients on daily care of their teeth

- Perform administrative duties, such as scheduling office visits, keeping patient records, and ordering dental supplies

Training Provided

Job training consists of 9 to 14 weeks of classroom instruction, including practice in dental care tasks. Course content typically includes:

- Preventive dentistry

- Radiology (X-ray) techniques

- Dental office procedures

- Dental hygiene procedures

Further training occurs on the job and through advanced courses.

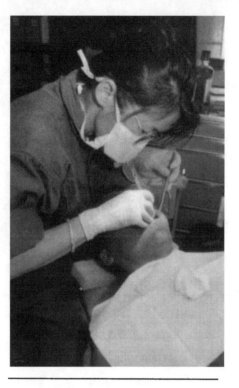

Helpful Attributes

Helpful school subjects include biology and chemistry. Helpful attributes include:

- Good eye-hand coordination

- Ability to follow spoken instructions and detailed procedures

- Interest in working with people

Physical Demands

Dental specialists must sometimes stand for long periods.

Work Environment

Dental specialists in the military usually work indoors in dental offices or clinics. Some specialists may be assigned to duty aboard ships.

Civilian Counterparts

Civilian dental specialists work in dental offices or clinics. Their work is similar to work in the military. They typically specialize in assisting dentists to treat patients, provide clerical support (dental assistants), or clean teeth (dental hygienists).

Opportunities

The military has about 6,000 dental specialists. Each year, the services need new specialists due to changes in personnel and the demands of the field. After job training, new specialists are assigned to dental offices or clinics, where they work under the supervision of dentists. With experience, dental specialists perform more difficult tasks involving patient care. In time, they may become responsible for assisting dental officers in the management of dental programs.

MILITARY CAREERS/SCORE	INTEREST CODE
The circled score shows the typical Military Careers Score of servicemembers in this occupation. 1 2 **③** 4 5 6 7 Compare this score to your Military Career Score to see how well your aptitudes, skills, and abilities match those of personnel currently in these positions. See your recruiter for more information about qualification requirements.	This occupation generally appeals to people whose primary Interest Code is *Realistic. Realistic* jobs: • Allow you to work with your hands • Let you see the results of your work • Involve using machines, tools, and equipment
Pages 8 and 9 explain the Military Careers Score and the Interest Codes	

MEDICAL CARE TECHNICIANS

Army
Navy
Air Force
Coast Guard

The military provides medical care to all men and women in the services. Medical care technicians work with teams of physicians, nurses, and other health care professionals to provide treatment to patients. They help give patients the care and treatment required to help them recover from illness or injury. They also prepare rooms, equipment, and supplies in hospitals and medical clinics.

What They Do

Medical care technicians in the military perform some or all of the following duties:

- Provide bedside care in hospitals, including taking the body temperature, pulse, and respiration rate of patients

- Feed, bathe, and dress patients

- Prepare patients, operating rooms, equipment, and supplies for surgery

- Make casts, traction devices, and splints according to physicians' instructions

- Give medication to patients under the direction of physicians and nurses

Helpful Attributes

Helpful school subjects include general science, biology, and psychology. Helpful attributes include:

- Interest in helping others

- Ability to work under stressful or emergency conditions

- Ability to follow directions precisely

Training Provided

Job training consists of 7 to 52 weeks of classroom instruction, including practice in patient care. Training length varies depending on specialty. Course content may include:

- Patient care techniques

- Emergency medical techniques

- Methods of sterilizing surgical equipment

- Plaster casting techniques

Further training occurs on the job and through advanced courses.

Physical Demands

Some specialties in this area require sufficient strength to lift and move patients, and some require a normal skin condition to guard against infection.

Work Environment

Medical care technicians work in hospitals and clinics on land or aboard ships. In combat situations, they may work in mobile field hospitals.

Civilian Counterparts

Civilian medical care technicians work in hospitals, nursing homes, rehabilitation centers, psychiatric hospitals, or physicians' offices. They perform similar duties to those performed in the military. They may be called nurses aides, orderlies, operating room technicians, orthopedic assistants, or practical nurses.

Opportunities

The services have about 10,000 medical care technicians. Each year, they need new technicians due to changes in personnel and the demands of the field. After job training, new technicians are assigned to hospitals or medical units where they work under close supervision. In time, they may advance to supervisory positions and help train others.

MILITARY CAREERS/SCORE	INTEREST CODE
The circled score shows the typical Military Careers Score of servicemembers in this occupation. 1 2 3 4 **(5)** 6 7 Compare this score to your Military Career Score to see how well your aptitudes, skills, and abilities match those of personnel currently in these positions. See your recruiter for more information about qualification requirements.	This occupation generally appeals to people whose primary Interest Code is ***Realistic. Realistic*** jobs: • Allow you to work with your hands • Let you see the results of your work • Involve using machines, tools, and equipment
Pages 8 and 9 explain the Military Careers Score and the Interest Codes	

MEDICAL LABORATORY TECHNICIANS

Army
Navy
Air Force
Coast Guard

Medical laboratories are an important part of the military health care system. The staffs of medical laboratories perform clinical tests required to detect and identify diseases in patients. Medical laboratory technicians conduct tests on the tissue, blood, and body fluids of medical patients.

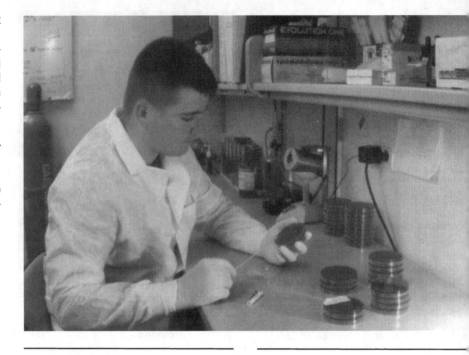

What They Do

Medical laboratory technicians in the military perform some or all of the following duties:

- Use lab equipment to analyze specimens (samples) of tissue, blood, and body fluids

- Examine blood and bone marrow under microscopes

- Test specimens for bacteria or viruses

- Draw blood from patients

- Assist in collecting specimens at autopsies (medical examinations of the dead)

- Record and file results of laboratory tests

Training Provided

Job training consists of 12 to 36 weeks of classroom and on-the-job instruction, including practice in testing specimens. Training length varies depending on specialty. Course content typically includes:

- Medical laboratory procedures

- Study of human parasites and diseases

- Laboratory administration and record keeping

Helpful Attributes

Helpful school subjects include biology, chemistry, and algebra. Helpful attributes include:

- Interest in scientific and technical work

- Ability to follow detailed procedures precisely

Physical Demands

Normal color vision is required to work with colored chemicals and dyes.

Work Environment

Medical laboratory technicians work in medical centers, clinics, and hospitals on land or aboard ships.

Civilian Counterparts

Civilian medical laboratory technicians usually work for privately owned laboratories, hospitals, clinics, or research institutions. They perform duties similar to military medical laboratory technicians.

Opportunities

The military has about 5,000 medical laboratory technicians. Each year, the services need new technicians due to changes in personnel and the demands of the field. After job training, technicians perform routine laboratory tests under close supervision. With experience, they do more complex testing and analysis and work more independently. After demonstrating job proficiency, medical laboratory technicians help train new technicians and supervise laboratory personnel. In time, they may advance to laboratory management positions.

MILITARY CAREERS/SCORE	INTEREST CODE
The circled score shows the typical Military Careers Score of servicemembers in this occupation. 1 2 3 4 5 6 **(7)** Compare this score to your Military Career Score to see how well your aptitudes, skills, and abilities match those of personnel currently in these positions. See your recruiter for more information about qualification requirements.	This occupation generally appeals to people whose primary Interest Code is **Realistic. Realistic** jobs: • Allow you to work with your hands • Let you see the results of your work • Involve using machines, tools, and equipment

Pages 8 and 9 explain the Military Careers Score and the Interest Codes

MEDICAL RECORD TECHNICIANS

Army
Navy
Air Force
Coast Guard

Medical records are important for health care delivery. To provide proper treatment, physicians need complete and accurate information about patient symptoms, test results, illnesses, and prior treatments. Medical record technicians prepare and maintain patient records, reports, and correspondence.

What They Do

Medical record technicians in the military perform some or all of the following duties:

Fill out admission and discharge records for patients entering and leaving military hospitals

Assign patients to hospital rooms

Prepare daily reports about patients admitted and discharged

Organize, file, and maintain medical records

Prepare reports about physical examinations, illnesses, and treatments

Prepare tables of medical statistics

Maintain libraries of medical publications

Helpful Attributes

Helpful school subjects include general science and business administration. Helpful attributes include:

Interest in work requiring accuracy and attention to detail

Ability to communicate well

Interest in using computers and other office machines

Work Environment

Medical record technicians work in admissions or medical records sections of hospitals and clinics. They work in land-based facilities and aboard ships.

Training Provided

Job training consists of 6 to 18 weeks of classroom instruction. Training length varies depending on specialty. Course content typically includes:

• Medical terminology

• Medical records preparation and maintenance

• Maintenance of medical libraries

• Basic computer skills

Civilian Counterparts

Civilian medical record technicians usually work for hospitals, clinics, and government health agencies. They perform duties similar to military medical record technicians. However, civilian medical record technicians tend to specialize in areas such as admissions, ward, or outpatient records. Those working in admission or discharge units are called admitting or discharge clerks.

Opportunities

The services have about 5,000 medical record technicians. Each year, they need new technicians due to changes in personnel and the demands of the field. After training, new technicians are assigned to hospitals or clinics, where they work under close supervision. With experience, they may assume supervisory positions and may manage medical record units or admission or discharge units.

MILITARY CAREERS/SCORE	INTEREST CODE
The circled score shows the typical Military Careers Score of servicemembers in this occupation. **1 2 3 ④ 5 6 7** Compare this score to your Military Career Score to see how well your aptitudes, skills, and abilities match those of personnel currently in these positions. See your recruiter for more information about qualification requirements.	This occupation generally appeals to people whose primary Interest Code is **Conventional. Conventional** jobs: • Require attention to detail • Require attention to accuracy
Pages 8 and 9 explain the Military Careers Score and the Interest Codes	

MEDICAL SERVICE TECHNICIANS

In emergencies or in combat, physicians are not always immediately available to treat the injured or wounded. When a physician is not available, medical service technicians provide basic and emergency medical treatment. They also assist medical officers in caring for sick and injured patients.

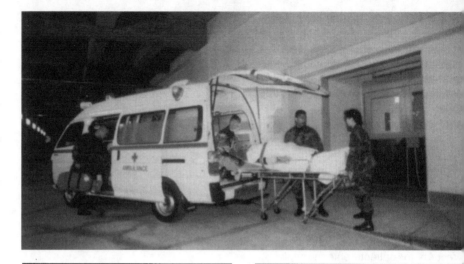

What They Do

Medical service technicians in the military perform some or all of the following duties:

- Examine and treat emergency or battlefield patients
- Interview patients and record their medical histories
- Take patients' temperature, pulse, and blood pressure
- Prepare blood samples for laboratory analysis
- Keep health records and clinical files up to date
- Give shots and medicines to patients

Training Provided

Job training consists of 16 to 54 weeks of classroom instruction, depending on specialty. Course content typically includes:

- Emergency medical treatment
- Basic nursing care
- Study of the human body
- Minor surgical procedures
- Clinical laboratory procedures
- Methods for diagnosing diseases

Further training occurs on the job and through advanced courses.

Work Environment

Medical service technicians usually work in hospitals and clinics on land or aboard ships. Medical service technicians may give emergency medical treatment in the field.

Physical Demands

Medical service technicians may have to lift and carry wounded or injured personnel during emergency situations. Air medical evacuation specialists must pass a flight physical exam.

Civilian Counterparts

Civilian medical service technicians work in hospitals, clinics, nursing homes, and rehabilitation centers. They perform duties similar to those performed by medical service technicians in the military. Civilian medical service technicians are known for the type of work they do: emergency medical technicians treat victims of accidents, fire, or heart attacks; medical assistants work for physicians and perform routine medical and clerical tasks; medication aides give shots and medicine under the close supervision of physicians; and physician assistants perform routine examinations and treatment for physicians.

Helpful Attributes

Helpful school subjects include chemistry, biology, psychology, general science, and algebra. Helpful attributes include:

- Interest in helping others
- Ability to communicate effectively
- Ability to work under stressful conditions

Opportunities

The services have about 27,000 medical service technicians. Each year, they need new technicians due to changes in personnel and the demands of the field. After job training, technicians are assigned to serve in their medical specialty. They work under the direction and supervision of medical officers and experienced medical service technicians. Eventually, they may advance to supervisory positions and help manage a medical facility.

MILITARY CAREERS/SCORE	INTEREST CODE
The circled score shows the typical Military Careers Score of servicemembers in this occupation. 1　2　3　**④**　5　6　7 Compare this score to your Military Career Score to see how well your aptitudes, skills, and abilities match those of personnel currently in these positions. See your recruiter for more information about qualification requirements.	This occupation generally appeals to people whose primary Interest Code is **Social**. **Social** jobs: • involve working with and helping others • Lets you teach others new skills

Pages 8 and 9 explain the Military Careers Score and the Interest Codes

Profile: Larry Roberts

Larry Roberts feels that his career as an Army medical service technician has made the most of his abilities. "I'm good with people," he says, "and I react well in emergencies." His first assignment was with the 65th Medical Group, near Yongsan, Korea. In the beginning, he worked in the dispensary (clinic), caring for patients under the direction of a physician. When needed, he was sent to the demilitarized zone (DMZ) to treat casualties. Within a year, he had been promoted from private first class through sergeant and had become a medical noncommissioned officer (NCO).

From Korea, Larry was assigned to Letterman Army Medical Center, CA, where he cared for patients in special care units and the emergency room. He gave medications, changed dressings, maintained supplies, and helped patients after surgery. Larry liked working in the emergency room best. "There was always something happening," he says. "It kept me sharp and nimble."

Even though he enjoyed his work, Larry decided at this point to leave the Army. He was a civilian for only 83 days. He realized he liked his military career; it interested him more than any others he saw, so he reenlisted.

Larry was sent back to the DMZ in Korea for a year to be in charge of a dispensary. He was then transferred to the 377th Medivac Squadron, a helicopter squadron that picked up patients from all over Korea. His job was to keep the patients alive until they got to the hospital. Back in the States, Larry was assigned to an Army medical center. He started in the emergency room where he performed emergency patient care and went on ambulance runs, and ended his tour in the burn unit.

Larry's next assignments took him more into administration. By this time, Larry had been promoted through staff sergeant to sergeant first class. His best experience, he feels, was at Letterman Army Medical Center, where he was NCOIC of the department of ambulatory care. "Everything came together there," he says. "I had a good group, and I felt good about what I could do."

Larry is now the career advisor NCO for medical service technicians. With 18 years of travel and adventure behind him, he uses his wide knowledge of the field in helping select people for schools and assignments.

SAMPLE CAREER PATH

Medical Services Coordinator   18–19 years

Medical services coordinators help medical staff plan and direct patient care and treatment. They oversee training, health care, and disaster control programs. Coordinators also recommend ways to improve facility operations and working conditions.

Medical Service Supervisor   8–11 years

Medical service supervisors plan and schedule work, personnel, and training assignments. They inspect medical service operations and write technical, personnel, and patient reports. Supervisors also help select sites and set up field medical facilities.

Medical Service Technician   4–6 years

Medical service technicians treat wounded, injured, or critically ill patients. They perform minor medical procedures, suture wounds, and apply casts to broken limbs. Technicians also prepare patients for surgery and perform preoperative and postoperative care.

Medical Service Aide

Medical service aides are assigned to a medical services unit. They assist in examining and treating patients who have minor injuries or common diseases. They collect blood, cultures, and record test results, patient histories and other basic information. Aides also provide emergency first aid and change bandages and dressings.

The years shown represent typical time-in-service before advancement to that level. Actual career advancement depends on individual experience and performance.

OPTOMETRIC TECHNICIANS

Optometry, or vision care, is one of the many health benefits available to military personnel. The military operates its own clinics to examine eyes and fit glasses or contact lenses. Optometric technicians assist optometrists in providing vision care. They work with patients and manage clinic offices.

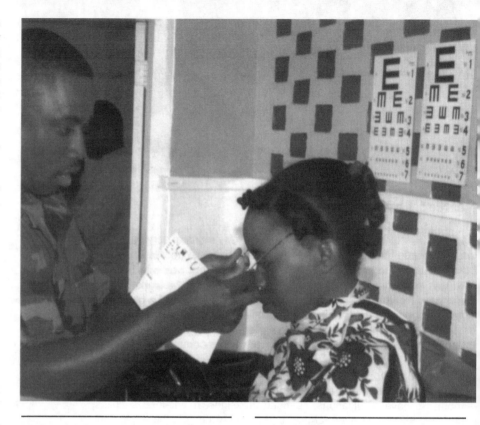

What They Do

Optometric technicians in the military perform some or all of the following duties:

- Use and maintain opthalmic instruments and equipment
- Perform screening tests
- Order eyeglasses and contact lenses from prescriptions
- Fit eyeglasses to patients
- Make minor repairs to glasses
- Place eyedrops and ointment into patients' eyes
- Keep records in optometry offices

Helpful Attributes

Helpful school subjects include algebra, geometry, biology, and related courses. Helpful attributes include:

- Interest in work requiring accuracy and attention to detail
- Ability to communicate effectively

Training Provided

Job training consists of 9 to 13 weeks of classroom instruction, including practice in optometric procedures. Course content typically includes:

- Preparing and fitting glasses and contact lenses
- Vision testing
- Maintenance of optometric instruments

Further training occurs on the job.

Work Environment

Optometric technicians normally work in optometric clinics.

Physical Demands

Normal color vision is required for some specialties to use optometric instruments.

Civilian Counterparts

Civilian optometric technicians work in private optometry offices, clinics, and government health agencies. They perform duties similar to those performed by military optometric technicians. Optometric technicians are also called optometric assistants.

Opportunities

The services have over 500 optometric technicians. Each year, they need new technicians due to changes in personnel and the demands of the field. After training, new technicians give simple vision tests under close supervision and perform office duties. As they gain experience, they work with less supervision and perform more difficult tasks. In time, they may help to manage optometric clinics.

MILITARY CAREERS/SCORE	INTEREST CODE
The circled score shows the typical Military Careers Score of servicemembers in this occupation.	This occupation generally appeals to people whose primary Interest Code is **Realistic. Realistic** jobs:

MILITARY CAREERS/SCORE: 1 2 3 4 (5) 6 7

Compare this score to your Military Career Score to see how well your aptitudes, skills, and abilities match those of personnel currently in these positions. See your recruiter for more information about qualification requirements.

INTEREST CODE:
- Allow you to work with your hands
- Let you see the results of your work
- Involve using machines, tools, and equipment

Pages 8 and 9 explain the Military Careers Score and the Interest Codes

PHARMACY TECHNICIANS

Prescription drugs and medicines are important to medical treatment. Patients and physicians depend on military pharmacies to fill their prescriptions accurately. Pharmacy technicians prepare and dispense prescribed drugs and medicines under the supervision of pharmacists or physicians. They also maintain pharmacy supplies and records.

What They Do

Pharmacy technicians in the military perform some or all of the following duties:

- Read physicians' prescriptions to determine the types and amount of drugs to prepare

- Weigh and measure drugs and chemicals

- Mix ingredients in order to produce prescription medications

- Prepare labels for prescriptions

- Dispense medications to patients

- Store shipments of drugs and medications

Physical Demands

Normal color vision is required as is the ability to speak clearly. Some specialties may involve heavy lifting.

Helpful Attributes

Helpful school subjects include algebra, chemistry, biology, physiology, and anatomy. Helpful attributes include:

- Interest in body chemistry

- Ability to work using precise measurements and standards

- Ability to follow strict procedures and directions

Training Provided

Job training consists of 12 to 17 weeks of classroom instruction. Course content typically includes:

- Pharmacy laws and regulations

- Drug types and uses

- Mixing and dispensing drugs

Work Environment

Pharmacy technicians usually work in hospitals and clinics on land or aboard ships. They may also work in field hospitals.

Civilian Counterparts

Civilian pharmacy technicians work in pharmacies, drug stores, hospitals, and clinics under the direction of pharmacists. They are usually known as pharmacy helpers and generally do not have responsibility for the compounding and dispensing of drugs. They perform simple tasks, such as storing supplies, cleaning equipment, and delivering prescriptions. While military pharmacy technicians generally have more job responsibilities than civilian pharmacy helpers, they do not have the qualifications needed to become civilian pharmacists. Pharmacists must complete a college pharmacy degree program, pass a state board exam, and serve in a pharmacy internship.

Opportunities

The services have over 2,000 pharmacy technicians. Each year, they need new technicians due to changes in personnel and the demands of the field. After job training, new technicians work under the supervision of experienced pharmacy technicians and pharmacists. With experience, they work more independently. Eventually, they may supervise other technicians and may manage military pharmacies.

MILITARY CAREERS/SCORE	INTEREST CODE
The circled score shows the typical Military Careers Score of servicemembers in this occupation. 1 2 3 4 **(5)** 6 7 Compare this score to your Military Career Score to see how well your aptitudes, skills, and abilities match those of personnel currently in these positions. See your recruiter for more information about qualification requirements.	This occupation generally appeals to people whose primary Interest Code is *Realistic*. *Realistic* jobs: • Allow you to work with your hands • Let you see the results of your work • Involve using machines, tools, and equipment
Pages 8 and 9 explain the Military Careers Score and the Interest Codes	

PHYSICAL & OCCUPATIONAL THERAPY SPECIALISTS

Physical and occupational therapy consists of treatment and exercise for patients disabled by illness or injury. Physical and occupational therapy specialists assist in administering treatment aimed at helping disabled patients regain strength and mobility and preparing them to return to work.

What They Do

Physical and occupational therapy specialists in the military perform some or all of the following duties:

- Test and interview patients to determine their physical and mental abilities

- Assist physical and occupational therapists in planning therapy programs and exercise schedules

- Fit artificial limbs (prostheses) and train patients in their use

- Provide massages and heat treatments to patients

- Teach patients new mobility skills

- Set up and maintain therapeutic equipment such as exercise machines and whirlpools

Physical Demands

Therapy specialists may have to lift and support patients during exercises and treatments.

Helpful Attributes

Helpful school subjects include general science, biology, physiology, and psychology. Helpful attributes include:

- Interest in working with and helping people

- Patience to work with people whose injuries heal slowly

- Ability to communicate effectively

Work Environment

Therapy specialists work in hospitals, clinics, and rehabilitation centers.

Training Provided

Job training consists of 11 to 31 weeks of classroom instruction, including practice in applying therapy techniques. Course content typically includes:

- Anatomy, physiology, and psychology (the study of the body, body functions, and the mind)

- Methods of therapy, including massage, electric therapy, and radiation therapy

- Handling and positioning of patients

- Principles of rehabilitation

Further training occurs on the job and through advanced courses.

Civilian Counterparts

Civilian therapy specialists work in hospitals, rehabilitation centers, nursing homes, schools, and community health centers. They perform duties similar to military therapy specialists. Civilian therapy specialists often specialize in treating a particular type of patient, such as children, the severely disabled, the elderly, or those who have lost arms or legs (amputees).

Opportunities

The services have over 500 physical and occupational therapy specialists. Each year, they need new specialists due to changes in personnel and the demands of the field. After job training, therapy specialists provide routine therapy care under the direction of supervisors. With experience, they work with patients with more serious problems. Eventually they may advance to supervisory positions.

MILITARY CAREERS/SCORE	INTEREST CODE
The circled score shows the typical Military Careers Score of servicemembers in this occupation. 1 2 3 4 5 **6** 7 Compare this score to your Military Career Score to see how well your aptitudes, skills, and abilities match those of personnel currently in these positions. See your recruiter for more information about qualification requirements.	This occupation generally appeals to people whose primary Interest Code is *Social*. *Social* jobs: • involve working with and helping others • Lets you teach others new skills
Pages 8 and 9 explain the Military Careers Score and the Interest Codes	

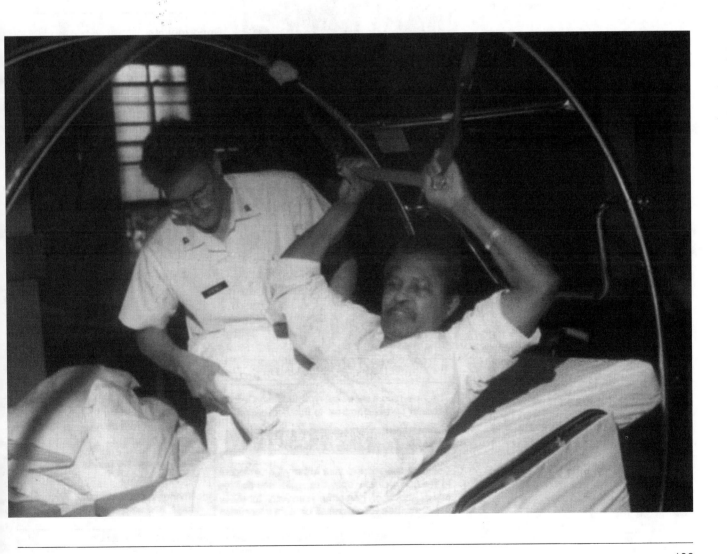

RADIOLOGIC (X-RAY) TECHNICIANS

Army
Navy
Air Force
Coast Guard

Radiology (the use of X-rays) is important in the diagnosis and treatment of medical conditions. X-rays and other diagnostic techniques, such as ultrasound and magnetic resonance imaging (MRI), help physicians detect injuries and illnesses. Radiology is also used to treat some diseases, such as cancer. Radiologic technicians operate X-ray and other imaging related equipment used in diagnosing and treating injuries and diseases. They work as part of a medical team of physicians and specialists to provide health care to patients. Radiologic technicians may specialize by the type of equipment they operate.

What They Do

Radiologic technicians in the military perform some or all of the following duties:

- Read requests or instructions from physicians to determine each patient's X-ray or imaging needs

- Position patients under radiologic equipment

- Operate imaging equipment

- Adjust equipment to the correct time and power of exposure

- Process X-ray pictures

- Prepare and administer radioactive solutions to patients

- Keep records of patient treatment

Helpful Attributes

Helpful school subjects include algebra, biology, and other science courses. Helpful attributes include:

- Interest in activities requiring accuracy and attention to detail

- Ability to follow strict standards and procedures

- Interest in helping others

Training Provided

Job training consists of 12 to 19 weeks of classroom instruction, including practice with radiologic equipment. Extensive on-the-job training is also provided. Training length varies depending on specialty. Course content typically includes:

- Operation of diagnostic imaging equipment

- Radioactive isotope therapy

- X-ray film processing

- Anatomy and physiology

Additional training occurs through advanced courses.

Work Environment

Radiologic technicians work in hospitals and clinics. In combat situations, they may work in mobile field hospitals. They follow strict safety procedures to minimize exposure to radiation.

Civilian Counterparts

Civilian radiologic technicians work in hospitals, diagnostic clinics, and medical laboratories. They perform duties similar to military radiologic technicians. They may specialize in various areas of radiology and may be called X-ray technologists, radiographers, sonographers, radiation therapy technologists, or nuclear medicine technologists.

Opportunities

The military has about 3,500 radiologic technicians. Each year, the services need new technicians due to changes in personnel and the demands of the field. After job training, technicians start operating routine imaging equipment. With experience, they may specialize in nuclear medicine and administer radiation and radioisotopic treatment and therapy. In time, they may advance to become supervisors of radiologic units.

MILITARY CAREERS/SCORE	INTEREST CODE
The circled score shows the typical Military Careers Score of servicemembers in this occupation.	This occupation generally appeals to people whose primary Interest Code is **Realistic. Realistic** jobs:
1 2 3 4 5 **6** 7	• Allow you to work with your hands • Let you see the results of your work
Compare this score to your Military Career Score to see how well your aptitudes, skills, and abilities match those of personnel currently in these positions. See your recruiter for more information about qualification requirements.	• Involve using machines, tools, and equipment
Pages 8 and 9 explain the Military Careers Score and the Interest Codes	

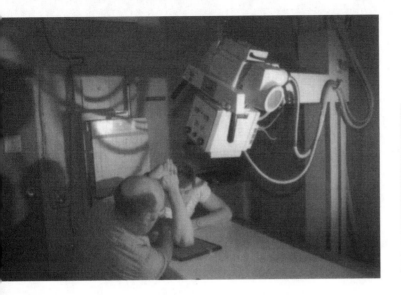

Profile: Ernie Hughes

When Ernie Hughes joined the Navy, he had a guarantee of training in the medical field. He knew he would eventually specialize, but following boot camp, he first went to school to become a hospital corpsman. At the Great Lakes Naval Training Center, Waukegan, IL, he got what he calls "a working knowledge" of anatomy, nursing, and pharmacological chemistry. His first assignment was at the Naval Regional Medical Center, Millington, TN, caring for patients in the intensive care unit. He also worked in medical records and the dispensary, checking throats, taking temperatures, and sending patients to a doctor if he found a problem.

After a year, Ernie was assigned to the medical records unit at the Naval Regional Medical Center, New Orleans, LA. He also worked part-time in the pediatric clinic and the emergency room. As an extra duty, he flew on sea/air rescue missions with the Coast Guard. For this, he was commended for work done above and beyond the call of duty. "My time spent flying with the Coast Guard," Ernie says, "was some of the best of my career."

With 3 years as a hospital corpsman behind him, Ernie began his training for a specialty in nuclear medicine. The training was in two parts. First, Ernie attended classes in math, chemistry, anatomy, physics, and radiopharmacy at the Naval School of Health Sciences, Bethesda, MD. Then he went to the Naval Regional Medical Center, San Diego, CA, for on-the-job training in his new specialty. Under guidance, he operated and maintained radioactive isotope therapy apparatus to do imaging, blood work, and laboratory tests.

Ernie's first, and current, assignment as a clinical nuclear medicine technician is at the Armed Forces Radiobiology Research Institute, Bethesda, MD. Ernie helps medical officers prepare and conduct radioactive isotope research. His work has included studies of the effects of various levels of radiation on organs of the body and research on neuroreceptors in the brain.

Petty Officer First Class Ernie Hughes likes his specialty. "I had to work hard to get here," he says, "but now I have a respected career that challenges me. I am in a position to make decisions and to work on my own."

SAMPLE CAREER PATH

Radiologic Services Coordinator   18–20 years

Radiological services coordinators oversee radiology programs and coordinate activities with other health specialists. They develop guidelines for conducting standard radiologic procedures, set work priorities, and inspect radiology departments.

Radiologic Supervisor   8–10 years

Radiologic supervisors give technical help to aides and technicians and assist doctors with difficult cases. They supervise radiation surveying, monitoring, and decontamination control duties. Supervisors also plan work assignments and prepare technical, personnel, and administrative reports.

Radiologic Technician   4–6 years

Radiologic technicians are assigned more difficult duties. They maintain and adjust imaging equipment and train new personnel. Technicians also operate imaging equipment and provide results to physicians. They evaluate and approve the radiograph techniques and computations of new technicians.

Radiologic Aide

Radiologic aides are assigned to radiology departments of hospitals, field units, or ship dispensaries. They prepare patients for X-rays and other diagnostic imaging procedures. They also position and operate imaging equipment.

The years shown represent typical time-in-service before advancement to that level. Actual career advancement depends on individual experience and performance.

Human Resource Development Occupations

Human resource development specialists recruit and place qualified personnel, and provide the training programs necessary to help people perform their jobs effectively. Personnel in this career area normally specialize by activity. Recruiting specialists, for example, provide information about military careers to young people, parents, schools, and local communities. They explain service employment and training opportunities, pay and benefits, and service life. Personnel specialists collect and store information about the people in the military, such as training, job assignment, promotion, and health information. Training specialists and instructors teach classes and give demonstrations to provide military personnel with the knowledge needed to perform their jobs.

- Personnel Specialists
  Profile: Donna Grant
- Recruiting Specialists
- Training Specialists and Instructors

PERSONNEL SPECIALISTS

Personnel management helps individuals develop their military careers. It also serves the military's need to fill jobs with qualified workers. Personnel specialists collect and store information about the people in the military, such as training, job assignment, promotion, and health information. They work directly with service personnel and their families.

What They Do

Personnel specialists in the military perform some or all of the following duties:

- Organize, maintain, and review personnel records

- Enter and retrieve personnel information using computer terminals

- Assign personnel to jobs

- Prepare correspondence, organizational charts and reports

- Provide career guidance

- Assist personnel and their families who have special needs

Training Provided

Job training consists of 7 to 9 weeks of classroom instruction. Course content typically includes:

- Preparation of military correspondence and forms

- Personnel records management

- Computer update and retrieval procedures

Further training occurs on the job and through advanced courses.

Helpful Attributes

Helpful school subjects include English, speech, and business administration. Helpful attributes include:

- Ability to follow detailed procedures and instructions

- Ability to compose clear instructions or correspondence

- Interest in working closely with others

Work Environment

Personnel specialists normally work in office settings on land or aboard ships.

Civilian Counterparts

Civilian personnel specialists work for all types of organizations, including industrial firms, retail establishments, and government agencies. They perform duties similar to military personnel clerks. However, specific jobs vary from company to company.

Opportunities

The services have about 20,000 personnel specialists. Each year, they need new specialists due to changes in personnel and the demands of the field. After job training, specialists process personnel actions and add information to records. In time, they may supervise other personnel specialists and eventually may manage personnel offices.

MILITARY CAREERS/SCORE	INTEREST CODE
The circled score shows the typical Military Careers Score of servicemembers in this occupation. 1 2 **(3)** 4 5 6 7 Compare this score to your Military Career Score to see how well your aptitudes, skills, and abilities match those of personnel currently in these positions. See your recruiter for more information about qualification requirements.	This occupation generally appeals to people whose primary Interest Code is ***Conventional. Conventional*** jobs: • Require attention to detail • Require attention to accuracy

Pages 8 and 9 explain the Military Careers Score and the Interest Codes

Profile: Donna Grant

Technical Sergeant Donna Grant gets shocked, but positive, reactions when people discover she is a career woman in the military. She likes the opportunities open to her in the military and feels that they are basically the same for women as they are for men. She believes that "if you give it everything you've got, the Air Force will give you all it has to offer."

Her first assignment was at Lowry Air Force Base (AFB), CO, where she scheduled testing for personnel eligible for promotion. She quickly advanced to airman and then to airman first class. At Lowry, she met and married her husband, who is also in the Air Force.

On her next assignment at the Royal Air Force in Upper Heyford, England, she was responsible not only for test scheduling, but also for reviewing, maintaining, and organizing records for all the enlisted and officer promotion programs. "At this point, I really dug into the career field, started learning things for myself, and began building a good work reputation." She achieved senior airman and sergeant and soon became the assistant noncommissioned officer in charge (NCOIC).

Over the next several years, Donna's assignments took her into various areas of personnel administration. At Offut AFB, NE, she was the NCOIC of processing base personnel leaving the Air Force. Here, she received the Meritorious Service Medal for the high quality of her work and was also promoted to Staff Sergeant. Donna was head of the quality work force section on her next assignment at Thule AFB, Greenland, a small base 600 miles south of the North Pole. "There were only a few people in our office, so we all had a lot of responsibility and got some really good experience. But our 4th of July baseball game was played in the snow."

Donna worked on separations and retirements on her next assignment at Davis Monthan AFB, AZ. As part of her duties, she implemented computer programs and gave briefings on promotions. Through her efforts, the base personnel office was able to make significant improvements in its promotions and testing process. Technical Sergeant Donna Grant is now the NCOIC of the promotion branch at Scott AFB, IL.

SAMPLE CAREER PATH

Personnel Supervisor   17–21 years

Personnel supervisors oversee the staff of a personnel office and advise commanders on personnel matters. Supervisors assign new personnel clerks and organize training programs. They also develop and track the budget.

Personnel Specialist   5–7 years

Personnel specialists supervise the processing of personnel action forms (promotions, awards, and reassignments) and the maintenance of service record files. They assign work to personnel clerks and monitor their job performance. Specialists also train and assist new personnel clerks.

Personnel Clerk

Personnel clerks perform routine clerical and administrative support duties to collect and maintain military personnel records. They process paperwork for promotions, retirements, reenlistments, separations (discharges), and reclassifications (changes in job specialties). They also prepare requests for orders, correspondence, personnel action forms, and related records and reports.

The years shown represent typical time-in-service before advancement to that level. Actual career advancement depends on individual experience and performance.

RECURITING SPECIALISTS

Attracting young people with the kinds of talent needed to succeed in today's military is a large task. Recruiting specialists provide information about military careers to young people, parents, schools, and local communities. They explain service employment and training opportunities, pay and benefits, and service life.

What They Do

Recruiting specialists in the military perform some or all of the following duties:

- Interview civilians interested in military careers

- Describe military careers to groups of high school students

- Explain the purpose of the ASVAB (Armed Services Vocational Aptitude Battery) and test results to students and counselors

- Participate in local job fairs and career day programs

- Talk about the military to community groups

- Counsel military personnel about career opportunities and benefits

Training Provided

Job training consists of 4 to 6 weeks of classroom instruction. Course content typically includes:

- Recruiting procedures

- Interviewing techniques

- Public speaking techniques

- Community relations practices

Further training occurs on the job and through advanced courses.

Work Environment

Recruiting specialists work in local recruiting offices, on high school campuses and career centers, and in local communities. They may have to travel often.

Helpful Attributes

Helpful school subjects include the social sciences, speech, psychology, and English. Helpful attributes include:

- Interest in working with youths

- Ability to speak before groups

- Ability to work independently

Civilian Counterparts

Civilian recruiting specialists work for businesses of all kinds searching for talented people to hire. Recruiters also work for colleges seeking to attract and enroll talented high school students.

Opportunities

The services have about 8,000 recruiting specialists. Normally, personnel must be in the service for several years before they are eligible to become recruiters. Each year, the services need new recruiters since some specialists spend only a few years in recruiting before returning to their primary occupational area. Those who choose to make a career of recruiting may, in time, supervise one or more recruiting offices.

MILITARY CAREERS/SCORE	INTEREST CODE
The circled score shows the typical Military Careers Score of servicemembers in this occupation. 1　2　3　**(4)**　5　6　7 Compare this score to your Military Career Score to see how well your aptitudes, skills, and abilities match those of personnel currently in these positions. See your recruiter for more information about qualification requirements.	This occupation generally appeals to people whose primary Interest Code is *Social*. *Social* jobs: • involve working with and helping others • Lets you teach others new skills
Pages 8 and 9 explain the Military Careers Score and the Interest Codes	

TRAINING SPECIALISTS AND INSTRUCTORS

The military trains new personnel in the job skills needed to begin their careers in the service. The military also offers advanced training and retraining to nearly all personnel. Instruction in electronics, health care, computer sciences, and aviation are just a few of the many vocational and technical areas for which the military has training programs. Training specialists and instructors teach classes and give demonstrations to provide military personnel with the knowledge needed to perform their jobs.

What They Do

Training specialists and instructors in the military perform some or all of the following duties:

- Prepare course outlines and materials to present during training

- Select training materials, such as textbooks and films

- Teach classes and give lectures in person, over closed-circuit TV, or on videotape

- Work with students individually when necessary

- Test and evaluate student progress

Helpful Attributes

Helpful school subjects include public speaking and English. Helpful attributes include:

- Interest in teaching

- Ability to communicate effectively, in writing and speaking

- Interest in counseling and promoting human relations

Work Environment

Training specialists and instructors in the military work either indoors or outdoors, depending on the type of training they provide and their specialty area.

Training Provided

Training consists of 2 to 14 weeks of classroom instruction, including practice teaching. Length of training varies depending on specialty. Course content typically includes:

- Lesson planning

- Instructional methods

- Communications skills

Physical Demands

Training specialists and instructors must be able to speak clearly and distinctly.

Civilian Counterparts

Civilian training specialists and instructors work for vocational and technical schools, high schools, colleges, businesses, and government agencies. Their duties are similar to those performed by military training specialists and instructors. Civilian training specialists and instructors may be called teachers, trainers, or training representatives.

Opportunities

The services have about 7,000 training specialists and instructors. Each year, they need new specialists and instructors due to changes in personnel and the demands of the field. Because training specialists and instructors must have an in-depth knowledge of a subject to be effective, only experienced personnel may become training specialists and instructors. Normally, training specialists and instructors are selected from those workers in each occupation who are both good in their work and have shown an ability to teach. Often, they divide their time between regular work and training duties.

MILITARY CAREERS/SCORE	INTEREST CODE
The circled score shows the typical Military Careers Score of servicemembers in this occupation. 1 2 3 4 **5** 6 7 Compare this score to your Military Career Score to see how well your aptitudes, skills, and abilities match those of personnel currently in these positions. See your recruiter for more information about qualification requirements.	This occupation generally appeals to people whose primary Interest Code is *Social*. *Social* jobs: • involve working with and helping others • Lets you teach others new skills
Pages 8 and 9 explain the Military Careers Score and the Interest Codes	

Machine Operator and Production Occupations

Machine operator and production careers include occupations that require the operation of industrial equipment, machinery, and tools to fabricate and repair parts for a variety of items and structures. They may also operate boilers, turbines, nuclear reactors, and portable generators aboard ships and submarines. Personnel may specialize by type of work performed. Welders, for instance, work with various types of metals to repair or form the structural parts of ships, submarines, buildings, or other equipment. Other specialists inspect, maintain, and repair survival equipment such as parachutes, and aircraft life support equipment.

- Machinists
  Profile: Nancy Tita
- Power Plant Operators
- Printing Specialists
- Survival Equipment Specialists
- Water and Sewage Treatment Plant Operators
- Welders and Metal Workers

MACHINISTS

Sometimes when engines or machines break down, the parts needed to repair them are not available. In these cases, the broken parts must be repaired or new ones made. Machinists make and repair metal parts for engines and all types of machines. They operate lathes, drill presses, grinders, and other machine shop equipment.

What They Do

Machinists in the military perform some or all of the following duties:

- Study blueprints or written plans of the parts to be made

- Set up and operate lathes to make parts such as shafts and gears

- Cut metal stock using power hacksaws and bandsaws

- Bore holes using drill presses

- Shape and smooth parts using grinders

- Measure work using micrometers, calipers, and depth gauges

Helpful Attributes

Helpful school subjects include math, general science, metal working, and mechanical drawing. Helpful attributes include:

- Preference for working with the hands

- Interest in making things and finding solutions to mechanical problems

- Ability to apply mathematical formulas

Work Environment

Machinists work in machine shops, which are often noisy.

Training Provided

Job training consists of 10 to 12 weeks of classroom instruction, including practice in machine operation. Course content typically includes:

- Machine types and uses

- Machine setup and operation

- Uses of different metals

- Safety procedures

Further training occurs on the job and through advanced courses.

Civilian Counterparts

Civilian machinists work for factories and repair shops in many industries, including the electrical product, automotive, and heavy machinery industries. They perform duties similar to military machinists.

Opportunities

The services have about 2,000 machinists. Each year, they need new machinists due to changes in personnel and the demands of the field. After job training, machinists perform routine repairs under close supervision. In time, they perform more difficult repairs and may train others. Eventually, they may become managers of one or more machine shops.

MILITARY CAREERS/SCORE	INTEREST CODE
The circled score shows the typical Military Careers Score of servicemembers in this occupation. 1 2 3 **4** 5 6 7 Compare this score to your Military Career Score to see how well your aptitudes, skills, and abilities match those of personnel currently in these positions. See your recruiter for more information about qualification requirements.	This occupation generally appeals to people whose primary Interest Code is *Realistic. Realistic* jobs: • Allow you to work with your hands • Let you see the results of your work • Involve using machines, tools, and equipment

Pages 8 and 9 explain the Military Careers Score and the Interest Codes

Profile: Nancy Tita

Staff Sergeant Nancy Tita has enjoyed her 10 years on active duty. She says her Army career has provided her the opportunity "to travel, meet different people, learn the latest technologies, and just have fun."

Nancy joined the Army Reserves for training so she could do something different from her civilian job as a clerk. After basic training, she went to Fort Sam Houston, TX, for training as a medical service technician. For a year, she worked several weekends a month with her Reserve unit; then she volunteered for active duty. "I enjoyed my time on duty, and I saw the Army as a place to get ahead," she explains.

When Nancy joined the Active Army, she asked to receive training as a machinist. She thought the work would be challenging and different and would allow her to prove herself. She went through initial training at Aberdeen Proving Ground, MD, where she learned the basic skills required of all machinists. Her first assignment was at Fort Eustis, VA, where she worked in the maintenance company, helping make repairs to everything from radios to helicopters. She was able to learn her trade quickly and became familiar with some of the other occupations in the maintenance shop.

At Fort Eustis, Nancy also worked for a year in her second specialty as a medical technician. She was then assigned to a maintenance company in Korea for a year where she was promoted to Sergeant. She returned to the States as a shop foreman in the services section of an armored division at Fort Knox, KY. In this position, she supervised a crew that repaired jeeps, tanks, and other armored equipment.

Nancy has been assigned to Aberdeen Proving Ground for the past five years as an instructor and Noncommissioned Officer (NCOIC) in Charge of student control. In addition to teaching metalworking courses, she processes students entering training and assigns them to their various classes. Nancy was recently promoted to Staff Sergeant and looks forward to being one of the top-ranking females in the maintenance field. When asked about being a female in a nontraditional job, Nancy replies, "I like the challenge of being the only female in the unit."

SAMPLE CAREER PATH

Mechanical Maintenance Superintendent   16–20 years

Mechanical maintenance superintendents oversee shop administration at a facility. They manage unit administration and plan personnel and equipment needs. Superintendents also develop quality and assurance and training programs.

Machine Shop Supervisor   7–8 years

Machine shop supervisors oversee shop operations. They design, make, and repair special machine tools, and inspect finished machined work for quality. Supervisors also plan project schedules and conduct training programs.

Senior Machinist   3–6 years

Senior machinists perform difficult machine setup and operation for precision work. They assist with complex machine jobs and interpret work orders and specifications. Senior machinists also assign work to machinists and train new personnel on machines. They lay out, mark, and make metal and nonmetal parts.

Machinist

Machinists learn to use metalworking machines to make and repair metal parts. They lay out work and set up standard machine tools. They prepare parts and materials for machining and operate lathes, grinders, shapers, and other machines. Machinists also test completed work using precision devices.

The years shown represent typical time-in-service before advancement to that level. Actual career advancement depends on individual experience and performance.

POWER PLANT OPERATORS

Army
Navy
Marine Corps
Coast Guard

Power plants generate electricity for ships, submarines, and military bases. The military uses many different types of power plants. Many ships and submarines have nuclear power plants. Power plant operators control power generating plants on land and aboard ships and submarines. They operate boilers, turbines, nuclear reactors, and portable generators.

What They Do

Power plant operators in the military perform some or all of the following duties:

- Monitor and operate control boards to regulate power plants
- Operate and maintain diesel generating units
- Monitor and control nuclear reactors that produce electricity and power ships and submarines
- Operate and maintain stationary engines, such as steam engines, air compressors, and generators
- Operate and maintain auxiliary equipment
- Inspect equipment for malfunctions
- Operate the steam turbines that generate power for ships

Training Provided

Job training consists of 12 to 25 weeks of classroom instruction, including practice in operating power plants. Course content typically includes:

- Operation of pressure boilers
- Operation and maintenance of reactor control systems
- Operation and maintenance of mechanical systems on nuclear powered ships and submarines

Nuclear specialties have training programs that last 1 year or more, covering all aspects of nuclear power plant operations.

Physical Demands

Power plant operators lift heavy parts or tools when maintaining power plants. They may also have to stoop and kneel and work in awkward positions while repairing.

Work Environment

Power plant operators usually work indoors. They are subject to high temperatures, dust, and noise.

Helpful Attributes

Helpful school subjects include math and shop mechanics. Helpful attributes include:

- Interest in working with large machinery
- Interest in nuclear power

Civilian Counterparts

Civilian power plant operators work for power companies, factories, schools, and hospitals. They perform duties similar to military power plant operators. Depending on the specialty, they may also be called boiler operators, stationary engineers, nuclear reactor operators, or diesel plant operators.

Opportunities

The services have about 13,000 power plant operators. Each year, they need new power plant operators due to changes in personnel and the demands of the field. After job training, power plant operators work under the close direction of supervisors. With experience, they may gain greater responsibility for plant operations and supervise other operators. Eventually, they may become superintendents of utilities for large bases or chiefs of ships' engineering departments.

MILITARY CAREERS/SCORE	INTEREST CODE
The circled score shows the typical Military Careers Score of servicemembers in this occupation.	This occupation generally appeals to people whose primary Interest Code is *Realistic*. *Realistic* jobs:
1 2 3 4 5 (6) 7	• Allow you to work with your hands
Compare this score to your Military Career Score to see how well your aptitudes, skills, and abilities match those of personnel currently in these positions. See your recruiter for more information about qualification requirements.	• Let you see the results of your work • Involve using machines, tools, and equipment
Pages 8 and 9 explain the Military Careers Score and the Interest Codes	

PRINTING SPECIALISTS

The military produces many printed publications each year, including newspapers, booklets, training manuals, maps, and charts. Printing specialists operate printing presses and binding machines to make finished copies of printed material.

What They Do

Printing specialists in the military perform some or all of the following duties:

- Reproduce printed matter using offset lithographic printing processes

- Prepare photographic negatives and transfer them to printing plates using copy cameras and enlargers

- Prepare layouts of artwork, photographs, and text for lithographic plates

- Produce brochures, newspapers, maps, and charts

- Bind printed material into hardback or paperback books using binding machines

- Maintain printing presses

Helpful Attributes

Helpful school subjects include shop mechanics and photography. Helpful attributes include:

- Preference for doing physical work

- Interest in learning about printing

Training Provided

Job training consists of 8 to 20 weeks of classroom instruction, including practice in operating printing presses. Training length varies by specialty. Course content typically includes:

- Photolithography techniques

- Operation of offset presses

- Techniques for making printing plates

- Binding techniques

Further training occurs on the job and through advanced courses.

Work Environment

Printing specialists work indoors in print shops and offices located on land or aboard ships.

Physical Demands

Normal color vision is required to enter some specialties in this occupation.

Civilian Counterparts

Civilian printing specialists work for commercial print shops, newspapers, insurance companies, government offices, or businesses that do their own printing. They perform duties similar to military printing specialists. They may be called offset printing press operators, lithograph press operators, offset duplicating machine operators, lithograph photographers, or bindery workers.

Opportunities

The military has about 500 printing specialists. Each year, the services need new specialists due to changes in personnel and the demands of the field. After job training, specialists normally operate printing and binding machines under direct supervision. With experience, they work more independently, setting up and operating machines. In time, printing specialists may become supervisors of printing plants.

MILITARY CAREERS/SCORE	INTEREST CODE
The circled score shows the typical Military Careers Score of servicemembers in this occupation.	This occupation generally appeals to people whose primary Interest Code is **_Realistic. Realistic_** jobs:
1 **(2)** 3 4 5 6 7	• Allow you to work with your hands
Compare this score to your Military Career Score to see how well your aptitudes, skills, and abilities match those of personnel currently in these positions. See your recruiter for more information about qualification requirements.	• Let you see the results of your work • Involve using machines, tools, and equipment
Pages 8 and 9 explain the Military Careers Score and the Interest Codes	

SURVIVAL EQUIPMENT SPECIALISTS

Military personnel often have hazardous assignments. They depend on survival equipment to protect their lives in case of emergencies. Survival equipment specialists inspect, maintain, and repair survival equipment such as parachutes, aircraft life support equipment, and air-sea rescue equipment.

What They Do

Survival equipment specialists in the military perform some or all of the following duties:

- Inspect parachutes for rips and tangled lines
- Pack parachutes for safe operation
- Repair life rafts and load them with emergency provisions
- Test emergency oxygen regulators on aircraft
- Stock aircraft with fire extinguishers, flares, and survival provisions
- Train crews in the use of survival equipment

Training Provided

Job training consists of 6 to 12 weeks of classroom instruction, including practice in working with survival equipment. Course content typically includes:

- Parachute rigging techniques
- Repair of inflatable rafts and other survival equipment
- Maintenance of oxygen equipment
- Maintenance of air-sea rescue equipment

Further training occurs on the job and through additional courses.

Helpful Attributes

Helpful school subjects include shop mechanics and science. Helpful attributes include:

- Interest in working for the safety of others
- Ability to do work requiring accuracy and attention to detail

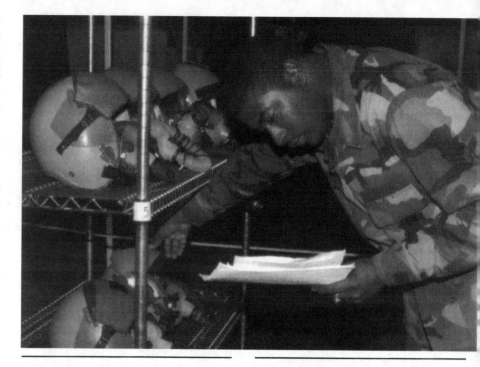

Work Environment

Survival equipment specialists in the military work in repair shops on land or aboard ships.

Civilian Counterparts

Civilian survival equipment specialists work for commercial airlines, parachute rigging and supply companies, survival equipment manufacturing firms, and some government agencies. They perform duties similar to military survival equipment specialists. Those that specialize in parachutes are called parachute riggers.

Physical Demands

Normal color vision is required to work with color-coded wiring and repair charts.

Opportunities

The military has about 5,000 survival equipment specialists. Each year, the services need new specialists due to changes in personnel and the demands of the field. After job training, survival equipment specialists work on survival equipment under the close direction of supervisors. With experience, they work with less supervision and perform more challenging tasks. In time, survival equipment specialists may become supervisors assisting in the management of survival equipment repair facilities.

MILITARY CAREERS/SCORE	INTEREST CODE
The circled score shows the typical Military Careers Score of servicemembers in this occupation. 1 2 **3** 4 5 6 7 Compare this score to your Military Career Score to see how well your aptitudes, skills, and abilities match those of personnel currently in these positions. See your recruiter for more information about qualification requirements.	This occupation generally appeals to people whose primary Interest Code is **Realistic. Realistic** jobs: • Allow you to work with your hands • Let you see the results of your work • Involve using machines, tools, and equipment
Pages 8 and 9 explain the Military Careers Score and the Interest Codes	

WATER AND SEWAGE TREATMENT PLANT OPERATORS

Army
Navy
Air Force
Marine Corps
Coast Guard

Military bases operate their own water treatment plants when public facilities cannot be used. These plants provide drinking water and safely dispose of sewage. Water and sewage treatment plant operators maintain the systems that purify water and treat sewage.

What They Do

Water and sewage treatment plant operators in the military perform some or all of the following duties:

- Operate pumps to transfer water from reservoirs and storage tanks to treatment plants

- Add chemicals and operate machinery that purifies water for drinking or cleans it for safe disposal

- Test water for chlorine content, acidity, oxygen demand, and impurities

- Regulate the flow of drinking water to meet demand

- Clean and maintain water treatment machinery

- Keep records of chemical treatments, water pressure, and maintenance

Helpful Attributes

Helpful school subjects include chemistry, math, and shop mechanics. Helpful attributes include:

- Interest in working with mechanical equipment

- Interest in chemistry and pollution control

Work Environment

Water and sewage treatment plant operators work indoors and outdoors. They may be exposed to strong odors.

Physical Demands

Normal color vision is needed to examine water for acidity and impurities.

Training Provided

Job training consists of 8 to 10 weeks of classroom instruction, including practice operating water and sewage treatment equipment. Course content typically includes:

- Operation of treatment systems

- Water testing and analysis

- Maintenance and repair of pumps, compressors, and other equipment

Further training occurs on the job and through advanced courses.

Civilian Counterparts

Civilian water and sewage treatment plant operators work for municipal public works and industrial plants. Their work is similar to military water and sewage treatment plant operators. Civilian plant operators usually specialize as water treatment plant operators, waterworks pump station operators, or wastewater treatment plant operators.

Opportunities

The services have over 3,000 water and sewage plant operators. Each year, they need new plant operators due to changes in personnel and the demands of the field. After job training, new operators work under close supervision in water or sewage treatment plants. With experience, they may supervise plant operations. Eventually, they may become base utilities superintendents.

MILITARY CAREERS/SCORE	INTEREST CODE
The circled score shows the typical Military Careers Score of servicemembers in this occupation. 1 2 **③** 4 5 6 7 Compare this score to your Military Career Score to see how well your aptitudes, skills, and abilities match those of personnel currently in these positions. See your recruiter for more information about qualification requirements.	This occupation generally appeals to people whose primary Interest Code is *Realistic. Realistic* jobs: • Allow you to work with your hands • Let you see the results of your work • Involve using machines, tools, and equipment
Pages 8 and 9 explain the Military Careers Score and the Interest Codes	

WELDERS AND METAL WORKERS

Sheet metal is used as a building material in many military construction projects. Ships, tanks, and aircraft are made of heavy metal armor. Welders and metal workers make and install sheet metal products, such as roofs, air ducts, gutters, and vents. They also make custom parts to repair the structural parts of ships, submarines, landing craft, buildings, and equipment.

What They Do

Welders and metal workers in the military perform some or all of the following duties:

- Weld, braze, or solder metal parts together

- Repair automotive and ship parts using welding equipment

- Measure work with calipers, micrometers, and rulers

Physical Demands

Welders and metal workers may have to lift heavy metal parts and work in crouching or kneeling positions. Good color vision is required for locating and marking reference points, setting and adjusting welding equipment, and matching paints.

Helpful Attributes

Helpful school subjects include auto mechanics and industrial arts. Helpful attributes include:

- Preference for physical work

- Interest in working with repair tools

Work Environment

Welders and metal workers work indoors in metalworking shops and aircraft hangars. They also work outdoors at construction sites, on ships, and in the field.

Training Provided

Job training consists of 4 to 15 weeks of classroom instruction. Training length varies depending on specialty. Course content typically includes:

- Sheet metal layout and duct work

- Procedures for cutting, brazing, and heat treating

- Operation and care of welding, soldering, and brazing equipment

Further training occurs on the job and through advanced courses.

Civilian Counterparts

Civilian welders and metal workers may work for metal repair shops, auto repair shops, construction companies, pipeline companies, aircraft manufacturing plants, shipyards, and marine servicing companies. They perform duties similar to military welders and metal workers.

Opportunities

The services have over 6,000 welders and metal workers. Each year, they need new welders and metal workers due to changes in personnel and the demands of the field. After job training, welders and metal workers begin to make and repair metal equipment under the direction of a supervisor. With experience, they may become managers of repair shops, maintenance depots, or shipyards.

MILITARY CAREERS/SCORE	INTEREST CODE
The circled score shows the typical Military Careers Score of servicemembers in this occupation.	This occupation generally appeals to people whose primary Interest Code is **Realistic. Realistic** jobs:
1 2 ③ 4 5 6 7	• Allow you to work with your hands
Compare this score to your Military Career Score to see how well your aptitudes, skills, and abilities match those of personnel currently in these positions. See your recruiter for more information about qualification requirements.	• Let you see the results of your work • Involve using machines, tools, and equipment
Pages 8 and 9 explain the Military Careers Score and the Interest Codes	

Media and Public Affairs Occupations

Media and public affairs careers include those occupations that are involved in the public presentation and interpretation of military information and events. Enlisted media and public affairs personnel take and develop photographs; film, record, and edit audio and video programs; present news and music programs; and produce graphic artwork, drawings, and other visual displays. Other public affairs specialists may act as interpreters and translators to convert written or spoken foreign languages into English or other languages.

- Audiovisual and Broadcast Technicians
- Broadcast Journalists and Newswriters
  Profile: Casondra Brewster
- Graphic Designers and Illustrators
- Interpreters and Translators
- Musicians
- Photographic Specialists

AUDIOVISUAL AND BROADCAST TECHNICIANS

Television and film productions are an important part of military communications. Films are used for training in many military occupations. They are also used to record military operations, ceremonies, and news events. These productions require the teamwork of many technicians. Audiovisual and broadcast technicians perform many specialized tasks, ranging from filming to script editing to operating audio recording devises.

What They Do

Audiovisual and broadcast technicians in the military perform some or all of the following duties:

Work with writers, producers, and directors in preparing and interpreting scripts

Plan and design production scenery, graphics, and special effects

Operate media equipment and special effect devices including cameras, sound recorders, and lighting

Follow script and instructions of film or TV directors to move cameras, zoom, pan, or adjust focus

Training Provided

Job training consists of 7 to 52 weeks of instruction. Training length varies depending on specialty. Course content typically includes:

- Motion picture equipment operation
- Audio recording
- Scripting and special effects techniques
- Maintenance of public address sound equipment

Further training occurs on the job and through advanced courses.

Physical Demands

Normal color vision and the ability to speak clearly are required for some specialties in this area.

Work Environment

Audiovisual and broadcast technicians work in studios or outdoors on location. They sometimes work from aircraft or ships. They travel and work in all climates.

Civilian Counterparts

Civilian audiovisual and broadcast technicians work for film production companies, government audiovisual studios, radio and television stations, and advertising agencies. Their duties are similar to those performed by military journalists and newswriters. They may be called motion picture camera operators, audiovisual production specialists, sound mixers, recording engineers, and broadcasting and recording technicians.

Helpful Attributes

Helpful school subjects include photography, graphics, art, speech and drama. Helpful attributes include:

- Interest in creative and artistic work
- Preference for working as part of a team
- Experience in school plays or making home movies

Opportunities

The services have about 1,000 audiovisual and broadcast technicians. Each year, they need new technicians due to changes in personnel and the demands of the field. After job training, new technicians assist with various production processes. With experience, they work more independently and, in time, may direct audiovisual productions.

MILITARY CAREERS/SCORE	INTEREST CODE
The circled score shows the typical Military Careers Score of servicemembers in this occupation.	This occupation generally appeals to people whose primary Interest Code is **Realistic. Realistic** jobs:
1 2 3 4 **5** 6 7	• Allow you to work with your hands
Compare this score to your Military Career Score to see how well your aptitudes, skills, and abilities match those of personnel currently in these positions. See your recruiter for more information about qualification requirements.	• Let you see the results of your work • Involve using machines, tools, and equipment
Pages 8 and 9 explain the Military Careers Score and the Interest Codes	

BROADCAST JOURNALISTS AND NEWSWRITERS

Army
Navy
Air Force
Marine Corps
Coast Guard

The military publishes newspapers and broadcasts television and radio programs for its personnel and the public. These services are an important source of general information about people and events in the military. Broadcast journalists and newswriters write and present news programs, music programs, and radio talk shows.

What They Do

Broadcast journalists and newswriters in the military perform some or all of the following duties:

- Gather information for military news programs and publications

- Write radio and TV scripts

- Develop ideas for news articles

- Arrange and conduct interviews

- Collect information for commercial media use

- Select photographs and write captions for news articles

- Write news releases, feature articles, and editorials

Work Environment

Broadcast journalists and newswriters work in broadcasting studios on land or aboard ships, or sometimes outdoors, depending upon the research needed for their articles.

Training Provided

Job training consists of 9 to 12 weeks of classroom instruction. Course content typically includes:

- Newswriting and research

- Newspaper format and layout

- Photojournalism (writing news stories featuring pictures)

- Radio and television programming and production

Physical Demands

Normal color vision and the passing of a voice audition are required for some specialties in this area.

Helpful Attributes

Helpful school subjects include English, journalism, speech, and media communications. Helpful attributes include:

- Ability to keep detailed and accurate records

- Interest in researching facts and issues for news stories

- Ability to write clearly and concisely

- Strong, clear speaking voice

Civilian Counterparts

Broadcast journalists and newswriters work for newspapers, magazines, wire services, and radio and television stations. Their duties are similar to those performed by military journalists and newswriters. They may be employed as newscasters, disc jockeys, writers, directors, producers, or correspondents.

Opportunities

The military has about 2,000 broadcast journalists and newswriters. Each year, the services need new journalists and newswriters due to changes in personnel and the demands of the field. After job training, they research and announce news stories and music programs. Eventually, they may become editors or editorial assistants or managers of broadcasting stations.

MILITARY CAREERS/SCORE	INTEREST CODE
The circled score shows the typical Military Careers Score of servicemembers in this occupation.	This occupation generally appeals to people whose primary Interest Code is ***Social. Social*** jobs:
1 2 3 4 5 6 **7**	• involve working with and helping others
Compare this score to your Military Career Score to see how well your aptitudes, skills, and abilities match those of personnel currently in these positions. See your recruiter for more information about qualification requirements.	• Lets you teach others new skills
Pages 8 and 9 explain the Military Careers Score and the Interest Codes	

Profile: Casondra Brewster

Casondra Brewster was on a scholarship working towards an associate's degree in journalism at Casper College in Wyoming. After leaving Casper College at the age of 26, Casondra wanted to continue her studies in journalism, but realized she could not afford it. She knew she wanted to be a journalist, and she turned to the Army to find her opportunity. She says, "I was getting antsy to really do something. The Army was always in the back of my head since many of my relatives and friends had been in the military."

Casondra entered the Army through a delayed entry program enabling her to complete her associate's degree and begin active duty with civilian acquired skills. She was able to start her military career as a public affairs specialist doing what she loved, writing articles and taking pictures. Her first tour took her to Europe where one of her assignments was to cover the 50th anniversary of World War II. This assignment took her all over Europe to important historic sites including Normandy, where she interviewed World War II veterans, wrote articles for use in military and civilian publications, and took historical photos. She also acted as a media escort for civilian journalists, reporters, and photographers as they viewed various military sites. While overseas, Casondra spent time in northern Iraq where she covered the Army's operations to provide humanitarian assistance to Kurdish refugees. She also performed public affairs duties in Bosnia and Macedonia. In a 3 year period, Casondra visited 12 countries. She often accompanied soldiers on their missions so that she could document what they were doing. She has patrolled the Serbian/Macedonian border and taken pictures from helicopters over Iraq. Of this experience she says, "My job is the best one in the Army because through it, I get to experience everyone else's job."

Even though Casondra loved her job in the Army, she made the decision to leave to start a family. After being out of the military, she really missed the camaraderie and lifestyle and says, "The military provides a community unlike any other I've experienced." After having her second child, she chose to return to the Army where she is now performing public affairs duties at Fort Belvoir in Virginia. In the next few months, she will be up for promotion, and she will also have the opportunity to further her skills by taking more advanced classes in photojournalism. She is happy to be back in the military and says, "I am in for the long haul now. It wasn't until I joined the military that I realized there was so much out there. I want my kids to have the same opportunities."

SAMPLE CAREER PATH

Public Affairs Coordinator   15–20 years

Public affairs coordinators assist staff officers in directing military public affairs operations. They plan, organize, and direct military news and information operations. They determine training needs and set up public affairs training programs. They also prepare administrative, personnel, and technical reports for officers.

Editor   7–8 years

Editors set work priorities and assign personnel to meet news deadlines, review work and give technical assistance. They also coordinate military and civilian news media and, prepare public affairs information. They may teach classes in the principles of journalism and writing styles and techniques

Senior Broadcast Journalist Newswriter   3–5 years

Senior broadcast journalists and newswriters plan and design layouts for newspapers, bulletins, and magazines. They conduct special interviews, news conferences, and tours for civilians. They also edit written material and taped interviews for radio and television.

Broadcast Journalist/Newswriter

Broadcast journalists and newswriters gather information and prepare news features and stories for military and civilian use. They interview individuals and write news stories and editorials. They also select photographs for publications and write captions for the pictures.

The years shown represent typical time-in-service before advancement to that level. Actual career advancement depends on individual experience and performance.

GRAPHIC DESIGNERS AND ILLUSTRATORS

Army
Navy
Air Force
Marine Corps

The military produces many publications, such as training manuals, newspapers, reports, and promotional materials. Graphic artwork is used in these publications and for signs, charts, posters, and TV and motion picture productions. Graphic designers and illustrators produce graphic artwork, drawings, and other visual displays.

What They Do

Graphic designers and illustrators in the military perform some or all of the following duties:

- Produce computer-generated graphics

- Draw graphs and charts to represent budgets, numbers of troops, supply levels, and office organization

- Develop ideas and design posters and signs

- Help instructors design artwork for training courses

- Draw illustrations and cartoons for filmstrips and animation for films

- Make silkscreen prints

- Work with TV and film producers to design backdrops and props for film sets

Training Provided

Job training consists of about 12 weeks of classroom instruction including practice in preparing graphic designs and illustrations. Course content typically includes:

- Introduction to graphics, lettering, drawing, and layout techniques

- Illustration and television graphic techniques

- Theory and use of color

Further training occurs on the job.

Work Environment

Graphic designers and illustrators usually work in offices on land or aboard ships.

Helpful Attributes

Helpful school subjects include art, drafting, and geometry. Helpful attributes include:

- Interest in artwork or lettering

- Ability to convert ideas into visual presentations

- Neatness and an eye for detail

Civilian Counterparts

Civilian graphic designers and illustrators work for government agencies, advertising agencies, print shops, engineering firms, and large organizations that have their own graphics departments. They may be known as graphic arts technicians or commercial artists.

Physical Demands

Coordination of eyes, hands, and fingers are needed to draw sketches. Normal color vision is required to work with paints and other art materials.

Opportunities

The services have about 1,000 graphic designers and illustrators. Each year they need new designers and illustrators due to changes in personnel and the demands of the field. After job training, graphic designers prepare tables, signs, and graphics under close supervision. With experience, they help formulate and produce more complex designs. In time, they may supervise others and lead large projects. Eventually, they may manage graphics departments.

MILITARY CAREERS/SCORE	INTEREST CODE
The circled score shows the typical Military Careers Score of servicemembers in this occupation. 1 2 3 **(4)** 5 6 7 Compare this score to your Military Career Score to see how well your aptitudes, skills, and abilities match those of personnel currently in these positions. See your recruiter for more information about qualification requirements.	This occupation generally appeals to people whose primary Interest Code is *Artistic. Artistic* jobs: • Allow you to be creative • Allow you to use your imagination to do original work

Pages 8 and 9 explain the Military Careers Score and the Interest Codes

INTERPRETERS AND TRANSLATORS

Army
Navy
Air Force
Marine Corps

Some members of the military must be able to read and understand the many languages of the world. Information from foreign language newspapers, magazines, and radio broadcasts is important to the nation's defense. Interpreters and translators convert written or spoken foreign languages into English or other languages. They usually specialize in a particular foreign language.

What They Do

Interpreters and translators in the military perform some or all of the following duties:

- Translate written and spoken foreign language material to and from English, making sure to preserve the original meaning

- Interview prisoners of war, enemy deserters, and civilian informers in their native languages

- Record foreign radio transmissions using sensitive communications equipment

- Prepare written reports about the information obtained

- Translate foreign documents, such as battle plans and personnel records

- Translate foreign books and articles describing foreign equipment and construction techniques

Physical Demands

Normal hearing and the ability to speak clearly and distinctly are usually required to enter this occupation.

Special Requirements

Fluency in a foreign language is required to enter most specialties within this occupation.

Training Provided

Job training consists of 7 to 20 weeks of classroom instruction including practice in interpretation. Training length varies depending on specialty. Longer training is necessary for specialties that do not require foreign language fluency prior to entry. For these specialties, foreign language training for 6 to 12 months is provided. Course content typically includes:

- Interrogation (questioning) methods

- Use and care of communications equipment

- Procedures for preparing reports

Further training occurs on the job and through advanced courses.

Helpful Attributes

Helpful school subjects include speech, communications, and foreign languages. Helpful attributes include:

- Talent for foreign languages

- Interest in working with people

- Interest in reading and writing

Work Environment

Interpreters and translators normally work on military bases, aboard ships, or in airplanes.

Civilian Counterparts

Civilian interpreters and translators work for government agencies, embassies, universities, and companies that conduct business overseas. Their work is similar to the work of military interpreters and translators.

Opportunities

The military has about 8,000 interpreters and translators. Each year, the services need new interpreters and translators due to changes in personnel and the demands of the field. After job training, interpreters and translators work under the direction of more experienced workers and supervisors. With experience, they work more independently. In time, interpreters and translators may become directors of translation for large bases.

MILITARY CAREERS/SCORE	INTEREST CODE
The circled score shows the typical Military Careers Score of servicemembers in this occupation. 1 2 3 4 5 6 (7) Compare this score to your Military Career Score to see how well your aptitudes, skills, and abilities match those of personnel currently in these positions. See your recruiter for more information about qualification requirements.	This occupation generally appeals to people whose primary Interest Code is ***Investigative. Investigative*** jobs: • Involve learning about a new subject area • Allow you to use your knowledge to solve problems or create things or ideas
Pages 8 and 9 explain the Military Careers Score and the Interest Codes	

MUSICIANS

Army
Navy
Air Force
Marine Corps
Coast Guard

Music is an important part of military life. Service bands and vocal groups have a strong tradition of performing at ceremonies, parades, concerts, festivals, and dances. Musicians and singers perform in service bands, orchestras, and small groups. They perform many types of music, including marches, classics, jazz, and popular music.

What They Do

Musicians in the military perform some or all of the following duties:

- Play in or lead bands, orchestras, combos, and jazz groups

- Sing in choral groups or as soloists

- Perform for ceremonies, parades, concerts, festivals, and dances

- Rehearse and learn new music when not performing

- Play brass, percussion, woodwind, or string instruments

Training Provided

Although musicians must be musically proficient to enter the service, music training is given to new band members. Job training consists of 11 to 24 weeks of classroom instruction, including practice playing instruments. Training length varies depending on musical specialty. Course content typically includes:

- Music theory

- Group instrumental techniques

- Sight-reading musical scores

- Dance band techniques

Further training occurs on the job through regular rehearsals and individual practice.

Special Requirements

To qualify for a service band, applicants must pass one or more auditions. They must be fairly accomplished musicians and be able to sight-read musical notations.

Work Environment

Musicians play indoors in theaters, concert halls, and at dances; outdoors at parades and open-air concerts. They also travel regularly.

Helpful Attributes

Helpful school subjects include band, music theory, harmony, and other music courses. Helpful attributes include:

- Poise when performing in public

- Ability to play more than one instrument

- Ability to sing

Civilian Counterparts

Civilian musicians work for many types of employers, including professional orchestras, bands, and choral groups. They work in nightclubs, concert halls, theaters, and recording studios.

Opportunities

The services have over 4,000 musicians. Each year, they need new musicians due to changes in personnel and the demands of the field. After job training, musicians are assigned to band units located with U.S. forces around the world. They perform as members of bands and vocal groups. In time, they may become heads of their instrument sections and, possibly, bandleaders or orchestra conductors. The most outstanding performers are selected for the official service bands or orchestras of their service.

MILITARY CAREERS/SCORE	INTEREST CODE
The circled score shows the typical Military Careers Score of servicemembers in this occupation. **1 2 3 4 5 6 (7)** Compare this score to your Military Career Score to see how well your aptitudes, skills, and abilities match those of personnel currently in these positions. See your recruiter for more information about qualification requirements.	This occupation generally appeals to people whose primary Interest Code is *Artistic. Artistic* jobs: • Allow you to be creative • Allow you to use your imagination to do original work
Pages 8 and 9 explain the Military Careers Score and the Interest Codes	

PHOTOGRAPHIC SPECIALISTS

The military uses photographs for many purposes, such as intelligence gathering and news reporting. The services operate photographic laboratories to develop the numerous photos taken by the military. Photographic specialists take and develop still color or black and white photographs.

What They Do

Photographic specialists in the military perform some or all of the following duties:

Select camera, film, and other equipment needed for assignments

Determine camera angles, lighting, and any special effects needed

Take still photos of people, events, military equipment, land areas, and other subjects

Develop, duplicate, or retouch film negatives, photos, or slides

Maintain photographic equipment

Training Provided

Job training consists of 7 to 24 weeks of classroom instruction, including practice in taking and developing photographs. Length of training varies depending on the specialty. Course content typically includes:

Photographic processing and reproduction

Principles of photojournalism

Operation and maintenance of photographic equipment

Further training occurs on the job and through advanced courses.

Helpful Attributes

Helpful school subjects include photography, chemistry, art, and mathematics. Helpful attributes include:

Ability to recognize and arrange interesting photo subjects

Accuracy and attention to detail

Physical Demands

Normal color vision is required to produce accurate color prints.

Civilian Counterparts

Civilian photographic specialists work for photography studios, newspapers, magazines, advertising agencies, commercial photograph developers, and large businesses. They perform duties similar to military specialists. Depending on the specialty, they may be known as photojournalists, aerial or still photographers, film developers, automatic print developers, or print controllers.

Work Environment

Photographic specialists work both indoors and outdoors while photographing their subjects. They may take photos from aircraft or ships. They process photographs in photographic laboratories on bases or aboard ships.

Opportunities

The services have about 1,500 photographic specialists. Each year, the services need new specialists due to changes in personnel and the demands of the field. After job training, specialists work under supervision. With experience, they are given more responsibility and, eventually, may supervise other photographic specialists.

MILITARY CAREERS/SCORE	INTEREST CODE
The circled score shows the typical Military Careers Score of servicemembers in this occupation. 1 2 3 4 **(5)** 6 7 Compare this score to your Military Career Score to see how well your aptitudes, skills, and abilities match those of personnel currently in these positions. See your recruiter for more information about qualification requirements.	This occupation generally appeals to people whose primary Interest Code is *Artistic. Artistic* jobs: • Allow you to be creative • Allow you to use your imagination to do original work

Pages 8 and 9 explain the Military Careers Score and the Interest Codes

Protective Service Occupations

Protective service personnel enforce military laws and regulations and provide emergency response to natural and man made disasters. Personnel normally specialize by function. Specialists in emergency management implement response procedures for all types of disasters, such as floods, earthquakes, hurricanes, or enemy attack. Military police control traffic, prevent crime, and respond to emergencies. Other law enforcement and security specialists investigate crimes committed on military property and guard inmates in military correctional facilities. Firefighters put out, control, and help prevent fires in buildings, aircraft, and aboard ships.

- Emergency Management Specialists
- Firefighters
- Law Enforcement and Security Specialists
  Profile: Charles Marren

EMERGENCY MANAGEMENT SPECIALISTS

The military prepares for emergencies or natural disasters by developing detailed warning, control, and evacuation plans. Emergency management specialists prepare emergency plans and respond to all types of disasters, such as floods, earthquakes, hurricanes, or enemy attack.

What They Do

Emergency management specialists in the military perform some or all of the following duties:

- Assist in preparing and maintaining disaster operations plans

- Train military and civilian personnel on what to do in an emergency

- Operate and maintain nuclear, biological, and chemical detection and decontamination equipment

- Conduct surveys to determine needs in the event of an emergency

- Monitor disaster preparedness activities and training operations

- Serve as members of emergency response teams

Helpful Attributes

Helpful school subjects include algebra, chemistry, physics, geometry, and trigonometry. Helpful attributes include:

- Ability to communicate effectively

- Ability to plan and organize

- Ability to work calmly under stress

Work Environment

Emergency management specialists work indoors when conducting training sessions and preparing disaster plans. Sometimes they work outdoors while operating decontamination equipment and monitoring disaster training.

Training Provided

Job training consists of 8 to 10 weeks of classroom instruction, including practice in the use of nuclear, biological, and chemical detection and decontamination equipment. Course content typically includes:

- Defensive procedures for nuclear, biological, and chemical warfare

- Preparation of emergency plans

Further training occurs on the job and through advanced courses.

Physical Demands

Normal color vision is needed to identify chemical agents.

Civilian Counterparts

Civilian emergency management specialists work for federal, state, and local governments, including law enforcement and civil defense agencies. They perform duties similar to military emergency management specialists.

Opportunities

The services have about 9,000 emergency management specialists. Each year, they need new specialists due to changes in personnel and the demands of the field. After job training, some prepare emergency plans under close supervision. With experience, they work more independently and assist in surveys and inspections. Other specialists conduct inspections and operate decontamination equipment. Eventually, they may become supervisors of emergency management programs.

MILITARY CAREERS/SCORE	INTEREST CODE
The circled score shows the typical Military Careers Score of servicemembers in this occupation. 1 2 **3** 4 5 6 7 Compare this score to your Military Career Score to see how well your aptitudes, skills, and abilities match those of personnel currently in these positions. See your recruiter for more information about qualification requirements.	This occupation generally appeals to people whose primary Interest Code is *Realistic. Realistic* jobs: • Allow you to work with your hands • Let you see the results of your work • Involve using machines, tools, and equipment
Pages 8 and 9 explain the Military Careers Score and the Interest Codes	

FIREFIGHTERS

Military bases have their own fire departments. Military firefighting units are responsible for protecting lives and property on base from fire. Firefighters put out, control, and help prevent fires in buildings, aircraft, and aboard ships.

What They Do

Firefighters in the military perform some or all of the following duties:

- Operate pumps, hoses, and extinguishers
- Force entry into aircraft, vehicles, and buildings in order to fight fires and rescue personnel
- Drive firefighting trucks and emergency rescue vehicles
- Give first aid to injured personnel
- Inspect aircraft, buildings, and equipment for fire hazards
- Teach fire protection procedures
- Repair firefighting equipment and fill fire extinguishers

Training Provided

Job training consists of 7 to 11 weeks of classroom training, including practice in fighting fires. Course content typically includes:

- Types of fires
- Firefighting equipment operations
- Firefighting procedures
- First aid procedures
- Rescue procedures

Further training occurs on the job.

Helpful Attributes

Helpful school subjects include health and general science. Helpful attributes include:

- Ability to remain calm under stress
- Willingness to risk injury to help others
- Ability to think and act decisively

Physical Demands

Good vision without glasses and a clear speaking voice are required to enter some specialties in this occupation. Firefighters have to climb ladders and stairs. They must also be able to lift and carry injured personnel.

Civilian Counterparts

Civilian firefighters work for city and county fire departments, other government agencies, and industrial firms. They perform duties similar to those performed by military firefighters, including rescue and salvage work.

Work Environment

Firefighters work indoors and outdoors while fighting fires. They are exposed to the smoke, heat, and flames of the fires they fight.

Opportunities

The services have about 8,000 firefighters. Each year, they need new firefighters due to changes in personnel and the demands of the field. After training, new firefighters perform work under close supervision. With experience, they work more independently and may supervise others. Eventually, they may become chiefs of base fire departments or similar units.

MILITARY CAREERS/SCORE	INTEREST CODE
The circled score shows the typical Military Careers Score of servicemembers in this occupation. 1 **2** 3 4 5 6 7 Compare this score to your Military Career Score to see how well your aptitudes, skills, and abilities match those of personnel currently in these positions. See your recruiter for more information about qualification requirements.	This occupation generally appeals to people whose primary Interest Code is *Realistic. Realistic* jobs: • Allow you to work with your hands • Let you see the results of your work • Involve using machines, tools, and equipment
Pages 8 and 9 explain the Military Careers Score and the Interest Codes	

LAW ENFORCEMENT AND SECURITY SPECIALISTS

Army
Navy
Air Force
Marine Corps
Coast Guard

The military services have their own law enforcement and police forces. These specialists investigate crimes committed on military property or that involve military personnel. Military police do many of the same things as civilian officers, control traffic, prevent crime, and respond to emergencies. They also guard military bases and inmates in military correctional facilities.

What They Do

Law enforcement and security specialists in the military perform some or all of the following duties:

- Investigate criminal activities and activities related to espionage, treason, and terrorism

- Interview witnesses and arrest suspects

- Guard correctional facilities and other military installations

- Patrol areas on foot, by car, or by boat

- Perform fire and riot control duties

Training Provided

Job training consists of 5 to 12 weeks of classroom instruction. Training length varies depending on specialty. Course content typically includes:

- Civil and military laws

- Investigation and evidence collection procedures and techniques

- Prisoner control and discipline

- Use of firearms and hand-to-hand defense techniques

- Traffic and crowd control procedures

Helpful Attributes

Helpful school subjects include government and speech. Helpful attributes include:

- Interest in law enforcement and crime prevention

- Willingness to perform potentially dangerous work

- Ability to remain calm under pressure

Work Environment

Law enforcement and security specialists in the military work both indoors and outdoors depending on their assignment. They may work outdoors while conducting investigations or patrolling facilities.

Civilian Counterparts

Civilian law enforcement and security specialists work for state, county, or city law enforcement agencies. They may also work in prisons, intelligence agencies, and private security companies. They perform similar duties to those performed in the military. They may be called police officers, detectives, private investigators, undercover agents, correction officers, or security guards.

Physical Demands

Normal color vision is necessary to enter some specialties in this area. Some specialties have minimum age and height requirements.

Opportunities

The military has about 30,000 law enforcement and security specialists. Each year, the services need new specialists due to changes in personnel and the demands of the field. After job training, they work under the direction of more experienced specialists. In time, they may supervise and train new workers or lead investigations. Eventually, they may become chiefs of detectives, chiefs of police, or superintendents of correctional facilities.

MILITARY CAREERS/SCORE	INTEREST CODE
The circled score shows the typical Military Careers Score of servicemembers in this occupation. 1 2 3 **(4)** 5 6 7 Compare this score to your Military Career Score to see how well your aptitudes, skills, and abilities match those of personnel currently in these positions. See your recruiter for more information about qualification requirements.	This occupation generally appeals to people whose primary Interest Code is ***Realistic. Realistic*** jobs: • Allow you to work with your hands • Let you see the results of your work • Involve using machines, tools, and equipment
Pages 8 and 9 explain the Military Careers Score and the Interest Codes	

Profile: Charles Marren

After completing one year of study in Criminal Justice at Northeastern University in Boston, Charles Marren began looking for a different kind of challenge. Charles felt as though he was doing many of the same things he had done in high school. Seeking a way to prove himself, Charles looked to the Marine Corps. In high school, he had admired the recent graduates who returned to his neighborhood after completing recruit training. He liked the respect they received from others, and more importantly, he wanted the confidence they possessed.

Charles began his Marine Corps enlistment as a Military Police Officer (MP) at Camp Pendleton where he performed base security duties. As he gained experience, he moved into the more challenging role of a patrol officer enforcing laws within the base community. In this position, Charles responded to emergency situations such as robberies, assaults, and accidents. During his career, Charles was fortunate to have the opportunity to attend the Federal Bureau of Investigation (FBI) National Academy where he received extensive investigative training. This preparation enabled him to advance further in the criminal investigation arena. As an investigator, Charles gathered crime evidence, interrogated suspects, and interviewed witnesses. He also served in the position of provost sergeant. In this assignment, he acted as an advisor to the senior law enforcement officer at Marine Corps Headquarters in Quantico, VA.

As a law enforcement officer, Charles had the opportunity to travel to many places, including Hawaii, Japan, and many locations within the continental United States.

As he looks to retirement in the near future, Master Sergeant Marren says "I am proud to have had the opportunity to serve my country for the past 20 years as a Marine." He feels that the training and experience he has acquired will enable him to easily transition to a civilian career in law enforcement.

SAMPLE CAREER PATH

Law Enforcement Superintendent 18–20 years

Law enforcement superintendents manage law enforcement and security forces on large bases. They set force goals and objectives and decide where law enforcement and security support is needed. Superintendents coordinate military police work with civilian agencies. They review accident reports and plan traffic safety programs.

Law Enforcement Supervisor 8–11 years

Law enforcement supervisors oversee several squads. They help with difficult cases and develop crime prevention programs. Supervisors also plan work schedules, make duty assignments, and prepare technical and personnel reports.

Squad Leader 4–6 years

Squad leaders oversee a small group of specialists. They carry out traffic safety programs and direct crowd control operations. Squad leaders also inspect squad members for proper uniform and equipment and give on-the-job training to new squad members.

Law Enforcement And Security Specialists

Law enforcement and security specialists are the military's police officers. They investigate accidents and crimes, and prepare reports on the incidents. They arrest suspects when necessary. Specialists also direct the movement of people and traffic.

The years shown represent typical time-in-service before advancement to that level. Actual career advancement depends on individual experience and performance.

Support Service Occupations

Support service occupations include subsistence services, and occupations that support the morale and well-being of military personnel and their families. Food service specialists prepare all types of food in dining halls, hospitals, and ships. Counselors help military personnel and their families deal with personal issues. They work as part of a team that may include social workers, psychologists, medical officers, chaplains, personnel specialists, and commanders. The military also provides chaplains and religious program specialists to help meet the spiritual needs of its personnel. Religious program specialists assist chaplains with religious services, religious education programs, and related administrative duties.

- Caseworkers and Counselors
- Food Service Specialists
  Profile: Dwayne Robinson
- Religious Program Specialists
  Profile: Mike Kowalski

CASEWORKERS AND COUNSELORS

Just like some civilians, some military personnel need assistance with various problems or concerns, including career decisions, family issues, substance abuse, or emotional problems. Caseworkers and counselors work with military personnel and their families to help them with their particular concerns. They may specialize by the type of counseling that they do, such as career guidance or alcohol and drug abuse prevention. They normally work as part of a team that may include social workers, psychologists, medical officers, chaplains, personnel specialists, and commanders.

What They Do

Caseworkers and counselors in the military perform some or all of the following duties:

- Interview personnel who request help or are referred by their commanders

- Identify problems and determine the need for professional help

- Counsel personnel and their families

- Administer and score psychological tests

- Help personnel evaluate and explore career opportunities

- Teach classes on human relations

- Keep records of counseling sessions

Helpful Attributes

Helpful school subjects include health, biology, psychology, sociology, social science, and speech. Helpful attributes include:

- Interest in working with people

- Patience in dealing with problems that take time and effort to overcome

- Sensitivity to the needs of others

Physical Demands

Caseworkers and counselors need to speak clearly and distinctly in order to teach classes and work with personnel who have problems.

Training Provided

Job training consists of 8 to 10 weeks of classroom instruction, including practice in counseling. Course content typically includes:

- Orientation to counseling and social service programs

- Interviewing and counseling methods

- Treatments for drug and alcohol abuse

- Psychological testing techniques

Further training occurs on the job and through advanced courses.

Work Environment

Caseworkers and counselors usually work in offices or clinics.

Civilian Counterparts

Civilian caseworkers and counselors work in rehabilitation centers, hospitals, schools, and public agencies. They are usually required to have a college degree in social work, psychology, or counseling. They may also be called employment counselors, social workers, human services workers, or substance abuse counselors.

Opportunities

The services have about 1,000 caseworkers and counselors. Each year, they need new caseworkers and counselors due to changes in personnel and the demands of the field. After job training, they work under close supervision. With experience, they work more independently and may supervise other caseworkers.

MILITARY CAREERS/SCORE	INTEREST CODE
The circled score shows the typical Military Careers Score of servicemembers in this occupation. 1 2 3 4 **(5)** 6 7 Compare this score to your Military Career Score to see how well your aptitudes, skills, and abilities match those of personnel currently in these positions. See your recruiter for more information about qualification requirements.	This occupation generally appeals to people whose primary Interest Code is *Social*. *Social* jobs: • involve working with and helping others • Lets you teach others new skills
Pages 8 and 9 explain the Military Careers Score and the Interest Codes	

FOOD SERVICE SPECIALISTS

Every day, more than one million meals are prepared in military kitchens. Some kitchens prepare thousands of meals at one time, while others prepare food for small groups of people. Food service specialists prepare all types of food according to standard and dietetic recipes. They also order and inspect food supplies and prepare meats for cooking.

What They Do

Food service specialists in the military perform some or all of the following duties:

- Order, receive, and inspect meat, fish, fruit, and vegetables
- Prepare standard cuts of meat using cleavers, knives, and bandsaws
- Cook steaks, chops, and roasts
- Bake or fry chicken, turkey, and fish
- Prepare gravies and sauces
- Bake breads, cakes, pies, and pastries
- Serve food in dining halls, hospitals, field kitchens, or aboard ship
- Clean ovens, stoves, mixers, pots, and utensils

Training Provided

Job training consists of 9 to 14 weeks of classroom instruction, including practice in food preparation. Training length varies depending on specialty. Course content typically includes:

- Standard and dietetic menus and recipes
- Preparation and cooking of various foodstuffs and bakery products
- Food and supply ordering
- Storage of meats, poultry, and other perishable items

Further training occurs on the job and through advanced courses.

Physical Demands

Food service specialists may have to lift and carry heavy containers of foodstuffs and large cooking utensils.

Helpful Attributes

Helpful school subjects include home economics, health, mathematics, accounting, and chemistry. Helpful attributes include:

- Interest in cooking
- Interest in working with the hands

Work Environment

Food service specialists normally work in clean, sanitary kitchens and dining facilities. They may sometimes work in refrigerated meat lockers. Sometimes they work outdoors in tents while preparing and serving food under field conditions.

Civilian Counterparts

Civilian food service specialists work in cafés, restaurants, and cafeterias. They also work in hotels, hospitals, manufacturing plants, schools, and other organizations that have their own dining facilities. Depending on specialty, food service specialists are called cooks, chefs, bakers, butchers, or meat cutters.

Opportunities

The services have about 28,000 food service specialists. Each year, they need new specialists due to changes in personnel and the demands of the field. After job training, food service specialists help prepare and serve food under close supervision. Some food service specialists specialize as bakers, cooks, butchers, or meat cutters. With experience, they work more independently and may train new food service specialists. Eventually, they may become head cooks, chefs, or food service supervisors.

MILITARY CAREERS/SCORE	INTEREST CODE
The circled score shows the typical Military Careers Score of servicemembers in this occupation. **① 2 3 4 5 6 7** Compare this score to your Military Career Score to see how well your aptitudes, skills, and abilities match those of personnel currently in these positions. See your recruiter for more information about qualification requirements.	This occupation generally appeals to people whose primary Interest Code is **Realistic. Realistic** jobs: - Allow you to work with your hands - Let you see the results of your work - Involve using machines, tools, and equipment
Pages 8 and 9 explain the Military Careers Score and the Interest Codes	

Profile: Dwayne Robinson

Dwayne Robinson joined the Navy right after high school. He and a friend joined the Navy to travel and to learn a trade. Dwayne found his career in his first assignment as a seaman apprentice – after spending part of his tour working in the mess hall, he discovered that cooking was what he wanted to do. His first assignment was on the USS *Waldron* in Norfolk, VA, where he worked in the ship's galley.

Dwayne reenlisted because the Navy gave him the opportunity to go to cooking school where he learned menu planning and nutrition and improved his cooking skills. After school, he spent a year and a half in the bakery at the Naval Hospital in Guam.

After his promotion to petty officer first class, Dwayne spent the next three years managing the inventory of a commissary store. He was not sure if his career in the Navy was going anywhere, but after some friendly advice from his Chief, he decided not to leave. His decision paid off. During his next assignment aboard the USS *O'Callahan*, he was in charge of running the entire mess, a duty he had always wanted. He was also promoted to Chief Petty Officer. Dwayne says the most important day of his career was the day he "put on the hat." (The lower ranks, Dwayne explains, wear sailor caps; only chiefs may wear "the hat.")

After making chief, Dwayne spent three years as an instructor in the Navy cooking school in San Diego. He and his fellow instructors won first place in the San Diego Culinary Show. On Saturdays, Dwayne ran a cooking school for Explorer Scouts. By the end of this assignment, he had been promoted to senior chief.

Dwayne has spent the past four years as food services supervisor on several ships. On the USS *New Orleans*, he managed a 35-person staff that fed 580 crew members and, at times, 1,800 Marines (nearly 7,000 meals a day). Aboard his last ship, the USS *Wadsworth,* he went on a 7-month cruise of the South Pacific, with stops in Hawaii, Guam, Korea, Hong Kong, the Philippines, Australia, New Zealand, and Samoa.

SAMPLE CAREER PATH

Food Service Supervisor   **15–21 years**

Food service supervisors set food service standards, policies, and work priorities. They prepare standard operating procedures and administrative reports on food service activities. Supervisors plan budgets, monitor food service expenses, and determine personnel, equipment, and food supply needs.

Chef   **7–13 years**

Chefs plan and prepare food menus and recipes. They direct kitchen staff in food preparation and develop work schedules. Chefs determine food and supply needs, and prepare order forms and records. They also conduct training classes and assign trainers to new cooks.

Cook

Cooks work under the supervision of experienced chefs. They prepare ingredients and cook basic dishes. Cooks maintain the kitchen and dinning areas in a clean orderly fashion.

The years shown represent typical time-in-service before advancement to that level. Actual career advancement depends on individual experience and performance.

RELIGIOUS PROGRAM SPECIALISTS

Army
Navy
Air Force

The military has personnel from many religions and faiths. The military provides chaplains and religious program specialists to help meet the spiritual needs of its personnel. Religious program specialists assist chaplains with religious services, religious education programs, and related administrative duties.

What They Do

Religious program specialists in the military perform some or all of the following duties:

- Assist chaplains in planning and religious programs and activities
- Assist chaplains in conducting religious services
- Prepare religious, educational, and devotional materials
- Organize charitable and public service volunteer programs
- Maintain relations with religious communities and public service organizations
- Perform administrative duties for chaplains

Helpful Attributes

Helpful school subjects include English, public speaking, accounting, and typing. Helpful attributes include:

- Interest in religious guidance
- Sensitivity to the needs of others
- Knowledge of various religious customs and beliefs
- Ability to express ideas clearly
- Interest in administrative work

Training Provided

Job training consists of 7 to 8 weeks of classroom instruction. Course content typically includes:

- Principles of religious support programs
- Guidance and counseling techniques
- Leadership skills
- Office procedures

Work Environment

Religious program specialists in the military usually work indoors. They also serve aboard ships or with land and air units in the field.

Civilian Counterparts

Civilian religious program specialists help manage churches and religious schools. Their duties are similar to those performed by military religious program specialists, including planning religious programs and preparing religious educational materials. They are also called directors of religious activities.

Physical Demands

The ability to speak clearly and distinctly is required to enter this occupation.

Opportunities

The services have about 1,000 religious program specialists. Each year, they need new specialists due to changes in personnel and the demands of the field. After job training, religious program specialists help chaplains and supervisors with administrative matters. With experience, they gain more responsibility for organizing activities and working in the local community. In time, they may supervise other specialists.

MILITARY CAREERS/SCORE	INTEREST CODE
The circled score shows the typical Military Careers Score of servicemembers in this occupation. 1 2 ③ 4 5 6 7 Compare this score to your Military Career Score to see how well your aptitudes, skills, and abilities match those of personnel currently in these positions. See your recruiter for more information about qualification requirements.	This occupation generally appeals to people whose primary Interest Code is **Social. Social** jobs: • involve working with and helping others • Lets you teach others new skills
Pages 8 and 9 explain the Military Careers Score and the Interest Codes	

Profile: Michael Kowalski

Sergeant First Class Michael (Mike) Kowalski enlisted in the Army for three reasons: "I wanted to serve God, serve my country, and get experience." As a chaplain assistant, he feels he is doing all three.

In training, Mike learned the two sides of his job: administration and religious support. On his first assignment at Fort Carson, CO, Mike supported the Jewish chapel program, which included maintaining a kosher kitchen. At his second job there, he supported programs at the division artillery chapel. This job also took him with the troops on training exercises. He helped set up the field chapel tent, organize field services, and provide moral support to the troops. "This is what the job is all about," Mike says, "helping support the individual soldier." During this assignment, Mike rose to the rank of sergeant.

Mike was next assigned to a military hospital in Landstuhl, West Germany, where he served as the noncommissioned officer in charge (NCOIC) of the hospital chaplain's office. This was a busy time for Mike and his wife. Not only did they provide support to hospital patients and their families, but they also organized a full-scale chapel program for the Landstuhl community. This included conducting chapel services, religious education programs, and activities in music and drama. Mike also supervised chaplain assistants and was responsible for the chaplains' fund.

Back in the States, Mike went to Fort Knox, KY, as the NCOIC of the main post chapel. As a staff sergeant, he provided support for all the chapel programs, supervised and trained the chaplain assistants, and took care of the chapel and its equipment. When Mike was switched to the staff chaplain's office, he handled budgeting and contracting for material and equipment for the 12 chapels on the post.

Mike is now assigned to the U.S. Army Chaplains' Center and School, Fort Monmouth, NJ, as an instructor. He teaches new chaplain assistants how to support chapel activities. Mike recently returned from the Army Airborne School, where he became parachute qualified.

Mike feels that his career has provided him a unique opportunity. "I love people," he says. "My job has given me a chance to be with them and help them."

SAMPLE CAREER PATH

Chapel Operations Coordinator   16–18 years

Chapel operations coordinators are responsible for religious program activities in subordinate commands. They set goals, objectives, and priorities for religious programs and prepare and conduct command briefings on programs. They coordinate programs with hospitals, welfare agencies, and confinement facilities. Coordinators also develop worship schedules and educational materials.

Chapel Supervisor   6–8 years

Chapel supervisors oversee religious program specialists. They train personnel and assign their duties. Supervisors coordinate recruitment and training of ushers, lay readers, and religious school teachers.

Religious Program Specialist

Religious program specialists assist chaplains in all aspects of their religious and social service duties. They prepare the chapel for religious services or special ceremonies, such as weddings, funerals, and memorial services. They also help recruit and train ushers and religious school teachers.

The years shown represent typical time-in-service before advancement to that level. Actual career advancement depends on individual experience and performance.

Transportation and Material Handling Occupations

Transportation and material handling specialists ensure the safe transport of people and cargo. Most personnel within this occupational group are classified according to mode of transportation (i.e. aircraft, automotive vehicle, or ship). Air crew members operate equipment on board aircraft during operations. Vehicle drivers operate all types of heavy military vehicles including fuel or water tank trucks, semi-tractor trailers, heavy troop transport, and passenger buses. Boat operators navigate and pilot many types of small water craft, including tugboats, gunboats, and barges. Cargo specialists load and unload military supplies and material using equipment such as forklifts and cranes.

- Air Crew Members
    - *Profile: Edward Barkley*
- Air Traffic Controllers
    - *Profile: David Martinez*
- Aircraft Launch and Recovery Specialists
    - *Profile: James DiMarco*
- Cargo Specialists
- Flight Engineers
- Petroleum Supply Specialists
- Quartermasters and Boat Operators
* Seamen
* Transportation Specialists
* Vehicle Drivers
- Warehousing and Distribution Specialists

AIR CREW MEMBERS

The military uses aircraft of all types and sizes to conduct combat and intelligence missions, rescue personnel, transport troops and equipment, and perform long-range bombing missions. Air crew members operate equipment on board aircraft during operations. They normally specialize by type of aircraft, such as bomber, intelligence, transport, or search and rescue.

What They Do

Air crew members in the military perform some or all of the following duties:

- Operate aircraft communication and radar equipment

- Operate and maintain aircraft defensive gunnery systems

- Operate helicopter hoists to lift equipment and personnel from land and sea

- Operate and maintain aircraft in-flight refueling systems

Training Provided

Job training consists of 7 to 9 weeks of classroom instruction, including practical experience in aircraft systems operation and maintenance. Course content varies by specialty and may include:

- Operation of aircraft gunnery systems

- Operation of aircraft in-flight refueling systems

- Cargo, munitions, and fuel load planning

- Rescue and recovery operations

Further training occurs on the job through actual flying time. There are additional courses covering air crew survival, scuba diving, parachuting, aircraft maneuvering, and combat crew training.

Physical Demands

Air crew members must be in excellent physical condition and pass a special physical exam in order to qualify for flight duty. They must be mentally sound and have normal hearing.

Work Environment

Air crew members work inside all sizes and types of aircraft based on land or aboard ships. They fly in all types of weather and in both hot and cold climates.

Helpful Attributes

Helpful school subjects include mathematics and mechanics. Helpful attributes include:

- Interest in flying

- Ability to work under stress

- Ability to work as a team member

Civilian Counterparts

There are no direct civilian equivalents to military air crew members. However, some of the skills gained in the military could be useful in civilian government and private agencies that provide emergency medical services. Also, weight and load computation skills are useful for civilian air transport operations.

Opportunities

The services have about 5,000 air crew members. Each year, they need new air crew members due to changes in personnel and the demands of the field. After receiving their "air crew qualified" rating, air crew members are assigned to a flying unit. They may work on one of many types of aircraft under direction of the aircraft commander. With experience, they may supervise and train other enlisted air crew members. They have the opportunity to become air crew chiefs, combat crew chiefs, or supervisors of rescue and recovery units.

MILITARY CAREERS/SCORE	INTEREST CODE
The circled score shows the typical Military Careers Score of servicemembers in this occupation. **① 2 3 4 5 6 7** Compare this score to your Military Career Score to see how well your aptitudes, skills, and abilities match those of personnel currently in these positions. See your recruiter for more information about qualification requirements.	This occupation generally appeals to people whose primary Interest Code is **Realistic. Realistic** jobs: • Allow you to work with your hands • Let you see the results of your work • Involve using machines, tools, and equipment

Pages 8 and 9 explain the Military Careers Score and the Interest Codes

Profile: Edward Barkley

At 22, Ed Barkley had finished high school and had been working for four years when he decided to join the Air Force. At first he thought he wanted to be an aircraft mechanic, but during basic training, he volunteered to go to loadmaster school. He says, "That way I could be a mechanic *and* I could fly." He completed three months of training in Savannah, GA, and then spent three more years maintaining air cargo and airdrop equipment. He also flew missions to drop supplies for use in field exercises.

After four years, Ed decided he wanted an Air Force career. He liked his job, the security it provided, and the opportunity it gave him to get ahead. By reenlisting, Ed also knew he would go overseas on his next assignment. For nearly two years, he was on crews that flew out of Okinawa, delivering food, supplies, and troops – sometimes dropping supplies to troops in the field.

For the past ten years, Ed has been assigned first to Travis Air Force Base (AFB), CA, then to McGuire AFB, NJ. During both of these assignments, he has held many different jobs and has traveled worldwide. He has also completed an associate's degree through courses offered on base and a bachelor's degree through a special on-base program run by a private college.

Ed has advanced during his career as a loadmaster. Shortly after arriving at Travis AFB, he became crew leader. He then worked his way up the ladder in his squadron, taking on more responsibility. As a trainer at McGuire AFB, he prepared new loadmasters for work on C-141 aircraft. He advanced to flight examiner and then to assistant chief of loadmasters. After two years, Ed became an air crew operations manager. This position brought him his most challenging assignment – managing all Air Force cargo and passenger equipment from the Mississippi River to Egypt. Ed made sure that the right type of equipment, from cargo containers to passenger seats, was available at the right airfield when it was needed. For the past several years, Ed has been the chief of loadmasters for several different squadrons, managing loadmasters carrying supplies throughout the world.

SAMPLE CAREER PATH

Air Crew Operations Supervisor   18–21 years

Air crew operations supervisors plan and organize air crew activities and assist in planning in-flight operations and training missions. They conduct mission briefings and prepare operations orders for crew members. Supervisors also inspect and evaluate unit activities, facilities, air crew records, and reports for accuracy and completeness.

Air Crew Leader   6–11 years

Crew leaders plan, schedule, and assign work duties. They also train air crew members, inspect aircraft systems and equipment, and prepare in-flight mission reports and logs.

Air Crew Member

Air crew members operate a variety of systems onboard an aircraft during flight. They are also responsible for pre and post flight duties such as loading and unloading aircraft fuel, cargo, and passengers and performing operational maintenance on specialized aircraft equipment.

The years shown represent typical time-in-service before advancement to that level. Actual career advancement depends on individual experience and performance.

AIR TRAFFIC CONTROLLERS

Every day, hundreds of military airplanes and helicopters take off and land all over the world. Their movements are closely controlled in order to prevent accidents. Air traffic controllers direct the movement of aircraft into and out of military airfields. They track aircraft by radar and give voice instructions by radio.

What They Do

Air traffic controllers in the military perform some or all of the following duties:

- Operate radio equipment to issue takeoff, flight, and landing instructions

- Relay weather reports, airfield conditions, and safety information to pilots

- Use radar equipment to track aircraft in flight

- Plot airplane locations on charts and maps

- Compute speed, direction, and altitude of aircraft

- Maintain air traffic control records and communication logs

Physical Demands

Normal color vision, normal hearing and a clear speaking voice are required to enter this occupation. Controllers must pass a special physical exam.

Training Provided

Job training consists of 7 to 13 weeks of classroom instruction. Training length varies depending on specialty. Course content typically includes:

- Air traffic control fundamentals

- Visual and instrument flight procedures

- Radar and other landing approach procedures

- Communication procedures

Additional training occurs on the job. Aircraft carrier air traffic controllers receive specialized training.

Work Environment

Air traffic controllers work in land-based and shipboard control centers.

Helpful Attributes

Helpful school subjects include general mathematics, English, and typing. Helpful attributes include:

- Ability to work under stress

- Skill in math computation

- Ability to make quick, decisive judgments

Civilian Counterparts

Civilian air traffic controllers work for the FAA in airports and control centers around the country. They perform duties similar to military air traffic controllers. They may specialize in specific areas, such as aircraft arrivals, departures, ground control, or en route flights.

Special Requirements

Certification by the Federal Aviation Administration (FAA) normally must be obtained during training.

Opportunities

The services have about 7,000 air traffic controllers. Each year, they need new controllers due to changes in personnel and the demands of the field. After job training, new controllers normally perform duties such as ground control or work in airfields with light air traffic. With experience, they perform more difficult controller duties. In time, they may become supervisors of other controllers.

MILITARY CAREERS/SCORE	INTEREST CODE
The circled score shows the typical Military Careers Score of servicemembers in this occupation. 1 2 3 4 5 **6** 7 Compare this score to your Military Career Score to see how well your aptitudes, skills, and abilities match those of personnel currently in these positions. See your recruiter for more information about qualification requirements.	This occupation generally appeals to people whose primary Interest Code is ***Realistic. Realistic*** jobs: • Allow you to work with your hands • Let you see the results of your work • Involve using machines, tools, and equipment

Pages 8 and 9 explain the Military Careers Score and the Interest Codes

Profile: David Martínez

David Martínez was concerned about his future career at the hometown paper mill in Maine. "I was married and had children. I needed some education and a job," he explains. So David enlisted in the Marine Corps with a guarantee to work in aviation. He was selected for air traffic control. After basic training, David went to school in Glencoe, GA, to learn tower and radar air traffic control. Since federal licenses are needed for this type of work, he also earned his Federal Aviation Administration (FAA) operator's certificate. Obtaining his FAA operator's license started David on the road toward becoming FAA qualified to work in air traffic control.

At his first assignment in New River, NC, David was a tower air traffic controller trainee. He started in ground control, but soon his duties expanded to include local control (control in the air within a 5-mile radius of the airfield). He also passed his test to become FAA qualified in tower control and for the New River tower. He then became watch supervisor at the facility. In his 2 years at New River, he advanced from private first class through sergeant.

David continued to expand his qualifications at his next duty station in Okinawa. He became qualified in radar control and facility rated, which meant that he could work any air traffic control position in the facility. He also spent a short time in Yuma, AZ, as a controller and was promoted to Staff Sergeant.

The next 8 years went fast. David's assignments were split between Japan and New River. Sometimes he only spent a year in one place, and he had to requalify to work at each new facility, but his career was taking off. He was promoted to Gunnery Sergeant and moved into positions of greater responsibility: from radar controller and assistant approach controller, to facility watch supervisor, to senior enlisted person at his facility. When he was finally assigned to a 3-year tour in Kaneohe, HI, it was as crew chief and radar approach controller.

Now Gunnery Sergeant Martínez is crew chief at Cherry Point, NC. He qualified in the radar air traffic control facility and is working to qualify as a radar approach controller as well. David will be retiring soon, but he believes he has done well in his sometimes hectic career. "I had no prior civilian job experience, but I worked hard and persevered," he says.

SAMPLE CAREER PATH

Facility Supervisor   **17–20 years**

Facility supervisors are in charge of air traffic operations at an airfield facility. They plan, direct, and organize air traffic control at an airfield. They also inspect airfields and direct air traffic control training programs.

Supervisor   **7–11 years**

Air traffic supervisors manage the operations of control towers or radar centers. They supervise shifts and brief staff on weather, local field conditions, runways to be used, and other situations affecting aircraft. They coordinate air traffic control with other airfields and inspect runways and airfield facilities.

Controller   **4–6 years**

Controllers take on difficult or emergency duties in addition to normal flight control duties. They conduct instrument flight approaches in bad weather and take radar control of aircraft during emergencies. Controllers also coordinate search and rescue missions with air crews and give on-the-job training to new air traffic controllers

Apprentice Controller

Apprentice controllers work under the direct supervision of an experienced controller. They track air traffic by sight or with radar equipment. Apprentice controllers contact pilots with takeoff, approach, and landing instructions or other vital flight information. They also direct vehicle and aircraft movement on runways and around airfields.

The years shown represent typical time-in-service before advancement to that level. Actual career advancement depends on individual experience and performance.

AIRCRAFT LAUNCH AND RECOVERY SPECIALISTS

Navy
Marine Corps
Coast Guard

The military operates thousands of aircraft that take off and land on aircraft carriers all over the world. The successful launch and recovery of aircraft is important to the completion of air missions and the safety of flight crews. Aircraft launch and recovery specialists operate and maintain catapults, arresting gear, and other equipment used in aircraft carrier takeoff and landing operations.

What They Do

Aircraft launch and recovery specialists in the military perform some or all of the following duties:

- Operate consoles to control launch and recovery equipment, including catapults and arresting gear
- Operate elevators to transfer aircraft between flight and storage decks
- Install and maintain visual landing aids
- Test and adjust launch and recovery equipment
- Install airfield crash barriers and barricades
- Direct aircraft launch and recovery operations

Helpful Attributes

Helpful school subjects include shop mechanics. Helpful attributes include:

- Interest in working on hydraulic and mechanical equipment
- Ability to use hand tools and test equipment
- Interest in aircraft flight operations

Training Provided

Job training consists of 9 to 13 weeks of classroom instruction, including practice in maintaining launch and recovery equipment. Course content typically includes:

- Operating and maintaining launch and recovery equipment
- Installing crash barriers and barricades

Work Environment

Aircraft launch and recovery specialists work outdoors aboard ships while operating and maintaining launch and recovery equipment or holding visual landing aids for incoming aircraft. They are exposed to noise and fumes from jet and helicopter engines.

Civilian Counterparts

There are no direct civilian counterparts to military aircraft launch and recovery specialists. However, many of the skills learned are relevant to jobs performed by ground crews at civilian airports.

Physical Demands

Normal color vision is required to work with color-coded parts and the wiring of launch and recovery equipment.

Opportunities

The services have about 2,500 aircraft launch and recovery specialists. Each year, they need new specialists due to changes in personnel and the demands of the field. After job training, specialists are assigned to an aircraft launch and recovery section aboard an aircraft carrier or at an airfield. Initially, they perform maintenance and repair on equipment, working under close supervision. With experience, they perform more complex activities. In time, they may train and supervise other specialists. Eventually, they may supervise activities on carrier flight and storage decks.

MILITARY CAREERS/SCORE	INTEREST CODE
The circled score shows the typical Military Careers Score of servicemembers in this occupation. **(1) 2 3 4 5 6 7** Compare this score to your Military Career Score to see how well your aptitudes, skills, and abilities match those of personnel currently in these positions. See your recruiter for more information about qualification requirements.	This occupation generally appeals to people whose primary Interest Code is *Realistic*. *Realistic* jobs: • Allow you to work with your hands • Let you see the results of your work • Involve using machines, tools, and equipment

Pages 8 and 9 explain the Military Careers Score and the Interest Codes

Profile: James DiMarco

James DiMarco's decision to follow his brothers into the service seemed the best answer to limited job opportunities. He joined the Navy with the idea of becoming an electrician, but his first assignment changed his mind. After basic training, he was assigned to the aircraft carrier USS *Coral Sea,* where he worked on the flight deck with a catapult crew. He enjoyed his work repairing and maintaining the mechanical equipment so much that he asked for formal training in this field. His request was granted, and he went to Philadelphia for classes in becoming a catapult operator.

James liked his new job; still, he left the Navy after his 4-year enlistment to go home and get married. Within 3 months, he had reenlisted because, as he puts it, "There were few jobs that offered me a chance to make something of myself." Following reenlistment, James spent nearly 2 years as catapult crew leader on the USS *Wasp,* where one of his older brothers was also assigned. He then spent a year in Lakehurst, NJ, as a crew leader testing new parts and newly designed catapult systems.

James's next assignment took him to the West Coast and the USS *Bennington.* He was responsible for a crew of 40 men who maintained and operated two catapults. One big job involved supervising work on the catapult system for a major ship overhaul. He also served aboard the USS *Ranger* on several cruises to Vietnam as supervisor of a catapult operation.

James was then selected to become an instructor at the Navy's school at Lakehurst. For 4 years, he taught the basics of operating and maintaining catapult systems to 250 students a year. He was also promoted to Chief Petty Officer – the goal he had set for himself when he joined the Navy. Following an assignment on the USS *Roosevelt,* James was promoted to flight deck supervisor and served on the USS *Independence* and then the USS *Forrestal,* where he managed a flight deck crew of up to 550 sailors.

For the past several years, James has been back at Lakehurst managing the launch and recovery school. James enjoys teaching and working with younger people to help them establish themselves in their careers. He believes he has made a significant contribution to the Navy. "But then," he says, "the Navy has rewarded me in turn."

SAMPLE CAREER PATH

Flight Deck Supervisor   19–20 years

Flight deck supervisors plan and direct operation, maintenance, and safety programs for all aspects of carrier launch and recovery work, including crash rescue, damage control, aircraft handling, and aviation fueling. They predict requirements for personnel, equipment, and materials and organize, schedule, and evaluate training programs. Deck supervisors also review the performance of aircraft handling, crash rescue, and damage control crews.

Crew Supervisor   7–8 years

Crew supervisors direct personnel in launch and recovery operations. They oversee equipment inspections, develop schedules for preventive maintenance, and analyze malfunctions to plan corrective action.

Launch and Recovery Specialist   3–4 years

Launch and recovery specialists perform more difficult tasks during operations and maintenance. They perform more complex repairs and prepare weekly preventive maintenance schedules. They are also responsible for inventorying supplies, spare parts, and equipment.

Apprentice Launch and Recovery Specialist

Apprentice launch and recovery specialists work under close supervision. They operate specialized equipment during launch and recovery operations and inspect equipment before and after use. They perform preventive maintenance, and update maintenance records.

The years shown represent typical time-in-service before advancement to that level. Actual career advancement depends on individual experience and performance.

CARGO SPECIALISTS

Army
Navy
Air Force
Coast Guard

The military delivers supplies, weapons, equipment, and mail to United States forces in many parts of the world. Military cargo travels by ship, truck, or airplane. It must be handled carefully to ensure safe arrival at the correct destination. Cargo specialists load and unload military supplies and material using equipment such as forklifts and cranes. They also plan and organize loading schedules.

What They Do

Cargo specialists in the military perform some or all of the following duties:

- Load supplies into trucks, transport planes, and railroad cars using forklifts

- Load equipment such as jeeps, trucks, and weapons aboard ships, using dockyard cranes

- Pack and crate boxes of supplies for shipping

- Inspect cargo for damage

- Plan and inspect loads for balance and safety

- Check cargo against invoices to make sure the amount and destination of material are correct

Training Provided

Job training consists of 2 to 6 weeks of classroom instruction, including practice in loading cargo. Course content typically includes:

- Operation and care of forklifts, power winches, and cranes

- Techniques for loading and storing cargo

- Techniques for planning and scheduling cargo shipments

- Safety procedures for handling potentially dangerous cargo

Further training occurs on the job.

Physical Demands

Cargo specialists must lift and carry heavy cargo.

Helpful Attributes

Helpful school subjects include general office and business mathematics. Helpful attributes include:

- Interest in working with forklifts and cranes

- Preference for physical work

Civilian Counterparts

Civilian cargo specialists work for trucking firms, air cargo companies, and shipping lines. They perform duties similar to military cargo specialists. Depending on specialty, they may also be called industrial truck operators, stevedores, longshoremen, material handlers, or cargo checkers.

Work Environment

Cargo specialists work outdoors on loading docks and indoors in warehouses.

Opportunities

The services have about 6,000 cargo specialists. Each year, they need new cargo specialists due to changes in personnel and the demands of the field. After job training, cargo specialists work in teams preparing and loading cargo for shipment under the direction of supervisors. In time, they may advance to become team leaders or supervisors of other cargo specialists. Eventually, they may become warehouse managers.

MILITARY CAREERS/SCORE	INTEREST CODE
The circled score shows the typical Military Careers Score of servicemembers in this occupation. 1 2 ③ 4 5 6 7 Compare this score to your Military Career Score to see how well your aptitudes, skills, and abilities match those of personnel currently in these positions. See your recruiter for more information about qualification requirements.	This occupation generally appeals to people whose primary Interest Code is *Realistic. Realistic* jobs: • Allow you to work with your hands • Let you see the results of your work • Involve using machines, tools, and equipment
Pages 8 and 9 explain the Military Careers Score and the Interest Codes	

FLIGHT ENGINEERS

The military operates thousands of airplanes and helicopters. Pilots and air crew members rely upon trained personnel to keep aircraft ready to fly. Flight engineers inspect airplanes and helicopters before, during, and after flights to ensure safe and efficient operations. They also serve as crew members aboard military aircraft.

What They Do

Flight engineers in the military perform some or all of the following duties:

- Inspect aircraft before and after flights
- Plan and monitor the loading of passengers, cargo, and fuel
- Assist pilots in engine start-up and shut-down
- Compute aircraft load weights and fuel distribution and consumption
- Monitor engine instruments and adjust controls following pilot orders
- Check fuel, pressure, electrical, and other aircraft systems during flight
- Inform pilot of aircraft problems and recommend corrective action

Helpful Attributes

Helpful school subjects include general mathematics and shop mechanics. Helpful attributes include:

- Skill in using wiring diagrams and maintenance manuals
- Interest in working with mechanical systems and equipment
- Strong desire to fly
- Ability to work as a member of a team

Work Environment

Flight engineers live and work on air bases or aboard ships in all areas of the world. They fly in hot and cold climates and in all types of weather.

Training Provided

Job training consists of 17 to 24 weeks of classroom instruction and practical experience in aircraft inspection. Course content typically includes:

- Operation of aircraft systems
- Inspection of aircraft engines, structures, and systems
- Preparation of records and logs

Further training occurs on the job during flight operations.

Physical Demands

Flight engineers, like pilots and navigators, have to be mentally alert and physically fit to perform their job. They must pass a special physical exam to qualify for flight duty.

Civilian Counterparts

Civilian flight engineers work for passenger and cargo airline companies. They perform the same duties as in the military.

Opportunities

The services have about 3,000 flight engineers. Each year, they need new flight engineers due to changes in personnel and the demands of the field. After receiving their "air crew qualified" rating, they are assigned to an airplane or helicopter flying unit. With experience, they work more independently and may supervise or train others. They may become flight engineer chiefs or air crew chiefs.

MILITARY CAREERS/SCORE	INTEREST CODE
The circled score shows the typical Military Careers Score of servicemembers in this occupation. 1 2 3 4 5 **6** 7 Compare this score to your Military Career Score to see how well your aptitudes, skills, and abilities match those of personnel currently in these positions. See your recruiter for more information about qualification requirements.	This occupation generally appeals to people whose primary Interest Code is **Realistic. Realistic** jobs: • Allow you to work with your hands • Let you see the results of your work • Involve using machines, tools, and equipment
Pages 8 and 9 explain the Military Careers Score and the Interest Codes	

PETROLEUM SUPPLY SPECIALISTS

Army
Navy
Air Force
Marine Corps
Coast Guard

Ships, airplanes, trucks, tanks, and other military vehicles require large amounts of fuel and lubricants. These and other petroleum products require special storage and handling. Petroleum supply specialists store, handle, and ship petroleum products, such as oil, fuel, compressed gas, and lubricants.

What They Do

Petroleum supply specialists in the military perform some or all of the following duties:

- Connect hoses and valves and operate pumps to load petroleum products into tanker trucks, airplanes, ships, and railroad cars
- Test oils and fuels for pollutants
- Repair pipeline systems, hoses, valves, and pumps
- Check the volume and temperature of petroleum and gases in tankers, barges, and storage tanks
- Prepare storage and shipping records
- Store and move packaged petroleum products using forklifts

Training Provided

Job training consists of 4 to 8 weeks of classroom instruction, including practice in using petroleum pumping equipment. Course content typically includes:

- Testing oil and fuels
- Operating airplane refueling systems and equipment
- Operating pumps, pipelines, and tanker equipment
- Planning and scheduling petroleum transport
- Safety regulations and procedures for handling dangerous materials

Further training occurs on the job and through advanced courses.

Helpful Attributes

Helpful school subjects include shop mechanics and business math. Helpful attributes include:

- Interest in working with machines and equipment
- Ability to follow spoken instructions
- Preference for physical work

Work Environment

Petroleum supply specialists work outdoors in all types of weather while filling storage tanks and refueling airplanes, ships, and tankers.

Physical Demands

Petroleum supply specialists may have to perform moderate to heavy lifting.

Civilian Counterparts

Civilian petroleum supply specialists work for oil refineries, pipeline companies, and tanker truck and ship lines. They may also refuel airplanes at large airports. They perform many of the same duties as military petroleum supply specialists.

Opportunities

The services have about 13,000 petroleum supply specialists. Each year, they need new specialists due to changes in personnel and the demands of the field. After training, specialists work in teams while performing oil and fuel pumping operations. Each team works under the direction of a supervisor. With experience, petroleum supply specialists may become team leaders, pipeline or pump station supervisors, or petroleum storage supervisors.

MILITARY CAREERS/SCORE	INTEREST CODE
The circled score shows the typical Military Careers Score of servicemembers in this occupation. 1 ② 3 4 5 6 7 Compare this score to your Military Career Score to see how well your aptitudes, skills, and abilities match those of personnel currently in these positions. See your recruiter for more information about qualification requirements.	This occupation generally appeals to people whose primary Interest Code is *Realistic*. *Realistic* jobs: • Allow you to work with your hands • Let you see the results of your work • Involve using machines, tools, and equipment
Pages 8 and 9 explain the Military Careers Score and the Interest Codes	

QUARTERMASTERS AND BOAT OPERATORS

The military operates many small boats for amphibious troop landings, harbor patrols, and transportation over short distances. Quartermasters and boat operators navigate and pilot many types of small watercraft, including tugboats, gunboats, and barges.

What They Do

Quartermasters and boat operators in the military perform some or all of the following duties:

Direct the course and speed of boats

Consult maps, charts, weather reports, and navigation equipment

Pilot tugboats when towing and docking barges and large ships

Operate amphibious craft during troop landings

Maintain boats and deck equipment

Operate ship-to-shore radios

Keep ship logs

Training Provided

Job training consists of 6 to 22 weeks of classroom instruction including practice in boat operations. Course content typically includes:

- Boat handling procedures

- Log and message-handling procedures

- Use of compasses, radar, charts, and other navigational aids

- Navigational mathematics

Helpful Attributes

Helpful school subjects include mathematics. Helpful attributes include:

- Ability to work with mathematical formulas

- Interest in sailing and navigation

- Ability to follow detailed instructions and read maps

Work Environment

Quartermasters and boat operators work aboard all types of boats and in all types of weather conditions. When not piloting boats, they may work on or below deck repairing boats and equipment or overseeing cargo storage. When ashore, they may work in offices that make nautical maps or in harbor management offices. Some boats are operated in combat situations.

Civilian Counterparts

Civilian quartermasters and boat operators may work for shipping and cruise lines, piloting tugboats, ferries, and other small vessels. Depending upon specialty, they may also be called tugboat captains, motorboat operators, navigators, or pilots.

Physical Demands

Quartermasters and boat operators may have to stand for several hours at a time. They must be able to speak clearly. Some specialties require normal depth perception and hearing.

Opportunities

The services have over 2,000 quartermasters. Each year, they need new quartermasters and boat operators due to changes in personnel and the demands of the field. After job training, they assist more experienced operators in maintaining logs and charts, and operating navigational equipment. After gaining experience, they perform more difficult tasks, such as operating navigational equipment and calculating ship position. In time, they pilot boats and help train new quartermasters and boat operators.

MILITARY CAREERS/SCORE	INTEREST CODE
The circled score shows the typical Military Careers Score of servicemembers in this occupation. 1 2 3 **4** 5 6 7 Compare this score to your Military Career Score to see how well your aptitudes, skills, and abilities match those of personnel currently in these positions. See your recruiter for more information about qualification requirements.	This occupation generally appeals to people whose primary Interest Code is *Realistic. Realistic* jobs: • Allow you to work with your hands • Let you see the results of your work • Involve using machines, tools, and equipment
Pages 8 and 9 explain the Military Careers Score and the Interest Codes	

SEAMAN

All ships must have teams of individuals with "jack-of-all-trades" skills who make things run smoothly above deck. Seamen perform many duties to help operate and maintain military ships, boats, and submarines.

What They Do

Seamen in the military perform some or all of the following duties:

- Operate hoists, cranes, and winches to load cargo or set gangplanks

- Operate and maintain on-deck equipment and ship rigging

- Supervise firefighting and damage control exercises

- Handle lines to secure vessels to wharves or other ships

- Stand watch for security, navigation, or communications

- Supervise crews painting and maintaining decks and sides of ships

Physical Demands

Seamen may have to climb ships' rigging and perform work at heights. Their work often involves moderate to heavy lifting.

Work Environment

Seamen and deckhands work aboard all types of ships and submarines. On ships, they often work outdoors on deck while servicing shipboard equipment.

Helpful Attributes

Helpful school subjects include mathematics and shop mechanics. Helpful attributes include:

- Ability to work closely with others

- Interest in sailing and being at sea

- Preference for physical work

Training Provided

Although classroom training of 6 to 12 weeks is provided to seamen, most training occurs on the job. Training programs vary depending on service and specialty.

Civilian Counterparts

Civilian seamen work primarily for shipping companies, sometimes called the Merchant Marine. They also work for cruise ship lines. They perform many duties similar to military seamen. They are called able seamen, deckhands, or boatswains.

Opportunities

The services have about 10,000 seamen. Each year, the services need new seamen due to changes in personnel and the demands of the field. New seamen work together on teams led by experienced supervisors. Through practice, they learn the many tasks they must perform. In time, seamen supervise one or more teams. Eventually, they may become managers responsible for planning and directing the work of many seamen. Often, seamen receive additional training that prepares them for other occupations in their service.

MILITARY CAREERS/SCORE	INTEREST CODE
The circled score shows the typical Military Careers Score of servicemembers in this occupation. 1 **(2)** 3 4 5 6 7 Compare this score to your Military Career Score to see how well your aptitudes, skills, and abilities match those of personnel currently in these positions. See your recruiter for more information about qualification requirements.	This occupation generally appeals to people whose primary Interest Code is *Realistic. Realistic* jobs: - Allow you to work with your hands - Let you see the results of your work - Involve using machines, tools, and equipment

Pages 8 and 9 explain the Military Careers Score and the Interest Codes

TRANSPORTATION SPECIALISTS

The military constantly moves passengers and cargo. Personnel often travel to meetings, training sessions, and new assignments. Supplies and equipment to support troops must be shipped regularly. Transportation specialists plan and assist in air, sea, and land transportation for people and cargo. Some assist passenger travel as gate agents and flight attendants.

What They Do

Transportation specialists in the military perform some or all of the following duties:

- Arrange for passenger travel via plane, bus, train, or boat
- Arrange for shipment and delivery of household goods
- Determine which vehicles to use based on freight or passenger-movement requirements
- Determine transportation and shipping routes
- Prepare transportation requests and shipping documents
- Check in passengers and baggage for military transport flights
- Serve as military airplane flight attendants
- Inspect cargo for proper packing, loading, and marking

Training Provided

Job training consists of 6 to 9 weeks of classroom instruction, including practice in making transportation arrangements. Course content typically includes:

- Planning transportation for personnel and cargo
- Proper cargo handling, shipping, and storing methods
- Analysis of transportation documents

Further training occurs on the job and through advanced courses.

Helpful Attributes

Helpful school subjects include mathematics and English. Helpful attributes include:

- Interest in arranging travel schedules
- Interest in using adding machines and computers
- Interest in serving people

Work Environment

Transportation specialists usually work in offices. They may work outdoors when escorting passengers or processing shipments. Flight attendants work on land and in airplanes.

Civilian Counterparts

Civilian transportation specialists work for airlines, shipping firms, and commercial freight lines. They perform duties similar to military transportation specialists. Civilian transportation specialists may also be called travel clerks, reservation clerks, or transportation agents.

Opportunities

The military has about 11,000 transportation specialists. Each year, the services need new specialists due to changes in personnel and the demands of the field. After job training, they make travel and shipping arrangements under direct supervision. Some may specialize as flight attendants and gate agents. With experience, they may become supervisors of other transportation specialists. In time, they may manage transportation offices.

MILITARY CAREERS/SCORE	INTEREST CODE
The circled score shows the typical Military Careers Score of servicemembers in this occupation. 1 **(2)** 3 4 5 6 7 Compare this score to your Military Career Score to see how well your aptitudes, skills, and abilities match those of personnel currently in these positions. See your recruiter for more information about qualification requirements.	This occupation generally appeals to people whose primary Interest Code is ***Conventional. Conventional*** jobs: - Require attention to detail - Require attention to accuracy
Pages 8 and 9 explain the Military Careers Score and the Interest Codes	

VEHICLE DRIVERS

The military uses numerous vehicles to transport its troops, equipment, and supplies. Together, the services own and operate about 50,000 heavy trucks and buses. Vehicle drivers operate all types of heavy military vehicles. They drive fuel or water tank trucks, semi-tractor trailers, heavy troop transports, and passenger buses.

What They Do

Vehicle drivers in the military perform some or all of the following duties:

• Read travel instructions to determine travel routes, arrival dates, and types of cargo

• Make sure vehicles are loaded properly

• Check oil, fuel and other fluid levels, and tire pressure

• Drive vehicles over all types of roads, traveling alone or in convoys

• Keep records of mileage driven and fuel and oil used

• Wash vehicles and perform routine maintenance and repairs

Training Provided

Job training consists of 7 to 8 weeks of classroom instruction, including practice in driving heavy military vehicles. Course content typically includes:

• Accident prevention

• Safety check procedures

• International road signs

• Basic vehicle maintenance

Work Environment

Vehicle driving involves long periods of sitting. Drivers sometimes must change heavy tires.

Helpful Attributes

Helpful school courses include driver education. Helpful attributes include:

• Interest in driving

• Interest in mechanics

Civilian Counterparts

Civilian vehicle drivers work for trucking companies, moving companies, bus companies, and businesses with their own delivery fleets. They perform duties similar to military vehicle drivers. They may specialize as tractor-trailer truck drivers, tank truck drivers, heavy truck drivers, or bus drivers.

Physical Demands

Normal color vision is required to read road maps.

Opportunities

The services have about 14,000 vehicle drivers. Each year, they need new vehicle drivers due to changes in personnel and the demands of the field. After job training, vehicle drivers are assigned to motor pools or motor transport units. They generally work without close supervision. In time, vehicle drivers may advance to supervisory positions assisting in the management of motor transport units.

MILITARY CAREERS/SCORE	INTEREST CODE
The circled score shows the typical Military Careers Score of servicemembers in this occupation. **①** 2 3 4 5 6 7 Compare this score to your Military Career Score to see how well your aptitudes, skills, and abilities match those of personnel currently in these positions. See your recruiter for more information about qualification requirements.	This occupation generally appeals to people whose primary Interest Code is *Realistic*. Realistic jobs: • Allow you to work with your hands • Let you see the results of your work • Involve using machines, tools, and equipment
Pages 8 and 9 explain the Military Careers Score and the Interest Codes	

WAREHOUSING AND DISTRIBUTION SPECIALISTS

The military maintains a large inventory of food, medicines, ammunition, spare parts, and other supplies. Keeping the military's supply system operating smoothly is an important job. The lives of combat troops in the field may depend on receiving the right supplies in time. Warehousing and distribution specialists receive, store, record, and issue military supplies.

What They Do

Warehousing and distribution specialists in the military perform some or all of the following duties:

Perform inventory and financial management procedures, including ordering, receiving, and storing supplies

Locate and catalog stock

Give special handling to medicine, ammunition, and other delicate supplies

Select the correct stock for issue

Load, unload, and move stock using equipment such as forklifts and hand trucks

Keep records on incoming and outgoing stock

Training Provided

Job training consists of 4 to 6 weeks of classroom instruction, including practice in handling and storing stock. Course content typically includes:

Stock control and accounting procedures

Procedures for shipping, receiving, storing, and issuing stock

Procedures for handling medical and food supplies

Movement, storage, and maintenance of ammunition

Further training occurs on the job and through advanced courses.

Work Environment

Warehousing and distribution specialists work in large general supply centers, small specialized supply rooms, or ship storerooms.

Physical Demands

Warehousing and distribution specialists may have to lift and carry heavy boxes of ammunition and other supplies. Normal color vision is required for specialties that handle color-coded parts, supplies, and ammunition.

Helpful Attributes

Helpful school subjects include math, bookkeeping, accounting and business administration. Helpful attributes include:

- Ability to keep accurate records
- Preference for physical work
- Interest in operating forklifts and other warehouse equipment
- Preference for work requiring attention to detail

Civilian Counterparts

Civilian Warehousing and distribution specialist work for factories, parts departments in repair shops, department stores, and government warehouses and stockrooms. They perform duties similar to military warehousing and distribution specialists. Civilian warehousing and distribution specialists may also be called stock control clerks, parts clerks, or storekeepers.

Opportunities

The services have about 65,000 warehousing and distribution specialists. Each year, they need new specialists due to changes in personnel and the demands of the field. After job training, specialists stock shelves, learn about different parts and supplies, and fill supply requests. In time, they also estimate needs, order stock, and supervise others. Eventually, they may become superintendents of supply centers.

MILITARY CAREERS/SCORE	INTEREST CODE
The circled score shows the typical Military Careers Score of servicemembers in this occupation. 1 (2) 3 4 5 6 7 Compare this score to your Military Career Score to see how well your aptitudes, skills, and abilities match those of personnel currently in these positions. See your recruiter for more information about qualification requirements.	This occupation generally appeals to people whose primary Interest Code is *Realistic*. *Realistic* jobs: • Allow you to work with your hands • Let you see the results of your work • Involve using machines, tools, and equipment
Pages 8 and 9 explain the Military Careers Score and the Interest Codes	

Vehicle and Machinery Mechanic Occupations

Vehicle and machinery mechanics conduct preventive and corrective maintenance on aircraft, automotive and heavy equipment, heating and cooling systems, marine engines, and powerhouse station equipment. They typically specialize by the type of equipment that they maintain. Aircraft mechanics inspect, service, and repair helicopters and airplanes. Automotive and heavy equipment mechanics maintain and repair vehicles such as jeeps, cars, trucks, tanks, self-propelled missile launchers, and other combat vehicles. They also repair bulldozers, power shovels, and other construction equipment. Heating and cooling mechanics install and repair air conditioning, refrigeration, and heating equipment. Marine engine mechanics repair and maintain gasoline and diesel engines on ships, boats, and other water craft. They also repair shipboard mechanical and electrical equipment. Powerhouse mechanics install, maintain, and repair electrical and mechanical equipment in power-generating stations.

- Aircraft Mechanics
  Profile: Brian Goelf
- Automotive and Heavy Equipment Mechanics
  Profile: Ron Johnson
- Heating and Cooling Mechanics
- Marine Engine Mechanics
  Profile: George Monch
- Powerhouse Mechanics

AIRCRAFT MECHANICS

Army
Navy
Air Force
Marine Corps
Coast Guard

Military aircraft are used to fly hundreds of missions each day for transport, patrol, and flight training. They need frequent servicing to remain safe and ready to fly. Aircraft mechanics inspect, service, and repair helicopters and airplanes.

What They Do

Aircraft mechanics in the military perform some or all of the following duties:

- Service and repair helicopter, jet, and propeller aircraft engines

- Inspect and repair aircraft wings, fuselages, and tail assemblies

- Service and repair aircraft landing gear

- Repair or replace starters, lights, wiring, and other electrical parts

Physical Demands

Some specialties require moderate to heavy lifting. Normal color vision is required to work with color-coded wiring.

Training Provided

Job training consists of 3 to 17 weeks of classroom instruction, including inspection and repair of aircraft engines and equipment. Training length varies depending upon the specialty. Course content typically includes:

- Engine disassembly and repair

- Repair of hydraulic, fuel, and electrical systems

- Repair of aluminum, steel, and fiberglass airframes and coverings

Further training occurs on the job and through advanced courses.

Helpful Attributes

Helpful school subjects include mathematics and shop mechanics. Helpful attributes include:

- Interest in work involving aircraft

- Interest in engine mechanics

- Ability to use hand and power tools

Work Environment

Aircraft mechanics work in aircraft hangars and machine shops located on air bases or aboard aircraft carriers.

Civilian Counterparts

Civilian aircraft mechanics work for aircraft manufacturers, commercial airlines, and government agencies. They perform duties similar to military aircraft mechanics. They may also be called airframe or power plant mechanics.

Opportunities

The services have about 70,000 aircraft mechanics. Each year, they need new mechanics due to changes in personnel and the demands of the field. After job training, mechanics are assigned to an aircraft maintenance unit, where they perform routine maintenance and simple repair jobs. In time, they may perform more difficult repairs and train and supervise new mechanics. Eventually, they may become inspectors, shop supervisors, or maintenance superintendents.

MILITARY CAREERS/SCORE	INTEREST CODE
The circled score shows the typical Military Careers Score of servicemembers in this occupation. `1  2  3  ④  5  6  7` Compare this score to your Military Career Score to see how well your aptitudes, skills, and abilities match those of personnel currently in these positions. See your recruiter for more information about qualification requirements.	This occupation generally appeals to people whose primary Interest Code is *Realistic. Realistic* jobs: • Allow you to work with your hands • Let you see the results of your work • Involve using machines, tools, and equipment

Pages 8 and 9 explain the Military Careers Score and the Interest Codes

Profile: Brian Goelf

When he graduated from high school, Brian Goelf got his parents' permission to join the Air Force. "I wanted to see different places," he says. After 23 years and 15 different locations, travel is still one of the aspects he likes most about his military career. Brian has lived in Canada, England, the Netherlands, Vietnam, Hawaii, and all over the United States.

Being mechanically inclined – he had always enjoyed working on cars – Brian asked to be trained in aircraft mechanics. After basic training, he went to aircraft mechanic's school and was assigned to Andrews Air Force Base (AFB) near Washington, DC. There he also completed an additional field training course on the Air Force T-33 trainer jet aircraft. After 2 years of performing unscheduled maintenance (pilot-reported problems), Brian went to Goose Bay, Canada, for another field training course on the F-102 aircraft.

Brian returned to the United States on an assignment to Scott AFB, IL, to work on the T-39 Saberliner, a private passenger jet. He went on flying status as the chief mechanic and flew around the country. He was also responsible for making or supervising repairs. Brian decided at this time to make his career in the military. Having just married, he saw the Air Force as a chance to get ahead. But, as Brian says, "It was having a job I really liked and being able to fly as well that really sold me."

Brian was promoted to Staff Sergeant and spent a year in Vietnam. In his first supervisory job, he coordinated flight line maintenance for a fighter squadron. Then, 2 years after his return to the States, he was selected as an instructor in aircraft mechanics. During this time, he earned another promotion and volunteered to go to Europe. Although most of his 4 years was spent in England and the Netherlands, he and his family were able to travel all over Europe.

Brian and his family had been home for only a year when he volunteered to go to Hawaii. He was promoted there to senior manager and served as the Pacific Air Force Command manager for several types of aircraft, ensuring that materials and supplies reached Air Force units in the Pacific. Brian recently returned to the mainland as assistant manager of a maintenance unit capable of supporting F-15 fighters anywhere in the world.

SAMPLE CAREER PATH

Aircraft Maintenance Supervisor   19–21 years

Aircraft maintenance supervisors are in charge of large aircraft maintenance and repair facilities. They plan and direct repair, inspection, maintenance, service, and modification of aircraft. They also develop training and safety programs and prepare technical, personnel, and administrative reports

Shop Supervisor   8–10 years

Shop supervisors are in charge of maintenance and repair for specific types of aircraft. They develop standard operating procedures and conduct on-the-job training programs. They also develop work schedules and prepare status reports.

Mechanic   4–5 years

Aircraft mechanics perform complex repairs and assist other mechanics. They perform complicated or unusual tests and disassemble aircraft engines to repair or replace parts. They also help apprentice mechanics identify malfunctions and fix problems.

Apprentice Aircraft Mechanic

Apprentice aircraft mechanics work under close supervision and perform routine repair and maintenance duties. They also record service, maintenance, and repairs in maintenance log records.

The years shown represent typical time-in-service before advancement to that level. Actual career advancement depends on individual experience and performance.

AUTOMOTIVE AND HEAVY EQUIPMENT MECHANICS

Keeping automotive and heavy equipment in good working condition is vital to the success of military missions. Automotive and heavy equipment mechanics maintain and repair vehicles such as jeeps, cars, trucks, tanks, and other combat vehicles. They also repair bulldozers, power shovels, and other construction equipment.

What They Do

Automotive and heavy equipment mechanics in the military perform some or all of the following duties:

• Troubleshoot problems in vehicle engines, electrical systems, steering, brakes, and suspensions

• Tune and repair engines

• Replace or repair damaged body parts, hydraulic arms or shovels, and grader blades

• Establish and follow schedules for maintaining vehicles

Training Provided

Job training consists of 8 to 29 weeks of classroom instruction. Training length varies depending on specialty. Course content typically includes:

• Engine repair and tune-up

• Troubleshooting mechanical and electrical problems

• Repairing and replacing body panels, fenders, and radiators

Further training occurs on the job and through advanced courses.

Helpful Attributes

Helpful school subjects include auto mechanics and industrial arts. Helpful attributes include:

• Preference for physical work

• Interest in troubleshooting and repairing mechanical problems

• Interest in automotive engines and how they work

Physical Demands

Automotive and heavy equipment mechanics have to lift heavy parts and tools. They sometimes have to work in cramped positions. Normal color vision is required for some specialties to work with color-coded wiring and to read diagrams.

Civilian Counterparts

Civilian automotive and heavy equipment mechanics may work for service stations, auto and construction equipment dealers, farm equipment companies, and state highway agencies. They perform duties similar to military automotive and heavy equipment mechanics. They may also be called garage mechanics, transmission mechanics, radiator mechanics, or construction equipment mechanics.

Work Environment

Automotive and heavy equipment mechanics usually work inside large repair garages. They work outdoors when making emergency repairs in the field.

Opportunities

The services have about 45,000 automotive and heavy equipment mechanics. Each year, they need new mechanics due to changes in personnel and the demands of the field. After job training, mechanics begin repairing equipment under the direction of a supervisor. In time, they have the opportunity to supervise other workers and possibly manage repair shops, motor pools, or maintenance units.

MILITARY CAREERS/SCORE	INTEREST CODE
The circled score shows the typical Military Careers Score of servicemembers in this occupation. 1 2 **(3)** 4 5 6 7 Compare this score to your Military Career Score to see how well your aptitudes, skills, and abilities match those of personnel currently in these positions. See your recruiter for more information about qualification requirements.	This occupation generally appeals to people whose primary Interest Code is **Realistic**. **Realistic** jobs: • Allow you to work with your hands • Let you see the results of your work • Involve using machines, tools, and equipment

Pages 8 and 9 explain the Military Careers Score and the Interest Codes

Profile: Ron Johnson

When Gunnery Sergeant Ron Johnson was a senior in high school, he knew he didn't want to go to college, but he wasn't sure what he wanted to do. So Ron enlisted in the Marine Corps. Joining the Marines offered him a break from the routine he saw in civilian life.

Ron entered the infantry even though he knew it was not what he wanted as a career. After basic and initial infantry training, he became a rifleman and was sent overseas to Okinawa, Japan. It was then that he found what he really wanted to do. On many marches, Ron saw trucks parked by the side of the road. When he asked why the trucks were not being used, he was told that they were deadlined (not working) and waiting for repair. He was frustrated because he wanted to be able to fix them. After four years in the infantry and reaching the rank of sergeant, he decided to reenlist. At the same time, he asked to switch his occupation to motor transport mechanic.

To qualify for his new occupation, Ron took the basic automotive maintenance course. He then began troubleshooting problems in jeeps, trucks, and trailers at Camp LeJeune, NC. Ron also used his training to help fix his friends' cars. In fact, they started calling him Johnson, M.D. (for Mechanical Doctor). Because of his good work, Ron was promoted to shop chief, responsible for supervising several mechanics.

After two years at Camp Lejeune as a mechanic and another promotion, David went back to Okinawa as a maintenance chief. He scheduled all vehicles for maintenance and ensured the safety of the shop. Even though he was overseas, he was able to play his favorite sports – tennis and football – on base. One year later, he moved to the Marine Corps Logistics Base in Albany, GA, as an inspector. He traveled to all the Reserve units from Texas to the East Coast inspecting vehicles. During his three years in Albany, Ron took the Motor Transport Staff Noncommissioned Officer (NCO) Course. On the series of tests he took there, he achieved the highest individual average in the school's history and graduated with honors. Ron was recently promoted to Gunnery Sergeant and reassigned to Marine Corps Headquarters.

SAMPLE CAREER PATH

Vehicle Repair Supervisor — 19–21 years

Vehicle repair supervisors direct repair operations for many different vehicles. They coordinate the activities of a major vehicle repair facility and identify ways to reduce costs for more effective programs. Supervisors monitor repair orders and the use of parts and supplies. They also ensure that proper records are kept on vehicles and shop personnel.

Shop Supervisor — 8–10 years

Shop supervisors direct the repairs of specific types of vehicles. They give technical assistance in troubleshooting difficult problems and inspect repaired vehicles. Supervisors design lay out of work stations and equipment, and assign work schedules. They also conduct training on the newest maintenance procedures and techniques.

Mechanic — 4–5 years

Mechanics take on troubleshooting and more difficult repairs. They isolate the causes of vehicle problems, determine repair needs, and perform major repairs and engine overhauls. They also prepare maintenance records and conduct on-the-job training for new mechanics.

Apprentice Mechanic

Apprentice mechanics are assigned to repair shops, where they perform routine maintenance and repairs. They perform service on vehicles and repair or replace parts as directed by senior mechanics.

The years shown represent typical time-in-service before advancement to that level. Actual career advancement depends on individual experience and performance.

HEATING AND COOLING MECHANICS

Army
Navy
Air Force
Marine Corps
Coast Guard

Air conditioning and heating equipment is used to maintain comfortable temperatures in military buildings, airplanes, and ships. Refrigeration equipment is used to keep food cold and to keep some missile fuels at sub-zero storage temperatures. Heating and cooling mechanics install and repair air conditioning, refrigeration, and heating equipment.

What They Do

Heating and cooling mechanics in the military perform some or all of the following duties:

- Install and repair furnaces, boilers, and air conditioners

- Recharge cooling systems with refrigerant gases

- Install copper tubing systems that circulate water or cooling gases

- Replace compressor parts such as valves, pistons, bearings, and electrical motors on refrigeration units

- Repair thermostats and electrical circuits

Training Provided

Job training consists of 8 to 22 weeks of classroom instruction, including practice in repair work. Training length varies depending on specialty. Course content typically includes:

- Refrigeration theory

- Installation and repair of refrigeration and air conditioning units

- Installation and repair of furnaces and boilers

- Use of diagrams and blueprints

Additional training is available on the job and in advanced courses.

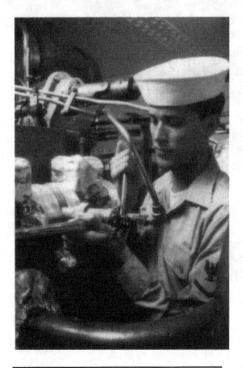

Work Environment

Heating and cooling mechanics may work inside repair shops. Frequently, they work wherever equipment is to be installed or repaired.

Physical Demands

Heating and cooling mechanics may have to lift or move heavy equipment. They are often required to stoop, kneel, and work in cramped positions. Normal color vision is required for locating and repairing color-coded wiring.

Helpful Attributes

Helpful school subjects include science, math, and shop mechanics. Helpful attributes include:

- Ability to use hand and power tools

- Interest in working on machines

- Interest in solving problems

Civilian Counterparts

Civilian heating and cooling mechanics work for contractors that install home furnaces and air conditioners or for firms that repair refrigerators and freezers in homes, grocery stores, factories, and warehouses. Heating and cooling mechanics in civilian life often specialize more than those in the military. They may be called heating, air conditioning, refrigeration, or climate control mechanics.

Opportunities

The military has about 7,000 heating and cooling mechanics. Each year, the services need new mechanics due to changes in personnel and the demands of the field. After job training, mechanics maintain and repair equipment under supervision. With experience, they may learn to diagnose mechanical problems and perform complicated repairs. Eventually, they may become superintendents of utilities for large bases.

MILITARY CAREERS/SCORE	INTEREST CODE
The circled score shows the typical Military Careers Score of servicemembers in this occupation. 1 2 **(3)** 4 5 6 7 Compare this score to your Military Career Score to see how well your aptitudes, skills, and abilities match those of personnel currently in these positions. See your recruiter for more information about qualification requirements.	This occupation generally appeals to people whose primary Interest Code is *Realistic*. *Realistic* jobs: • Allow you to work with your hands • Let you see the results of your work • Involve using machines, tools, and equipment
Pages 8 and 9 explain the Military Careers Score and the Interest Codes	

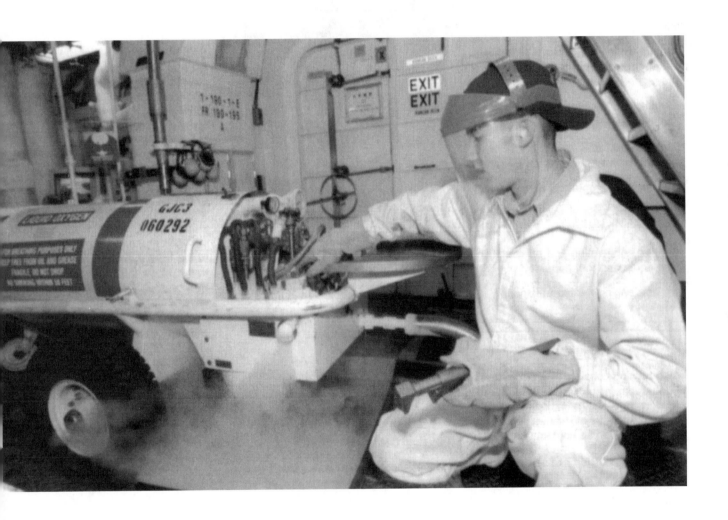

MARINE ENGINE MECHANICS

Army
Navy
Marine Corps
Coast Guard

The military operates many types of watercraft from small motor launches to large ships. Many of these vessels are powered by gasoline or diesel engines. Marine engine mechanics repair and maintain gasoline and diesel engines on ships, boats, and other watercraft. They also repair shipboard mechanical and electrical equipment.

What They Do

Marine engine mechanics in the military perform some or all of the following duties:

- Repair and maintain shipboard gasoline and diesel engines
- Locate and repair machinery parts, including valves and piping systems
- Repair ship propulsion machinery
- Repair and service hoisting machinery and ship elevators
- Repair refrigeration and air conditioning equipment on ships
- Repair engine-related electrical systems

Training Provided

Job training consists of 9 to 24 weeks of classroom instruction, including practice in marine engine maintenance and repair. Training length varies depending on specialty. Course content typically includes:

- Internal combustion engine theory
- Repair of shipboard electronic and electrical machinery systems
- Service and repair of fuel injection systems
- Use and care of hand and power tools

Further training occurs on the job and through advanced courses.

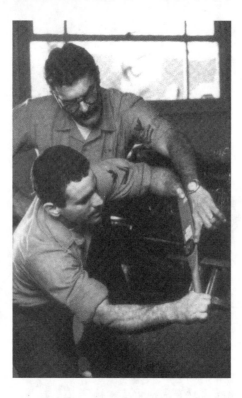

Helpful Attributes

Helpful school subjects include shop mechanics. Helpful attributes include:

- Interest in fixing engines and machinery
- Ability to use hand and power tools
- Preference for doing physical work

Physical Demands

Normal color vision is required to work with color-coded diagrams and wiring.

Work Environment

Marine engine mechanics work aboard ships, normally in the engine or power rooms. Sometimes they work in repair centers on land bases. Working conditions in engine rooms tend to be noisy and hot.

Civilian Counterparts

Civilian marine engine mechanics work in many industries, including marine transportation, commercial fishing, and oil exploration and drilling. They perform duties similar to military marine engine mechanics.

Opportunities

The military has about 7,000 marine engine mechanics. Each year, the services need new mechanics due to changes in personnel and the demands of the field. After job training, they work under close supervision in repair centers or shipboard engine rooms. With experience, they work more independently and may supervise other mechanics. In time, marine engine mechanics may become supervisors of marine engine repair centers or shipboard maintenance sections.

MILITARY CAREERS/SCORE	INTEREST CODE
The circled score shows the typical Military Careers Score of servicemembers in this occupation. 1 2 3 4 5 **(6)** 7 Compare this score to your Military Career Score to see how well your aptitudes, skills, and abilities match those of personnel currently in these positions. See your recruiter for more information about qualification requirements.	This occupation generally appeals to people whose primary Interest Code is *Realistic. Realistic* jobs: • Allow you to work with your hands • Let you see the results of your work • Involve using machines, tools, and equipment

Pages 8 and 9 explain the Military Careers Score and the Interest Codes

188

Military Careers

Profile: George Monch

George Monch grew up in Cape May, NJ, home of the Coast Guard Training Center. His love for the sea and familiarity with the Coast Guard directed him toward a Coast Guard career. Even now, after 16 years, Chief Monch still says, "I can't be too far from the water."

Out of boot camp, George went to Yorktown, VA, for a 4-month course in engineering. His first assignment was back home in Cape May aboard the cutter Alert. As George explains it, his first duty assignment was "basic engine cleaning." However, it was not long before he was promoted in both rank and responsibility. He was assigned to overhauling small boilers and maintaining the fresh water system. He also helped repair auxiliary engine equipment (engines that are used in place of the sails).

George's next assignment was a 1-year tour in Japan. He started out as a watchstander and advanced to supervise the overhaul of engines and auxiliary equipment. He then returned to Cape May to become part of the Aids to Navigation Team, responsible for operating and maintaining several boats, lighthouses, and navigation buoys.

George left active duty after 8 years, but stayed in the Coast Guard Reserve, working weekends as a small boat operator on search and rescue missions. Three years later, seeking greater job security, he decided to go back on active duty. He was assigned to the Eagle, the Coast Guard Academy's training vessel. In the winter, George supervised the modernization of the ship's auxiliary equipment. In the summer, as the Eagle sailed across the Caribbean and the Atlantic to Europe, he gave the cadets instruction in seamanship and the ship's auxiliary equipment.

George's next assignment was on the West Coast where he was the engineering supervisor on the Point Ledge, a vessel used for search and rescue and drug enforcement along the California coast.

For the past 2 years, Chief Monch has worked at the Coast Guard shipyard in Baltimore, MD. In charge of equipment for a variety of vessels, he orders parts and advises the ship's crew on how to replace broken parts and repair equipment.

SAMPLE CAREER PATH

Marine Engine Superintendent   17–20 years

Marine engine superintendents plan and direct maintenance and repair activities of marine engine mechanics on ships or at repair centers. They determine personnel, equipment, and material needs. They organize training, long-range maintenance and safety programs. Superintendents also review and update requirements for watchstanding qualifications.

Engine Room Supervisor   8–9 years

Engine room supervisors oversee the maintenance and repair of engines and shipboard mechanical equipment. They prepare reports on machinery repairs and performance and adjust work assignments for personnel development. Supervisors give technical advice and lead an engine room watch.

Marine Engine Mechanic   4–5 years

Mechanics perform complicated engine repairs and help apprentice mechanics. They clean, inspect, and repair mechanical and hydraulic devices, and perform engine checks. They also instruct mechanics in operational procedures and damage control.

Apprentice Marine Engine Mechanic

Apprentice mechanics perform basic maintenance and repair. They inspect and repair engine parts and verify clearances between parts, using gauges and micrometers. Apprentices also study blueprints and drawings to trace, locate, and inspect parts and systems.

The years shown represent typical time-in-service before advancement to that level. Actual career advancement depends on individual experience and performance.

POWERHOUSE MECHANICS

**Army
Navy
Air Force
Marine Corps
Coast Guard**

Power generating stations (powerhouses) provide electric power for military bases, ships, and field camps. There are many types of powerhouses, from small gas generators to large nuclear reactors. Powerhouse mechanics install, maintain, and repair electrical and mechanical equipment in power generating stations.

What They Do

Powerhouse mechanics in the military perform some or all of the following duties:

- Install generating equipment, such as gasoline and diesel engines, turbines, and air compressors

- Repair and maintain nuclear power plants

- Inspect and service pumps, generators, batteries, and cables

- Tune engines using hand tools, timing lights, and combustion pressure gauges

- Diagnose (troubleshoot) engine and electrical system problems

- Replace damaged parts such as fuel injectors, valves, and pistons

Training Provided

Job training for non-nuclear specialties consists of 12 to 24 weeks of classroom instruction, including practice in repairing power generating equipment. Training length varies depending on the specialty. Course content typically includes:

- Principles of electricity

- Gas and diesel engine theories

- Hydraulic (fluid pressure) and pneumatic (air pressure) system maintenance

Nuclear specialties have training programs that last 1 year or more, covering all aspects of nuclear power plant operations. Further training occurs on the job and through advanced courses.

Physical Demands

Powerhouse mechanics may have to lift and move heavy electrical generators or batteries. Normal color vision is required to work with color-coded wiring and cables.

Helpful Attributes

Helpful school subjects include shop mechanics and math. Helpful attributes include:

- Interest in repairing machines and equipment

- Preference for doing physical work

- Interest in nuclear power

Work Environment

Powerhouse mechanics work in equipment repair shops, power plant stations, or power generating rooms aboard ships. Sometimes they work outdoors while repairing substation generating equipment.

Civilian Counterparts

Civilian powerhouse mechanics work for a wide variety of employers, such as utility and power companies, manufacturing companies, and others that operate their own power plants. They perform duties similar to military powerhouse mechanics.

Opportunities

The services have about 12,000 powerhouse mechanics. Each year, they need new mechanics due to changes in personnel and the demands of the field. After job training, mechanics perform routine maintenance tasks under close supervision. With experience, they perform more complex repair work. In time, they may become powerhouse repair crew supervisors or power plant operations managers.

MILITARY CAREERS/SCORE	INTEREST CODE
The circled score shows the typical Military Careers Score of servicemembers in this occupation. 1 2 3 **(4)** 5 6 7 Compare this score to your Military Career Score to see how well your aptitudes, skills, and abilities match those of personnel currently in these positions. See your recruiter for more information about qualification requirements.	This occupation generally appeals to people whose primary Interest Code is **Realistic.** *Realistic* jobs: • Allow you to work with your hands • Let you see the results of your work • Involve using machines, tools, and equipment

Pages 8 and 9 explain the Military Careers Score and the Interest Codes

Military Officer Occupations

General Information on Officer Occupations

For the latter half of the 20th century, the potential for global war with the former Soviet Union and its allies shaped the military's personnel requirements and overall strategies. In response to continuing changes in areas such as Eastern Europe, Africa, and the former Soviet Union, the military services have refocused their strategies to address smaller regional conflicts and the growing need for peacekeeping and humanitarian aid missions. As the military moves into the 21st century, it will need a multidimensional workforce that will be able to take advantage of new technologies and adapt quickly to new requirements.

New officers are usually college graduates with bachelor's degrees. They must meet the physical, academic, and moral standards set by their service to be accepted into programs for becoming an officer (commissioning programs). The qualifications required for acceptance into the various programs are described in this section on page 194.

Officers usually begin their careers gaining experience in their chosen occupational field. Working closely with more senior officers, they also begin supervising small groups of enlisted people. As officers become more experienced and advance in responsibility and rank, they direct more enlisted personnel, begin to lead other officers, and may eventually become the senior leaders and managers of the military. Commanding officers are responsible for every detail of U.S. ground and naval forces, ships, flying squadrons, and amphibious assault forces.

MILITARY OFFICER OCCUPATIONS

Officers lead and manage activities in every occupational specialty in the military. They must be able to learn detailed information quickly to be effective in the changing assignments and environments they will experience during their careers.

One of the characteristics of a successful leader is willingness to serve. Officers serve their country daily, sometimes placing themselves in danger. They are responsible for the well-being, training, and readiness of the people they lead.

Officers are also trained in specific occupational skills. They manage the military supply system and care for the health of combat and support personnel and their dependents. They analyze military intelligence and lead technicians on land or aboard ships.

Some officers, such as infantry and submarine officers, work in jobs directly related to combat. These occupations are open only to men. In other occupations, certain combat-related duty assignments may be closed to women.

A large number of men and women in the military work in occupations that support the combat forces. They are essential to the readiness and strength of the combat forces.

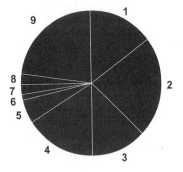

Figure 5
Distribution of Officers by Occupational Groups

1. Combat Specialty
2. Engineering, Science, and Technical
3. Executive, Administrative, and Managerial
4. Health Care
5. Human Resource Development
6. Media and Public Affairs
7. Protective Service
8. Support Service
9. Transportation

Together, the five services offer employment opportunities in over 1,500 officer job specialties. To help you explore military officer careers, these specialties are grouped into 59 occupations in this book. The 59 occupations are organized into nine broad groups or job families:

- Combat Specialty
- Engineering, Science, and Technical
- Executive, Administrative, and Managerial
- Health Care
- Human Resource Development
- Media and Public Affairs
- Protective Service
- Support Service
- Transportation

Figure 5 shows the distribution of officers across the nine occupational groups.

Over two-thirds of all military officer occupations have counterparts in the civilian world-of-work. For example, there are personnel managers, optometrists, electrical engineers, lawyers, and management analysts in both the military and civilian work forces.

The services offer training and advancement opportunities in each occupation. No matter which occupation newly commissioned officers enter, they find a well-defined career path leading to increased responsibility and higher pay.

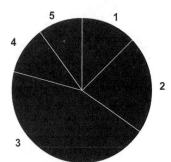

Figure 6
Pathways to Newly Commissioned Officers

1. Service Academies
2. Officer Candidate School (OCS)
   and Officer Training School (OTS)
3. Reserve Officers' Training Corps (ROTC)
4. Direct Appointments
5. Enlisted Commissioning Programs

GENERAL QUALIFICATION REQUIREMENTS

Each year, approximately 20,000 men and women become commissioned officers in the military. The term "commissioned" refers to the certification that officers receive upon meeting all qualification requirements. The certification confers military rank, authority, and obligation. To join the military as a commissioned officer, applicants must have a four-year college degree. Certain scientific, technical, and professional fields require an advanced degree. In addition, mental aptitude, physical requirements, and moral standards must be met. The general qualification requirements for military officers are presented in Table 5 on page 195. Specific requirements vary by service. For additional information on officer qualification requirements, see the "Service Information on Officer Occupations" section beginning on page 209. For detailed questions, it is necessary to contact a recruiter.

Pathways to Becoming an Officer

There are four main pathways to becoming a commissioned officer:

- Service Academies
- Officer Candidate School (OCS) and Officer Training School (OTS)
- Reserve Officers' Training Corps (ROTC)
- Direct Appointments.

An indirect pathway to becoming an officer is through Enlisted Commissioning Programs.

Figure 6 shows the percentage of newly commissioned officers who became officers through these pathways. A description of each pathway follows:

Service Academies

The four service academies are:

- United States Military Academy at West Point, New York (Army)
- United States Naval Academy at Annapolis, Maryland (Navy and Marine Corps)
- United States Air Force Academy at Colorado Springs, Colorado (Air Force)
- United States Coast Guard Academy at New London, Connecticut (Coast Guard)

The competition for entry into the academies is keen. Among candidates who meet all the eligibility requirements, the academies offer admission to only the most qualified. To be eligible for admission to any of the academies, a young person must be at least 17 years of age, a citizen of the United States, of good moral character, and academically and physically qualified. In addition, candidates for the Army, Navy, and Air Force Academies must have a nomination to be considered for admission. Nominations are not necessary for admission to the Coast Guard Academy. Most candidates seek a nomination from their members of Congress. It is not necessary to know Senators or Representatives personally to receive a nomination from them. The recommended time to apply for nomination is the spring of the junior year in high school.

The academies all offer a four-year program of study leading to a bachelor of science degree in one of many disciplines. Students, called cadets or midshipmen, receive free tuition, room, board, medical and dental care, and a

---

Table 5 – General Officer Qualifications*

Age: Must be between 19 and 29 years for Officer Candidate School (OCS) and Officer Training School (OTS); 17 and 21 years for Reserve Officers' Training Corps (ROTC); 17 and 22 years for the service academies..

Citizenship Status: Must be U.S. citizen.

Physical Condition: Must meet minimum physical standards listed below. Some occupations have additional physical standards.

Height –	Maximum	Minimum
For males:	6'5"/190.5 cm	5'0"/152.4 cm
For females:	6'5"/190.5 cm	4'10"/147.3 cm

Weight – There are minimum and maximum weights for the various services according to height, wrist size, and/or percentage of body fat.

	Maximum	Minimum
For males:	243 lb/110.4 kg	100 lb/45.35 kg
For females:	205 lb/93.18 kg	90 lb/40.82 kg

Vision – The requirements are specific for each service and are determined by job specialty. In general, service members must have at least 20/400 or 20/200 vision that can be corrected to 20/20 with eyeglasses or contacts lenses. The vision requirements are also based on depth perception as well as color blindness.

Overall Health – Must be in good health and pass a medical exam. Certain diseases or conditions may exclude persons from enlistment, such as diabetes, severe allergies, epilepsy, alcoholism, and drug addiction.

Education: Must have a four-year college degree from an accredited institution. Some occupations require advanced degrees or four-year degrees in a particular field.

Aptitude: Must achieve the minimum entry score on the Armed Services Vocational Aptitude Battery (ASVAB). Minimum entry scores vary by service and occupation.

Aptitude: Must achieve the minimum entry score on an officer qualification test. Each service uses its own officer qualification test.

Moral Character: Must meet standards designed to screen out persons unlikely to become successful officers. Standards cover court convictions, juvenile delinquency, arrests, and drug use.

Marital Status and Dependents: May be either single or married for ROTC, OCS/OTS, and direct appointment pathways. Must be single to enter and graduate from service academies. Single persons with one or more minor dependents are not eligible for officer commissioning.

Waivers: On a case-by-case basis, exceptions (waivers) are granted by individual services for some of the above qualification requirements.

* Each service sets its own qualification requirements for officers. For additional information on a particular service's requirements, refer to the "Service Information on Officer Occupations" section beginning on page 209, or contact a military recruiter.

monthly allowance. Graduates receive a commission as a military officer and must serve on active duty for at least six years. Each year, about 13 percent of the military's new officers are graduates of these four academies. For more information about the service academies, see the "Service Information on Officer Occupations" section beginning on page 209 and your school counselor.

Officer Candidate/Training School

Each service offers a program for college graduates with no prior military training who wish to become military officers. These programs are called Officer Candidate School (OCS) or Officer Training School (OTS), depending on the service. Interested candidates should apply through a local recruiter in the fall of their senior year of college. After graduation, young men and women selected for OCS/OTS join the military as enlisted members for the duration of their OCS/OTS training. Depending on the service, OCS/OTS lasts up to 20 weeks. After successful completion, candidates are commissioned as military officers and have a minimum active-duty service obligation of three years. Each year, about 21 percent of the military's new officers are commissioned through OCS/OTS. For more information, contact a recruiter.

Reserve Officers' Training Corps

Undergraduate students in public or private colleges or universities may receive training to become officers under the Reserve Officers' Training Corps (ROTC). ROTC programs for the Army, Navy, Air Force, and Marine Corps are available in over 1,400 colleges and universities nationwide.

Depending on the service and ROTC option selected, students train for two, three, or four years. Often, they receive scholarships for tuition, books, fees, uniforms, and a monthly allowance. In addition to their military and college course work, ROTC candidates perform drills for several hours each week and participate in military training exercises for several weeks each summer. Graduating ROTC candidates become commissioned as military officers and either go on active duty or become members of Reserve or National Guard units. Each year, about 44 percent of the military's new officers are gained through ROTC programs. For more information about service ROTC programs, see the "Service Information on Officer Occupations" section beginning on page 209. For information on the colleges and universities that offer ROTC programs for a particular service, contact a recruiter from that service.

Direct Appointments

Medical, legal, engineering, and religious professionals who are fully qualified in their field may apply to receive direct appointments as military officers. These individuals enter military service and begin practicing their profession with a minimum of military training. The service obligation for officers entering through direct appointment is two years. Some scholarship programs are available to assist students in these fields with their professional schooling in return for several years of service. Each year, direct appointments make up about 11 percent of the military's new officers. For information about opportunities for direct appointment in a particular service, contact a recruiter from that service.

Enlisted Commissioning Programs

In addition to the four main pathways described above, the services each have programs for qualified enlisted personnel to earn commissions as officers. Once selected to an enlisted commissioning program, enlisted personnel must follow one of the four major pathways described above in order to receive their commission. These programs are exclusive, as they account for only 10 percent of newly commissioned officers each year.

SERVICE SUPPORT FOR CAREER ADVANCEMENT

From the time officers are commissioned until the last day of duty, the services play an important role in supporting their career development. The military offers a wide range of training and development opportunities to help each officer build a career. However, to succeed, officers must take advantage of the opportunities provided.

Officer Training and Education

Training and education are ongoing throughout a military officer's career. Although each service has its own programs for officer professional development, all services view training and education, followed by practical experience, as the normal course for officer development. The military provides five kinds of training and educational opportunities to its officers:

- Basic officer training
- Job training
- Advanced training
- Professional military education
- Leadership training.

These five types of training are discussed on the following pages.

1) Basic Officer Training

An important part of every pathway leading to officer commissioning is training on the basic knowledge required to become an officer. The topics covered in this training include:

- Roles and responsibilities of the officer
- Military laws and regulations
- Service traditions
- Military customs and courtesies
- Career development
- Military science
- Administrative procedures.

In addition, most commissioning pathways involve physical conditioning consisting of calisthenics, running, and drills.

The duration and timing of officer training may vary with the commissioning pathway followed. For example, ROTC candidates receive basic officer training over the course of their two- to four-year ROTC programs. The same is true for cadets or midshipmen at the service academies. In contrast, OCS/OTS candidates receive their basic officer training in the 12- to 20-week OCS/OTS programs they attend after graduation from college or after spending time as an enlisted member.

2) Job Training

After earning their commissions, officers normally receive job training in preparation for their first duty assignment. Depending on the occupational field entered, initial job training may last from several weeks to two years. Officer training, however, does not end after this initial training.

Because officers are the professional leaders of the military, they must develop knowledge of the broad areas they might command. For example, supply officers must understand the entire supply system, from contracting to warehouse man-

agement, to one day command supply operations for an entire base. Therefore, supply officers are assigned to several different jobs during their careers. Throughout a career, the services provide training to allow officers to maintain and increase their skills. In addition to technical training, the services provide training that focuses on military strategy and history as well as developing the leadership, communication, and management skills required for positions of greater responsibility.

For certain occupations, the military does not provide job training. Doctors, veterinarians, nurses, therapists, lawyers, engineers, social workers, and other professionals may only enter the military after they have been fully trained and, in most cases, certified by a state board.

3) Advanced Training

There are advanced training courses for virtually every officer occupation. These courses fall into two basic categories. In the first category are those courses that teach the technical or administrative skills needed for an officer's next assignment. For example, transportation officers with truck and vehicle experience may receive training in landing craft maintenance management before they are transferred to a landing craft assignment.

In the second category are the courses that train officers in the overall mission of their occupations. For example, infantry officers need instruction in coordinating combat actions with artillery and aircraft units, while ship officers need to learn how to coordinate operations of ships and aircraft to hunt submarines.

4) Professional Military Education

Professional military education (PME) prepares officers for the increasingly challenging leadership, planning, operations, and management responsibilities they assume as they rise in rank. PME is highly recommended for career-oriented officers, regardless of their occupational specialties.

PME courses teach techniques for combat-support operations in battle. Officers study military history, strategy, tactics (how to maneuver forces on the battlefield), planning, and organization. They learn how each service supports the others, and how the services work together to defend our nation.

PME is divided into two courses of study that correspond to specific points in career development. Officers may be selected to attend full-time resident programs to complete PME. If not, they are strongly encouraged to complete the courses by correspondence. Resident PME courses are usually taught at service "war colleges." Each service has its own PME programs, but the levels of instruction and many subjects are similar. There are even opportunities for members of one service to attend full-time resident programs at the school of another service.

5) Leadership Training

Officers receive leadership training throughout their careers. There are formal courses of leadership and management, and leadership is discussed in many occupational courses. Additionally, officers receive advice and on-the-job instruction in leadership from more senior officers.

Continuing Education

Continuing education is an important part of an officer's professional development. It allows officers to broaden their knowledge and earn advanced degrees in military science, technical subjects related to their occupations, management techniques, and subjects in which they are interested. Although having an advanced degree does not guarantee career advancement, it can be an important factor.

Figure 7
Officer Insignia of the United States Armed Forces

The services offer several programs for officer continuing education:

Service Colleges and Postgraduate Schools

Service-oriented institutions, like the Naval Postgraduate School and the Air Force Institute of Technology, offer advanced degree programs in many fields. Both correspondence courses and resident programs are available. There is intense competition for entrance into these programs, and selections are based on service need as well as officer preference.

Tuition Assistance

Up to 75 percent of tuition costs at state and private institutions may be reimbursed for officers enrolled in night school or correspondence courses. To participate, officers must meet the entrance requirements of the institution and meet service guidelines. In some cases, the service will select officers to attend graduate degree programs full-time and pay all costs plus their salaries. Opportunities are limited, and selections are based on service need.

OFFICER PROMOTION

Officers can progress through 10 officer pay grades during their careers. Figure 7 contains information on the relationship between pay grade and rank and also illustrates the insignia for the ranks in each service.

PAY GRADE / SERVICE	ARMY	NAVY	AIR FORCE	MARINE CORPS	COAST GUARD
O-10	GENERAL	ADMIRAL	GENERAL	GENERAL	ADMIRAL
O-9	LIEUTENANT GENERAL	VICE ADMIRAL	LIEUTENANT GENERAL	LIEUTENANT GENERAL	VICE ADMIRAL
O-8	MAJOR GENERAL	REAR ADMIRAL (UPPER HALF)	MAJOR GENERAL	MAJOR GENERAL	REAR ADMIRAL (UPPER HALF)
O-7	BRIGADIER GENERAL	REAR ADMIRAL (LOWER HALF)	BRIGADIER GENERAL	BRIGADIER GENERAL	REAR ADMIRAL (LOWER HALF)
O-6	COLONEL	CAPTAIN	COLONEL	COLONEL	CAPTAIN
O-5	LIEUTENANT COLONEL	COMMANDER	LIEUTENANT COLONEL	LIEUTENANT COLONEL	COMMANDER
O-4	MAJOR	LIEUTENANT COMMANDER	MAJOR	MAJOR	LIEUTENANT COMMANDER
O-3	CAPTAIN	LIEUTENANT	CAPTAIN	CAPTAIN	LIEUTENANT
O-2	FIRST LIEUTENANT	LIEUTENANT JUNIOR GRADE	FIRST LIEUTENANT	FIRST LIEUTENANT	LIEUTENANT JUNIOR GRADE
O-1	SECOND LIEUTENANT	ENSIGN	SECOND LIEUTENANT	SECOND LIEUTENANT	ENSIGN

Officers in the pay grade of O-1 advance by the action of their local commander. Commanders ensure that all necessary qualifications are being completed and that officers have spent the required time in grade.

Officers are continually evaluated by more senior officers. Individual performance is compared with the performance of all other officers in similar pay grades. A selection board thoroughly examines every aspect of each officer's career performance to select only the most qualified officers for promotion.

Selection boards are made up of experienced senior officers. Each selection board evaluates performance from the time each officer entered the service to the time the board meets. The members of the selection board evaluate each officer's record for promotion. Factors that qualify officers for promotion include:

- Career-long performance of job duties, leadership, and management
- Pursuit of, and success in, positions of increasing responsibility
- Successful completion of required qualifications and professional military education
- Appearance and behavior.

By selecting the most qualified officers for promotions, the services ensure they have the best possible leadership.

Excellent performance reports are essential to career advancement. Although a series of excellent performance reports does not guarantee an individual's promotion, a less-than-excellent record severely limits chances for advancement. Since the number of officer positions is limited by Congress, the competition at senior levels is intense.

Figure 8 shows the average time an officer has been in the military (time-in-service) when he or she is promoted to each pay grade. For example, most officers will advance to O-2 in two years and to O-4 in 10 years. A very few outstanding officers may be selected for promotion earlier than indicated.

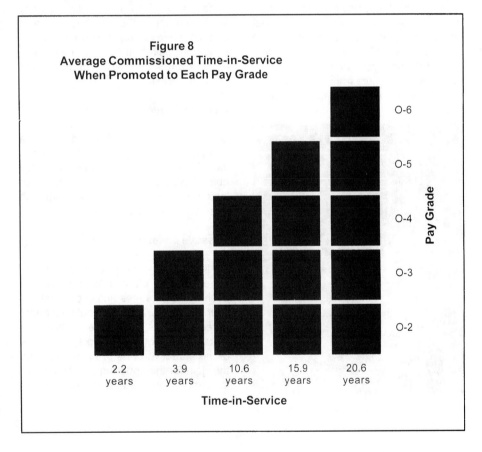

Figure 8
Average Commissioned Time-in-Service
When Promoted to Each Pay Grade

DUTY ASSIGNMENT

The five services have similar systems for assigning personnel to jobs. Each system is designed to satisfy the present and future staffing needs of the particular service. For example, if the service needs a physician or pilot at a remote location, officers in those occupations will be assigned there. However, at the same time, the services also attempt to meet the desires of individuals and provide the best opportunity for career development. The duty assignment process determines where officers work, how often they move, and the opportunities available to them.

Assignment Decisions

The services use mid- to senior-level officers who are familiar with a particular occupation to manage assignments for officers in that occupation. Assignment officers try to assign officers to different units to give them a broad range of experience. Both range and depth of experience are important to officer advancement. Although these officers cannot always meet each person's needs or desires, they try to make duty assignments that will enhance each officer's career.

Length of Tours

The time that an officer spends at a particular duty assignment is called a tour. The length of a tour varies by service and geographic location. Typically, a tour lasts from three to four years, although there are many exceptions.

Possible Location

All services require their officers to travel. Military officers are stationed in each of the 50 states and in countries all over the world. They are routinely transferred after one-, two-, three-, or four-year tours of duty. To many people, this is one of the attractive parts of service life and they join for the opportunity to travel, live in foreign countries, and see different

parts of the United States. Nearly three-quarters of all service personnel are assigned to duty in the United States. Every service also has people stationed overseas; most of them are located in Europe, in countries such as Germany, Great Britain, and Italy. Many officers are also assigned to the Pacific Islands, including countries such as Japan. Typically, officers will have two overseas assignments during their careers.

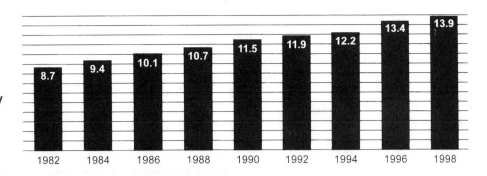

**Figure 9
Percentage of Active Duty
Women Officers
1982 – 1998**

1982	1984	1986	1988	1990	1992	1994	1996	1998
8.7	9.4	10.1	10.7	11.5	11.9	12.2	13.4	13.9

WOMEN OFFICERS

Military women are recognized today for the important contributions that they make to national defense. As shown in Figure 9, the percentage of active duty officers that are women has increased to about 14 percent.

According to federal laws and policies, women may not be assigned to duty that involves a high probability of exposure to direct ground combat. Through studies, the services have determined which occupations have the highest probability of exposure to hostile fire and physical contact with the enemy. Examples of these occupations include infantry officer, artillery officer, and tank officer.

Despite federal laws and policies that restrict women from entering direct ground combat-related occupations, the scope of women's opportunities in the military has expanded. Women are currently eligible to enter about 90 percent of all military career fields. Examples of the many occupations in which women serve include airplane pilot, environmental health and safety officer, civil engineer, and intelligence officer. The outlook for women officers in the military suggests that the future will provide even greater opportunities.

RESERVE FORCES

Seven forces make up the Reserves:

- Army Reserve
- Navy Reserve
- Air Force Reserve
- Marine Corps Reserve
- Coast Guard Reserve
- Army National Guard
- Air National Guard.

Reserve Forces Role

The Reserves have an important role in our national defense. Their primary mission is to stay prepared to respond to events that threaten our country's security. In a national emergency, the Reserves can be "called up" to serve temporarily on active duty to expand our regular armed forces.

In peacetime, the Reserves perform many duties to support the regular active-duty forces, such as air patrols, search and rescue missions, air defense watch, installation and repair of communications equipment, transport of troops and supplies, and provision of medical services.

In addition to serving the national defense, National Guard units serve their states and communities during natural disasters and civil emergencies. Guard members have been called upon to rescue flood and hurricane victims, fight forest fires, and assist local authorities during evacuations.

Becoming a Reserve Forces Officer

Currently, there are nearly 160,000 officers in the seven Reserve Forces. Each year, the Reserves need approximately 20,000 new officers. Although most Reserve Forces officers have prior experience as officers in the active-duty forces, young men and women without prior military experience may join the Reserves if they qualify. The basic qualification requirements are the same as for active-duty officers, shown in Table 5 on page 195.

There are several pathways to becoming a Reserve Forces officer, including ROTC and National Guard training. For more information, refer to the "Service Information on Officer Occupations" section beginning on page 209, or contact a military recruiter.

Service Obligation

To become a Reserve Forces officer, individuals without prior experience as active-duty officers must commit themselves to an eight-year service obligation and undergo an initial training program at a military base. This training lasts between six and 18 weeks, depending on the Reserve Force selected.

After initial training is successfully completed, Reserve Forces officers live and work as civilians in their own communities and train part-time with a nearby Reserve unit.

Reserve Unit Training

Reservists in organized units are required to attend training assemblies regularly throughout the year. Reserve units are required to conduct a minimum of 48 training assemblies a year. These assemblies are held on the weekends or evenings or a combination of both. One weekend is the equivalent of four training drills.

Reservists must also spend from 12 to 17 days in full-time training each year. The annual training period is normally scheduled during the summer and may be conducted at a site away from the member's community.

Reserve Pay

A Reservist's pay is based on the same pay grade and length of service as military personnel on active duty. Members receive one day's pay for each drill attended. In addition, they receive one day's pay for each day of annual training.

PAY AND BENEFITS

Military officers in all five services are paid according to the same pay scale and receive the same basic benefits. Military pay and benefits are set by Congress, which normally grants a cost-of-living pay increase once each year. In addition to pay, the military provides many of life's necessities, such as food, clothing, and housing. The following sections describe officer pay, allowances, and benefits in more detail.

Officer Pay Grades

Officers can progress through 10 officer pay grades during their careers. Pay grade and length of service determine an officer's pay. Figure 7 on page 200 contains information on the relationship between pay grade and rank and also illustrates the insignia for the ranks in each service.

Most newly commissioned officers begin at pay grade O-1. Those who have certain professional qualifications and receive direct appointment may enter at a higher pay grade. After two years, officers usually move up to O-2. After an additional two years, the military generally promotes officers to O-3 if job performance is satisfactory and other requirements are met.

Basic Pay

The major part of an officer's paycheck is basic pay. Pay grade and total years of service determine an officer's basic pay. Table 6 contains information on annual basic pay as of 2000. Cost-of-living increases generally occur once a year. Using this table, you can find that a person who has been in the service for eight years, and advanced to pay grade O-3, receives a basic pay of $43,826 per year.

Incentives and Special Pay

The military offers incentives and special pay (in addition to basic pay) for certain types of duty. For example, incentives are paid for submarine and flight duty. Other types of hazardous duty with monthly incentives include parachute jumping, flight deck duty, and explosives demolition. In addition, the military gives special pay for sea duty, diving duty, duty in some foreign countries, and duty in areas subject to hostile fire. Special pay is also provided for officers in certain occupations, such as physicians, dentists, and life scientists.

Table 6 – 2000 Basic Pay for Officers (Annual Figures)

	Under 2 yrs	2	3	4	6	8	10	...	26
				Years of Service					
O-10	*	*	*	*	*	*	*	...	$135,821
O-9	*	*	*	*	*	*	*	...	119,837
O-8	*	*	*	*	*	*	*	...	108,576
O-7	*	*	*	*	*	*	*	...	95,825
O-6	*	*	*	$57,053	$57,053	$57,053	$57,053	...	84,186
O-5	$38,881	$45,767	$48,935	48,935	48,935	48,935	50,404	...	*
O-4	32,854	40,007	42,674	42,674	43,466	45,382	48,485	...	*
O-3	30,528	34,132	36,483	40,378	42,311	43,826	46,202	...	*
O-2	26,625	29,077	34,931	36,108	36,853			...	*
O-1	23,118	24,059	29,077	*	*	*	*	...	*

* Military Personnel with this many years of service will probably not be in this pay grade. (Pay scale between 10 and 26 years not shown.)

Allowances

Many officers and their families live free of charge in military housing on the base where they are assigned. Those living off base receive a quarters (housing) allowance in addition to their basic pay. In 2000, the monthly housing allowance ranged from $397 to $1,114, depending on pay grade and if the officer had dependents. Each officer also received a subsistence (food) allowance of $158 per month. Because allowances are not taxed as income, they provide a significant tax savings in addition to their cash value.

When added together, housing and food allowances, along with their tax savings, are substantial additions to basic pay. Table 7 contains information on the total value of basic pay, allowances, and tax savings, called Regular Military Compensation. The table represents the amount of pay a civilian worker would have to earn to realize the same "take home" pay as a military officer. These figures provide a more realistic comparison between military and civilian salaries than the figures in Table 6.

Table 7 – 2000 Regular Military Compensation (Annual Figures)

	Years of Service								
	Under 2 yrs	2	3	4	6	8	10	...	26
O-10	*	*	*	*	*	*	*	...	$137,357
O-9	*	*	*	*	*	*	*	...	137,267
O-8	*	*	*	*	*	*	*	...	129,841
O-7	*	*	*	*	*	*	*	...	117,274
O-6	*	*	*	$76,876	$76,876	$76,876	$76,876	...	103,847
O-5	$56,349	$63,201	$66,631	66,631	66,631	66,631	68,250	...	*
O-4	48,471	55,334	57,935	57,935	58,712	60,648	63,898	...	*
O-3	43,485	47,111	49,377	53,082	54,928	56,392	58,767	...	*
O-2	37,037	39,607	45,691	46,814	47,523	*	*	...	*
O-1	32,074	32,976	38,324	*	*	*	*	...	*

Regular Military Compensation reflects basic pay, allowances, and the value of the tax advantage for allowances.

* Military Personnel with this many years of service will probably not be in this pay grade. (Pay scale between 10 and 26 years not shown.)

Employment Benefits

Military officers receive substantial benefits in addition to their pay and allowances. While they are in the service, officers' benefits include health care, vacation time, legal assistance, recreational programs, educational assistance, and commissary/exchange (military store) privileges. Families of officers also receive some of these benefits. Table 8 contains a summary of these employment benefits.

Retirement Benefits

The military offers one of the best retirement programs in the country. After 20 years of active duty, officers may retire and receive a monthly payment equal to 40 percent of their average basic pay for their last five years of active duty. Officers who retire with more than 20 years of active service receive higher pay. Other retirement benefits include medical care and commissary/exchange privileges.

Veterans' Benefits

Veterans of military service are entitled to certain veterans' benefits set by Congress and provided by the Veterans Administration. In most cases, these include guarantees for home loans, hospitalization, survivor benefits, educational benefits, disability benefits, and assistance in finding civilian employment.

Table 8 – Summary of Employment Benefits for Officers

Vacation	Leave time of 30 days per year.
Medical, Dental and Eye Care	Full medical, hospitalization, dental, and eye care services for officers and most health care costs for family members.
Continuing Education	Voluntary educational programs for undergraduate and graduate degrees or for single courses, including tuition assistance for programs at colleges and universities.
Recreational Programs	Programs include athletics, entertainment, and hobbies: Softball, basketball, football, swimming, tennis, golf, weight training, and other sports — Parties, dances, and entertainment — Club facilities, snack bars, game rooms, movie theaters, and lounges — Active hobby and craft clubs, book and music libraries.
Exchange and Commissary Privileges	Food, goods, and services are available at military stores, generally at lower costs than regular retail stores.
Legal Assistance	Many free legal services are available to assist with personal matters.

Service Information on Officer Occupations

Army

OVERVIEW

Today's Army is composed of a highly trained team of individuals. The individual soldier, the noncommissioned officer (NCO), and the officer make the Army's sophisticated technology work. They operate tanks, fly helicopters, and launch missiles. They build bridges, calibrate and operate computers, and apply state-of-the-art tools and methods to solve critical problems. Working together, these elements enable the Army to accomplish its mission to deter war and be prepared to fight and win should deterrence fail.

The Army is made up of nearly 500,000 bright, well-trained men and women on active duty, including more than 66,000 officers and 12,000 warrant officers. These men and women compose the best-trained, best-disciplined, and most self-assured Army in recent history. The Army needs about 7,000 new officers each year.

BECOMING AN OFFICER

You may become an officer in the U.S. Army through one of four commissioning programs: The United States Military Academy, The Army Reserve Officers' Training Corps (ROTC), the Officer Candidate School (OCS), or direct appointment. All require, as a minimum, that the applicant be a high school graduate, pass a medical and physical exam, and be at least 17 years old. In order to be competitive for these programs, an individual needs to be working toward or already have acquired a four-year college degree.

U.S. Military Academy

The United States Military Academy, located at West Point, New York, offers bachelor of science degrees with majors in both engineering and liberal arts. Graduates earn a commission as a Second Lieutenant in the U.S. Army.

Admission to the academy is very competitive. Appointments are generally made through nominations from United States Senators and Representatives. Applicants should begin their quest for entry into the academy no later than the middle of their junior year in high school.

Army Reserve Officers' Training Corps (ROTC)

Army ROTC is the primary source of college-trained officers for the Army. The ROTC program is currently offered at 270 institutions with partnership agreements allowing for participation at more than 900 other colleges and universities.

Army ROTC is divided into two parts—the Basic Course and the Advanced Course. The Basic Course covers the freshman and sophomore years of college. Non-scholarship students may withdraw at any time during the Basic Course and no military obligation is incurred. Four-year scholarship recipients may participate for one year without obligation. Successful Basic Course graduates may enroll in the Advanced Course during the final two years of college. Students in the Advanced Course receive uniforms, $450 towards textbooks, and a subsistence allowance of up to $1,500 each year. Cadets are scheduled for a five-week Advanced Camp during the summer between their junior and senior years of college.

Educational assistance in the form of highly competitive scholarships are available for two, three, or four years. The scholarship will pay 100 percent of tuition and educational fees up to $16,000 annually. Additional benefits include a variety of incentives offered by the institutions. These incentives range from in state tuition and academic credit to free room and board.

Officer Candidate School (OCS)

Officer Candidate School (OCS) is a 14-week course to train enlisted personnel, Warrant Officers, and civilians with a college degree to be Army officers. Enlisted soldiers and Warrant Officers must have 60 hours of college before applying for OCS. Civilian applicants must have a bachelor's degree.

Direct Appointment

The Army offers direct appointment opportunities for specialists from selected legal, medical, ministerial, and technical career fields. Professional experience can even earn a higher entry grade for qualified applicants.

Warrant Officers

An Army Warrant Officer is an officer appointed by warrant of the Secretary of the Army, based on a sound level of technical and tactical competence. The Warrant Officer is a highly specialized expert and trainer who gains progressive levels of expertise and leadership by operating, maintaining, administering and managing the Army's equipment, support activities, or technical systems for an entire career.

Becoming a Warrant Officer requires great skill in a specific occupational specialty. Army Warrant Officers must demonstrate leadership abilities and have the desire and dedication to perfect their technical proficiency through professional development, training, and education. Through schooling, experience, assignments and promotions, they are trained to perform effectively in the highest, most demanding positions within their career specialties. A local Army recruiter can provide up-to-date information about how to qualify to become a Warrant Officer.

OFFICER TRAINING

Newly commissioned officers attend an Officer Basic Course (OBC), which prepares them for their first assignment. OBC contains a mix of classroom education and physical training. Much of the time is devoted to practicing leadership skills in a work-like environment. During OBC, which lasts about four months, Lieutenants also participate in a vigorous physical fitness program. OBC instruction is provided by the branch of the Army that utilizes an officer's specialty. For example, newly commissioned infantry officers attend OBC at the U.S. Army Infantry School at Fort Benning, Georgia.

Special skills that may be needed by new officers are developed at a functional training course. Pilots complete their flight training after OBC. Army infantry lieutenants may volunteer for Airborne (parachute) or Ranger training. Some infantry officers complete certification courses as Bradley fighting vehicle commanders if they are being assigned to units equipped with that vehicle.

Army officers are also provided advanced training and refresher instruction to meet the needs of the Army or their next assignment. These courses usually are not more than six months in length. For example, Army supply officers can take advanced courses in material management, air delivery of cargo, and food services management. Specialized courses are available in every career area.

At various points during a career as an Army officer, there are opportunities to participate in professional military education such as the Combined Arms Services Staff School or the Command and General Staff School. These programs prepare officers for the increasing responsibilities associated with career advancement to the more senior grades in the Army. They are primarily the study of how to be an officer and provide the command and staff knowledge required to be a professional officer.

ADVANCEMENT

Most new Army officers begin their careers as Second Lieutenants. A few officers receive a direct appointment to a higher grade. There are established points (time-in-grade) at which time an officer is considered for promotion. Army officers are selected for advancement based on their being qualified to meet the requirements of the Army. The Army promotion process is designed to ensure advancement of the best officers, promote career development, and promote officers with the greatest demonstrated potential.

Promotion to the grade of First Lieutenant usually occurs at two years of service. After an additional two years of service, the best qualified officers are promoted to Captain. After being in the Army a total of nine to 11 years, an officer becomes eligible for promotion to Major. This and subsequent promotions are more competitive. While all officers compete with each other for promotion, the Army recognizes a need to retain the right number of officers with the skills to meet Army requirements. A selection board evaluates the potential of all eligible officers and recommends the best qualified in each career area for promotion. There are provisions for early promotions of outstanding performers (limited to no more than 10 percent of promotions).

EDUCATION PROGRAMS

Advanced education is a goal for most Army officers. Some officers may be selected to pursue full-time studies toward a master's or doctorate degree through programs paid by the Army. Many officers pursue advanced education on their own time. Here are some of the programs offered by the Army for the advanced education of its officers:

Advanced Degree Program

The Army Educational Requirements System determines the Army's need for officers with advanced degrees. Selected officers are provided an opportunity to attend graduate school for up to three years in a discipline required by the Army. After completing their graduate studies, these officers are assigned to positions that utilize their education. These officers can also anticipate future assignments that capitalize on their specialized knowledge. Officers are considered for this program after completing six to eight years of active duty.

Fully Funded Legal Education Program (FLEP)

The Judge Advocate General's Funded Legal Education Program allows up to 25 officers to be selected each year to attend a regular course of instruction leading to a Juris Doctor (J.D.) or Bachelor of Law (LL.B.) degree at an approved civilian law school. These programs are provided at government expense and usually last three academic years. Upon completion of schooling, the officer is required to accept an appointment in the Judge Advocate General's Corps for the period of active-duty obligation.

Training With Industry (TWI) Program

The TWI program provides training in industrial procedures and practices not available through military or civilian schools. It provides officers with vital knowledge, experience and perspective in management and operational techniques. This experience is necessary to fill positions of significant responsibility in Army commands and activities that normally deal with civilian industry. Currently, these programs are concentrated in the areas of artificial intelligence, aviation logistics, communications-electronics, finance, marketing, ordnance, physical security, procurement, public affairs, research and development, systems automation, and transportation. These programs are normally one year long, with a predetermined follow-on assignment.

RESERVE OFFICERS

In thousands of cities and towns across America, men and women work full-time in their communities and serve their nation part-time in one of the Army's reserve components. There are more than 7,000 units of the Army Reserve and the Army National Guard. These units are trained and equipped to accomplish Army missions worldwide on very short notice. They are a vital part of the total Army team, often training alongside active-duty Army personnel at home and overseas.

There are about 11,000 officers currently serving in Army National Guard and Army Reserve units. They serve in all career fields found in the active component of the Army. Often they serve in a career field that is the same as their civilian profession. Many serve in military units that offer them an exciting and demanding change from their full-time job. Most reservists will agree that the skills and qualities that are necessary for success in civilian life are enhanced by their military training and experience.

FOR FURTHER INFORMATION

Students who wish to learn more about specific military occupations are encouraged to use this book to the fullest. In addition, many career information systems found in high schools and libraries have information about Army careers. The most up-to-date information about Army commissioning programs is available from an Army recruiter. Feel free to contact the one nearest you. There is no obligation.

Navy

OVERVIEW

The Navy operates throughout the world to help preserve peace. Navy cruisers, destroyers, frigates, submarines, aircraft carriers, and support ships are ready to maintain the freedom of the seas. Navy sea and air power are available to assist in the defense of our allies or engage enemy forces in the event of war.

The United States Navy is a large and complex organization. Over 371,000 officers and enlisted personnel make up today's Navy. Many of the nearly 54,000 officers serve as ship or submarine officers, pilots, flight officers, nuclear power instructors, and special warfare officers. Others perform specialized duties in intelligence, engineering, law, medicine, and scientific careers. Between 5,000 and 6,000 men and women join the Navy as officers every year.

BECOMING AN OFFICER

A Navy officer must be a mature person capable of assuming a wide variety of duties at sea, in the air, and ashore. Applicants must be physically fit, at least 19 years old, and United States citizens. They must have at least a bachelor's degree. The major fields of study required vary depending on the officer specialty.

There are several ways to become a Navy officer. Commissioning programs are available for students still in college and for college graduates. Specialists in certain professional and scientific fields may qualify for a direct commission. Programs leading to a commission as a Navy officer include the Naval Reserve Officers' Training Corps and the U.S. Naval Academy.

Naval Reserve Officers' Training Corps

The Naval Reserve Officers' Training Corps (NROTC) program offers tuition and other financial benefits worth up to $100,000 at 57 Units which include more than 140 of the country's leading colleges and universities. Two-year and four-year subsidized scholarships are offered. Participants receive a monthly cash allowance.

Two-year and four-year nonsubsidized NROTC programs are also offered. These are referred to as college programs and provide for monthly cash allowances during the junior and senior years.

U.S. Naval Academy

The United States Naval Academy (USNA) provides a free four-year undergraduate education program. The USNA program leads to a bachelor's degree in a wide range of major subjects and a commission as a Navy or Marine Corps officer. Students are paid a monthly salary while attending the academy.

Students must be single with no children and must serve on active duty for at least five years after graduation, depending on follow-on training and designation. Admission to the Naval Academy is made through nominations from United States Senators, Representatives, the President and Vice President of the United States, and the Secretary of the Navy.

Nuclear Propulsion Officer Candidate Programs

The Nuclear Propulsion Officer Candidate (NUPOC) program is for college juniors and seniors pursuing a bachelor's degree in physics, chemistry, mathematics, or an engineering discipline. College graduates with a bachelor's or higher degree may also qualify for the NUPOC program. Cash bonuses are offered for joining and completing the Navy's NUPOC program.

The only Navy requirement is that the student maintain excellent grades in required subjects and earn a degree. While in the NUPOC program, the student can enjoy many of the same benefits received by regular Navy officers. Upon graduation from college, NUPOCs begin their naval officer training at Officer Candidate School (OCS) in Pensacola, Florida.

Aviation Officer/Naval Flight Officer Programs

Aviation Officer Candidate (AOC) and Naval Flight Officer Candidate (NFOC) programs are for college seniors and graduates interested in becoming Navy pilots or flight officers. If qualified and accepted, they attend the Officer Candidate School in Pensacola, Florida.

Warrant Officers

The Warrant Officer Program is open to all enlisted Navy people with the rank of Chief Petty Officer or above and have completed at least 12 years of naval service. Warrant Officers are senior to all enlisted Chief Petty Officers and junior to all Ensigns.

Limited Duty Officers

The Limited Duty Officer Program is open to warrant officers with more than two years of service as warrants and to enlisted people who are Petty Officers with at least eight years of naval service. If qualified, they earn a Navy officer commission because of their high quality and experience in a specialty, but are limited to duties of that specialty.

Direct Commission

Direct commission (appointment) may be attained by a professional person who is already established in his or her specialty field, but who is interested in the challenging and rewarding career and lifestyle of a Navy officer. The Navy has programs to help medical, dental, law, and theology students complete their professional training and earn commissions as Navy officers.

OFFICER TRAINING

Before receiving their first active-duty assignment, all new Navy officers go through a period of initial training. This training is designed to acquaint individuals with the Navy way of life, its rules, regulations, and responsibilities. The training also covers naval operations, organization, and administrative procedures. NROTC candidates and Naval Academy midshipmen receive this training as part of their college program. Other prospective officers are required to go to one of two schools – Officer Candidate School (OCS) in Pensacola Florida or Officer Indoctrination School (OIS) in Newport, Rhode Island.

Each school consists of a full schedule of academic studies and rigorous physical training. OCS is a course for new surface warfare, nuclear submarine, aviation, engineering, supply, intelligence officers, aviation maintenance officers, and diving and salvage officers. OIS is a course for officers who have received a direct commission in the field of medicine or law.

Navy officers also go through specialized or technical training before their initial assignment. Initial advanced training after being commissioned an officer is usually at the Navy specialty school that pertains to the officer's major field of education or for which he or she qualified when entering the Navy. Here the new officers learn how to apply that specialty to naval operations.

For instance, cryptology officers go to the Naval Security Group orientation course; intelligence officers go to the Navy and Marine Corps Intelligence School; supply corps officers go to the Navy Supply School; civil engineer corps officers go to the Civil Engineer Corps School; and Navy chaplains go to the Chaplains' School. Pilots and naval flight officers receive their flight training and learn to operate the complex communications and weapons systems on Navy aircraft.

These schools may be several months to more than a year in length, depending on the complexity of the specialty and the advanced training needed. Other than the Navy aviation team, officers in the nuclear power program have the longest overall training period. After OCS, they go to Nuclear Power School for 24 weeks, then to a nuclear power training unit for 26 weeks, then to either the Submarine Officer Basic Course for 13 weeks or the Surface Warfare Officer School for 17 weeks before being assigned aboard a nuclear-powered vessel. The Navy's nuclear power training program is the broadest and most comprehensive anywhere.

Navy officers are also given short courses of special and refresher instruction to meet the needs of the service and their assignment. These courses usually are not more than six months in length. Specialized courses offered to Navy officers are in communications, basic and advanced electronics, civil engineering, transportation management, naval justice, and petroleum products and supply.

Navy officers are also provided an opportunity to attend one of the service colleges. These are considered necessary for higher command leadership. A naval officer should possess a thorough knowledge of the principles and methods of naval strategy and tactics and of joint operations with other branches of the armed forces. To achieve these objectives, courses are given at the Armed Forces Staff College, the Inter-American Defense College, the National Defense University, the Naval War College, and Foreign Service Colleges.

ADVANCEMENT

Most college graduates begin their Navy officer career as an Ensign. After two years, they are eligible for promotion to Lieutenant Junior Grade. Another two-year period makes them eligible for promotion to Lieutenant. After being in the Navy a total of nine to 11 years, an officer becomes eligible for promotion to Lieutenant Commander. A Lieutenant Commander must have 15 to 17 years of service to be eligible to become a Commander. A Commander must have been in the Navy 21 to 23 years to be promoted to Captain.

Promotion to the ranks of Lieutenant Commander and above are very competitive, and only the best officers are selected for advancement. A selection board evaluates the past performance of each eligible officer and recommends the best qualified for promotions.

Each Navy officer is given a new assignment, or tour, as it is called, every few years. Every effort is made to match personal desires with the needs of the Navy. Assignments may be in the officer's chosen field or in a different field where there is a need.

EDUCATION PROGRAMS

Education and training are a continuous process throughout a Navy officer's career. As an officer's career develops, he or she may have the opportunity to take advantage of an advanced educational program. Presented below are some of the opportunities offered by the Navy in the professional development of its officers.

Postgraduate Education Program

The goal of the Navy's Postgraduate Education Program is to provide specialized education at the master's and doctorate level in technical and nontechnical fields of study. The program is conducted mainly at the Naval Postgraduate School in Monterey, California. The program is supplemented by using civilian universities for many courses. It also makes use of appropriate courses provided by other agencies of the Department of Defense.

Correspondence and Extension Courses

Correspondence and extension courses are encouraged for all Navy officers. Most of the courses are provided by the Naval Correspondence Course Center. Others are offered by the Naval War College, the Industrial College of the Armed Forces, military medical and dental schools, the Defense Intelligence School, and the Naval Submarine School.

Officers may also enroll in courses given by other services and in graduate and undergraduate level education offered by colleges and universities.

THE NAVAL RESERVE

Navy officers who leave active duty for civilian careers can retain many of the benefits of a Navy career by joining the Naval Reserve Force.

The Naval Reserve Force is a team of highly trained people available in a national emergency to meet the expanded needs of the regular Navy. Most Reservists serve in a part-time status, consisting of one weekend a month and an annual two-week period of duty, called annual training (AT). These training periods can be taken on an individual basis or with a Reserve unit.

A Naval Reserve Force medical program works the same way for medical specialists who wish to serve their country and at the same time continue their civilian medical practice.

The Naval Reserve Force numbered more than 24,000 officers in mid-1986, and rose to approximately 47,000 in 1993.

FOR FURTHER INFORMATION

The occupational information in Military Careers can be useful in exploring career opportunities in the Navy. Many career information systems found in high schools and libraries have similar information about military careers. However, to obtain detailed information about the latest commissioning programs, contact your local officer programs recruiter. There is no obligation. The Navy's toll free number for recruiter information is 1-800-USA-NAVY. Another strong source of information is the Navy recruiting website at www.navyjobs.com.

Air Force

OVERVIEW

The United States Air Force is the primary aerospace arm of our nation's armed forces. The men and women of the Air Force fly, maintain, and support the world's most technically advanced aerospace vehicles, including long-range bombers, supersonic fighters, Airborne Warning and Control System (AWACS) aircraft, and many others. These forces are used whenever and wherever necessary to protect the interests of the United States and our allies. The Air Force is made up of nearly 400,000 men and women – disciplined, dedicated, and professionally trained officers and airmen – from all walks of life. Some 76,000 officers pilot multimillion-dollar aircraft, launch satellites, gather sensitive intelligence data, manage maintenance and other logistical support, or do one of many tasks vital to the Air Force mission. The Air Force currently commissions about 5,000 male and female officers each year to fill openings in a wide variety of challenging careers.

BECOMING AN OFFICER

The Air Force commissions only United States citizens who possess a bachelor's degree from an accredited college. Depending on the career field an applicant selects, additional academic qualifications may be required (e.g., a graduate degree, specific courses). Applicants for a commission must also be physically fit and of high moral character. Typically, men and women may earn commissions through one of three precommissioning sources: The U.S. Air Force Academy, Air Force Reserve Officer Training Corps (AFROTC), or Officer Training School (OTS). Individuals in some professions may obtain a direct commission without attending one of the above commissioning programs.

U.S. Air Force Academy

Located at the foot of the Rocky Mountains near Colorado Springs, Colorado, the Air Force Academy annually accepts about 1,200 young men and women into its four-year program. Graduates earn a bachelor of science degree and an Air Force commission.

The program is intense, with a well-balanced curriculum that includes the physical and social sciences, humanities, and math. In addition, the academy provides cadets with a background in space operations through courses such as astrodynamics and aeroengineering.

Admission to the Air Force Academy is generally made through nominations from United States Senators or Representatives, but other avenues to receive an admission appointment are available.

Air Force Reserve Officer Training Corps (AFROTC)

This program gives college students a unique opportunity to earn a commission while they complete their degree requirements. The AFROTC offers four- and two-year programs (in selected fields) at more than 1,000 colleges and universities across the nation. You apply for the four-year AFROTC program by simply enrolling in the aerospace studies course at the time you register for your other freshman courses. You may apply for the two-year AFROTC program if you have at least two years of undergraduate work remaining. Each cadet receives $150 a month tax free during the final two academic years. See your AFROTC representative about details on AFROTC program opportunities.

Scholarships are available for all programs on a competitive basis. Scholarships pay for most tuition, laboratory and incidental fees, and textbooks. Scholarship cadets also receive $150 tax free each month during the school year. High school students interested in the four-year scholarship should apply late in their junior year or early in their senior year of high school. College freshman and sophomores can apply by contacting the professor of aerospace studies at their college or university.

Officer Training School

The Officer Training School (OTS) at Maxwell AFB near Montgomery, Alabama, is a great opportunity for those who already have a bachelor's degree. Its rigorous 14-week program guides college graduates or airmen with degrees to commissions as Second Lieutenants. OTS cadets acquire the knowledge to perform as effective Air Force officers.

Direct Appointment

The Air Force directly commissions men and women in certain professions. Individuals are eligible for direct appointment if they are fully qualified in certain medical, legal, or religious fields. Individuals who believe they may be qualified for a direct commission should contact their nearest Air Force recruiter.

OFFICER TRAINING

Most new officers attend a technical training course immediately after coming on active duty. Technical training equips new officers with the specific skills required by their job specialty. Depending on the specialty, technical training lasts from a few weeks to over a year. (Some officers go directly to their first assignment without attending technical training.) Technical training centers are located at military installations throughout the United States. Upon completion of initial technical training, officers are assigned to an Air Force unit where they put their newly acquired skills to work.

At various points during a career as an Air Force officer, there is an opportunity to participate in professional military education – such as Squadron Officer School, Air Command and Staff College, and the Air War College. These programs prepare officers for the increasing responsibilities associated with career progression to the more senior grades in the Air Force. In addition, they provide the command and staff knowledge required to be a professional officer. Other educational opportunities are also available to Air Force officers.

ADVANCEMENT

Most newly commissioned officers enter the Air Force as Second Lieutenants. A few officers receive a direct appointment to a higher grade. There are established points when an officer is considered for promotion. Air Force promotions are based on future potential as demonstrated by past and current performance. Promotion to the grade of First Lieutenant usually occurs after two years of service. After an additional two years of service, most officers are promoted to Captain.

Subsequent promotions are competitive, and only the best-qualified officers are selected for promotion. Most officers compete for promotions without regard to their specific career specialty, though some officers (physicians, dentists, nurses, lawyers, chaplains, etc.) compete within their own specialties. There are provisions for early promotion of outstanding performers.

Most young officers (Lieutenants) start out in small units. As they gain experience and progress in rank (Captain), they are assigned to larger units, overseeing the operation of several smaller units. More senior officers (Majors and Lieutenant Colonels) are usually assigned as commanders of squadrons and are responsible for accomplishing that squadron's mission, as well as for the welfare of the men and women under their command. Colonels typically command large units or head major staff functions. Generals command combat organizations and oversee thousands of personnel and hundreds of millions of dollars in aircraft, supplies, and equipment.

EDUCATION PROGRAMS

The Air Force sponsors advanced education for qualified officers. Officers attending graduate school in their off-duty time can have the Air Force pay up to 75 percent of their tuition. The Air Force also sponsors officers' advanced education at the Air Force Institute of Technology (AFIT) or at one of the many civilian colleges throughout the country. The Air Force pays for all tuition, fees, books, and equipment and continues to provide full pay and benefits. AFIT provides scientific, technological, and other specialized education to satisfy Air Force requirements. Air Force-sponsored education leads to degrees in engineering, management, social sciences, and many other fields.

RESERVE FORCES

The reserve forces consist of two components, the Air National Guard and the Air Force Reserve. Their primary mission is to provide trained units and qualified personnel for active duty in the Air Force in time of war or national emergency and at such other times as the national security requires.

The reserve forces are highly trained, combat ready, and available for immediate call up to serve on active duty. They train (drill) regularly and provide a significant contribution to the daily operations of the Air Force as a by-product of their training. Guard and Reserve air crews currently fly the Air Force's front line aircraft.

Air National Guard

The Air National Guard (ANG) provides 89 major flying units and several hundred mission support units, with at least one flying unit in every state. During peacetime, the Guard also has a state mission that includes disaster relief, maintaining peace and order, and civilian defense. Guard units are under the control of the state governors through their Adjutants General. There are approximately 115,000 men and women in the ANG.

Criteria for appointment as an officer in the ANG are similar to those for active Air Force officers and are spelled out in Air Force instructions. However, selection and appointment to fill ANG unit vacancies are prerogatives of the states, with the Air Force granting federal recognition as reserve officers of the Air Force. Nonprior-service line officers selected for appointment in the ANG must attend six weeks of precommissioning training at the ANG Academy of Military Science, McGhee-Tyson AB, Knoxville, Tennessee, where they are prepared for their initial commissioned service in the ANG. Upon commissioning, many new ANG officers are scheduled to attend further Air Force training in their specialty. There are approximately 14,000 ANG officers, of which over 4,200 are pilots.

Air Force Reserve

The Air Force Reserve is a federal force. It provides 58 flying squadrons and nearly 400 mission support units. The Air Force Reserve has both "equipped" units with their own aircraft and "associate" units that fly and maintain active force aircraft and augment their active force counterparts during wartime or times of crisis.

The Air Force Reserve consists of approximately 78,000 men and women who train regularly, either in the units or as Individual Mobilization Augmentees (IMAs). IMAs are individual Reservists who train with active-duty Air Force organizations and who will augment those organizations for wartime, contingency, and limited peacetime requirements. There are approximately 12,400 IMAs.

Criteria for appointment as an officer in the Air Force Reserve are similar to those for active-duty Air Force officers and are discussed elsewhere in this guide. Nonprior-service personnel selected to be candidates for pilot or navigator training or to become engineers are sent to the Officer Training School along with the active-force line officer candidates. Reserve nonprior-service personnel who are not rated attend the Air National Guard Academy of Military Science. Medical officers attend an active-force short course at bases near Montgomery, Alabama. Each year, a small number of "deserving airmen" are selected to be commissioned from the enlisted ranks of the Air Force Reserve. They attend a two-week course at Maxwell AFB, Alabama, to learn officer skills.

There are approximately 15,000 Air Force Reserve officers (including IMAs). Approximately 2,300 are pilots and 350 are navigators. Over 21 percent of Reserve officers are women. The vast majority of the officer corps of the Air Force Reserve consists of prior-service officers who were commissioned through the Air Force Reserve Officer Training Corps, the Air Force Academy, or the Officer Training School and who served several years in the active Air Force before leaving extended active duty and joining the Air Force Reserve.

The focal point for recruiting officers in the Air Force Reserve and Air National Guard is the unit, since officers are basically recruited from each unit's local area. The Military Personnel Flights, located at each flying unit, are aware of all officer vacancies in both the flying units and the mission support units they service.

FOR FURTHER INFORMATION

High school guidance counselors and Air Force Recruiters can give you advice and information on Air Force ROTC programs, Officer Training School, and the Air Force Academy. Local Air Force selection officers have the latest information on commissioning programs and career opportunities; contact them if you have questions.

Marine Corps

OVERVIEW

The United States Marine Corps was created on November 10, 1775, by a resolution of the Continental Congress. Since then, the Marine Corps has grown to be one of the most elite fighting forces in the world. The Marine Corps' mission is unique among the five services; Marines serve on U.S. Navy ships, protect naval bases, guard U.S. embassies abroad, and serve as an ever-ready strike force to quickly protect the interests of the U.S. and its allies anywhere in the world. To perform the many duties of the Marine Corps, approximately 174,000 officers and enlisted Marines in the Corps fly planes and helicopters; operate radar equipment; drive armored vehicles; gather intelligence; survey and map territory; maintain and repair computers, jeeps, radios, trucks, tanks, and aircraft; and perform hundreds of other challenging jobs. Each year, the Marine Corps accepts approximately 1,600 new officers into its ranks to maintain its approximately 16,500-person officer corps.

BECOMING AN OFFICER

The Marine Corps recruits young men and women of high moral standards who have or will have a four-year college degree, are physically fit, and have demonstrated potential for leadership. Applicants must be U.S. citizens and pass the initial Marine Corps physical fitness test. Additionally, applicants must take either the SAT, ACT, or ASVAB aptitude tests. Minimum acceptable scores are: SAT – combined verbal and math scores of 1000; ACT – 45; and ASVAB – Electronics Repair composite – 115. The only age requirement is that a person must be at least 20 and less than 28 (waiverable to 35) years of age at the time of commissioning. Applicants for law programs must score a minimum of 30 on a 50-point scale, or 150 on a 180-point scale, of the LSAT.

Marine Corps officers are selected from various sources, including the Naval Reserve Officers' Training Corps (NROTC) Program, the United States Naval Academy, the Platoon Leaders Class (PLC) Program, and the Officer Candidate Class (OCC) Program.

Naval Reserve Officers' Training Corps

The NROTC Scholarship Program offers tuition and other financial benefits worth as much as $70,000 at one of more than 62 of the country's leading colleges and universities. Four-year NROTC scholarships are available to high school graduates on a competitive selection process in which consideration is given to such factors as high school record, college board scores, extracurricular activities, and leadership qualities.

Two- and three-year NROTC scholarships are available to college freshmen, sophomores, and juniors meeting basic requirements. Recipients are selected in a competitive process similar to that for the four-year scholarship.

U.S. Naval Academy

Since 1883, Marine Corps officers have been commissioned from the U.S. Naval Academy, where graduating midshipmen earn a bachelor of science degree either in one of seven different engineering programs or in one of eleven disciplines offered with an engineering emphasis. Annually, nearly 17 percent of each graduating class receives a regular Marine Corps commission.

Platoon Leaders Class

The Platoon Leaders Class (PLC) Program is for those college freshmen, sophomores, and juniors who have made the decision to pursue a Marine Corps officer commission. Application to this program may be made upon successful completion of the first semester or quarter of the freshman year. Applicants must be pursuing a four-year baccalaureate degree from an accredited college. They are eligible to receive $150 per month in financial assistance after successful completion of their first summer of training.

PLC officer candidates attend summer training sessions at the Marine Corps Officer Candidates School in Quantico, Virginia. Freshmen and sophomores participate in two six-week sessions, and juniors participate in one 10-week session.

Aviation guarantees in the PLC-Aviation Program are available to those who qualify. In this program, individuals can receive real flight experience and instruction to familiarize themselves with flying before military flight training begins.

PLC-Law is a post-baccalaureate degree program for law school attendees. Active duty is postponed until a student obtains a law degree and passes the bar examination.

Officer Candidate Class

The Officer Candidate Class (OCC) Program is pre-commission training for college seniors and graduates who desire to be Marine Corps officers. Upon graduation from college, candidates attend one 10-week officer training course and receive a reserve commission upon successful completion of training.

Women Officer Candidate Program

The Women Officer Candidate (WOC) Program is open to women in their junior and senior years of college or who have graduated from a four-year accredited institution. Training consists of a 10-week summer course in consolidated officer candidate companies. Women candidates participate in many of the same rigorous screening programs as their male counterparts, and when they successfully complete training, they receive a reserve commission as well.

In addition to the programs described above, the Marine Corps has programs for qualified enlisted personnel to earn commissions as officers. These programs include the Marine Enlisted Commissioning Education Program (MECEP), the Enlisted Commissioning Program (ECP), and the Meritorious Commissioning Program (MCP).

OFFICER TRAINING

The Marine Corps has developed career patterns to prepare its officers to assume progressively higher command and staff responsibilities. These career patterns are designed to provide individual training and education, followed by operational assignments. They allow officers to learn their professions and progress to sequentially more demanding assignments.

Officer training can generally be divided into three types. First, the Marine Corps maintains a system of professional military education that is progressive in nature. This education prepares officers for the increasing responsibilities associated with career progression to more senior grades in the Marine Corps. It is primarily the study of how to be an officer and apply the command and staff knowledge required of a professional. Examples of this type of training are the 23-week Basic Officers Course, which all newly commissioned officers attend, and the 43-week Command and Staff College for midgrade officers.

The second type of training encompasses the many specific skill-producing courses that are conducted to enable the officer to perform in a specialized area immediately upon assignment. Most Marine Corps officers attend one of these courses sponsored by the Corps, but they may also attend others conducted by the Navy or another service. An example of this type of initial training is pilot training conducted by the Navy. An example of follow-on skill progression training is the Weapons and Tactics Instructor Course designed for highly qualified aviation and command and control officers.

The third type of training provided to selected officers is either in-house or civilian advanced academic education. This type of training is designed to meet the Marine Corps' need for officers trained in specific technical, scientific, engineering, or managerial fields. Examples of this type of training are the U.S. Naval Post Graduate School and U.S. Naval Test Pilot School.

Each Marine Corps officer's training begins with the physically and mentally demanding Basic Officers Course and progresses to individual training specifically designed for his or her military occupational specialty (MOS). This unique training of the Marine Corps air-ground team provides all Marine Corps officers with a common background that is independent of their MOS.

ADVANCEMENT

Marine Corps officers are selected for advancement based on their qualifications to fully meet the needs of the Marine Corps. Each individual's qualifications and performance of duty must clearly demonstrate that he or she would be capable of performing the duties normally associated with the next higher permanent grade. Every aspect of an officer's performance is carefully evaluated during the selection process to ensure that those selected for promotion are truly the best qualified.

The Marine Corps has an established career counseling system to provide officers with proper career guidance and counsel. Broad guidelines help to channel all officers to a rewarding, successful career.

After initial qualification in an MOS, officers are offered continued professional education, various duty assignments, and further MOS training. Junior officers can expect to perform not only as leaders, but as technicians and managers. Commonly, junior officers are put in charge of units consisting of anywhere from three or four, to over 100, Marines.

As junior officers become more proficient in their fields, opportunities arise for more challenging assignments and increased responsibility. Performance in these challenging situations directly relates to the continuance of a Marine Corps career. Although promotion boards review many factors, performance is the key to advancement.

EDUCATION PROGRAMS

The Marine Corps offers career education at every level in the officer ranks. Not only is formal schooling provided to enhance the professional development of officers, but the Marine Corps has an extensive correspondence course program available to all officers.

Especially inviting are the various graduate education programs made available to qualified officers; the Special Education Program, the Advanced Degree Program, the Excess Leave Program-Law, and the Funded Law Education Program.

Special Education Program

The Special Education Program (SEP) is a fully funded program designed to build up the Marine Corps' pool of officers with specialties in both technical and non-technical disciplines. Officers accepted into and completing the program earn master's degrees in designated disciplines by attending the Naval Postgraduate School, the Air Force Institute of Technology, or approved civilian schools.

Advanced Degree Program

Under the Advanced Degree Program (ADP), expenses for the cost of a master's degree are partially funded. Officers are selected to study in a particular technical or non-technical discipline and may attend the accredited school of their choice. While in this and the SEP program, officers continue to receive all pay and allowances.

A sample of the types of disciplines officers may study while in either the ADP or the SEP includes space systems operations, defense systems analysis, management, public relations, computer science, electronic engineering, and telecommunications management.

Excess Leave Program-Law

The Excess Leave Program-Law (ELP-L) provides qualified Marine Corps officers the opportunity to take time off from active duty to attend an accredited law school at their own expense. While participating in the ELP-L, officers receive no pay or allowances.

Funded Law Education Program

Under the Funded Law Education Program (FLEP), Marine Corps officers attend an accredited law school of their choice, with the Marine Corps paying their tuition and expenses. Full pay and allowances are provided to those officers in the FLEP.

RESERVE OFFICERS

The Marine Corps Reserve plays a vital role in the augmentation of the regular force. Hard work and dedication are keys to maintaining a combat-ready force capable of responding, at any time, to the call to active duty. Reserve officers have an especially challenging role in maintaining this ready force.

Currently, 8,000 Reserve officers serve on active duty, and 8,054 Reserve officers are assigned to Selected Marine Corps Reserve (SMCR) units or the Individual Ready Reserve (IRR).

Reserve officers serve in the same types of duties and job assignments as their regular counterparts. The main difference is that they serve part-time, one weekend each month and two weeks of continuous duty each year. Regular officers serve full-time, all year round.

FOR FURTHER INFORMATION

The above information is only a broad overview of the exciting challenges available to Marine Corps officers. Young men and women desiring more information about Marine Corps officer opportunities should contact a local Marine Corps officer selection officer by calling 1-800-MARINES or by sending a message by e-mail to recruiting@MQG-SMTP3.USMC.MIL.

Coast Guard

OVERVIEW

The United States Coast Guard regularly performs many functions vital to maritime safety. The Coast Guard's most visible job is saving lives and property in and around American waters. The Coast Guard also enforces customs and fishing laws, protects marine wildlife, fights pollution on our lakes and along the coastline, and conducts the International Ice Patrol. The Coast Guard is also responsible for monitoring traffic in major harbors, keeping shipping lanes open on ice-bound lakes, and maintaining lighthouses and other navigation aids.

The Coast Guard is a part of the U.S. Department of Transportation. In time of war it may be placed under the command of the Navy, which operates within the Department of Defense. A vital part of the Armed Services, the Coast Guard has participated in every major American military campaign. The Coast Guard is the smallest of the armed services. Currently there are over 5,580 commissioned officers and 1,490 warrant officers. Coast Guard officers perform in many different occupations to support the mission of the Coast Guard. Each year, the Coast Guard has openings for about 300 new officers (in addition to Academy) in a wide range of challenging careers.

BECOMING AN OFFICER

There are four programs leading to a commission as an officer in the U.S. Coast Guard – the Coast Guard Academy, Officer Candidate School, direct commissioning, and appointment as a chief warrant officer. Applicants for all programs must be physically qualified, U.S. citizens, and possess high moral character.

The U.S. Coast Guard Academy

The U.S. Coast Guard Academy, located in New London, Connecticut, accepts about 250 young men and women into its program each year. The four-year academic program leads to a bachelor of science degree in a variety of majors. Approximately 75 percent of the academy graduates earn degrees in technical areas such as engineering, sciences, and mathematics.

Each major provides a sound undergraduate education in a field of interest to the Coast Guard and prepares the cadet to assume initial duty as a junior officer. Upon graduation, the cadet is commissioned as an Ensign in the Coast Guard.

Appointment as a cadet is based solely on an annual nationwide competition. It is not necessary to obtain a nomination from a Senator or Representative. The competition includes either the College Board Scholastic Aptitude Test (SAT) or the American College Testing Assessment (ACT), high school rank in class, community service, and leadership qualities. Interested students should apply during the fall of their senior year in high school.

Officer Candidate School

The Officer Candidate School (OCS) is pre-commissioning training for college graduates who want to become Coast Guard officers. Candidates attend a 17-week officer training course at New London, Connecticut. The physical and academic curriculum is demanding. In addition to physical training, OCS candidates study navigation, cutter operations, seamanship, Coast Guard orientation, and leadership. After completing OCS, candidates are commissioned as Ensigns in the Coast Guard Reserve.

Direct Commissions

Graduates from a law school accredited by the American Bar Association are eligible to receive commissions as Lieutenant Junior Grade in the Coast Guard Reserve. The applicant must be admitted to the bar of a state or federal court within one year of receiving a commission. Qualified graduates of state and federal maritime academies may also be eligible for a commission as an Ensign or Lieutenant Junior Grade in the Coast Guard Reserve. Engineers are highly sought after and may be directly commissioned up to the rank of Lieutenant. Occasionally, direct commissions may be available for ROTC/NROTC/AFROTC students at selected colleges and universities, prior military officers, and qualified military pilots. Qualified military pilots may compete for direct commissions as aviators in the rank of Ensign or Lieutenant Junior Grade in the Coast Guard Reserve.

TRAINING

Newly commissioned officers are offered a wide variety of mission opportunities for their first assignment. This duty will be in one of the Coast Guard's primary missions, such as search and rescue, marine law enforcement, drug interdiction, or aids to navigation. All officers are encouraged to apply for postgraduate education or specialized training. The Coast Guard provides training in a range of career areas. Coast Guard pilot training is available to selected graduates of the Coast Guard Academy or Officer Candidate School. Pilot trainees attend 14 months of basic and advanced flight training at naval air stations in Pensacola, Florida, Mobile, Alabama, or Corpus Christi, Texas. Many other courses are provided to instruct officers in specific skills needed for a particular assignment. In addition, there are opportunities to participate in professional military education at schools such as the Armed Forces Staff College, the Industrial College of the Armed Forces, or one of the colleges run by another branch of the service.

College Student Pre-commissioning Initiative (CSPI)

The College Student Pre-commissioning Initiative (CSPI) is available to students attending Historically Black Colleges and Universities, member schools of the Hispanic Association of Colleges and Universities, and other approved institutions of higher learning. CSPI Requirements include the following:

- Score a 1000 on the SAT, 1100 on the SAT II, 21 on the ACT, or an ASVAB General Technical of 110 or higher.

- Be between 21 and 26 years of age at the time of your college graduation

- Be a United States citizen

- Be a sophomore or junior enrolled in a four-year degree program at an HBCU, HACU or other approved institution

- Meet all physical requirements for a Coast Guard commission

- Maintain a 2.5 GPA or better.

EDUCATION PROGRAMS

The Coast Guard believes strongly in the continued education of its members. The Coast Guard offers several education assistance programs, including the Tuition Assistance Program, the Physician's Assistant Program, and the Postgraduate Education Program.

Tuition Assistance Program

The Coast Guard sponsors a tuition assistance program for off-duty education within the limits of available funds. This program allows Coast Guard members to enroll in off-duty courses at accredited colleges and universities. The tuition is paid by the Coast Guard for all courses not in excess of six credits per semester (or quarter) or for any course not extending beyond one semester or a maximum of 17 weeks, whichever is longer.

Physician's Assistant Program

The Physician's Assistant Program is a two-year, full-time course of study at Sheppard AFB, Wichita Falls, Texas, offered to warrant officers in the medical specialty. The program includes 12 months of study and 12 months of clinical rotation at an Air Force hospital. Upon successful completion, Coast Guard graduates receive their certificates as physician's assistants and promotion to Lieutenant (O-3). Completion of the program results in a bachelor's degree in Health Science.

Postgraduate Education Program

The Coast Guard offers qualified officers an opportunity to obtain advanced education on a full-time basis at the Coast Guard's expense. Each year, approximately 125 officers are selected for this program. They attend various colleges and universities in over 30 major curriculum areas. Entry into this program is competitive, and only the best qualified officers are selected.

FOR FURTHER INFORMATION

Although the preceding section gives a general overview of the Coast Guard and its programs, it by no means covers the wide range of opportunities available in the Coast Guard. Your local Coast Guard recruiter would be pleased to supply you with more detailed Coast Guard career information. The Coast Guard toll-free information number is 1-877-NOW-USCG, ext. 1704.

Officer Occupational Descriptions

Combat Specialty Occupations

Combat specialty officers plan and direct military operations, oversee combat activities, and serve as combat leaders. This category includes officers in charge of tanks and other armored assault vehicles, artillery systems, special forces, and infantry. They normally specialize by the type of unit that they lead. Within the unit, they may specialize by the type of weapon system. Artillery and missile system officers, for example, direct personnel as they target, launch, test, and maintain various types of missiles and artillery. Special forces officers lead their units in offensive raids, demolitions, intelligence gathering, and search and rescue missions.

- Amored Assault Vehicle Officers
  Profile: Gideon Gravatt
- Artillery and Missile Officers
- Combat Mission Support Officers
- Infantry Officers
  Profile: Wayne Garvey
- Special Forces Officers

ARMORED ASSAULT VEHICLE OFFICERS

In peacetime, armored units stay ready to defend the country anywhere in the world. In combat, they operate tanks, armored vehicles, amphibious and other types of assault vehicles to engage and destroy the enemy. Armored assault vehicle officers lead tank and armor units. They normally specialize by type of unit, such as armor, light armor (cavalry), or amphibious assault.

What They Do

Armored assault vehicle officers in the military perform some or all of the following duties:

- Gather and evaluate intelligence on enemy strength and positions
- Formulate battle plans
- Coordinate actions with infantry, artillery, and air support units
- Plan and direct communications
- Direct operations of tanks, amphibious assault vehicles, support equipment, and troops
- Plan and supervise tactical and technical training of an armored unit
- Direct unit administrative activities

Physical Demands

Armor officers must meet the same demanding physical requirements as the troops they command. They must be physically fit and able to hold up under the stress of combat conditions.

Special Requirements

A 4-year college degree is normally required to enter this occupation. This occupation is open only to men.

Helpful Attributes

Helpful fields of study include engineering, geography, physical sciences, history, and business or public administration. Helpful attributes include:

- Ability to motivate and lead others
- Willingness to accept a challenge and face danger
- Decisiveness
- Ability to work well under stress
- Interest in armored equipment and battlefield strategy

Work Environment

Tank officers work and train in all climates and weather conditions. To remain ready for combat, tank units must regularly train under simulated combat conditions. During these exercises, tank officers are on the move, working, eating, and sleeping outdoors and in tents. When not in training, tank officers perform administrative duties in offices.

Training Provided

Job training consists of 4 to 20 weeks of classroom and field training. Training length varies depending on specialty. Course content typically includes:

- Weapons and equipment maintenance
- Armor operations, principles, and tactics
- Night maneuvers
- Role of the platoon leader

Further training occurs on the job and through specialized courses.

Civilian Counterparts

Although the job of armored assault vehicle officer has no equivalent in civilian life, the leadership and administrative skills it provides are similar to those used in many civilian managerial occupations.

Opportunities

The services have about 4,500 armored assault vehicle officers. Each year, they need new armor officers due to changes in personnel and the demands of the field. New tank officers are assigned to tank and armor units as platoon leaders. Advancement in armor is based on ability to lead. Armor officers with proven ability to lead may assume command positions.

INTEREST CODE

This occupation generally appeals to people whose primary Interest Code is *Enterprising. Enterprising* jobs:

- Are fast-paced
- Require that you take on a lot of responsibility

Pages 8 and 9 explain the Interest Codes

Profile: Lt. Gideon Gravatt

Gideon Gravatt was raised with his brothers and sister by a single mother in St. Louis. For much of his childhood, the family struggled on welfare often wondering where the next meal was coming from. When Gideon was 17, a Marine Corps recruiter called him and asked if he had considered the military. Gideon and his older brother had both talked about the military as a way to a new and better life. Although Gideon excelled in high school, graduating in the top 10% of his class, he was not ready to pursue further education right away. He decided to enlist in the Marine Corps and went to boot camp in San Diego the summer after he graduated. After boot camp, Gideon attended combat training at Camp Pendleton and then went to Fort Knox to learn to become a tank mechanic. While at Fort Knox, Gideon was surprised to learn that he had been selected to enter the Reserve Officers' Training Corps (ROTC).

Although he initially had decided he was not ready to go to college, he did not want to pass up the opportunity for a free education. He was able to choose the college program of his choice and decided to attend Purdue University where he obtained a bachelor's degree in history. During his summers, he attended military training which took him to different locations including England, France, Spain, Italy, and Greece.

After graduating from college, Gideon received further training from the Marine Corps preparing to be an armor officer. His first assignment was as a platoon commander at Twentynine Palms Marine Corps Combat Center in California. As a platoon commander, Gideon was responsible for leading his tank unit in combat simulation exercises. These training exercises were essential to ensure that they would be ready to respond in the event of a real battle. Gideon also had the opportunity to participate in training exercises overseas in Kuwait where he described the "thrill of driving his tank at 50 miles per hour across the desert firing on the move." After serving as a platoon commander, he acted as the company commander in charge of several tank platoons.

Gideon is currently stationed at Marine Corps Headquarters in Quantico, Virginia where he is increasing his skills and experience in the areas of technology and communications. Prior to starting his next field assignment, he will have the opportunity to receive advanced training in armor or amphibious warfare.

SAMPLE CAREER PATH

Battalion Commander　　　　15–18 years

Battalion commanders are in charge of an armor battalion consisting of several companies, usually around 56 armored vehicles and several hundred men. They plan training exercises or missions and instruct company commanders on mission assignments and objectives. They coordinate battle plans with other combat, intelligence and support units.

Armor Staff Officer　　　　9–11 years

Armor staff officers assist their battalion commander in administration and management duties. They manage a specialized function such as logistics or operations for a battalion or headquarters staff and advise senior commanders on armor operations and readiness. They also resolve unit supply, maintenance, or personnel problems. They may also teach armored vehicle training courses.

Company Commander　　　　4 years

Company commanders lead an armor company consisting of several platoons, around 16 armored vehicles. They develop and carry out training plans, field exercises and battle plans to support battalion objectives. They explain plans and exercises to platoon leaders and assign unit objectives.

Platoon Leader

Platoon leaders train and lead an armored assault vehicle platoon of 4 vehicles and 12-16 soldiers and inspect vehicles, troops, barracks, and equipment. They also plan daily conditioning programs for their platoon and lead the in combat training exercises. Platoon leaders direct the care and maintenance of vehicles, radios, and other equipment assigned to their unit.

(This sample career path is for tank officers. Career paths for amphibious assault and other types of armored assault vehicle officers may be different.)

The years shown represent typical time-in-service before advancement to that level. Actual career advancement depends on individual experience and performance.

ARTILLERY AND MISSILE OFFICERS

The United States military uses some of the most technologically advanced weapon systems in the world from artillery weapons such as cannons and rockets to guided missiles that can be launched from land, air, or sea. The effective use of these systems requires technical expertise and sound military judgement. Artillery and missile officers direct artillery and missile crew members as they position, target, and fire weapons. They normally specialize by type of weapon system.

What They Do

Artillery and missile officers in the military perform some or all of the following duties:

- Direct training activities of artillery and missile crew members
- Direct fire control operations and firing procedures
- Select location of artillery and missile strikes and coordinate their use with other combat units
- Direct maintenance of artillery and missile system equipment
- Direct testing and inspection of artillery and missile systems
- Direct security operations at missile sites

Physical Demands

Physical requirements vary depending upon the type of weapon system to which the officer is assigned. In most instances artillery and missile officers must meet very demanding physical requirements. They must be able to perform effectively for long periods of time under stressful conditions.

Special Requirements

A 4-year college degree is normally required to enter this occupation. Some specialties within this occupation are closed to women, and for others a master's degree in management is preferred.

Helpful Attributes

Helpful fields of study include engineering, physics, chemistry, computer science, and business or public administration. Also, some helpful attributes include:

- Ability to motivate and lead others
- Ability to remain calm in stressful situations
- Ability to learn and perform complex procedures
- Decisiveness

Training Provided

Job training consists of between 3 to 19 weeks of classroom instruction and field training. Training length varies depending upon specialty. Course content typically includes:

- Artillery tactics
- Ammunition handling procedures
- Fire direction control procedures
- Missile targeting
- Security coding and authentication procedures
- Launch operations
- Maintenance programs

Further training occurs on the job and through advanced courses.

Work Environment

Artillery and missile officers work under different conditions depending on the type of weapon system they are responsible for. Some artillery officers spend a lot of time in field training exercises, where they work, eat, and sleep outdoors and in tents. Others live and work aboard ships. Missile system officers may work in locations such as underground launch command centers, or submarines.

Civilian Counterparts

Although the job of artillery and missile officer has no equivalent in civilian life, the leadership skills it provides are similar to those desired by many civilian employers.

Opportunities

The services have about 12,000 artillery and missile officers. Each year, they need new artillery and missile officers due to changes in personnel and the demands of the field. After initial job training, new artillery and missile officers usually work under the direction of more experienced officers as they direct artillery units or gain more experience in missile operations. After demonstrating leadership ability, they may advance to senior management and command positions.

INTEREST CODE

This occupation generally appeals to people whose primary Interest Code is *Enterprising. Enterprising* jobs:

- Are fast-paced
- Require that you take on a lot of responsibility

Pages 8 and 9 explain the Interest Codes

COMBAT MISSION SUPPORT OFFICERS

Military combat operations require careful planning and coordination of combat resources. Combat mission support officers ensure that everything is in the right place at the right time during military operations. They provide battle management from specialized aircraft, ground locations, and ships. Combat mission support officers normally specialize according to their area of expertise.

What They Do

Combat mission support officers in the military perform some or all of the following duties:

- Develop plans, policies, and procedures for battle management

- Train, establish standards, and conduct evaluations of unit personnel

- Advise commanders of ground, air, and naval units on deployment of combat forces

- Assist in the planning and execution of combat operations

- Direct the movement of resources within the combat zone

Physical Requirements

Combat mission support officers must meet different physical requirements depending on their specialty. Those that work on an aircraft, for example, must pass a special physical exam to quality for flight duty.

Helpful Attributes

Helpful attributes include:

- Ability to coordinate with others

- Ability to make decisions in stressful situations

- Ability to absorb large amounts of data in a short period of time

- Ability to manage a large staff

Special Requirements

A 4-year college degree is normally required to enter this occupation.

Training Provided

Job training consists of classroom instruction and field training under simulated combat situations. Training length varies depending on position. Course content typically includes:

- Battle tactics and management

- Relationships among air, ground, and naval forces

- Capabilities of weapon systems

- Communications systems

Work Environment

Combat mission support officers work in a variety of settings. Some work in offices or command and control centers. Others work primarily outdoors in the field during training exercises and actual combat situations. Depending on the service branch and specialty, combat mission support officers may work in aircraft, and aboard ships.

Civilian Counterparts

There are no direct civilian counterparts for combat mission support officer specialties. However, their leadership ability and management skills are sought after by many organizations in the public and private sector.

Opportunities

The services have about 2,000 combat mission support officers. Each year, they need new officers due to changes in personnel and the demands of the field. After job training, combat mission support officers typically assist commanders in battle management activities. Based on performance and demonstrated leadership ability, they may become responsible for larger forces.

INTEREST CODE

This occupation generally appeals to people whose primary Interest Code is *Enterprising. Enterprising* jobs:

- Are fast-paced
- Require that you take on a lot of responsibility

Pages 8 and 9 explain the Interest Codes

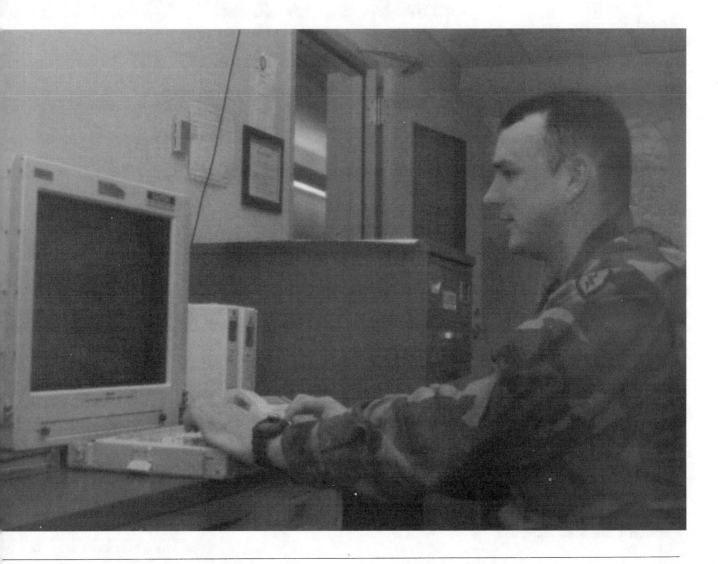

INFANTRY OFFICERS

In peacetime, the infantry stays ready to defend the country anywhere in the world. In combat, the infantry is deployed to capture or destroy enemy forces on the ground and to repel enemy invasions. Infantry officers direct, train, and lead infantry units.

What They Do

Infantry officers in the military perform some or all of the following duties:

- Gather and evaluate intelligence on enemy strength and positions

- Develop offensive and defensive battle plans

- Coordinate plans with armor, artillery, and air support units

- Direct construction of bunkers, fortifications, and obstacles to support and camouflage infantry positions

- Direct the use of infantry weapons and equipment, such as machine guns, mortars, rocket launchers, and armored personnel carriers

- Develop and supervise infantry unit training

- Direct administrative activities

Physical Demands

Infantry officers must meet the same demanding physical requirements as the infantrymen they command. They must be in excellent physical condition to perform strenuous activities over long periods of time, sometimes without sleep or rest.

Helpful Attributes

Helpful fields of study include engineering, history, physical education, and business or public administration. Helpful attributes include:

- Ability to motivate and lead others

- Willingness to accept a challenge and face danger

- Interest in land battle history and strategy

Special Requirements

A 4-year college degree is normally required to enter this occupation. This occupation is open only to men.

Work Environment

Because infantry officers must be prepared to lead their troops anywhere in the world that the infantry is needed, they work and train in all climates and weather conditions. During training exercises, as in real combat situations, infantry officers work, eat, and sleep outdoors and in tents. When not in the field, infantry officers perform administrative and management duties in offices.

Training Provided

Job training consists of 8 to 14 weeks of classroom instruction and field training under simulated combat conditions. Training length varies depending on specialty. Course content typically includes:

- Infantry leadership roles

- Infantry squad and platoon tactics

- Modern offensive and defensive combat techniques

Civilian Counterparts

Although the job of infantry officer has no equivalent in civilian life, the leadership and administrative skills it provides are similar to those used in many civilian managerial occupations.

Opportunities

The services have about 7,000 infantry officers. Each year, they need new infantry officers due to changes in personnel and the demands of the field. After job training, infantry officers are assigned to infantry units as platoon leaders. They direct training and tactical exercises for wargames. Advancement in the infantry is based on ability to lead. Infantry officers with proven ability to lead may assume command positions.

INTEREST CODE

This occupation generally appeals to people whose primary Interest Code is *Enterprising. Enterprising* jobs:

- Are fast-paced

- Require that you take on a lot of responsibility

Pages 8 and 9 explain the Interest Codes

Profile: Wayne Garvey

Growing up in a small town in Texas, Wayne Garvey enjoyed working outdoors and knew he would like the life of a soldier. During his ROTC training at the Virginia Military Institute (VMI), Wayne heard an infantry officer talk about his profession. "I was impressed by his orientation to people and the emphasis the Army places on individual and team effort, professionalism, and dedication."

Wayne graduated from VMI, earning a commission in the Reserves. He qualified for a delayed entry to active duty, and used the time to go to law school. After admission to the bar, he began active duty. His first assignment following basic infantry and airborne training was to the 101st Airborne, Fort Campbell, KY, as a weapons platoon leader. Wayne also served as a company executive officer and as battalion adjutant, monitoring administration.

His next tour was in the Middle East as a platoon leader during Operation Desert Storm. Wayne led his platoon into many combat actions and earned several decorations, including the Silver Star, the nation's third highest award for gallantry. He also spent part of his tour on the headquarters staff before returning home. During this tour, he advanced to captain.

With his service obligation complete, Wayne left the Army. He practiced law and was very successful. "But," he says, "I missed the Army every day of those 2 years." He and his wife made the decision together to return to Army life.

Shortly after his return to the Army, Wayne was assigned to the Army Military Academy at West Point where he taught military tactics.

Since West Point, Wayne has served several tours on various Army staffs; in one tour he assigned infantry officers to positions throughout the world. He also commanded an infantry battalion in Korea. "This was a real milestone," he says, "a real highlight of my career to date."

Recently selected for the highest level officers' courses at the Army War College, Wayne says about his service, "Even the bad days have been good. I have really enjoyed my career!"

SAMPLE CAREER PATH

Battalion Commander — 15-18 years

Battalion commanders are in charge of a battalion consisting of several companies, usually between 500 and 1,000 men. They plan training exercises or missions and instruct company commanders on mission assignments and objectives. They also coordinate battle plans with other combat, intelligence and support units.

Infantry Staff Officer — 9-11 years

Infantry staff officers assist their battalion commander in administration and management duties. They manage a specialized function such as logistics or operations and advise senior commanders on infantry operations and readiness. They may also teach infantry courses.

Company Commander — 4 years

Company commanders lead an infantry company consisting of several platoons. They develop and carry out training plans, field exercises, and battle plans to support battalion objectives. They also explain plans and exercises to platoon leaders and assign unit objectives.

Platoon Leader

Platoon leaders train and lead an infantry platoon of 30 to 50 soldiers. They conduct inspections, plan daily conditioning programs, and lead combat exercises. Platoon leaders also direct the care and maintenance of weapons, radios, and other equipment assigned to their unit.

The years shown represent typical time-in-service before advancement to that level. Actual career advancement depends on individual experience and performance.

SPECIAL FORCES OFFICERS

Each service has specially trained forces to perform rapid strike missions. These elite forces stay in a constant state of readiness to strike anywhere in the world on a moment's notice. Special forces officers lead special operations forces in offensive raids, demolitions, intelligence gathering, and search and rescue missions. Due to the wide variety of missions, special forces officers are trained swimmers, parachutists, and survival experts.

What They Do

Special forces officers in the military perform some or all of the following duties:

- Train personnel in parachute, scuba diving, and special combat techniques

- Plan missions and coordinate plans with other forces as needed

- Train personnel for special missions using simulated mission conditions

- Lead special forces teams in accomplishing mission objectives

- Direct and supervise administrative activities of special forces units

Physical Demands

Special forces officers must meet very demanding physical requirements. Good eyesight, night vision, and physical conditioning are required to reach mission objectives by parachute, over land, or under water. Good eye-hand coordination is required to detonate or deactivate explosives. In most instances, special operations officers are required to be qualified swimmers, parachutists, and endurance runners.

Special Requirements

A 4-year college degree is normally required to enter this occupation. Selection as a special operations officer is very competitive. This occupation is open only to men.

Helpful Attributes

Helpful fields of study include physical education, engineering, physical sciences, history, and business or public administration. Helpful attributes include:

- Ability to remain calm and decisive under stress

- Willingness to accept a challenge and face danger

- Willingness to stay in top physical condition

- Determination to complete a very demanding training program

Work Environment

Because special forces officers must be prepared to go anywhere in the world they are needed, they train and work in all climates, weather conditions, and settings. They may work in cold water and dive from submarines or small underwater craft. They may also be exposed to harsh temperatures, often without protection, during missions into enemy-controlled areas.

Training Provided

Job training consists of up to 20 weeks of formal classroom training and practical experience. Training length varies depending on specialty. Course content typically includes:

- Physical conditioning, scuba diving, swimming, and parachuting

- Mission planning techniques

- Handling and using explosives

- Reconnaissance techniques

Additional training occurs on the job. Basic skills are kept sharp through planning and conducting exercises under simulated mission conditions.

Civilian Counterparts

Although the job of special forces officer has no equivalent in civilian life, the leadership and administrative skills it provides are similar to those used in many civilian management occupations, particularly law enforcement.

Opportunities

The services have about 2,500 special forces officers. Each year, they need new special forces officers due to changes in personnel and the demands of the field. After training, special forces officers usually assist commanders in directing special operations forces. After demonstrating leadership ability, they may assume command positions.

INTEREST CODE

This occupation generally appeals to people whose primary Interest Code is *Enterprising. Enterprising* jobs:

- Are fast-paced

- Require that you take on a lot of responsibility

Pages 8 and 9 explain the Interest Codes

Engineering, Science, and Technical Occupations

Engineering, science, and technical officers have a wide range of responsibilities based on their area of expertise. They lead or perform activities in areas such as information technology, environmental health and safety, and engineering. For instance, these officers may direct the operations of communications centers or the development of complex computer systems. Environmental health and safety officers study the air, ground, and water to identify and analyze sources of pollution and its effects. They also direct programs to control safety and health hazards in the work place. Other personnel may work as aerospace engineers to design and direct the development of military aircraft, missiles, and spacecraft.

- Aerospace Engineers
- Civil Engineers
  - *Profile: Philip Thompson*
- Communications Managers
  - *Profile: Larry Cannon*
- Computer Systems Officers
- Electrical and Electronics Engineers
- Environmental Health and Safety Officers
- Industrial Engineers
- Intelligence Officers
  - *Profile: Teresa Alvarez*
- Lawyers and Judges
  - *Profile: Samuel E. Jackson*
- Life Scientists
- Marine Engineers
- Nuclear Engineers
- Ordnance Officers
- Physical Scientists
- Space Operations Officers

AEROSPACE ENGINEERS

Although private companies build the military's aerospace equipment, military engineers are responsible for seeing that all equipment meets service needs. Aerospace engineers design and direct the development of military aircraft, missiles, and spacecraft.

What They Do

Aerospace engineers in the military perform some or all of the following duties:

- Plan and conduct research on aircraft guidance, propulsion, and weapons systems

- Study new designs for aircraft, missiles, and spacecraft

- Help select private companies to build military aircraft, missiles, and spacecraft

- Monitor production of aircraft, missiles, and spacecraft

- Decide what tests should be conducted of prototypes (full-scale test models)

- Conduct stress analysis and wind tunnel tests with aircraft and missile prototypes

Special Requirements

A 4-year college degree in aeronautical, astronautical, or mechanical engineering is required to enter this occupation.

Helpful Attributes

Helpful attributes include:

- Interest in concepts and principles of engineering

- Interest in working with mathematical formulas

- Interest in planning and directing research projects

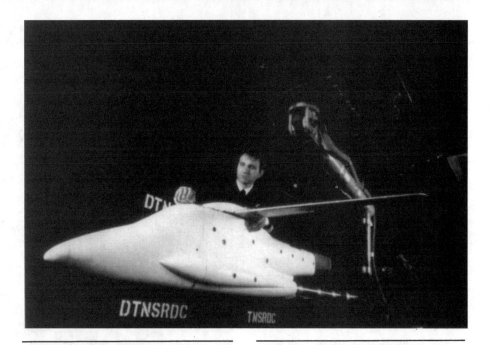

Work Environment

Aerospace engineers work in offices or laboratories.

Training Provided

No initial job training is provided to officers in this occupation.

Civilian Counterparts

Civilian aerospace engineers usually work in the aircraft manufacturing industry. Some work for the Department of Defense, the National Aeronautics and Space Administration (NASA), and other government agencies. As in the military, civilian aerospace engineers may specialize in one type of aerospace product, such as aircraft, missiles, or space vehicles. They may also specialize in engineering specialties such as product design, testing, or production research. Depending on their specialty, they may be called aeronautical engineers, aeronautical test engineers, or stress analysts.

Opportunities

The services have about 1,600 aerospace engineers. Each year, they need new engineers due to changes in personnel and the demands of the field. Newly commissioned aerospace engineers are usually assigned to engineering research and development units or laboratories. They work under the direction of experienced officers conducting research. With experience, they may serve as research and development managers or laboratory managers.

INTEREST CODE

This occupation generally appeals to people whose primary Interest Code is *Investigative. Investigative* jobs:

- Involve learning about a new subject area

- Allow you to use your knowledge to solve problems or create things or ideas

Pages 8 and 9 explain the Interest Codes

CIVIL ENGINEERS

Airfields, roads, bridges, buildings, power plants, docks, and water treatment plants on military bases around the world are continually being built, repaired, and improved. Civil engineers plan, design, and direct the construction of military facilities.

What They Do

Civil engineers in the military perform some or all of the following duties:

- Study the need for roads, airfields, buildings, and other facilities

- Direct surveys of construction areas

- Design construction projects

- Help select contractors to build facilities

- Check construction progress to see that it meets plans

- Plan and direct facility maintenance and modernization

- Plan temporary facilities for use in emergencies

- Keep master plans for military bases up to date

Special Requirements

A 4-year college degree in civil, architectural, sanitary, or environmental engineering, or another closely related field is required to enter this occupation.

Helpful Attributes

Helpful attributes include:

- Interest in engineering principles and concepts

- Interest in working with mathematical formulas

Work Environment

Civil engineers work in offices when designing projects or reviewing reports. They work outdoors when overseeing survey or construction activities.

Training Provided

No initial job training is provided to officers in this occupation. However, advanced courses are offered to support medical service and environmental control building programs.

Civilian Counterparts

Civilian civil engineers work for engineering firms, construction companies, and government agencies. Some may work for public utilities, railroads, and manufacturing firms. Civilian civil engineers perform duties similar to those performed in the military; however, they often specialize in certain types of projects.

Opportunities

The services have about 7,000 civil engineers. Each year, they need new engineers due to changes in personnel and the demands of the field. Newly commissioned civil engineers usually assist senior engineering officers in planning and design. With experience, they may manage construction projects and eventually, engineering offices. In time they may advance to senior management or command positions in the engineering field.

INTEREST CODE

This occupation generally appeals to people whose primary Interest Code is *Investigative. Investigative* jobs:

- Involve learning about a new subject area

- Allow you to use your knowledge to solve problems or create things or ideas

Pages 8 and 9 explain the Interest Codes

Profile: Philip Thompson

Phil Thompson joined the Navy Reserves while he was in college studying civil engineering. "I looked into the Navy's Civil Engineer Corps," he says, "and liked what I saw." After graduation, he went to Officer Candidate School in Newport, RI, and then to Civil Engineer Corps Officer School in Port Hueneme, CA.

Phil's first assignment was to Guam. As a new Civil Engineer Corps ensign (O-1), Phil had 400 civilians working for him. He also had a large budget and responsibility for maintaining all Navy and Marine buildings and housing on the island. In his second year he was assigned as the Activities Civil Engineer (ACE). He managed a budget of $4 million and a large number of civilian workers. Phil liked the job so much that he asked to extend his tour of duty.

Phil enjoyed the public works side of civil engineering. For his next assignment, he went to the Naval Air Station Whidbey Island, WA. There, he directed facility maintenance forces, maintained three runways, two outlying airfields, roads, water, power, transportation, and everything needed to keep the base operating year-round.

Phil's most memorable tour was at the naval base at Guantanamo Bay, Cuba. He directed contractors building a water desalinization plant and an addition to the power plant. But his greatest satisfaction came from completely remodeling every home on the base. "We gutted and remade hot, uncomfortable houses into modern, fully air-conditioned units. It was really appreciated by the Navy and Marine Corps personnel and dependents living at Guantanamo," Phil says.

From his post in the Pentagon, where he monitors Navy planning and construction in the entire continental United States, Commander Phil Thompson is looking forward to taking some time off when he retires this fall. Looking back he says, "It's been 22 years of fun."

SAMPLE CAREER PATH

Director of Engineering   **15–18 years**

Directors of engineering command combat engineering or construction battalions of 500 to 750 military personnel. They direct all civil engineering operations at a military base and advise base or area commanders on civil engineering matters. They also direct planning and management of major engineering projects and evaluate construction bids submitted by civilian contractors.

Engineering Staff Officer   **9–11 years**

Engineering staff officers analyze and recommend design specifications for buildings, and other structures and determine construction project costs. They also lead other civil engineers and advise senior commanders on combat engineering or general construction matters.

Senior Engineer   **4 years**

Senior engineers plan and manage programs to maintain utilities, buildings, or roads on a military base and review plans and designs for engineering projects. They also command combat engineering companies of 65 to 200 enlisted personnel.

Civil Engineer

Civil engineers direct personnel in maintaining and constructing buildings and train enlisted personnel in construction techniques. They may also lead combat engineers in missions such as building fortifications, assembling mobile bridges, or preparing mine fields.

The years shown represent typical time-in-service before advancement to that level. Actual career advancement depends on individual experience and performance.

COMMUNICATIONS MANAGERS

Instant worldwide communication among air, sea, and land forces is vital to military operations. The services operate some of the largest and most complex communications networks in the world. Communications managers plan and direct the operation of military communication systems. They also manage personnel in communications centers and relay stations.

What They Do

Communications managers in the military perform some or all of the following duties:

- Develop rules and procedures for sending and receiving communications

- Direct personnel who operate computer systems and electronic telecommunications and satellite communications equipment

- Develop ways to track and ensure the security of communications equipment

- Direct personnel who maintain and repair communications equipment

- Develop budgets for communications centers.

Special Requirements

A 4-year college degree, preferably in engineering, mathematics, computer science, or related field, is usually required to enter this occupation.

Helpful Attributes

Helpful attributes include:

- Interest in working with computers, radios, and electronic equipment

- Interest in technical work

- Interest in planning and directing the work of others

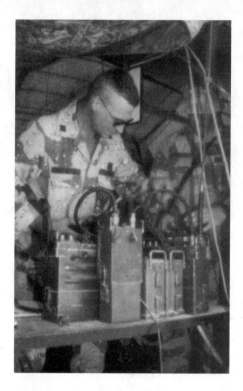

Training Provided

Job training consists of 12 to 32 weeks of classroom instruction. Training length varies depending on the specialty. Course content typically includes:

- Communications theory and security

- Communications-electronics management

- Satellite communications

- Electronic principles, technologies, and systems

- Tactical combat communications systems

Further training occurs on the job and through advanced courses.

Work Environment

Communications managers usually work in communications centers on land or aboard ships.

Civilian Counterparts

Civilian communications managers work for organizations in business and government to plan, develop, and manage their communications systems and networks. For example, large global companies with offices around the world often have their own systems and networks to make it easier for managers and employees to share information and communicate by phone, e-mail, or teleconference. With the exception of duties related to combat situations, civilian communications managers perform duties similar to their military counterparts.

Opportunities

The services have about 2,000 communications managers. Each year, they need new communications managers to meet the changing demands in the field. After job training, communications managers are assigned to manage or assist in managing a communications center. With experience, they may advance to senior management or command positions.

INTEREST CODE

This occupation generally appeals to people whose primary Interest Code is *Enterprising. Enterprising* jobs:

- Are fast-paced
- Require that you take on a lot of responsibility

Pages 8 and 9 explain the Interest Codes

Profile: Larry Cannon

Larry Cannon grew up on a farm in North Carolina. In high school, Larry excelled in both academics and athletics, but he did not have any real plans for the future. At the suggestion of one of his coaches, he applied for and received an athletic scholarship to Fayetteville State University. After a short time there, Larry found that although he loved sports, he did not enjoying playing in the college environment. He returned to his home town and spent some time working on the farm. He soon realized that living on the farm was definitely not what he wanted. When some of Larry's friends were making a trip to a local college, they convinced him to give college life another try. After he enrolled, Larry got a part-time job to help finance his studies. His manager had been in the military and talked a lot about the benefits of being in the Air Force. Larry wanted to know more about what the military had to offer, so he spoke to one of the Reserve Officer Training Corps (ROTC) instructors at his school. Larry did well on the Air Force Officer Qualification Test and was awarded a full ROTC scholarship.

Upon graduation from college, the Air Force sent Larry to electronics school to prepare him for his first assignment leading a mobile communications unit. His days were filled with the excitement of constant movement, travelling day or night by helicopter, tank, or jeep to set up communications equipment wherever and whenever needed.

Larry's next assignment took him to the Pacific island of Okinawa. As the Chief of the Communication Maintenance section, Larry managed millions of dollars in communications equipment and more than 300 personnel. The most rewarding part of the experience for Cannon and his family was the cultural exchange that came from living in a foreign country and making friends with local residents. Larry's next few assignments in California, Wyoming, and Washington broadened his expertise in communications management, and systems research and development (R&D). Larry had the opportunity to work as an advisor on communications issues on a design team for a missile system. Larry also spent time at the Pentagon in Washington, DC planning communications strategies.

Presently, Colonel Cannon is the Commander of the Communications Group at Andrew Air Force Base in Maryland where he manages a unit of over 500 personnel.

In addition to serving his country and excelling in his career field, Colonel Cannon is thankful for the opportunities he has had to travel to new places, meet new people, and continue his participation in sports as both a coach and a player.

SAMPLE CAREER PATH

Communications Director　　　**15–18 years**

Communications directors oversee the communications systems for a large facility or command. They determine the communications needs of large forces and plan the development of the needed systems. Directors also plan and manage the communications budget and workload. They are responsible for briefing top-level military leaders on communications matters.

Communications Staff Officer　　　**9–11 years**

Communications staff officers brief senior-level staff on communications and information capabilities. They oversee quality assurance and system security efforts. Communications staff officers also serve as a technical representatives and consultants on communications and information systems matters.

Senior Communications Managers　　　**4 years**

Senior communications managers oversee the operations of communications units. They gather functional needs for communications and computer systems and translate these into standard and cost efficient technical requirements. Senior officers also train new officers and assign work to subordinates.

Communications Managers

Communications managers plan, direct and supervise the installation and use of communications equipment and systems. They test, evaluate and accept modifications to existing systems and new equipment. Communications managers also plan, design and manage the integration of diverse types of communications and information systems.

The years shown represent typical time-in-service before advancement to that level. Actual career advancement depends on individual experience and performance.

COMPUTER SYSTEMS OFFICERS

The military uses computers in almost every aspect of its operations. Military computers are used to process payroll and personnel information, control the targeting and firing of weapons systems, account for money, and make it easier to communicate around the world. Computer systems officers direct the operations of computer centers and are involved in the planning and development of computer systems.

What They Do

Computer systems officers in the military perform some or all of the following duties:

- Assess information technology needs and develop plans and budgets

- Evaluate bids and monitor contracts for information technology products and services

- Plan and manage computer and network system security programs

- Analyze mission requirements and translate them into computer system requirements

- Lead the design, development, testing, and maintenance of computer software programs and data bases

- Plan and oversee the installation of new systems and equipment

- Direct teams of computer systems specialists

Training Provided

Job training consists of 5 to 18 weeks of classroom instruction. Training length varies depending on specialty. Course content typically includes:

- Fiscal and contract management

- Assessment of computer equipment needs

- Computer systems development and project management

Work Environment

Computer systems officers in the military work in offices or at computer sites on military bases or aboard ships.

Helpful Attributes

Helpful attributes include:

- Interest in technical work

- Interest in planning and directing the work of others

- Good organizational and management skills

Special Requirements

A 4-year college degree in computer science, computer or industrial engineering, business administration, or a related field is required to enter this occupation. Some specialties require a master's degree.

Civilian Counterparts

Civilian computer systems officers work for a wide variety of employers, such as banks, hospitals, manufacturers, financial firms, government agencies, and firms that design computer systems. They perform duties similar to those performed by military computer systems officers. They may also be called information systems directors, computer systems engineers, software engineers, or systems analysts.

Opportunities

The services have over 4,000 computer systems officers. Each year, they need new computer systems officers due to changes in personnel and the demands of the field. After job training, computer systems officers are assigned to units where they work in teams of engineers, systems analysts, and computer programmers. With experience and demonstrated leadership, they may advance to senior management or command positions in the computer systems field.

INTEREST CODE

This occupation generally appeals to people whose primary Interest Code is *Enterprising. Enterprising* jobs:

- Are fast-paced
- Require that you take on a lot of responsibility

Pages 8 and 9 explain the Interest Codes

ELECTRICAL AND ELECTRONICS ENGINEERS

Equipment such as radar, missile guidance systems, and communication equipment depends on advanced electronics. Electrical and electronics engineers design, develop, and test electrical and electronic equipment. They also direct equipment installation and repair.

What They Do

Electrical and electronics engineers in the military perform some or all of the following duties:

- Direct research to improve and develop computer, navigation, and other electronic systems
- Direct equipment installation and repair
- Develop test standards and operating instructions for electrical and electronic systems
- Design and develop test instruments
- Test new or modified equipment to check its performance and reliability
- Review test data, report results, and recommend actions

Special Requirements

A 4-year college degree in electrical or electronics engineering is required to enter this occupation.

Helpful Attributes

Helpful attributes include:

- Interest in engineering concepts and principles
- Interest in planning and directing research projects
- Interest in working with mathematical formulas

Work Environment

Electrical and electronics engineers usually work in offices while planning research studies and designing electronic systems. They may work outdoors when overseeing the installation of new equipment.

Training Provided

Initial training is usually provided on the job. Classroom training is provided for some specialties in this occupation. Course content typically includes:

- Combat and tactical systems and networks
- Weapon system electronics

Civilian Counterparts

Civilian electrical and electronics engineers work for manufacturers of electrical and electronic equipment. Many work for government agencies, public utilities, and engineering firms. Civilian electrical and electronics engineers perform duties similar to those performed in the military. However, they usually specialize in product areas, such as computers, communications, or aerospace systems. They may also be called electronics design engineers and electronics test engineers.

Opportunities

The services have about 1,000 electrical and electronics engineers. Each year, they need new engineers due to changes in personnel and the demands of the field. After job training, electrical and electronics engineers are usually assigned to engineering research and development units or to communications centers. Initially, they conduct studies and supervise research and development staff. With experience, they may advance to senior management positions, such as engineering staff officer, or research and development manager.

INTEREST CODE

This occupation generally appeals to people whose primary Interest Code is *Investigative. Investigative* jobs:

- Involve learning about a new subject area
- Allow you to use your knowledge to solve problems or create things or ideas

Pages 8 and 9 explain the Interest Codes

ENVIRONMENTAL HEALTH AND SAFETY OFFICERS

The services take great care to ensure safe working conditions and a clean environment. A clean, safe, and healthy environment results in happier employees and better work. Environmental health and safety officers study the air, ground, and water to identify and analyze sources of pollution and its effects. They also direct programs to control safety and health hazards in the work place.

What They Do

Environmental health and safety officers in the military perform some or all of the following duties:

- Determine methods to collect environmental data for research projects and surveys

- Analyze data to identify pollution problem areas

- Inspect food samples to detect any spoilage or disease

- Develop pollution control plans and policies

- Conduct health education programs

- Work with civilian public health officials in performing studies and analyzing results

Special Requirements

A 4-year college degree is normally required to enter this occupation. A degree in biomedical or biological science is required to enter some specialties in this occupation.

Helpful Attributes

Helpful fields of study include chemistry, biology, environmental sciences, soil science, civil engineering, and veterinary science. Helpful attributes include:

- Interest in protecting the environment

- Interest in conducting research or analytical studies

- Interest in work requiring accuracy and attention to detail

Work Environment

Environmental health and safety officers normally work in offices or research laboratories. They work outdoors while conducting environmental studies and surveys or inspecting facilities.

Training Provided

No initial job training is provided to officers in this occupation.

Civilian Counterparts

Civilian environmental health and safety officers work for engineering firms, manufacturing firms, and government agencies. They perform duties similar to those performed by military environmental health and safety officers. Depending on their specialty, they may be called environmental scientists, air pollution analysts, soil analysts, industrial hygienists, or water quality analysts.

Opportunities

The services have about 1,300 environmental health and safety officers. Each year, they need new health and safety officers due to changes in personnel and the demands of the field. Positions for environmental health and safety officers in the Coast Guard are filled by U.S. Public Health Service Officers. New environmental health and safety officers are assigned to environmental health teams. After demonstrating leadership qualities, they may advance to senior management or command positions.

INTEREST CODE

This occupation generally appeals to people whose primary Interest Code is *Investigative. Investigative* jobs:

- Involve learning about a new subject area

- Allow you to use your knowledge to solve problems or create things or ideas

Pages 8 and 9 explain the Interest Codes

INDUSTRIAL ENGINEERS

In the military, people need to know that the equipment they are using will perform as expected when a crisis arises. Industrial engineers manage quality control programs to ensure that the military develops and uses high quality products and systems. They also do research to determine the most effective ways for the military to use its people and equipment.

What They Do

Industrial engineers in the military perform some or all of the following duties:

- Use mathematical analysis to study operations and improve the way work is done

- Calculate the human and material resources required to produce an end product in the desired time

- Plan and direct quality control and production control programs

- Conduct studies to determine performance and reliability of equipment or systems

- Design, implement, and test new systems for managing production processes

- Study how people work with machines or computers and determine effects of human factors

- Develop mathematical models to perform various types of cost analyses

- Coordinate production activities with other organizations and contractors to ensure requirements are satisfied

Helpful Attributes

Helpful attributes include:

- Interest in technical work
- Ability to plan and organize studies
- Interest in working with mathematical models and formulas
- Interest in working closely with people

Work Environment

Industrial engineers usually work in offices. They may work outdoors while performing field studies or overseeing the installation of equipment and systems.

Training Provided

Job training is offered for some specialties. Training length varies from 8 to 16 weeks of classroom instruction, depending on the specialty. Course content typically includes:

- Management standards, principles, and policies

- Problem analysis and decision making

- Production and purchasing methods

Special Requirements

A 4-year college degree in industrial engineering, industrial management, or a related field is required to enter this occupation.

Civilian Counterparts

Civilian industrial engineers work primarily in manufacturing and consulting firms. They also work in other industries and businesses, including insurance companies, retail stores, banks, public utilities, and hospitals. Civilian industrial engineers perform duties similar to those performed in the military. Depending on the specialty, they may also be called production engineers, safety engineers, production planners, or quality control engineers.

Opportunities

The services have over 2,000 industrial engineers. Each year, they need new engineers due to changes in personnel and the demands of the field. After job training, industrial engineers are usually assigned to an engineering, management evaluation, or procurement unit. With experience, they may advance to command or policy-making positions in engineering, administration, or other fields.

INTEREST CODE

This occupation generally appeals to people whose primary Interest Code is *Investigative. Investigative* jobs:

- Involve learning about a new subject area

- Allow you to use your knowledge to solve problems or create things or ideas

Pages 8 and 9 explain the Interest Codes

INTELLIGENCE OFFICERS

Information about the size, strength, location, and capabilities of enemy forces is essential to military operations and national defense. To gather information, the services rely on aerial photographs, human observation, and electronic monitoring using radar and supersensitive radios. Intelligence officers gather technical intelligence needed for military planning.

What They Do

Intelligence officers in the military perform some or all of the following duties:

- Direct sea, ground, and aerial surveillance
- Prepare plans to intercept foreign communications transmissions
- Direct the analysis of aerial photos and other intelligence data
- Oversee the writing of intelligence reports
- Brief commanders on intelligence findings
- Help plan military missions
- Gather and analyze technical intelligence

Training Provided

Job training consists of 23 to 26 weeks of classroom instruction. Course content typically includes:

- Air, ground, and sea intelligence operations
- Photograph interpretation
- Use of surveillance equipment
- Reconnaissance equipment and weapons systems

Further training occurs on the job and through advanced courses.

Special Requirements

A 4-year college degree is normally required to enter this occupation.

Physical Demands

Normal color vision is required to work with map overlays and color photos.

Helpful Attributes

Helpful fields of study include cryptology, computer science, mathematics, and engineering. Helpful attributes include:

- Interest in solving problems
- Interest in analyzing data
- Ability to organize and manage activities
- Ability to work with abstract problems

Work Environment

Intelligence officers work in offices on land and aboard ships. They may work in the field on maneuvers and military exercises.

Civilian Counterparts

Civilian intelligence officers generally work in federal agencies, such as the Central Intelligence Agency (CIA) and Federal Bureau of Investigations (FBI). They perform duties similar to those performed by military intelligence officers.

Opportunities

The services have about 10,000 intelligence officers. Each year, they need new intelligence officers due to changes in personnel and the demands of the field. After job training, intelligence officers are assigned to intelligence units, military operations sections, or command posts. With experience, they may become commanders of intelligence units or directors of information gathering sections.

INTEREST CODE

This occupation generally appeals to people whose primary Interest Code is *Investigative. Investigative* jobs:

- Involve learning about a new subject area
- Allow you to use your knowledge to solve problems or create things or ideas

Pages 8 and 9 explain the Interest Codes

Profile: Teresa Alvarez

Teresa (Teri) Alvarez signed up for a Marine training program one summer in college. "It sounded interesting," she says, "and it carried no obligation." Teri and 6 friends went to training that summer. After graduation, three of them went on to Officer Candidate School and became Marine officers.

Teri decided to enter the intelligence field as an interrogator/translator. She was assigned to Hawaii as an intelligence analyst for Southeast Asia. As part of her duties, she prepared and gave briefings to senior officers served by her unit.

To further develop her leadership abilities, she was assigned to the Officer Candidate School in Quantico, VA. There, Teri taught several classes and counseled women officer candidates. She says, "I watched the women walk in and become Marine officers – leaving more confident and professional. It was one of my most enjoyable assignments."

After attending a special 9-month intelligence school to prepare her for assignment to the Defense Intelligence Agency (DIA), Teri reported for duty in Washington, DC as a Marine Captain. In this post she developed a situational model to alert intelligence planners to developing threats all over the world. She also prepared a training course for threat analysts in different intelligence agencies. For her work during this tour, she was awarded the newly authorized Defense Meritorious Service Medal.

After being selected for promotion to Major, Teri went full-time to Command and Staff College. She was then assigned as the first woman to hold a position as a division level (G-2) intelligence officer. She directed the group that provided intelligence services to the 2nd Marine Division, roughly one-third of the Marine Corps fighting force.

Later assignments included Okinawa and the Marine Headquarters in Washington, DC, where she works now, planning and analyzing Marine Corps intelligence activities. As a Lieutenant Colonel, she is looking forward to her next assignment. She says, "I am eager for more responsibility. I really like the challenge and the opportunity to advance in a field that is so important to the Marine Corps and the nation."

SAMPLE CAREER PATH

Intelligence Operations Director   15–18 years

Intelligence operations directors oversee intelligence services for air, land, or sea commands and coordinate their efforts with other military and civilian intelligence agencies. They determine the intelligence needed to support large combat forces and evaluate intelligence sources for accuracy and usefulness. They are responsible for briefing top-level military leaders.

Intelligence Staff Officer   9–11 years

Intelligence staff officers brief senior-level staff and combat commanders on activities of enemy forces. They also direct teams of officers and enlisted personnel, compiling and analyzing intelligence information from all sources. Intelligence staff officers confer with intelligence officers from other services and nations to share information and coordinate efforts.

Senior Intelligence Officer   4 years

Senior intelligence officers analyze information from multiple sources and prepare briefings or reports to support combat exercises and maneuvers. They also identify potential security problems.

Intelligence Officer

Intelligence officers research enemy forces and analyze their strengths and weaknesses. They also direct small teams of enlisted personnel in intelligence gathering operations. Intelligence officers debrief air crews or ground combat teams returning from missions or patrols.

The years shown represent typical time-in-service before advancement to that level. Actual career advancement depends on individual experience and performance.

LAWYERS AND JUDGES

The military has its own system of laws and courts. Lawyers in the various services Judge Advocate General (JAG) Corps administer activities within the military judicial system. They also perform legal research, prosecute and defend court cases, and are judges in military courts. They provide legal services for military personnel and represent the services in civil and international legal matters.

What They Do

Lawyers in the military perform some or all of the following duties:

- Give legal advice about government real estate, commercial contracts, patents, and trademarks

- Prepare pretrial advice for clients in court-martial cases

- Act as prosecuting attorney, defense attorney, or judge in court cases

- Prepare legal documents, such as wills and powers of attorney

- Interpret laws, directives, regulations, and court decisions

- Preside over court cases and make judgments based on the Uniform Code of Military Justice

- Help train new military lawyers

Helpful Attributes

Helpful attributes include:

- Interest in working with and researching legal concepts

- Ability to write clearly and concisely

- Ability to speak effectively in public

- Attention to detail

- Sensitivity to the needs of others

Work Environment

Lawyers and judges work in legal offices and courtrooms on land and aboard ships.

Training Provided

Job training consists of 8 to 12 weeks of classroom instruction. Training length varies depending on specialty. Course content typically includes:

- Military trial procedures

- Application of the Uniform Code of Military Justice

- Methods of obtaining evidence

- Courts-martial advocacy techniques

Further training occurs on the job and through advanced courses.

Civilian Counterparts

Civilian lawyers work in private practice and for law firms, government, corporations, and nonprofit groups. They perform duties similar to those performed by military lawyers. Civilian lawyers, however, usually specialize in a particular field. Judges in the civilian sector preside over courts of law and determine the rulings in cases that are brought before them.

Special Requirements

A degree in law is required to enter this occupation. In addition, most specialties require a membership to the bar in either federal court or the highest court of a state.

Opportunities

The services have about 3,800 lawyers and judges. Each year, they need new lawyers and judges to meet changes in demand in the field. In time, lawyers may advance to senior management positions in the legal field. With experience, some lawyers may be appointed military judges.

INTEREST CODE

This occupation generally appeals to people whose primary Interest Code is *Enterprising. Enterprising* jobs:

- Are fast-paced

- Require that you take on a lot of responsibility

Pages 8 and 9 explain the Interest Codes

Profile: Samuel E. Jackson

While Samuel Jackson was a freshman at Southern University in Louisiana, he met a Marine Corps officer who left a lasting impression on him due to his stately appearance and exceptional communication skills. He knew then that he wanted to be a Marine. He says, "I wanted to join the Marine Corps because I was looking for a challenge…not a lot of places give you the opportunity to test yourself like the Marine Corps." Shortly thereafter, he signed up for the Marine Corps Platoon Leaders Class (PLC) Program. As part of this program, Samuel attended training at Marine Corps Officer Candidate School in Quantico, VA for a total of 12 weeks. He was able to do this training while finishing his undergraduate degree in computer science and history. He says, "The challenges I faced in Officer Candidate School have helped prepare me for everything else I've done in my life."

Samuel initially started out wanting to be a pilot, but after scoring very high on the Law School Admissions Test (LSAT) exam, the Marine Corps gave him the opportunity to transfer to a law program. Upon graduation from Southern University, Samuel attended Tulane University School of Law as a Second Lieutenant in the Marine Corps on inactive duty status.

Prior to reporting to his first tour at Camp Pendleton in California, Samuel received additional training at the Navy Justice School to become certified as a Marine Corps judge advocate. During his first 18 months at Camp Pendleton, Samuel worked as a defense counsel defending more than 160 servicemembers in cases ranging from minor crimes or misdemeanors, such as theft, to felonies, such as murder. After completing his defense counsel assignment, Samuel worked as a legal assistance attorney, providing legal advice to individuals and their families in areas such as estate planning, immigration, family law, and consumer protection. He also worked as the Officer in Charge of the Camp Pendleton Tax office where he provided advice on state and federal tax matters and supervised a staff of 150 tax preparers.

In his current position at Headquarters in Quantico, VA, Major Jackson leads the Marine Corps' effort to recruit law students and lawyers. After he completes his current assignment, the Marine Corps will pay for him to obtain an advanced law degree. Samuel can then use this degree to further his Marine Corps career in an area that he chooses, such as international law or criminal law.

Of his military experience, Major Jackson says "Being in the Marine Corps has given me the opportunity to gain more experience in the legal profession than I would have been able to obtain during the same time period in the civilian world."

SAMPLE CAREER PATH

Legal Staff Director   **15–18 years**

Legal staff directors are in charge of JAG offices supporting local operational commands. They advise senior staff and combat commanders on legal matters and set up prosecution or defense in court-martial cases. They may also serve as military judges.

Legal Staff Officers   **9–11 years**

Legal staff officers develop expertise in specific legal areas such as contract, labor, maritime, or international law and advise commanders on matters in these areas. They also defend or prosecute personnel in court-martial cases that require lawyers of senior rank or specific expertise. They direct lawyers and enlisted legal specialists and review the legal aspects of military contracts.

Senior Lawyer   **4 years**

Senior lawyers advise commanders and senior officers on general legal issues and ensure that policies and procedures comply with civil and military law. They also investigate liability claims and advise military personnel on legal matters.

Lawyer

Judge Advocates General's (JAG) Corps lawyers prosecute and defend military personnel. They also research cases, interview defendants and witnesses, and prepare personal legal documents for military personnel.

The years shown represent typical time-in-service before advancement to that level. Actual career advancement depends on individual experience and performance.

LIFE SCIENTISTS

The military conducts studies of human and animal diseases to understand their causes and to find treatments. Harmful pests and bacteria are studied to find ways to protect people and food against illness or infection. Life scientists study the biology and chemistry of living organisms.

What They Do

Life scientists in the military perform some or all of the following duties:

- Study bacteria and parasites to determine how they invade and affect humans or animals

- Study the effects of diseases, poisons, and radiation on laboratory animals

- Study the effects of drugs, chemicals, and gases on living organisms

- Study ways of protecting humans through immunization from disease

- Direct blood banks and study blood chemistry

- Study the effects of aerospace flight, temperature, and movement on human physiology

- Study food storage and handling methods

- Study ways of keeping bases and ships free from pests and contagious diseases

- Conduct experiments and write technical reports

Special Requirements

A 4-year college degree is normally required to enter this occupation. Some specialties require a master's degree or medical degree.

Work Environment

Life scientists work in medical, clinical, and research laboratories and, at times, in food processing or storage plants. They may work outdoors while conducting field work on land or aboard ships.

Training Provided

No initial job training is provided to officers in this occupation. However, advanced courses are available in some specialties.

Helpful Attributes

Helpful fields of study include biochemistry, biology, microbiology, and pharmacology. Helpful attributes include:

- Interest in scientific work

- Ability to express ideas clearly and concisely

- Interest in mathematics, chemistry, biology, and medical research

Civilian Counterparts

Civilian life scientists work for universities, government agencies, medical laboratories, blood banks, pharmaceutical firms, chemical companies, or in private practice. They perform duties similar to those performed by military life scientists. Depending on their specialty, civilian life scientists may be called biochemists, biologists, entomologists, immunologists, medical technologists, pharmacologists, physiologists, toxicologists, or veterinarians.

Opportunities

The services have about 1,500 life scientists. Each year, they need new scientists due to changes in personnel and the demands of the field. Newly commissioned life scientists are normally ssigned to a laboratory, where they conduct research under the direction of more experienced scientists. In time, they may manage their own research projects and direct other officers. Eventually, they may become directors of research laboratories or hold other senior management positions in the health research field.

INTEREST CODE

This occupation generally appeals to people whose primary Interest Code is *Investigative. Investigative* jobs:

- Involve learning about a new subject area

- Allow you to use your knowledge to solve problems or create things or ideas

Pages 8 and 9 explain the Interest Codes

Ships and submarines must be designed for speed, strength, stability, and safety. Improvements in ship equipment, hull design, and deck layout can improve operations. Marine engineers design ships, submarines, and other watercraft for military use. They also oversee the construction and repair of ships and marine equipment.

What They Do

Marine engineers in the military perform some or all of the following duties:

- Study new ways of designing and building ship hulls

- Develop and test shipboard combat and salvage equipment

- Oversee the construction, maintenance, and repair of ship hulls and equipment

- Manage research programs to solve naval engineering problems

- Oversee the installation, operation, and repair of marine equipment and systems

- Evaluate marine research data and prepare technical reports

Special Requirements

A 4-year college degree in marine engineering is required to enter this occupation.

Work Environment

Marine engineers do much of their work outdoors at shipyards while overseeing shipbuilding and repair activities. They work in offices while directing vessel design and development activities.

Training Provided

No initial job training is provided to officers in this occupation.

Helpful Attributes

Helpful attributes include:

- Interest in technical work

- Ability to plan and organize research projects

- Interest in ships and shipbuilding

Civilian Counterparts

Civilian marine engineers work in the shipbuilding industry. They also work for government agencies and ship machinery manufacturers. Civilian marine engineers perform duties similar to those performed in the military. They may also be called marine equipment research engineers, marine architects, marine equipment design engineers, marine surveyors, and port engineers.

Opportunities

The services have over 500 marine engineers. Each year, they need new engineers due to changes in personnel and the demands of the field. Newly commissioned engineers may be assigned to engineering or marine research and development laboratories. They may also be assigned to work in shipyards with vessel maintenance and repair units. With experience, marine engineers may advance to senior engineering management and command positions.

INTEREST CODE

This occupation generally appeals to people whose primary Interest Code is *Investigative*. *Investigative* jobs:

- Involve learning about a new subject area

- Allow you to use your knowledge to solve problems or create things or ideas

Pages 8 and 9 explain the Interest Codes

NUCLEAR ENGINEERS

The military has been a pioneer in the use of nuclear energy. The military uses nuclear energy for power plants, strategic weapons, and defense systems. Nuclear engineers direct research and development projects to improve military uses of nuclear energy. They also direct nuclear power plant operations.

What They Do

Nuclear engineers in the military perform some or all of the following duties:

- Direct projects to improve nuclear power plants in ships and submarines

- Direct research on the uses and effects of nuclear weapons

- Develop safety procedures for handling nuclear weapons

- Assist high-level officials in creating policies for developing and using nuclear technology

- Direct operations and maintenance of nuclear power plants

Special Requirements

A 4-year college degree in physics, chemistry, or nuclear engineering is required to enter this occupation. Some specialties in this occupation require a master's degree.

Helpful Attributes

Helpful attributes include:

- Interest in scientific and technical work

- Interest in planning and directing complex research projects

- Interest in working with mathematical formulas

- Interest in concepts and principles of engineering

Work Environment

Nuclear engineers work in offices, research laboratories, and power plant control centers, either on land or aboard nuclear-powered ships and submarines.

Training Provided

No initial job training is provided to officers in this occupation. However, advanced training is available.

Civilian Counterparts

Civilian nuclear engineers work for firms that build and operate nuclear power plants and that develop and manufacture nuclear weapons. Many also work for public utilities, government agencies, and colleges and universities. Civilian nuclear engineers perform duties similar to those performed in the military.

Opportunities

The services have over 200 nuclear engineers. Each year, they need new engineers due to changes in personnel and the demands of the field. Newly commissioned nuclear engineers are usually assigned to nuclear research laboratories, nuclear power plants (on shore or aboard ships), or other defense facilities. With experience, they may advance to senior management or command positions.

ORDNANCE OFFICERS

Army
Navy
Air Force
Marine Corps
Coast Guard

Ordnance is a military term for all types of ammunition and weapons, such as missiles, guns, and chemical munitions. Ammunition and weapons are hazardous materials that require special handling to ensure their reliability and safety. Ordnance officers make decisions regarding the purchase, handling, storage, maintenance, use, and disposal of ordnance. They also supervise and train ordnance personnel assigned to their unit.

What They Do

Ordnance officers in the military perform some or all of the following duties:

- Manage and direct the inspection, repair, and maintenance of weapon systems
- Direct the handling, transportation, storage, and disposal of all types of ammunition, missiles, and explosives
- Detect, identify, and report chemical, nuclear, biological, and chemical contamination
- Supervise the loading and unloading of weapons and ammunition on aircraft, ships, and other transport systems
- Instruct personnel in explosive ordnance disposal methods and proper procedures for handling all types of ordnance

Special Requirements

A 4-year college degree is usually required to enter this occupation. Normal color vision is required for some specialties in this occupation.

Helpful Attributes

Helpful fields of study include chemistry, physics and other physical sciences. Helpful attributes include:

- Good organizational and management skills
- Attention to detail
- Ability to remain calm in stressful situations

Training Provided

Job training consists of 12-15 weeks of classroom instruction and practical exercises. Training length varies depending on the specialty. Course content typically includes:

- Ordnance transportation, handling and storage
- Maintenance and repair of weapons systems and ordnance
- Arming/disarming techniques
- Ordnance disposal
- Chemical and nuclear detection and defense

Civilian Counterparts

There are no direct civilian counterparts for most of the ordnance officer specialties. However, their experience in handling hazardous materials and proven ability to manage personnel in tense situations translate to strong leadership and managerial skills. Additionally, the expertise of some ordnance officers is similar to the knowledge used by bomb disposal experts and other emergency management personnel.

Work Environment

Ordnance officers usually work on bases or ships. Due to the need to keep forces supplied with weapons and munitions, ordnance officers may spend time outdoors in all types of weather.

Opportunities

The services have about 5,000 ordnance officers. Each year, they need new ordnance officers due to changes in personnel and the demands of the field. After job training, ordnance officers are usually assigned to field units that maintain ordnance supplies. In time, they may advance to senior management positions in ordnance.

INTEREST CODE

This occupation generally appeals to people whose primary Interest Code is *Enterprising. Enterprising* jobs:

- Are fast-paced
- Require that you take on a lot of responsibility

Pages 8 and 9 explain the Interest Codes

PHYSICAL SCIENTISTS

The military conducts physical sciences research to develop new technologies, materials, and equipment for use in a variety of areas including, medicine, and engineering. They also study physical characteristics of the atmosphere and environment to support military operations. Physical scientists conduct and manage research in fields such as chemistry, physics, meteorology, and oceanography. Depending on area of specialization, physical scientists may be involved in building new weapons systems, developing weather forecasts, or evaluating the effects of biological, and chemical agents.

What They Do

Physical scientists in the military perform some or all of the following duties:

- Conduct research in their specialty area

- Plan and conduct experiments in aerodynamics, optics, geophysics, biophysics, and astrophysics

- Conduct research on the effects of water and atmosphere on military warning and weapons systems

- Analyze strength, flexibility, weight, and properties of various types of materials

- Analyze and evaluate scientific data

- Teach/train other military personnel

- Manage laboratories or field staff to conduct experiments

Special Requirements

A 4-year college degree specific to the individual's area of focus is required to enter this occupation.

Helpful Attributes

Helpful attributes include:

- Interest in scientific and technical work

- Interest in collecting and analyzing data

Work Environment

Physical scientists in the military work in a variety of settings both indoors and outdoors depending on the area of specialization. Many physical scientists perform their work primarily in laboratories, or offices. Other physical scientists spend extensive hours outdoors collecting and analyzing data in the field. Although they observe strict safety precautions, some physical scientists may be exposed to hazardous substances.

Civilian Counterparts

Physical scientists are widely employed within the civilian workforce and enjoy a diverse set of opportunities within the federal government and the private sector. The federal government employs many physical scientists to conduct research on weather patterns, ground water supply, and a host of other issues directly impacting our way of life. Additionally, the private sector relies on physical scientists to develop new fuel sources (such as nuclear and solar energy) or medical applications. Depending on their specialty, civilian physical scientists may be called meteorologists, oceanographers, chemists, or physicists.

Training Provided

In general, no initial job training is provided to officers in this occupation. In some cases, additional military training may be provided depending upon the specialty area.

Opportunities

The services have about 2,000 physical scientists. Each year, they need new scientists due to changes in personnel and the demands of the field. New officers may work as part of research teams. With experience, they may lead research projects of their own. After demonstrating leadership abilities, they may advance to senior management positions in a variety of scientific fields.

INTEREST CODE

This occupation generally appeals to people whose primary Interest Code is **Investigative. Investigative** jobs:

- Involve learning about a new subject area

- Allow you to use your knowledge to solve problems or create things or ideas

Pages 8 and 9 explain the Interest Codes

SPACE OPERATIONS OFFICERS

Orbiting satellites and other space vehicles are used for national security, communications, weather forecasting, and space exploration. Space operations officers manage space flight planning, training, mission control, and other activities involved in launching and recovering spacecraft. They may also be astronauts who command space flights or who serve as crew members.

What They Do

Space operations officers in the military perform some or all of the following duties:

- Manage activities of the flight control facility, including mission planning and training

- Manage operation of guidance, navigation, and propulsion systems for ground and space vehicles

- Develop space flight simulation exercises to train astronauts

- Plan space stations

- Direct space center launch and recovery activities

- Command and pilot space shuttles

- Perform in-orbit tasks and experiments aboard spacecraft

- Monitor foreign space flights and missile launches

Physical Demands

Astronaut testing and training are very physically demanding. Officers must be in top physical shape to qualify for the astronaut shuttle program. Space operations officers must have normal color vision to read charts, graphics, and control panels.

Special Requirements

A 4-year college degree in science or engineering is required to enter the space operations field. A bachelor of science degree in engineering, mathematics, physical science, or life science is required to qualify as an astronaut.

Training Provided

Job training for mission control officers consists of about 1 year of classroom instruction and practical experience. Course content typically includes:

- Evaluation of space transport systems

- Development of space mission plans

- Methods for conducting space flight training programs

- Development of space flight simulation exercises

Further training occurs on the job and through academic courses. Astronauts must complete the NASA astronaut candidate training school. They also receive 1 year of practical training in space transport systems.

Helpful Attributes

Helpful attributes include:

- Interest in scientific research

- Decisiveness

- Ability to work well as part of a team

- Interest in space travel

Work Environment

Launch and mission control space operations officers work in offices. Astronauts are required at times to work in a zero gravity environment in training as well as in space flight.

Civilian Counterparts

Most civilian space operations officers work for the National Aeronautics and Space Administration (NASA) in launch and mission control. They perform duties similar to those performed by military space operations officers. Some civilian space operations officers work for private corporations and firms that operate space satellites.

Opportunities

The services have fewer than 500 space operations officers. The field is very competitive due to the limited number of specialties in this area. The services sometimes need new space operations officers because of changes in personnel and changes in the demands of the field. After job training, new officers are assigned to space operations, launch and mission control centers, or research facilities. With experience and special training, they have the opportunity to work in various areas such as astronautics or space flight control. Eventually, they may manage a missile warning facility, a satellite command center, a space launch system, a space systems analysis facility, or a manned space flight.

INTEREST CODE

This occupation generally appeals to people whose primary Interest Code is *Investigative*. *Investigative* jobs:

- Involve learning about a new subject area

- Allow you to use your knowledge to solve problems or create things or ideas

Pages 8 and 9 explain the Interest Codes

Executive, Administrative, and Managerial Occupations

Executive, administrative, and managerial officers oversee and direct military activities in key functional areas, such as finance, accounting, health administration, logistics, and supply. Health services administrators, for instance, are responsible for the overall quality of care provided at the hospitals and clinics they operate. They must ensure that each department works together to provide the highest quality of care. As another example, the military buys billions of dollars worth of equipment, supplies, and services from private industry each year. Purchasing and contracting managers negotiate and monitor contracts for purchasing equipment, materials, and services.

- Administrative Officers
- Finance and Accounting Managers
  Profile: Dwayne Johnson
- Health Services Administrators
- International Relations Officers
  Profile: Jack Devers
- Logisticians
- Management Analysts and Planners
- Purchasing and Contracting Managers
- Store Managers
- Supply and Warehousing Managers
  Profile: Benjamin Travis

ADMINISTRATIVE OFFICERS

The military is a large organization that performs a wide range of activities in locations all over the world. The success of many military activities and operations depends on the effective management and coordination of administrative functions. Administrative officers direct administrative functions and services, such as mail distribution and delivery, records management, and facilities management. Other officers who specialize by functional area, such as finance or personnel, are described under their respective occupational titles in this publication.

What They Do

Administrative officers in the military perform some or all of the following duties:

- Develop and implement administrative plans, policies, and procedures

- Coordinate administrative matters and direct administrative support staff and services

- Manage postal operations

- Develop and monitor programs for safeguarding classified materials

- Establish records and forms management programs

- Prepare responses to special correspondence

- Determine needs for supplies and equipment

- Manage the maintenance and use of facilities

Special Requirements

A 4-year college degree is usually required to enter this occupation.

Work Environment

Administrative officers normally work in offices on military bases or aboard ships.

Helpful Attributes

Helpful attributes include:

- Good organizational and management skills

- Ability to work effectively with people

- Attention to detail

- Ability to coordinate several activities at once

- Strong communication skills

- Ability to analyze and solve problems quickly

Civilian Counterparts

Civilian administrative services managers perform a range of duties in a variety of organizations. They coordinate and direct support services, such as secretarial and reception, conference planning and travel, mail distribution, and facilities management. They may work as property or real estate managers, office managers, or postal service managers.

Training Provided

Job training is offered for some specialties. Training length varies, depending on the specialty. Most specialties involve significant on-the-job training.

Opportunities

The services have about 1,000 administrative officers. Each year, they need new administrative officers due to changes in personnel and the demands of the field. After job training, officers are normally assigned to manage a section within a branch or department. As they gain experience, they take on more management responsibility and may eventually manage the administrative support operations of an entire installation.

INTEREST CODE
This occupation generally appeals to people whose primary Interest Code is **Enterprising. Enterprising** jobs: • Are fast-paced • Require that you take on a lot of responsibility
Pages 8 and 9 explain the Interest Codes

FINANCE AND ACCOUNTING MANAGERS

Each year, the services spend billions of dollars on personnel, equipment, and supplies. Only through careful management can military funds be put to their best use. Finance and accounting managers direct and manage the financial affairs of the military. They also advise commanders on financial and accounting matters.

What They Do

Finance and accounting managers in the military perform some or all of the following duties:

- Set policies for the use of military funds

- Direct the preparation of budgets and financial forecasts

- Advise management personnel on accounting, budgeting, and fiscal matters

- Develop ways to track financial transactions

- Prepare and examine financial records and reports

- Direct the activities of finance and accounting staff

Training Provided

Job training consists of 2 to 16 weeks of classroom instruction. Training length varies depending on specialty. Course content typically includes:

- Financial management techniques, including budget preparation and review

- Financial management techniques

- Military accounting

- Duties of finance and accounting managers

- Personnel management and payroll procedures

- Statistical analysis and fiscal planning

Special Requirements

A 4-year college degree in accounting, finance, or a related field is required to enter this occupation. Some specialties require a master's degree in business administration or recognition as a Certified Public Accountant (CPA).

Helpful Attributes

Helpful attributes include:

- Preference for working with numbers and statistics

- Interest in work requiring accuracy and attention to detail

- Interest in planning and directing the work of others

Civilian Counterparts

Civilian finance and accounting managers work for businesses, accounting firms, universities, hospitals, or government agencies. They perform duties similar to those performed by military finance and accounting managers. They usually specialize in certain areas of finance and accounting, such as budgets, internal auditing, or cost accounting. In large business firms, they may be called executive controllers or company treasurers.

Work Environment

Finance and accounting managers work primarily in offices.

Opportunities

The services have about 2,800 finance and accounting managers. Each year, they need new finance and accounting managers due to changes in personnel and the demands of the field. After job training, managers are assigned to finance and accounting offices. Initially, they perform work in accounting, auditing, or finance management operations. With experience, they may advance to senior management and command positions.

INTEREST CODE
This occupation generally appeals to people whose primary Interest Code is **Enterprising. Enterprising** jobs: • Are fast-paced • Require that you take on a lot of responsibility
Pages 8 and 9 explain the Interest Codes

Profile: Dwayne Johnson

Dwayne Johnson saw football as his ticket to a successful life, but when an auto accident limited his chances of playing professionally, he refocused his attention on academics. His father was a Colonel in the Army, so it was only natural for him to join the Army Reserve Officers' Training Corps (ROTC) while in college. Dwayne decided to major in accounting and pursue a career in the financial area.

In his first assignment as a newly commissioned Army officer, Dwayne worked at an Army Major Command Headquarters, overseeing a $100 million missile system contract. He was stunned by the importance of his first assignment and realized the Army would make a great career. "No one could match the level of responsibility I received as a new lieutenant," Dwayne says. His next assignment was in Korea, where he was in charge of payroll disbursements for an infantry division of 17,000 soldiers. This duty included bringing payroll cash to troops in the Demilitarized Zone between North and South Korea.

After Korea, Dwayne went to Fort Harrison in Indiana for a five month advanced finance course. Dwayne was able to apply what he learned at the finance course at his next assignment in Fort Knox, Kentucky where he was a Cash Control Officer. While at Fort Knox, he also received a Masters in Business Administration in finance. After Fort Knox, Dwayne was posted to Izmir, Turkey where he was an auditor for a North Atlantic Treaty Organization (NATO) joint command. He and his family especially enjoyed the cultural aspects of their stay.

After two years in Turkey, Dwayne, returned to Fort Harrison as an instructor. Dwayne enjoyed this role because he was able to "impact the soldiers of tomorrow." Dwayne next became the Executive Officer of a finance battalion in Hawaii that supported the deployment of troops abroad. While there, he was promoted to Major and made the Division Comptroller.

Lt. Colonel Johnson is currently living in the Washington, DC area where he is the officer in charge of assignments and career development for the Army Finance and Accounting Corps. He will soon be promoted to Colonel and become Commander of a finance battalion with personnel in Texas and Bosnia.

SAMPLE CAREER PATH

Finance and Accounting Director   15–18 years

Finance and accounting directors oversee the finance and accounting functions of a large facility or command. They determine the financial needs of their command. Directors also plan and manage the workload of finance and accounting units and ensure proper use of funds. They are responsible for briefing military and civilian leaders on budget matters.

Finance and Accounting Staff Officer   9–11 years

Finance and accounting staff officers advise senior-level staff on finance and budget matters. They review and analyze the financial needs of commands and coordinate proposals among multiple commands. They oversee comprehensive internal control and audit programs.

Senior Finance and Accounting Officers   4 years

Senior finance and accounting officers plan, develop, and coordinate budgets for their unit or command. They advise local commanders on financial and budget matters. Senior finance and accounting officers review budget reports and requests from subordinate units. They also train new officers in budget management procedures.

Finance and Accounting Officers

Finance and accounting officers control the flow of funds within the armed forces. They monitor budgets and disburse funds. They also oversee internal controls to ensure proper use of funds.

The years shown represent typical time-in-service before advancement to that level. Actual career advancement depends on individual experience and performance.

HEALTH SERVICES ADMINISTRATORS

In hospitals and clinics, all of the departments – emergency, X-ray, nursing, maintenance, administration, and food service – must work together to provide quality health care. Health services administrators manage hospitals, clinics, and other health care facilities. They also manage individual departments or specific health care programs within a hospital.

What They Do

Health services administrators in the military perform some or all of the following duties:

- Develop and manage budgets for health care facilities or programs

- Meet with hospital department heads to plan services and keep the health care facility running smoothly

- Direct personnel activities, such as hiring, employee evaluation, staff development, and recordkeeping

- Plan for delivering health services during emergencies and test these plans during exercises

- Direct the day-to-day operations of the nursing department

- Direct the operations of support departments, such as maintenance, food services, or administration

Training Provided

Job training is provided for some specialties in this occupation. This training consists of 10 to 12 weeks of classroom instruction and practical exercises. Course content typically includes:

- Planning and directing health services

- Patient unit management

- Nursing service administration

Helpful Attributes

Helpful attributes include:

- Interest in planning and directing the work of others

- Interest in working closely with people

- Ability to express ideas clearly and concisely

- Interest in health care

Special Requirements

A 4-year college degree in health care, public health, business, nursing administration, or a related field is required to enter most of the specialties in this occupation. Some specialties require further education or prior experience in the health services field.

Civilian Counterparts

Civilian health services administrators usually work for hospitals, clinics, nursing homes, health maintenance organizations (HMOs), or other health care facilities. They may also work for colleges and universities, public health agencies, insurance companies, or health management firms. Civilian health services administrators perform duties similar to those performed in the military. Depending on the programs or facilities they manage, civilian health services administrators may also be called hospital administrators, nursing services directors, emergency medical services coordinators, and outpatient services directors.

Work Environment

Health services administrators work in hospitals, clinics, and other health care facilities. Most work at facilities on land, but some work aboard hospital ships and ships with large sick bays.

Opportunities

The services have about 5,000 health services administrators. Each year, they need new health administrators due to changes in personnel and the demands of the field. After job training, health services administrators may be assigned to a variety of positions depending on their specialty. Usually, they work under the direction of experienced officers. With experience, they may manage one or more departments in a facility. In time, they may direct a health services facility. Eventually, they may advance to senior management positions responsible for planning health services at many facilities.

INTEREST CODE

This occupation generally appeals to people whose primary Interest Code is *Enterprising. Enterprising* jobs:

- Are fast-paced

- Require that you take on a lot of responsibility

Pages 8 and 9 explain the Interest Codes

INTERNATIONAL RELATIONS OFFICERS

Information about the military capabilities of foreign countries is vital to our national defense. Our leaders need to know the strengths and weaknesses of both friendly and unfriendly countries. International relations officers collect, analyze, and report information about foreign countries to be used for military planning.

What They Do

International relations officers in the military perform some or all of the following duties:

* Collect and report information about the military forces of foreign countries

* Hold meetings with foreign military and government officials

* Analyze political, social, and economic matters in foreign countries

* Project foreign political trends

* Advise commanders about situations in foreign countries

Special Requirements

A 4-year college degree is normally required to enter this occupation. Some specialties require an advanced degree. Knowledge of the people and language of one or more foreign countries may be required.

Helpful Attributes

Helpful fields of study include political science, history, and international affairs. Helpful attributes include:

* Ability to express ideas clearly and concisely

* Interest in collecting and analyzing data

* Interest in living and working in a foreign country

* Interest in working closely with people

Work Environment

International relations officers work mainly in offices of U.S. embassies and missions located overseas.

Training Provided

Job training is provided in some specialties. Training length varies by entry requirements and specialty area. Course content typically includes:

* Political and cultural awareness

* Development of foreign area expertise

* Organization and functions of diplomatic missions

Further training occurs on the job.

Civilian Counterparts

Civilians who perform work similar to the work of international relations officers are employed mainly by government agencies, such as the Department of State. Called foreign service officers, they work in U.S. embassies and missions overseas. Other civilian counterparts include political scientists, university instructors, and advisors to corporations doing business overseas.

Opportunities

The services have about 500 international relations officers. Each year, they need new international relations officers due to changes in personnel and the demands of the field. Normally, international relations officers are selected from among officers who have several years of military experience. They are selected from a variety of military career fields. These officers usually return to their main career field after several years of duty as international relations officers.

INTEREST CODE

This occupation generally appeals to people whose primary Interest Code is *Social. Social* jobs:

* involve working with and helping others

* Lets you teach others new skills

Pages 8 and 9 explain the Interest Codes

Profile: Jack Devers

After completing his college degree in education from the University of Wisconsin, Jack Devers worked abroad in Morocco for a foundation that provides housing and assistance to handicapped youth. During his time in Morocco, Jack learned Arabic and worked directly with the native people. After that experience, he knew he wanted a career that would allow him to live overseas again.

When Jack returned from North Africa, he decided he wanted to serve his country. He looked into opportunities in the military with hopes of accomplishing two goals, obtaining a master's degree and getting a chance to do more travel. Upon joining the Air Force, Jack went to Monterey, CA where he worked as an executive officer for the Asian School at the Defense Language Institute. This position gave him the opportunity to work with a culturally diverse group of people in an international environment. The Air Force also provided him with tuition assistance so he could pursue a master's degree.

It wasn't long before Jack got his wish to go abroad again. He arrived in Riyadh, Saudi Arabia shortly after the Gulf War ended to help set up training programs with the Saudis. To coordinate operations and conduct inspections, Jack traveled to embassies in places such as Pakistan, Egypt, Sudan, and Seychelles.

After Riyadh, Jack had the unique opportunity to act as a United Nations (UN) military observer on the Kuwait and Iraq border. His primary role as a UN observer was to help keep the peace by acting as a liaison between the Kuwaitis and Iraqis. For Jack, the highlight of this experience was having the chance to live and work closely with UN military personnel from 34 nations including China, Russia, the United Kingdom, France, Fiji, Nigeria, Argentina, Indonesia, and Uruguay.

Over the last several years, Jack's Air Force career has taken him to many other locations, including Somalia, the Western Sahara, and Vietnam. In each location, he was able to work with the local people to help the Air Force accomplish its mission. Jack's stay in Vietnam was of particular significance to him because he was able to be directly involved with the Vietnamese government on issues related to Missing in Action (MIA) and Prisoner of War (POW) affairs.

Currently, Major Devers is in Washington, DC where he is the Chief Foreign Area Officer, Academic Programs. In this position, he is responsible for making sure that foreign area officers are enrolled in the appropriate training and academic programs. When this assignment ends, Jack hopes to go overseas again to further his experience in the international arena.

SAMPLE CAREER PATH

International Relations Director   15–18 years

International relations directors oversee the foreign affairs functions of a large installation or command. They advise government representatives involved in negotiations with foreign governments. They also represent the United States military in meetings and negotiations.

Foreign Area Staff Officer   9–11 years

Foreign area staff officers advise senior commanders and civilian officials on foreign affairs. They maintain liaisons with government agencies concerned with international affairs and advise diplomatic staff on military issues. Staff officers also provide guidance on international aspects of military plans and policies.

Senior Foreign Area Officers   4 years

Senior foreign area officers oversee a foreign relations team that focuses on a specific region of the world. They represent the United States military on international staffs, projects, and missions. Senior officers participate in treaty and agreement negotiations affecting the military. They also conduct research on world or area political situations and advise their superiors on political situations in their region of expertise.

Foreign Area Officers

Foreign area officers provide foreign language competency and regional expertise essential to interaction with foreign militaries and governments. They analyze and prepare reports on international political situations, foreign culture, and foreign militaries. Foreign area officers often work directly with foreign personnel. They also provide assistance to U.S. active, retired, and reserve military personnel present in the host country.

Since international relations is often an additional skill area that supplements a person's primary occupation, the career paths of individuals may vary significantly.

The years shown represent typical time-in-service before advancement to that level. Actual career advancement depends on individual experience and performance.

LOGISTICIANS

In order for the military to operate successfully, the proper materials, equipment, and people need to be in the right place at the right time. Logisticians develop, review, and implement plans for coordinating many different variables such as, requirements for and availability of supplies, equipment, personnel, and transportation. In developing their plans, they also take into account maintenance and scheduling considerations, and cost factors. Some logisticians specialize in an area such as, aviation logistics.

What They Do

Logisticians in the military perform some or all of the following duties:

- Negotiate and buy goods and services

- Track inventory levels, process orders, and help determine when to make purchases

- Distribute and dispose of resources

- Coordinate with other groups to ensure the continued flow of materials and personnel

- Coordinate transportation and maintenance schedules for the safe deployment of personnel and materials

- Use computers and mathematical models to predict and solve logistical problems

Helpful Attributes

Helpful fields of study include management, operations research, resource allocation, statistics, and business or public administration. Helpful attributes include:

- Interest in solving problems

- Ability to express ideas clearly and concisely

- Ability to coordinate the efforts of multiple individuals or groups

Special Requirements

A 4-year college degree is normally required to enter this occupation.

Training Provided

Training consists of 8 to 12 weeks of classroom exercises and practical exercises. Course content typically includes:

- Purchasing and contracting

- Resource allocation

- Transportation and personnel coordination

Civilian Counterparts

Civilian logisticians work in all types of public and private organizations from hospitals to large manufacturing companies. They perform duties similar to those of military logisticians. Civilian logisticians may also be called logistics engineers, logistics analysts, and logistics planners.

Work Environment

Logisticians normally work in offices, although they may also work in a variety of other locations depending on their assignment.

Opportunities

The services have over 1,000 logisticians. Each year, they need new logisticians due to changes in personnel and the demands of the field. After job training, logisticians are normally assigned to a logistics unit where they use and refine their purchasing, allocation and coordination skills. In time, they may advance to senior management positions in logistics.

INTEREST CODE

This occupation generally appeals to people whose primary Interest Code is *Enterprising. Enterprising* jobs:

- Are fast-paced

- Require that you take on a lot of responsibility

Pages 8 and 9 explain the Interest Codes

MANAGEMENT ANALYSTS AND PLANNERS

Good management and planning reduces waste and inefficiency. By improving its management techniques, the military makes the best use of its human and material resources. Management analysts and planners study operations and organizations, identify and evaluate problems, and develop recommendations based on their findings.

What They Do

Management analysts and planners in the military perform some or all of the following duties:

Study organizations and their functions to determine personnel, information systems, finances, or equipment needs

Gather data for studies using a variety of methods

Develop and implement plans and policies that support organizational objectives

Determine organizational structures for new or existing offices

Perform comparison studies to review alternative options and determine the impacts of different factors

Analyze work processes and resource usage patterns

Design rules or procedures for work activities or information flow

Helpful Attributes

Helpful fields of study include management, organizational planning, operations research, and business or public administration. Helpful attributes include:

Interest in solving problems

Interest in collecting and analyzing data

Ability to express ideas clearly and concisely both verbally and in writing

Special Requirements

A 4-year college degree is normally required to enter this occupation.

Training Provided

Job training consists of 6 to 10 weeks of classroom instruction. Training length varies depending on specialty. Course content typically includes:

• Management engineering techniques

• Methods of statistical analysis

• Internal review and analysis techniques

• Systems analysis procedures

• Organizational planning

Civilian Counterparts

Civilian management analysts and planners often work in private management consulting firms. Many others work in hospitals, universities, government agencies, or manufacturing firms. Civilian management analysts and planners perform duties similar to those performed in the military. They are sometimes called management consultants. Some consultants specialize by industry, such as banking, health care, or transportation. Others specialize by business functional area, such as human resources, or information systems management.

Work Environment

Management analysts and planners normally work in offices, although they sometimes study work that occurs outdoors.

Opportunities

The services have about 2,000 management analysts and planners. Each year, they need new analysts and planners due to changes in personnel and the demands of the field. After job training, management analysts are assigned to analysis teams. With experience, they may advance to senior management or command positions.

INTEREST CODE

This occupation generally appeals to people whose primary Interest Code is *Enterprising. Enterprising* jobs:

• Are fast-paced

• Require that you take on a lot of responsibility

Pages 8 and 9 explain the Interest Codes

PURCHASING AND CONTRACTING MANAGERS

Army
Navy
Air Force
Marine Corps
Coast Guard

The military buys billions of dollars worth of equipment, supplies, and services from private industry each year. The services must make sure their purchases meet military specifications and are made at a fair price. Purchasing and contracting managers negotiate, write, and monitor contracts for purchasing equipment, materials, and services.

What They Do

Purchasing and contracting managers in the military perform some or all of the following duties:

- Review requests for supplies and services to make sure they are complete and accurate
- Prepare bid invitations or requests for proposals for contracts with civilian firms
- Review bids or proposals and award contracts
- Prepare formal contracts, specifying all terms and conditions
- Review work to make sure that it meets the requirements of contracts

Training Provided

Job training consists of 3 to 10 weeks of classroom instruction. Training length varies depending on specialty. Course content typically includes:

- Purchasing and accounting procedures
- Use of computers in contract administration
- Supply and financial management

Further training occurs through advanced courses.

Helpful Attributes

Helpful fields of study include management and business or public administration. Helpful attributes include:

- Ability to develop detailed plans
- Interest in work requiring accuracy and attention to detail
- Interest in negotiating

Special Requirements

A 4-year college degree is normally required to enter this occupation.

Work Environment

Purchasing and contracting managers work in offices.

Civilian Counterparts

Civilian purchasing and contracting managers work for a wide variety of employers, including engineering, manufacturing, and construction firms. They perform duties similar to those performed by military purchasing and contract managers. They may also be called procurement services managers, purchasing directors, contracts administrators, or material control managers.

Opportunities

The services have about 4,000 purchasing and contracting managers. Each year, they need new contracting managers due to changes in personnel and the demands of the field. After training, purchasing and contracting managers work with and advise commanders on contract proposals. With experience they may advance to senior management and command positions.

INTEREST CODE

This occupation generally appeals to people whose primary Interest Code is **Enterprising. Enterprising** jobs:

- Are fast-paced
- Require that you take on a lot of responsibility

Pages 8 and 9 explain the Interest Codes

STORE MANAGERS

The military operates retail stores for the convenience of service men and women. In some areas, particularly overseas, the goods and services offered at military stores, laundries, and barbershops are not otherwise available. Store managers direct the operation of retail service, food, and merchandise outlets. They also manage personnel who store food, supplies, and equipment.

What They Do

Store managers in the military perform some or all of the following duties:

- Direct personnel in purchasing, pricing, and selling food, supplies, and equipment

- Direct personnel in receiving, storing, and issuing supplies and equipment

- Supervise the inspection, care, and testing of products before their use or sale

- Plan training programs for new workers

- Direct inventory, accounting, and other record-keeping activities

- Plan and prepare store budgets

Special Requirements

A 4-year college degree is normally required to enter this occupation.

Helpful Attributes

Helpful fields of study include management, accounting, marketing, business administration, and industrial management. Helpful attributes include:

- Interest in planning work schedules

- Interest in managing a business

- Interest in planning and directing the work of others

Work Environment

Store managers work in retail stores or warehouses on land and aboard ships.

Training Provided

Job training consists of 5 to 10 weeks of classroom instruction. Training length varies depending on specialty. Course content typically includes:

- Accounting and record keeping

- Inventory control

- Retail store and warehouse management

- Personnel and office administration

- Budget management

Civilian Counterparts

Civilian store managers may work in many kinds of retail businesses. Some manage grocery, department, discount, and other large stores. Others manage warehouses that receive, store, and issue merchandise and supplies for retail outlets. Civilian store managers perform duties similar to those performed in the military. They may also be called retail store managers and distribution warehouse managers.

Opportunities

The services have close to 1,000 store managers. Each year, they need new store managers due to changes in personnel and the demands of the field. After job training, store managers are assigned to supply, exchange, or food service units. With experience, they may advance to senior management and command positions.

SUPPLY AND WAREHOUSING MANAGERS

The military needs vast amounts of supplies to feed and supply its personnel. Tons of materials such as food, fuel, medicine, and ammunition must be ordered, stored, and distributed each day. Supply and warehousing managers plan and direct personnel who order, receive, store, and issue equipment and supplies.

What They Do

Supply and warehousing managers in the military perform some or all of the following duties:

- Analyze the demand for supplies and forecast future needs

- Direct personnel who receive, inventory, store, and issue supplies and equipment

- Manage the inspection, shipping, handling, and packaging of supplies and equipment

- Direct the preparation of reports and records

- Evaluate bids and proposals submitted by potential suppliers

- Study ways to use space and distribute supplies efficiently

Special Requirements

A 4-year college degree is normally required to enter this occupation.

Helpful Attributes

Helpful fields of study include business administration, inventory management, and operations research. Helpful attributes include:

- Interest in planning and directing the work of others

- Ability to express ideas clearly and concisely

Training Provided

Job training consists of 2 to 16 weeks of classroom instruction. Training length varies depending on specialty. Course content typically includes:

- Warehousing and storage procedures

- Handling and packaging procedures

- Administrative procedures

- Field supply management

- Planning for future supply needs

Work Environment

Supply and warehousing managers usually work in offices and warehouses. At times, they may be exposed to loud noise from machines and equipment.

Civilian Counterparts

Civilian supply and warehousing managers work for storage companies, manufacturers, hospitals, schools, and government agencies. They perform duties similar to those performed by military supply and warehousing managers. They may also be called warehouse managers or operations managers.

Opportunities

The services have about 6,000 supply and warehousing managers. Each year they need new managers due to changes in personnel and the demands of the field. After job training, supply and warehousing managers are assigned to positions in supply or munitions management. With experience, they may advance to senior management or command positions.

INTEREST CODE

This occupation generally appeals to people whose primary Interest Code is *Enterprising. Enterprising* jobs:

- Are fast-paced
- Require that you take on a lot of responsibility

Pages 8 and 9 explain the Interest Codes

Profile: Benjamin Travis

Benjamin (Ben) Travis wanted to serve in the military. He also wanted a college education and a chance to play college basketball. So he applied for and was selected to attend the U.S. Coast Guard Academy, where he lettered in basketball 3 years.

Like many Coast Guard officers, Ben served two tours of general duty before he specialized. He requested for his first assignment a tour as gunnery (or weapons) officer on a Coast Guard cutter. His ship gave gunfire support to U.S. soldiers and Marines on land.

Back in the States, Ben married his girlfriend whom he had met while he was a cadet at the Academy. They enjoyed living in Miami Beach, the site of his next tour. Here, Ben commanded a 95-foot patrol boat and a crew of 15 men. He and his crew rescued stranded boats and enforced customs and maritime law in the Miami area.

Ben's next assignment was to graduate school, where he earned an M.B.A. in one intense year of study. Always interested in finance, he specialized in supply and warehousing management. (The Coast Guard calls supply officers "comptrollers.")

As a Lieutenant, his first comptroller assignment was with the 7th Coast Guard District in Miami, developing and managing a budget of $35–$45 million. Ben says, "I really enjoyed the independence and responsibility of that job."

As he advanced, he served in positions of more authority. As a Lieutenant Commander in Washington, DC, he briefed congressmen, senators, and other government officials on Coast Guard budget and procurement plans. He also enjoyed several general duty tours outside his occupational specialty. He especially enjoyed a tour as executive officer of a large Coast Guard cutter.

Now in Washington, DC, with the rank of Commander, Ben develops comptroller policies for the Coast Guard and oversees procurement of every item the Coast Guard buys, anywhere in the world. Reflecting on his career he says, "So far, I honestly haven't had an assignment that I didn't enjoy. The variety, the challenges, and the responsibility have been tremendously rewarding."

SAMPLE CAREER PATH

Supply and Warehousing Director   15–18 years

Supply and Warehousing Directors command a supply facility or direct the supply operations at a military base. They act as advisors to senior service commanders and conduct inspections of supply units.

Supply Staff Officer   9–11 years

Supply staff officers assist the supply and warehousing directors in administrative and management duties. They plan supply requirements for operational missions and analyze purchasing and distribution patterns. They also direct and evaluate studies to improve supply methods.

Senior Supply Officer   4 years

Senior supply officers manage a supply or warehouse operation, directing other officers and enlisted personnel. They advise commanding officers on supply requirements, inspect the facilities under their command, and train new supply officers.

Supply Officer

Supply officers direct civilian and enlisted military personnel in ordering, receiving, and issuing equipment and supplies. They also inspect storage facilities and give instructions on material handling and safety.

The years shown represent typical time-in-service before advancement to that level. Actual career advancement depends on individual experience and performance.

Health Care Occupations

Health care officers provide health services at military facilities based on their area of specialization. Officers who examine, diagnose, and treat patients with illness, injury, or disease include physicians, registered nurses, and dentists. Other health care officers provide therapy, rehabilitative treatment, and other services for patients. For example, physical and occupational therapists plan and administer therapy to help patients adjust to disabilities, regain independence, and prepare to return to work. Speech therapists evaluate and treat patients with hearing and speech problems. Dietitians manage medical food service facilities and plan meals for hospital patients and outpatients who need special diets. Pharmacists manage the purchasing, storing, and dispensing of drugs and medicines.

- Dentists
- Dietitians
- Optometrists
- Pharmacists
- Physical and Occupational Therapists
- Physician Assistants
- Physicians and Surgeons
    Profile: Anthony Rugieri
- Psychologists
- Registered Nurses
    Profile: Janice Kendall
- Speech Therapists

DENTISTS

Army
Navy
Air Force
Coast Guard

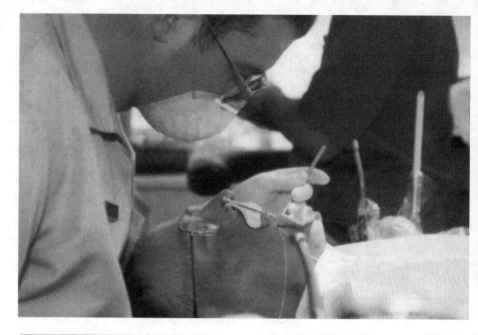

Dental care is a basic health service provided to men and women in the military. Military dentists examine, diagnose, and treat diseases and disorders of the mouth. They may practice general dentistry or work in one of several specialties.

What They Do

Dentists in the military perform some or all of the following duties:

- Examine patients' teeth and gums to detect signs of disease or tooth decay

- Examine X-rays to determine the soundness of teeth and the alignment of teeth and jaws

- Locate and fill tooth cavities

- Perform oral (mouth) surgery to treat problems with teeth, gums, or jaws

- Develop and fit dentures (artificial teeth) to replace missing teeth

- Construct and fit dental devices, such as braces and retainers, for straightening teeth

- Plan dental health programs for patients to help prevent dental problems

Special Requirements

A doctor of dentistry degree and additional training in a dental specialty are required to enter this occupation.

Helpful Attributes

Helpful attributes include:

- Desire to help others

- Good eye-hand coordination

Work Environment

Dentists work in hospitals and dental clinics on land and aboard ships.

Training Provided

No initial job training is provided to officers in this occupation.

Civilian Counterparts

Civilian dentists work in private practice, public health facilities, and dental research organizations. They perform duties similar to those performed in the military and specialize in similar areas. Depending on their specialty, dentists may also be called oral pathologists, endodontists, oral surgeons, orthodontists, pedodontists, prosthodontists, periodontists, or public health dentists.

Opportunities

The military has about 3,000 dentists. Each year, the services need new dentists to meet the changing demands in the field. Newly commissioned dentists are assigned to dental clinics to practice general dentistry or a dental specialty. Positions for dentists in the Coast Guard are filled by U.S. Public Health Service Officers. Dentists who demonstrate leadership and managerial qualities may advance to administer dental facilities and programs.

INTEREST CODE

This occupation generally appeals to people whose primary Interest Code is *Investigative. Investigative* jobs:

- Involve learning about a new subject area

- Allow you to use your knowledge to solve problems or create things or ideas

Pages 8 and 9 explain the Interest Codes

DIETITIANS

Dietitians are part of the military's health care staff. They are experts in the nutritional needs of hospital patients and outpatients. Dietitians manage medical food service facilities and plan meals for hospital patients and outpatients who need special diets.

What They Do

Dietitians in the military perform some or all of the following duties:

- Set policies for hospital food service operations

- Inspect hospital food service and preparation areas to be sure they meet sanitation and safety standards

- Plan and organize training programs for medical food service personnel

- Develop special diets for patients based on instructions from doctors

- Plan menus for hospital meals

- Interview patients to determine whether they are satisfied with their diet

- Develop hospital food service budgets

- Provide information on nutrition to the military community

Special Requirements

A 4-year college degree in food and nutrition or institutional management is required to enter this occupation. Some specialties require completion of a general dietetic internship.

Helpful Attributes

Helpful attributes include:

- Desire to help others

- Interest in nutrition and food preparation

- Interest in interpreting scientific and medical data

Work Environment

Dietitians work in hospitals, clinics, and aboard ships.

Training Provided

No initial job training is provided to officers in this occupation. However, the Air Force and Army offer internship programs in dietetics that are approved by the American Dietetic Association.

Civilian Counterparts

Civilian dietitians work in hospitals, clinics, and other health care facilities. They perform duties similar to those performed by military dietitians. Dietitians also work for college food services, restaurants, industrial food services, and research institutions. Civilian dietitians may specialize in specific areas of dietetics, such as consultation, clinical dietetics, and community health.

Opportunities

The services have about 300 dietitians. Each year, they need new dietitians due to changes in personnel and the demands of the field. Newly commissioned dietitians are assigned to military hospitals, clinics, or ships, where they plan and direct the work of food service personnel. They may advance to senior management positions in hospital food service programs.

INTEREST CODE

This occupation generally appeals to people whose primary Interest Code is *Investigative. Investigative* jobs:

- Involve learning about a new subject area

- Allow you to use your knowledge to solve problems or create things or ideas

Pages 8 and 9 explain the Interest Codes

OPTOMETRISTS

Army
Navy
Air Force

Eye care is part of the full health coverage provided to military personnel. The most common eye problem is the need for corrective lenses. Optometrists examine eyes and treat vision problems by prescribing glasses, contact lenses, or other corrective treatments. They refer patients with eye diseases to ophthalmologists (eye medical doctors).

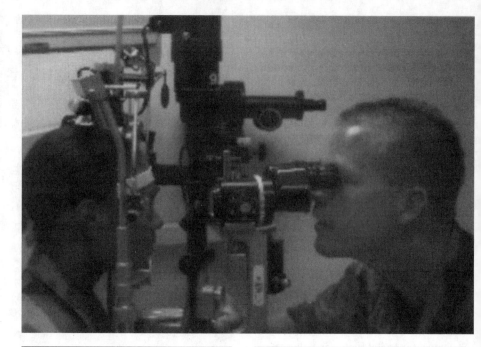

What They Do

Optometrists in the military perform some or all of the following duties:

- Check patient vision using eye charts

- Examine eyes for glaucoma and other diseases

- Measure patient nearsightedness, farsightedness, depth perception, and other vision problems using optical instruments

- Prescribe corrective lenses or other corrective treatments

- Prescribe training exercises to strengthen weak eye muscles

- Instruct patients on how to wear and care for glasses and contact lenses

Special Requirements

A doctor of optometry degree and a state license to practice optometry are required to enter this occupation.

Helpful Attributes

Helpful attributes include:

- Preference for working closely with people

- Desire to help others

- Interest in work requiring accuracy and attention to detail

Work Environment

Optometrists work in clinics and hospitals.

Training Provided

No initial job training is provided to officers in this occupation.

Civilian Counterparts

Most civilian optometrists work in private practice. Some work for hospitals, clinics, public health agencies, or optical laboratories. Civilian optometrists perform duties similar to those performed in the military.

Opportunities

The services have about 400 optometrists. Each year, they need new optometrists due to changes in personnel resources and the demands of the field. Newly commissioned optometrists are assigned to clinics or hospitals. In time, they may advance to senior management positions in the health service field.

INTEREST CODE

This occupation generally appeals to people whose primary Interest Code is *Investigative. Investigative* jobs:

- Involve learning about a new subject area

- Allow you to use your knowledge to solve problems or create things or ideas

Pages 8 and 9 explain the Interest Codes

284

Military Careers

PHARMACISTS

Drugs and medicines are sometimes prescribed by doctors when treating patients in military hospitals and clinics. Pharmacists manage the purchasing, storing, and dispensing of drugs and medicines.

What They Do

Pharmacists in the military perform some or all of the following duties:

• Manage pharmacy technicians who prepare, label, and dispense orders for drugs and medicines

• Advise doctors and patients on the proper use and side effects of drugs and medicines

• Train medical, nursing, and pharmacy staffs on the use of drugs

• Consult on drug and medicine research programs

• Check drug and medicine supplies and reorder when necessary

• Direct pharmacy record keeping

Special Requirements

A 4-year college degree in pharmacy and a state license to practice pharmacy are required to enter this occupation.

Helpful Attributes

Helpful attributes include:

• Interest in understanding the effects of drugs and medicines

• Interest in chemical formulas

• Interest in work requiring accuracy and attention to detail

Work Environment

Pharmacists work in hospitals and clinics on land and aboard ships.

Training Provided

No initial job training is provided to officers in this occupation.

Civilian Counterparts

Civilian pharmacists work for pharmacies, drug stores, and drug departments of stores and supermarkets. They also work for hospitals, nursing homes, and clinics. They perform duties similar to those performed by military pharmacists. Civilian pharmacists who specialize in radioactive drugs (radioisotopes) are known as radiopharmacists.

Opportunities

The services have over 500 pharmacists. Each year, they need new pharmacists due to changes in personnel and the demands of the field. Newly commissioned pharmacists are assigned to military hospitals or clinics, where they manage daily operations. Positions for pharmacists in the Coast Guard are filled by U.S. Public Health Service Officers. In time, pharmacists plan and direct pharmacy or other health programs.

INTEREST CODE

This occupation generally appeals to people whose primary Interest Code is *Investigative. Investigative* jobs:

• Involve learning about a new subject area

• Allow you to use your knowledge to solve problems or create things or ideas

Pages 8 and 9 explain the Interest Codes

PHYSICAL AND OCCUPATIONAL THERAPISTS

Army
Navy
Air Force
Coast Guard

Physical and occupational therapies are programs of treatment and exercise for patients disabled from illness or injury. Physical and occupational therapists plan and administer therapy to help patients adjust to disabilities, regain independence, and prepare to return to work.

What They Do

Physical and occupational therapists in the military perform some or all of the following duties:

- Test and interview patients to determine the extent of their disabilities

- Plan and manage individual physical or occupational therapy programs

- Consult with doctors and other therapists to discuss appropriate therapy and evaluate patients' progress

- Administer exercise programs and heat and massage treatments

- Counsel patients and their families to help create a positive attitude for recovery

Special Requirements

A 4-year college degree in physical or occupational therapy and completion of a clinical program in physical or occupational therapy are required to enter this occupation. Depending on specialty, a state physical therapy license or eligibility for registration with the American Occupational Therapy Association may also be required.

Helpful Attributes

Helpful attributes include:

- Desire to help others

- Interest in developing detailed plans and treatments

- Patience to work with people whose injuries heal slowly

- Ability to communicate effectively

Work Environment

Physical and occupational therapists work in hospitals, clinics, rehabilitation centers, and other medical facilities.

Physical Demands

Physical and occupational therapists may have to lift and support patients during exercises and treatments.

Training Provided

No initial job training is provided in this occupation.

Civilian Counterparts

Civilian physical and occupational therapists work in hospitals, rehabilitation centers, nursing homes, schools, and community mental health centers. They perform duties similar to those performed by military therapists. Civilian physical and occupational therapists often specialize in treating a particular type of patient, such as children, the elderly, the severely disabled, or those who have lost arms or legs (amputees).

Opportunities

The services have over 500 physical and occupational therapists. Each year, they need new therapists due to changes in personnel and the demands of the field. Positions for physical and occupational therapists in the Coast Guard are filled by U.S. Public Health Service Officers. Physical and occupational therapists have the opportunity to advance to senior management or command positions in medical administration.

INTEREST CODE

This occupation generally appeals to people whose primary Interest Code is *Investigative. Investigative* jobs:

- Involve learning about a new subject area

- Allow you to use your knowledge to solve problems or create things or ideas

Pages 8 and 9 explain the Interest Codes

PHYSICIAN ASSISTANTS

Physician assistants provide routine health care for patients, freeing physicians to concentrate on more serious health problems. Physician assistants examine, diagnose, and treat patients under the supervision of medical doctors.

What They Do

Physician assistants in the military perform some or all of the following duties:

- Record medical histories, examine patients, and make initial diagnoses

- Treat common illnesses or injuries, calling in supervising physicians for serious health problems

- Perform routine physical examinations and collect specimens for laboratory tests

- Order laboratory studies, such as blood tests, urinalysis, and X-rays

- Provide information to patients about diet, family planning, use of drugs, and the effect of treatments

- Provide emergency care in situations where doctors are not available

Special Requirements

Graduation from an accredited training program for physician assistants that is recognized by the services is normally required to enter this occupation. Depending upon the service, however, military job training may be available.

Helpful Attributes

Helpful attributes include:

- Self-confidence and the ability to remain calm in stressful situations

- Patience with others, especially those in pain or stress

- Desire to help others

- Ability to express ideas clearly and concisely

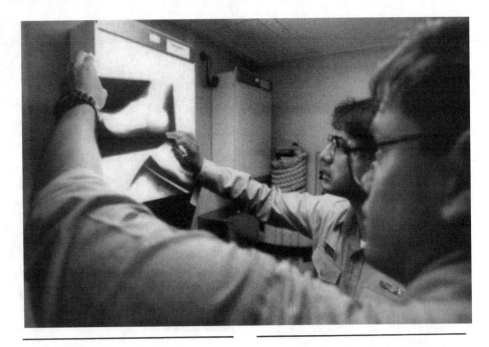

Work Environment

Physician assistants work in hospitals and clinics on land and aboard ships.

Training Provided

Job training, when available from the services, consists of about 40 weeks of classroom instruction, including practice in providing patient health care. Course content typically includes:

- Fundamental medical care procedures

- Principles of behavioral and dental science

- Health care administration techniques

Civilian Counterparts

Civilian physician assistants work in hospitals, clinics, doctor's offices, and nursing homes. They perform duties similar to those performed by military physician assistants.

Opportunities

The services have over 1,000 physician assistants. Each year, they need new physician assistants due to changes in personnel and the demands of the field. After job training, physician assistants provide health care under close supervision. With experience, they work more independently, although they remain under the supervision of a doctor. In time, they may advance to management positions in the military health care field.

INTEREST CODE

This occupation generally appeals to people whose primary Interest Code is *Investigative. Investigative* jobs:

- Involve learning about a new subject area

- Allow you to use your knowledge to solve problems or create things or ideas

Pages 8 and 9 explain the Interest Codes

PHYSICIANS AND SURGEONS

Army
Navy
Air Force
Coast Guard

Military physicians and surgeons represent all of the major fields of medical specialization. Physicians and surgeons are the chief providers of medical services to military personnel and their dependents. They examine patients, diagnose their injuries or illnesses, and provide medical treatment.

What They Do

Physicians and surgeons in the military perform some or all of the following duties:

- Examine patients to detect abnormalities in pulse, breathing, or other body functions

- Determine presence and extent of illness or injury by reviewing medical histories, X-rays, laboratory reports, and examination reports

- Develop treatment plans that may include medication, therapy, or surgery

- Perform surgery to treat injuries or illnesses

- Advise patients on their health problems and personal habits

- Coordinate the activities of nurses, physician assistants, medical specialists, therapists, and other medical personnel

- Conduct medical research

Special Requirements

A doctor of medicine or osteopathy degree and advanced training in a medical specialty are required to enter this occupation.

Helpful Attributes

Helpful attributes include:

- Desire to help others

- Ability to express ideas clearly and concisely

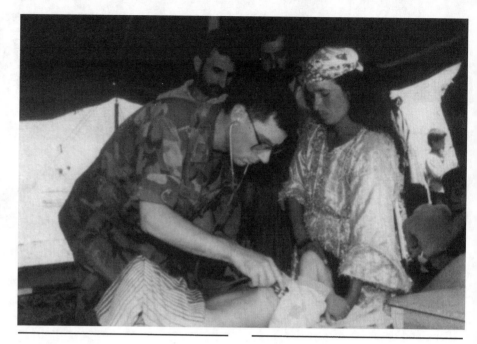

Work Environment

Physicians and surgeons work in hospitals and clinics on land and aboard ships.

Opportunities

The services have a total of about 12,000 physicians and surgeons, including all general practitioners and specialists. Each year, they need new physicians and surgeons due to changes in personnel and the demands of the field. The services give several hundred scholarships yearly to attend civilian medical schools or the Uniformed Services University of the Health Sciences in Bethesda, Maryland, in return for an obligated period of military service after graduation. The services normally hire physicians who have completed medical school and their internships. However, some services have programs to grant early officer commissions to civilians who are in medical school, internship, or residency status in return for an obligated period of service. Positions for physicians and surgeons in the Coast Guard are filled by U.S. Public Health Service Officers. After gaining experience in the military, physicians and surgeons may advance to senior management or command positions in the services' medical corps.

Training Provided

No initial job training is provided to officers in this occupation. However, advanced courses and programs in medical specialties are available. In addition, scholarships for advanced medical training are available in return for an obligated period of military service.

Civilian Counterparts

Civilian physicians work for hospitals or clinics or in private practice. They perform the same duties and work in the same areas of specialization as military physicians.

INTEREST CODE

This occupation generally appeals to people whose primary Interest Code is *Investigative. Investigative* jobs:

- Involve learning about a new subject area

- Allow you to use your knowledge to solve problems or create things or ideas

Pages 8 and 9 explain the Interest Codes

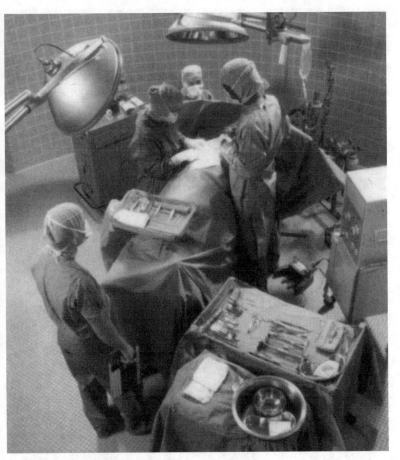

Profile: Anthony Rugieri

Anthony Rugieri enjoyed biology and wanted to become a doctor. He chose the Army because of the educational opportunities it offered for obtaining a medical degree. "The Army internship gave doctors a chance to rotate in departments and to practice many medical specialties," he says. Anthony's first assignment was directing emergency room services at a large hospital near Washington, DC.

In his next assignment, Anthony went to the Middle East for Operation Desert Storm. He found the life of a combat doctor challenging. After this tour, he decided to "stay awhile" in Army medicine.

Returning from the Middle East, Anthony was selected for a fully-funded advanced training program in internal medicine. He stayed on at the hospital where he trained and served a year as staff physician in internal medicine.

After a tour with the Office of the Army Surgeon General in Washington, DC, Anthony and his family enjoyed a tour in Germany together. Anthony was the chief of internal medicine at an Army hospital and followed this assignment with a position as chief of hospital clinics and community health services.

In Germany, Anthony qualified for certification in family practice medicine. This was a new program in military medicine. As one of the first doctors qualified, Anthony returned to the United States and became the chief of family services at a large hospital on the East Coast. He also directed a residency program for doctors in advanced training.

Today, Anthony is a Colonel, directing quality assurance for the Surgeon General of the Army. Anthony says, "One of the best things about my career has been the opportunity to work in many different jobs. I am always looking forward to my next assignment."

SAMPLE CAREER PATH

Medical Director   **15–18 years**

Medical Directors are in charge of administering medical services at a military hospital or large clinic. They confer with staff doctors to verify diagnoses and treatments. They also direct training and residency programs and evaluate staff doctors.

Staff Doctor   **9–11 years**

Staff doctors practice in their specialty at a hospital, clinic, or on a ship and serve as the chief of a clinic or department. They supervise and advise residents, general medical officers, interns, and students.

Resident Doctor   **2– 4 years**

Residents are doctors who have returned to military or civilian teaching hospitals to gain medical specialties. They complete rigorous programs of study in a specialty while instructing and supervising interns and students and caring for their own patients.

General Medical Officer   **2 years**

General medical officers are doctors assigned to hospitals, clinics, or large ships. They examine patients and diagnose and treat illnesses. They also conduct medical "rounds" to review patient progress.

Intern

Interns work in a supervised program of medical practice training for medical school graduates. They accompany resident and staff doctors on medical "rounds" and assist with patient evaluation and diagnosis, and treatment.

The years shown represent typical time-in-service before advancement to that level. Actual career advancement depends on individual experience and performance.

PSYCHOLOGISTS

Psychological research and treatment are important to national defense. Research can show how to improve military training, job assignment, and equipment design. Treatment can help personnel cope with stress. Psychologists conduct research on human behavior and treat patients with mental problems.

What They Do

Psychologists in the military perform some or all of the following duties:

- Conduct research on human and animal behavior, emotions, and thinking processes

- Conduct research on aptitude and job performance

- Give psychological tests and interpret results to diagnose patients' problems

- Treat patients individually and in groups

- Conduct experiments to determine the best equipment design, work procedures, and training course content

- Write research reports

- Direct research projects performed by outside contractors

Special Requirements

A 4-year college degree in psychology is required to enter this occupation. Some specialties require a master's degree.

Helpful Attributes

Helpful attributes include:

- Desire to help others

- Interest in scientific research

- Interest in mathematics and statistics

Work Environment

Psychologists usually work in offices, hospitals, clinics, and other medical facilities on land and aboard ships.

Training Provided

No initial job training is provided for officers in this occupation. Advanced courses are available in some specialties.

Civilian Counterparts

Some civilian psychologists treat patients in private practice, hospitals, school systems, and mental health centers. They are called clinical psychologists, counseling psychologists, or educational psychologists. Other civilian psychologists conduct research work for universities, research firms, and government agencies. They are called experimental psychologists, social psychologists, and psychometricians.

Opportunities

The services have over 800 psychologists. Each year, they need new psychologists due to changes in personnel and the demands of the field. With experience, they may lead projects of their own. New clinical psychologists may treat patients in military clinics. Eventually, both research and clinical psychologists may become directors of offices or laboratories.

INTEREST CODE

This occupation generally appeals to people whose primary Interest Code is *Investigative*. *Investigative* jobs:

- Involve learning about a new subject area

- Allow you to use your knowledge to solve problems or create things or ideas

Pages 8 and 9 explain the Interest Codes

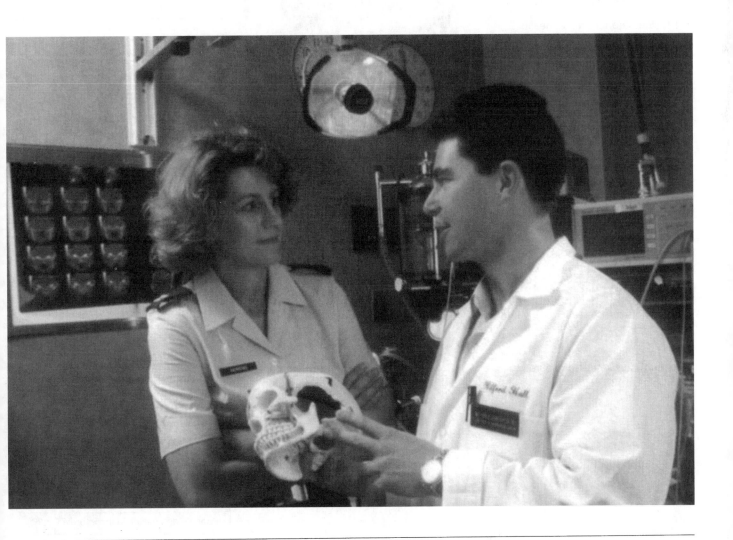

REGISTERED NURSES

Nurses are a key part of the staff at military hospitals and clinics. Registered nurses direct nursing teams and give patients individual care to help them recover from illness or injury.

What They Do

Registered nurses in the military perform some or all of the following duties:

- Help physicians treat patients

- Give injections of pain killers, antibiotics, and other medicines as prescribed by physicians

- Change bandages and dressings

- Assist physicians during surgery

- Provide life support treatment for patients needing emergency care

- Provide care for mental health patients

- Keep records of patients' condition

- Supervise practical nurses, nurse aides, and other support personnel

Special Requirements

Graduation from an accredited school of nursing and a license to practice nursing are required to enter this occupation.

Helpful Attributes

Helpful attributes include:

- Desire to help others

- Ability to express ideas clearly and concisely

- Self-confidence and the ability to remain calm under pressure

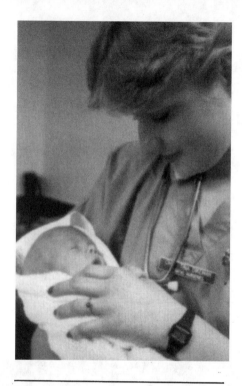

Training Provided

Job training consists of 14 to 27 weeks of classroom instruction. Training length varies depending on specialty. Course content typically includes:

- Practices and principles of military nursing

- Care of emotionally disturbed patients

- Health care for children

- Nursing techniques

- Anesthesia, respiratory therapy, and cardiopulmonary resuscitation

Work Environment

Registered nurses work in hospitals and clinics. Some work in sick bays aboard ships or in mobile field hospitals. Others work in airplanes that transfer patients to medical centers.

Civilian Counterparts

Civilian registered nurses work in hospitals, clinics, and private medical facilities. They also work for public health agencies, nursing homes, and rehabilitation centers. Civilian registered nurses perform duties similar to those performed in the military. They often specialize and may be known as public health nurses, nurse practitioners, or general duty nurses.

Opportunities

The services have close to 11,000 nurses. Each year, they need new nurses due to changes in personnel and the demands of the field. Positions for registered nurses in the Coast Guard are filled by U.S. Public Health Service Officers. Depending on the prior experience that nurses bring with them to the military, their job assignments may vary. After job training, inexperienced nurses work under close supervision. Experienced nurses normally work under less supervision. In time, nurses may become nurse supervisors. Eventually, they may become directors of nursing in hospitals or advance to senior health service management positions.

INTEREST CODE

This occupation generally appeals to people whose primary Interest Code is *Social. Social* jobs:

- involve working with and helping others

- Lets you teach others new skills

Pages 8 and 9 explain the Interest Codes

Profile: Janice Kendall

When she was 3 years old, Navy Captain Janice Kendall had an attack of appendicitis. She spent months in the hospital. She says, "I was so impressed with the nurses who cared for me that I knew I wanted to be one too."

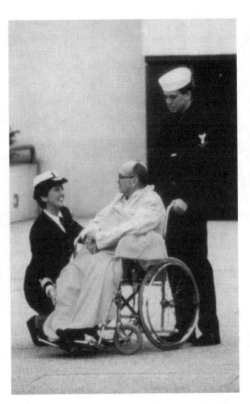

Janice went to diploma school in Canada, then did more work to train in psychiatric nursing. After practicing several years, an uncle in the Navy suggested she try Navy nursing. Feeling the 2-year commitment wasn't too bad, Janice joined. She began her career monitoring seven psychiatric wards as part of a close-knit team with the psychiatrist at the Navy hospital in San Diego.

Her second tour was in Subic Bay, the Philippines. The hours were long but rewarding. During this assignment she used her leave to tour the Far East – Hong Kong, Bangkok, India, and Japan. She also met her husband when he was on leave from Vietnam.

Janice was recognized not only as an outstanding nurse, but as an excellent leader. Her next few tours took her to hospitals where she directed other nurses and trained Navy hospital corpsmen. Training the hospital corpsmen has been a favorite activity for Janice. Navy corpsmen are often the only medical people on board submarines, small ships, and marine combat units.

Janice was selected for further education. After earning her baccalaureate degree in nursing, she was assigned to Camp Pendleton, CA, and then to Okinawa, a Japanese island. In Okinawa she served as assistant director of nursing services and director of family advocacy for all Navy and Marine Corps families on the island.

Today, Janice assists the Admiral who directs the Navy Nurse Corps. She has been at the hub of Navy nursing activity over the past several years. She says, "My experience has given me a lot to share with the young nurses I will be directing in my next tour." She is looking forward to serving as assistant director of nursing at one of the largest naval hospitals in the world.

Looking back over 24 years of service, she says, "I like everything about it. It's never the same, you constantly gain experience, see new places, and never lose seniority."

SAMPLE CAREER PATH

Director of Nursing Care   **15–18 years**

Directors of Nursing Care activities at hospitals or other medical treatment facilities manage all nursing services at their hospital or facility. They advise medical staff and hospital administration on nursing services. They also direct nursing orientation and training programs.

Patient Care Coordinator   **9–11 years**

Patient Care Coordinators administer nursing services for wards or clinics. They assign nurses to shifts and accompany doctors on medical "rounds." They also track the adequacy of nursing care, supervise the ordering of supplies, and monitor the maintenance of medical records.

Charge Nurse   **4 years**

Charge Nurses are responsible for all nursing activity on a hospital ward. They assign staff nurses to patients and participate in training programs. They also consult with patient care coordinators on unusual nursing problems and manage special or unusual patient needs.

Staff Nurse

Registered Nurses start their military careers assigned to patient care duty at a clinical service ward of a hospital or medical center. They provide specialized patient care and direct enlisted medical and nursing technicians in routine patient care.

The years shown represent typical time-in-service before advancement to that level. Actual career advancement depends on individual experience and performance.

SPEECH THERAPISTS

Speech therapists work as part of military medical teams. Speech therapists evaluate and treat patients with hearing and speech problems.

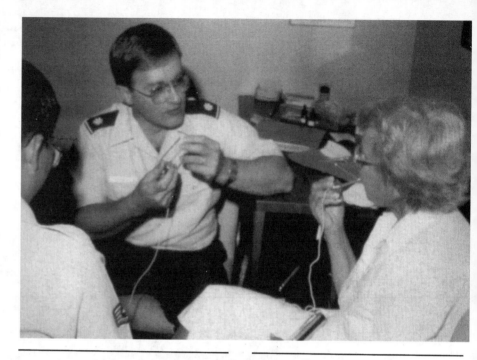

What They Do

Speech therapists in the military perform some or all of the following duties:

• Talk with patients to discuss hearing and speaking problems and possible causes and treatment

• Identify speaking and language problems

• Examine the ears, including the entire auditory (hearing) system

• Evaluate examination and test data to determine the type and amount of hearing loss

• Treat hearing problems using hearing aids and other treatments

• Assist patients in selecting and using hearing aids

• Conduct programs to help patients improve their speaking skills

• Research new techniques for treating hearing and speaking problems

Special Requirements

A master's degree in either audiology or speech therapy is required to enter this occupation depending on the occupational specialty.

Helpful Attributes

Helpful attributes include:

• Desire to help others

• Interest in scientific work

• Patience to work with people whose injuries heal slowly

Work Environment

Speech therapists work in therapy labs, clinics, and medical centers.

Training Provided

No initial job training is provided to officers in this occupational group.

Civilian Counterparts

Civilian speech therapists work in hospitals, clinics, schools, and research centers. They perform duties similar to those performed by military speech therapists. Depending on their specialty, civilian speech therapists may also be called audiologists or speech pathologists.

Opportunities

The services have about 100 speech therapists. Each year, they need new therapists due to changes in personnel and the demands of the field. Positions for speech therapists in the Coast Guard are filled by U.S. Public Health Service Officers. After displaying leadership abilities, speech therapists may advance to senior management and command positions in the medical field.

INTEREST CODE

This occupation generally appeals to people whose primary Interest Code is *Social. Social* jobs:

• involve working with and helping others

• Lets you teach others new skills

Pages 8 and 9 explain the Interest Codes

Human Resource Development Occupations

Human resource development officers manage recruitment, placement, and training strategies and programs in the military. Personnel in this area normally specialize by activity. Recruiting managers direct recruiting efforts and provide information about military careers to young people, parents, schools, and local communities. Personnel managers direct military personnel functions such as job assignment, staff promotion, and career counseling. Training and education directors identify training needs and develop and manage educational programs designed to keep military personnel current in the skills they need to perform their jobs.

- Personnel Managers
- Recruiting Managers
- Teachers and Instructors
- Training and Education Directors

Profile: Barry Forsythe

PERSONNEL MANAGERS

As with civilian employers, the military tries to find the best person for each job and encourages each individual to realize his or her full potential. Personnel managers direct programs to attract and select new personnel for the services, assign them to jobs, provide career counseling, and maintain personnel records.

What They Do

Personnel managers in the military perform some or all of the following duties:

- Plan recruiting activities to interest qualified young people in the military
- Direct testing and career counseling for military personnel
- Classify personnel according to job aptitude, interest, and service need
- Direct the assignment of personnel to jobs and training
- Direct personnel recordkeeping operations
- Establish standards to determine the number of people to assign to activities
- Study military jobs to see how they can be improved and kept up-to-date with technology
- Plan for hiring, training, and assigning personnel for the future
- Develop programs to prevent and resolve equal opportunity problems

Helpful Attributes

Helpful fields of study include personnel management, organizational development, industrial psychology, and labor relations. Helpful attributes include:

- Interest in working closely with people
- Interest in planning and directing the work of others
- Interest in working with computers

Work Environment

Personnel managers work in offices.

Training Provided

Job training consists of 5 to 16 weeks of classroom instruction. Course content typically includes:

- Military personnel policies and objectives
- Automated personnel systems
- Career development programs
- Equal opportunity problems
- Management and organizational concepts

Further training occurs in advanced courses.

Civilian Counterparts

Civilian personnel managers work for all types of businesses and industries, as well as for government agencies. They perform duties similar to those performed by military personnel managers. Depending on their specialty, they may also be called employment relations directors, employment managers, occupational analysts, industrial relations directors, equal employment opportunity representatives, or affirmative action coordinators.

Special Requirements

A 4-year college degree is normally required to enter this occupation.

Opportunities

The services have about 4,500 personnel managers. Each year, they need new managers due to changes in personnel and the demands of the field. After job training, personnel managers may be assigned to many different types of work, depending on their specialties. Usually, they begin by working under experienced personnel managers. In time, they may advance to senior management and command positions.

INTEREST CODE

This occupation generally appeals to people whose primary Interest Code is *Social*. *Social* jobs:

- involve working with and helping others
- Lets you teach others new skills

Pages 8 and 9 explain the Interest Codes

RECRUITING MANAGERS

Each year, over 300,000 young men and women enlist in the military, making it the country's largest employer of youth. The services recruit young people with the kinds of talent needed to succeed in today's military. Recruiting managers plan and direct the activities of recruiting specialists who provide information to young people about military careers.

What They Do

Recruiting managers in the military perform some or all of the following duties:

- Plan programs to inform young people about military careers

- Direct staff in local recruiting offices who carry out programs to inform the public about military careers

- Speak with local civic groups, schools, parents, and young people about military careers

- Prepare reports and brief commanders on recruiting goals and results

Special Requirements

A 4-year college degree is normally required to enter this occupation.

Helpful Attributes

Helpful fields of study include personnel management, communications, and public relations. Helpful attributes include:

- Interest in working closely with people

- Ability to speak effectively to large and small groups of people

Work Environment

Recruiting managers usually work in offices.

Training Provided

No initial job training is provided to officers in this occupation.

Civilian Counterparts

Civilian recruiting managers work for human resources or personnel departments for a variety of organizations in areas such as business, government, and the health care industry. Civilian recruiting managers develop staffing plans and manage efforts to hire people with the right skills for the work that needs to be performed. They may also work for search firms that specialize in finding employees for other companies.

Opportunities

The services have about 300 recruiting managers. Normally, officers must be in the military for a few years before they are eligible to become recruiting managers. Each year, the services need new recruiting managers since some officers enter the field of recruiting as a temporary position to gain experience in a management area before returning to their primary occupation. Officers remaining in recruiting may advance to senior management or command positions in this field.

INTEREST CODE

This occupation generally appeals to people whose primary Interest Code is *Social. Social* jobs:

- involve working with and helping others

- Lets you teach others new skills

Pages 8 and 9 explain the Interest Codes

TEACHERS AND INSTRUCTORS

The military provides training and educational opportunities for all personnel. Teachers and instructors conduct classes in such academic subjects as engineering, physical science, social science, and nursing. Teachers and instructors teach military personnel subjects that are related to their military occupations.

What They Do

Teachers and instructors in the military perform some or all of the following duties:

- Develop course content, training outlines, and lesson plans

- Prepare training aids, assignments, and demonstrations

- Deliver lectures

- Conduct laboratory exercises and seminars

- Give tests and evaluate student progress

- Diagnose individual learning difficulties and offer help

Special Requirements

A 4-year college degree is normally required to enter this occupation. Some specialties require a master's degree.

Helpful Attributes

Helpful attributes include:

- Ability to express ideas clearly and concisely

- Interest in teaching

- Preference for working closely with people

Work Environment

Teachers and instructors usually work in classrooms and lecture halls.

Training Provided

No initial job training is provided to officers in this occupation.

Civilian Counterparts

Civilian teachers and instructors work in junior colleges, colleges, and universities. They perform duties similar to those performed in the military. They may teach several different courses within the same field of study.

Opportunities

The services have about 4,000 officers working as teachers or instructors. They are usually selected from officers trained and working in a military occupation. Since some officers return to their regular occupations after teaching, the services need new teachers and instructors each year. Eventually, teachers may become tenured professors at the service academies or other military colleges or managers of education programs.

INTEREST CODE

This occupation generally appeals to people whose primary Interest Code is *Social. Social* jobs:

- involve working with and helping others

- Lets you teach others new skills

Pages 8 and 9 explain the Interest Codes

TRAINING AND EDUCATION DIRECTORS

The military places great importance on training to prepare service men and women for their military careers. Programs include training in technical skills, physical fitness, academic subjects, and leadership development. Training and education directors plan, develop, and manage education and training programs for military personnel.

What They Do

Training and education directors in the military perform some or all of the following duties:

- Plan and direct instructional programs for military personnel

- Develop training and educational policies and objectives

- Develop new training courses and evaluate new teaching methods

- Review and approve course material and training outlines prepared by instructors

- Assign duties to instructors, curriculum planners, and training aids specialists

- Train instructors in course subject matter

- Coordinate training for military personnel at civilian schools or through correspondence courses

- Evaluate the progress of students and instructors

Special Requirements

A 4-year college degree is normally required to enter this occupation. Some specialties require a master's or other postgraduate degree.

Work Environment

Education and training directors work in offices and classroom training facilities. Those directing physical training work in gyms or outdoor settings.

Helpful Attributes

Helpful fields of study include education, organizational development, personnel management, and industrial psychology. Helpful attributes include:

- Interest in developing educational programs

- Preference for working with people

- Interest in work involving many subject areas

Civilian Counterparts

Civilian training and education directors work in schools, colleges, universities, vocational and technical schools, and training departments in business and industry. They perform duties similar to those performed by military training and education directors. They may also be called education administrators, educational program directors, and vocational training directors.

Training Provided

No initial job training is provided to officers in this occupation.

Opportunities

The services have over 1,000 officers working as training and education directors. They need new training directors each year due to changes in personnel and the demands of the field. Training and education directors are usually selected from officers in many different occupational fields. They may direct training in their own or another occupational field. This occupation is normally available to officers who have had experience in an occupation besides education.

INTEREST CODE

This occupation generally appeals to people whose primary Interest Code is *Enterprising. Enterprising* jobs:

- Are fast-paced
- Require that you take on a lot of responsibility

Pages 8 and 9 explain the Interest Codes

Profile: Barry Forsythe

As the son of an Infantry Officer, Barry Forsythe grew up wanting to lead infantrymen in the US Army. In preparation for this responsibility, Barry attended the United States Military Academy (USMA) at West Point in New York. As a student at West Point, Barry earned his B.S. in Engineering. Following graduation, he was commissioned as an officer of an infantry division. Barry had continued in his father's footsteps.

Barry's first assignment came in 1970 in Berlin, Germany. As an infantry officer it was his responsibility to ensure his men were prepared for any battle situation, and at the height of the Vietnam conflict this was a real possibility. Barry dedicated himself to providing his men with the best training possible to prepare them for what they might encounter as a soldier in Vietnam or elsewhere. As the division leader, Barry felt a growing interest for what he was doing and the courses he developed were well received by his peers and students.

After three years in Berlin, Barry went to Korea where he furthered his knowledge and experience as an instructor and course developer. Barry knew then that he wanted to commit himself to the training and instruction of soldiers. To further this goal, Barry returned to school at the University of North Carolina where he received an M.S. degree in Social Psychology followed by a Ph.D. in Education. After finishing his class work, Barry returned to West Point as a rotating faculty member. Barry continued to experience the "absolute joy" that came from the opportunity to teach cadets and train them to become leaders in the U.S. Army. As a rotating faculty member, Barry was given the additional responsibility of developing the USMA's core class in Psychology. Every cadet who graduates from West Point takes the class developed by Dr. Forysthe. Barry's commitment to the Psychology program, West Point, and the US Army enabled him to secure a full-time teaching position at the Academy. Dr. Forsythe considers himself lucky to have had the rare opportunity to be one of only 23 full-time professors at the USMA.

In his current position as Vice Dean of the USMA, Barry takes seriously his responsibility to upholding the reputation and traditions of the USMA. Barry now focuses on his passion - curriculum development, as well as program evaluation, library services, and student support. He is driven to ensure West Point remains a "progressive learning environment".

SAMPLE CAREER PATH

Training and Education Administrators   15–18 years

Training and education directors oversee educational programs and administrative functions at military training facilities and service schools, colleges, and academies. They manage the development of curriculum, and they set examination and grading standards. Directors administer activities involving scheduling, discipline, enrollment, and budget matters. They are responsible for briefing senior military and civilian leaders on training or education efforts.

Training and Education Staff Officers   9–11 years

Training and education staff officers establish training objectives and manage the development of coursework, educational project outlines, and lesson plans. They may conduct research to develop new programs. Staff officers also oversee instructor training programs.

Senior Training and Education Officers   4 years

Senior training and education officers coordinate training programs in addition to developing and teaching their own courses. They consult with education and training officers on texts, project training outlines, entrance requirements, and test procedures. They also oversee preparation of coursework and training manuals. Senior instructors advise education and training staff officers on the revision of coursework and standards.

Training and Education Officers

Training and education officers teach personnel in a wide variety of subjects. They organize and prepare instructional materials, training project outlines, and daily and weekly lesson plans. Instructors prepare assignments, laboratory exercises, and demonstrations. They administer and grade examinations and test.

The years shown represent typical time-in-service before advancement to that level. Actual career advancement depends on individual experience and performance.

Media and Public Affairs Occupations

Media and public affairs officers oversee the development, production, and presentation of military information or events for the public. These officers may produce and direct motion pictures, videotapes, and TV and radio broadcasts that are used for training, news, and entertainment. They may also plan, develop, and direct the activities of military bands. Public affairs officers respond to inquiries about military activities and prepare news releases and reports to keep the public informed.

- Audiovisual and Broadcast Directors
- Music Directors
- Public Information Officers
  Profile: Dan Carroll

AUDIOVISUAL AND BROADCAST DIRECTORS

The services produce many motion pictures, videotapes, and TV and radio broadcasts. These productions are used for training, news, and entertainment. Audiovisual and broadcast directors manage audiovisual projects. They may direct day-to-day filming or broadcasting or manage other directors.

What They Do

Audiovisual and broadcast directors in the military perform some or all of the following duties:

- Plan and organize audiovisual projects, including films, videotapes, TV and radio broadcasts
- Determine the staff and equipment needed for productions
- Set production controls and performance standards for audiovisual projects
- Direct the preparation of scripts and determine camera-shooting schedules
- Direct actors and technical staff during performances

Training Provided

Job training consists of 15 to 99 weeks of classroom instruction. Training length varies depending on specialty. Course content typically includes:

- Public information management principles
- Management of military broadcasting facilities
- Motion picture and television production management

Work Environment

Audiovisual and broadcast directors usually work in studios or offices. They may direct film crews on location in military camps or combat zones.

Special Requirements

A 4-year college degree is normally required to enter this occupation.

Helpful Attributes

Helpful fields of study include audiovisual production, cinematography, communications, and graphic arts. Helpful attributes include:

- Interest in organizing and planning activities
- Interest in planning and directing the work of others
- Ability to transform ideas into visual images

Civilian Counterparts

Civilian audiovisual and broadcast directors work for television networks and stations, motion picture companies, public relations and advertising firms, and government agencies. They perform duties similar to those performed by military audiovisual and broadcast directors.

Opportunities

The services have about 1,000 audiovisual and broadcast directors. Each year, they need new directors due to changes in personnel and the demands of the field. After job training, audiovisual and broadcast directors work in production units directing the work of audiovisual technicians and specialists. In time, they may advance to management positions in the broadcasting and public affairs fields.

INTEREST CODE
This occupation generally appeals to people whose primary Interest Code is *Enterprising*. *Enterprising* jobs:

- Are fast-paced
- Require that you take on a lot of responsibility

Pages 8 and 9 explain the Interest Codes

MUSIC DIRECTORS

Bands have a long tradition in the armed services. Military bands all over the world provide music for marching and parade activities, concerts, and stage presentations. Music directors plan, develop, and direct the activities of military bands. They also conduct band performances during concerts and parades.

What They Do

Music directors in the military perform some or all of the following duties:

- Plan musical programs

- Lead bands and choirs in performances

- Supervise training and rehearsal of musicians and choirs

- Determine funding needs for bands and choirs

- Plan purchases of instruments, equipment, and facilities

- Provide commanders with ideas for musical programs and ceremonies

Physical Demands

A "good ear" for musical notes is required.

Special Requirements

A 4-year college degree in music or music education is required to enter this occupation.

Helpful Attributes

Helpful attributes include:

- Interest in music theory

- Appreciation for many types of music, including marches, classics, pop, and jazz

- Interest in planning and organizing the work of others

Work Environment

Music directors usually work in offices and band halls. They may work outdoors when conducting or practicing for parades.

Training Provided

Job training consists of 20 to 40 weeks of classroom instruction. Training length varies depending on specialty. Course content typically includes:

- Band arranging and conducting

- Concert and marching band styles and techniques

- Band administration and management

Civilian Counterparts

Many civilian music directors work for college and high school music departments and civic and community orchestras. Others work in the motion picture, television, and studio recording industries. Civilian music directors perform duties similar to those performed in the military. They may also be called band directors, band leaders, orchestra leaders, or conductors.

Opportunities

The services have about 100 music directors. Each year, they need new directors due to changes in personnel and the demands of the field. After job training, music directors are assigned to military band units, where they plan and direct musical programs. With experience, they may assume command of larger military bands or direct the activities of several bands.

INTEREST CODE

This occupation generally appeals to people whose primary Interest Code is **Enterprising. Enterprising** jobs:

- Are fast-paced

- Require that you take on a lot of responsibility

Pages 8 and 9 explain the Interest Codes

PUBLIC INFORMATION OFFICERS

The services have public information officers to keep the public informed about the military. These officers answer questions from the news media, members of Congress, private citizens, and service personnel. They also prepare reports and news releases about activities on military bases and service policies and operations.

What They Do

Public information officers in the military perform some or all of the following duties:

- Supervise the preparation of reports and other releases to the public and the military

- Brief military personnel before they meet with the public and the news media

- Provide information to newspapers, TV and radio stations, and civic organizations

- Schedule and conduct interviews and news conferences

- Plan activities to improve public relations

Special Requirements

A 4-year college degree is normally required to enter this occupation.

Helpful Attributes

Helpful fields of study include journalism, communications, public relations, and advertising. Helpful attributes include:

- Ability to write clearly and simply

- Ability to speak effectively in public

- Interest in news and current events

Work Environment

Public information officers usually work in offices.

Training Provided

Job training consists of 8 weeks of classroom instruction. Course content typically includes:

- Department of Defense policies

- Principles of public information and community relations

Civilian Counterparts

Civilian public information officers work for large corporations, government agencies, colleges and universities, and community groups. They perform duties similar to those performed by military public information officers. They may also be called public relations representatives and corporate communications specialists.

Opportunities

The services have about 800 public information officers. Each year, they need new public information officers due to changes in personnel and the demands of the field. After job training, public information officers normally direct specialists who gather information for reports, respond to requests for information, and write news releases. With experience, public information officers prepare and give briefings, speeches, and interviews. Eventually, they may advance to senior public affairs positions.

INTEREST CODE

This occupation generally appeals to people whose primary Interest Code is **Enterprising. Enterprising** jobs:

- Are fast-paced
- Require that you take on a lot of responsibility

Pages 8 and 9 explain the Interest Codes

Profile: Dan Carroll

After finishing high school, Dan Carroll held various jobs in construction, and law enforcement to help pay for his education at a small Christian college. When he graduated from college, Dan spent four years working at a textile company in Georgia where he was being groomed for a position in management. At this point in his life, Dan knew that he wanted more than what his management career had to offer. He had four brothers in the Air Force who often spoke about the travel, adventure, and benefits of the military way of life. After speaking with a recruiter about different military opportunities, Dan decided that he really wanted to have the chance to serve his country just as his brothers did.

After completing basic officer training, Dan's first Air Force assignment was at a security police unit in Arkansas where he managed administrative operations. While he was there, he also became a licensed minister providing services in homeless outreach programs and prison ministries.

Dan's next assignment took him overseas to England where he quickly progressed to Chief of Protocol. In this position, he was responsible for ensuring that proper etiquette and procedures were followed for events involving dignitaries, VIPs, and the media. After leaving Europe, Dan went to Langley Air Force Base in Virginia where he trained chiefs of protocol and handled itineraries for visitors such as the first Russian delegation to the United States. At Langley, Dan's other duties included responding to public inquiries about military operations such as Desert Storm and Desert Shield.

After his tour in Virginia, Dan had the unique opportunity to manage a multi-million dollar budget for advertising publicity in Los Angeles. In this position, he put together television ads, arranged guest speakers, and worked with the Hollywood Screen Actors Guild. While in Los Angeles, Dan was also the Chief of Community Relations for the Space and Missile Systems Center where he wrote speeches, and gave information about key space issues to the media. Dan left Los Angeles to be the Director of Protocol for the Air Force Academy where his division handled visits from the President and foreign dignitaries.

Colonel Carroll is currently the Chief of Public Affairs at Andrews Air Force Base in Maryland where he coordinates with the press and media on important issues and events. Of his career, Dan says, "What I like about public affairs more than any other job is that you get to see the big picture and understand the key messages of the Air Force." In his free time, Colonel Carroll continues his ministry work and likes to pursue outdoor activities such as whitewater rafting.

SAMPLE CAREER PATH

Public Information Director   15–18 years

Public information directors oversee the public affairs efforts of a large facility or command. They determine the public and media relations needs of their command. Directors also plan and manage the public information budget and workload. They are responsible for briefing top-level military leaders on public affairs matters.

Public Information Staff Officer   9–11 years

Public information staff officers advise senior-level staff on public affairs issues and capabilities. They oversee public information groups and implement national policies on public access to information.

Senior Public Information Officers   4 years

Senior public information officers lead local public relations or broadcasting units. They coordinate access to military personnel by the news media and produce television segments for local and military-wide use. Senior public information officers also analyze public and internal attitudes and implement programs to improve moral.

Public Information Officers

Public information officers respond to requests for information on the armed forces from the news media, public and military personnel and their families. They provide information on training exercises, military engagements and events taking place at military facilities to interested parties.

The years shown represent typical time-in-service before advancement to that level. Actual career advancement depends on individual experience and performance.

Protective Service Occupations

Protective service officers are responsible for the safety and protection of individuals and property on military bases and vessels. Emergency management officers plan and prepare for all types of natural and man made disasters. They develop warning, control, and evacuation plans to be used in the event of a disaster. Law enforcement and security officers enforce all applicable laws on military bases and investigate crimes when the law has been broken.

- Emergency Management Officers
- Law Enforcement and Security Officers

EMERGENCY MANAGEMENT OFFICERS

Army
Navy
Air Force
Marine Corps
Coast Guard

The military must be prepared for all types of emergencies, from natural disasters, such as floods, earthquakes, and hurricanes, to enemy attacks. Emergency management officers prepare warning, control, and evacuation plans. They also coordinate emergency response teams during natural disasters.

What They Do

Emergency management officers in the military perform some or all of the following duties:

- Organize emergency teams for quick responses to disaster situations

- Research ways to respond to possible disaster situations

- Conduct training programs for specialized disaster response teams

- Develop joint disaster response plans with local, state, and federal agencies

- Obtain supplies, equipment, and protective gear

- Develop warning systems and safe shelters

- Direct disaster control centers

Helpful Attributes

Helpful fields of study include physical and environmental sciences, engineering, law enforcement, and business or public administration. Helpful attributes include:

- Interest in developing detailed plans

- Ability to remain calm in stressful situations

- Ability to express ideas clearly and concisely

Work Environment

Emergency management officers usually work in offices while developing disaster response plans. They work outdoors while inspecting shelters or directing emergency response teams.

Special Requirements

A 4-year college degree is normally required to enter this occupation.

Training Provided

Job training consists of 2 to 9 weeks of classroom instruction. Training length varies depending on specialty. Course content typically includes:

- Disaster planning

- Procedures for nuclear, biological, and chemical decontamination

- Effects of radiation

- Procedures for nuclear accident teams

Civilian Counterparts

Civilian emergency management officers work for federal, state, and local governments, including law enforcement and civil defense agencies. They perform duties similar to those performed by military emergency management officers.

Opportunities

The services have about 800 emergency management officers. Each year they need new emergency management officers due to changes in personnel and the demands of the field. After job training, emergency management officers are assigned to command centers or planning sections, where they develop emergency plans and training programs. In time, they may advance to senior management positions.

INTEREST CODE

This occupation generally appeals to people whose primary Interest Code is *Enterprising*. *Enterprising* jobs:

- Are fast-paced
- Require that you take on a lot of responsibility

Pages 8 and 9 explain the Interest Codes

LAW ENFORCEMENT AND SECURITY OFFICERS

Army
Navy
Air Force
Marine Corps
Coast Guard

The military services have their own police forces to protect lives and property on military bases and to patrol our coastal waters. Law enforcement and security officers command military police units that enforce laws and investigate crimes. They also plan and direct programs to protect property, communications, and classified information.

What They Do

Law enforcement and security officers in the military perform some or all of the following duties:

- Direct the enforcement of military law

- Develop policies and programs to prevent crime and reduce traffic accidents

- Supervise the arrest, custody, transfer, and release of offenders

- Plan and direct criminal investigations and investigations of suspected treason, sabotage, or espionage

- Plan for the security of military bases and office buildings and direct security procedures

- Manage military correctional facilities

- Help in ballistics, forgery, fingerprinting, and polygraph (lie detector) examinations

Special Requirements

A 4-year college degree is normally required to enter this occupation. Some specialties require further education or prior experience in law enforcement and security.

Helpful Attributes

Helpful fields of study include business administration, criminal justice, psychology, sociology, and public administration. Helpful attributes include:

- Interest in law enforcement and crime prevention

- Interest in planning and directing the work of others

Work Environment

Law enforcement and security officers in the military usually work in offices while planning and directing law enforcement and security activities. They may work outdoors while directing investigations, observing prisoners, and inspecting security systems.

Training Provided

Job training consists of 7 to 28 weeks of classroom instruction. Training length varies depending on specialty. Course content typically includes:

- Law enforcement administration

- Management of security problems

- Investigation procedures and reporting

- Military law

Civilian Counterparts

Civilian law enforcement and security officers work in federal, state, and local prisons, intelligence and law enforcement agencies, and private security companies. Some also operate their own security firms or become private detectives. They perform duties similar to those performed in the military. They may also be called police chiefs, chief inspectors, prison wardens, security managers, or chief deputy sheriffs.

Opportunities

The services have about 3,500 law enforcement and security officers. Each year, they need new officers due to changes in personnel and the demands of the field. After job training, officers are assigned to command police, security, or investigative units. Depending on ability and experience, law enforcement and security officers may be assigned to direct one or more large law enforcement units.

INTEREST CODE

This occupation generally appeals to people whose primary Interest Code is *Enterprising. Enterprising* jobs:

- Are fast-paced
- Require that you take on a lot of responsibility

Pages 8 and 9 explain the Interest Codes

Support Service Occupations

Support service officers include personnel who manage food service activities and perform services in support of the morale and well being of military personnel and their families. Food service managers oversee the preparation and delivery of food services within dining facilities located on military installations and vessels. Social workers focus on improving conditions that cause social problems, such as drug and alcohol abuse, racism, and sexism. Chaplains conduct military worship services for military personnel and perform other spiritual duties covering beliefs and practices of all religious faiths.

- Chaplains
- Food Service Managers
- Social Workers

CHAPLAINS

Army
Navy
Air Force

The military provides for the spiritual needs of its personnel by offering religious services, moral guidance, and counseling. Chaplains conduct worship services for military personnel and perform other spiritual duties covering the beliefs and practices of all religious faiths.

What They Do

Chaplains in the military perform some or all of the following duties:

- Conduct worship services in a variety of religious faiths

- Perform religious rites and ceremonies, such as weddings and funeral services

- Visit and provide spiritual guidance to personnel in hospitals and to their families

- Counsel individuals who seek guidance

- Promote attendance at religious services, retreats, and conferences

- Oversee religious education programs, such as Sunday school and youth groups

- Train lay leaders who conduct religious education programs

- Prepare religious speeches and publications

Special Requirements

A master's degree in theology is required to enter this occupation. Ordination and ecclesiastical endorsement from a recognized religious denomination are also required.

Helpful Attributes

Helpful attributes include:

- Ability to express ideas clearly and concisely

- Interest in planning and directing the work of others

- Sensitivity to the needs of others

Work Environment

Chaplains in the military usually work in offices, hospitals, and places of worship. Those assigned to sea duty work aboard ships. Those assigned to land combat units sometimes work outdoors.

Training Provided

Job training consists of 3 to 7 weeks of classroom instruction. Course content typically includes:

- Role and responsibility of military chaplains

- Administration and leadership techniques

- Training and education methods

- Procedures for planning programs

- Pastoral counseling methods

Further training occurs on the job and through advanced courses.

Civilian Counterparts

Civilian chaplains work in places of worship, hospitals, universities, and correctional institutions. They perform duties similar to those performed in the military. However, they are almost always affiliated with a particular religious faith. Chaplains are also called clergy, ministers, preachers, priests, or rabbis.

Opportunities

The services have about 3,500 chaplains of various faiths. Each year, they need new chaplains due to changes in personnel and the demands of the field. Military chaplains may advance to become directors of religious programs in their services.

INTEREST CODE

This occupation generally appeals to people whose primary Interest Code is *Social. Social* jobs:

- involve working with and helping others

- Lets you teach others new skills

Pages 8 and 9 explain the Interest Codes

FOOD SERVICE MANAGERS

The military serves food to hundreds of thousands of service members each day. Meals must be carefully planned and prepared to ensure good nutrition and variety. Food service managers direct the facilities that prepare and serve food.

What They Do

Food service managers in the military perform some or all of the following duties:

- Manage the cooking and serving of food at mess halls

- Direct the operation of officers' dining halls

- Determine staff and equipment needed for dining halls, kitchens, and meat-cutting plants

- Set standards for food storage and preparation

- Estimate food budgets

- Maintain nutritional and sanitary standards at food service facilities

Special Requirements

A 4-year college degree is normally required to enter this occupation.

Helpful Attributes

Helpful fields of study include food service management, nutrition, and business administration. Helpful attributes include:

- Interest in nutrition and food preparation

- Interest in planning and directing the work of others

Work Environment

Food service managers usually work in food service facilities. They may manage facilities in field camps or aboard ships.

Training Provided

Job training consists of 12 to 16 weeks of classroom instruction. Course content typically includes:

- Food service operations and management

- Resource management

- Nutritional meal planning

- Hotel management

Civilian Counterparts

Civilian food service managers work for hotels, restaurants, and cafeterias. They perform duties similar to those performed by military food service managers.

Opportunities

The services have about 500 food service managers. Each year, they need new managers due to changes in personnel and the demands of the field. After job training, food service managers may work independently or under the supervision of other officers. With experience, they may manage one or more large facilities. In time, they may advance to senior management positions.

INTEREST CODE

This occupation generally appeals to people whose primary Interest Code is *Enterprising. Enterprising* jobs:

- Are fast-paced

- Require that you take on a lot of responsibility

Pages 8 and 9 explain the Interest Codes

SOCIAL WORKERS

The military needs close cooperation and a spirit of teamwork among its men and women. Social workers focus on improving conditions that cause social problems, such as drug and alcohol abuse, racism, and sexism.

What They Do

Social workers in the military perform some or all of the following duties:

- Counsel military personnel and their family members

- Supervise counselors and caseworkers

- Survey military personnel to identify problems and plan solutions

- Plan social action programs to rehabilitate personnel with problems

- Plan and monitor equal opportunity programs

- Conduct research on social problems and programs

- Organize community activities on military bases

Physical Demands

Social workers need to be able to speak clearly and distinctly to work with clients.

Special Requirements

A 4-year college degree in social work or related social sciences is required to enter this occupation. Some specialties require a master's degree.

Helpful Attributes

Helpful attributes include:

- Desire to help others

- Sensitivity to the needs of others

- Ability to express ideas clearly and concisely

- Interest in research and teaching

Work Environment

Social workers in the military usually work in offices or clinics.

Training Provided

Job training consists of 16 to 24 weeks of instruction. Course content typically includes:

- Ways of controlling drug and alcohol abuse among military personnel

- Management of equal opportunity programs

Civilian Counterparts

Civilian social workers work for hospitals, human service agencies, and federal, state, county, and city governments. They perform duties similar to those performed by military social workers. However, civilian social workers usually specialize in a particular field, such as family services, child welfare, or medical services. They may also be called social group workers, medical social workers, psychiatric social workers, and social welfare administrators.

Opportunities

The services have about 300 social workers. Each year, they need new social workers due to changes in personnel and the demands of the field. After job training, social workers are assigned to counseling or assistance centers. With experience, they may advance to senior management positions.

INTEREST CODE

This occupation generally appeals to people whose primary Interest Code is *Social. Social* jobs:

- involve working with and helping others

- Lets you teach others new skills

Pages 8 and 9 explain the Interest Codes

Transportation Occupations

Officers in transportation occupations manage and perform activities related to the safe transport of military personnel and material by air, road, rail, and water. Officers normally specialize by mode of transportation or area of expertise since, in many cases, there are licensing and certification requirements. Pilots in the military fly various types of specialized airplanes and helicopters to carry troops and equipment and execute combat missions. Navigators use radar, radio and other navigation equipment to determine their position and plan their route of travel. Officers on ships and submarines work as a team to manage the various departments aboard their vessels. Transportation officers must also direct the maintenance of transportation equipment.

- Air Traffic Control Managers
- Airplane Navigators
- Airplane Pilots
    - *Profile: Lance Hogan*
- Helicopter Pilots
- Ship and Submarine Officers
    - *Profile: James Stoddard*
- Ship Engineers
- Transportation Maintenance Managers
- Transportation Managers
    - *Profile: Douglas Kronchek*

AIR TRAFFIC CONTROL MANAGERS

Air traffic control centers often have several sections giving instructions to military aircraft. One section gives take-off and landing instructions. Another gives ground instructions. A third section tracks planes in flight. Air traffic control managers direct the operations of air traffic control centers.

What They Do

Air traffic control managers in the military perform some or all of the following duties:

- Plan work schedules for air traffic controllers
- Manage air traffic control center operations to ensure safe flights
- Inspect control center facilities and equipment
- Direct tests of radar equipment and controller procedures
- Investigate and solve problems in control center operations
- Control air traffic using radar and radios

Training Provided

Job training consists of 6 to 11 weeks of classroom instruction. Training length varies depending on specialty. Course content typically includes:

- Air traffic control management
- Operational procedures for air traffic control
- Communications and radar procedures
- Aircraft recognition
- Take-off, landing, and ground control procedures

Physical Demands

Air traffic control personnel must pass a demanding physical exam as required by the Federal Aviation Administration.

Work Environment

Air traffic control managers work in air traffic control towers and centers at airfields and aboard ships.

Helpful Attributes

Helpful fields of study include aeronautical engineering, computer science, and liberal arts. Helpful attributes include:

- Interest in work requiring accuracy and attention to detail
- Ability to remain calm in stressful situations
- Decisiveness
- Ability to manage in accordance with strict standards

Special Requirements

A 4-year college degree is normally required to enter this occupation. Certification by the FAA must usually be obtained during military training.

Civilian Counterparts

Civilian air traffic control managers work at commercial airports. They perform duties similar to those performed by military air traffic control managers.

Opportunities

The services have about 1,800 air traffic control managers. Each year, they need new managers due to changes in personnel and the demands of the field. After job training, managers are assigned to air traffic control centers at airfields or aboard ships, where they gain experience in air traffic control management. They may advance to senior management and command positions in the aviation field.

INTEREST CODE

This occupation generally appeals to people whose primary Interest Code is *Enterprising. Enterprising* jobs:

- Are fast-paced
- Require that you take on a lot of responsibility

Pages 8 and 9 explain the Interest Codes

AIRPLANE NAVIGATORS

Navy
Air Force
Marine Corps
Coast Guard

Pilots rely on the precision and skill of the navigator to keep the aircraft on course. Airplane navigators use radar, radio and other navigation equipment to determine position, direction of travel, intended course, and other information about their flights.

What They Do

Airplane navigators in the military perform some or all of the following duties:

- Direct aircraft course using radar, sight, and other navigation methods

- Operate radios and other communication equipment to send and receive messages

- Locate other aircraft using radar equipment

- Operate bombardier systems during bombing runs

- Inspect and test navigation and weapons systems before flights

- Guide tankers and other airplanes during in-flight refueling operations

- Provide pilots with instrument readings, fuel usage, and other flight information

Helpful Attributes

Helpful fields of study include cartography, geography, and surveying. Helpful attributes include:

- Ability to read maps and charts

- Interest in work requiring accuracy and attention to detail

- Ability to respond quickly to emergencies

- Strong desire to fly

Physical Demands

Airplane navigators, like pilots, have a physically and mentally demanding job. Navigators are required to have excellent vision and must be in top physical shape.

Special Requirements

A 4-year college degree is required to enter this occupation. Although there are women airplane navigators, some specialties are open only to men.

Work Environment

Airplane navigators perform their work in aircraft. They may be stationed at airbases or aboard aircraft carriers anywhere around the world.

Training Provided

Job training consists of 6 to 12 months of classroom instruction. Course content typically includes:

- Principles and methods of navigation

- Operation of communication, weapon, and radar systems

- Inspection and testing of navigation equipment and systems

- Combat and bombing navigation procedures and tactics

Practical experience in navigation is gained through training in aircraft simulators and through about 100 hours of actual flying time. Further training occurs on the job and through advanced courses.

Civilian Counterparts

Civilian airplane navigators work for passenger and cargo airlines. With the exception of duties that are combat-related, their duties are similar to those performed by military navigators.

Opportunities

The services have about 6,000 airplane navigators. Each year, they need new navigators due to changes in personnel and the demands of the field. After job training, airplane navigators are assigned to flying sections for duty. They work as officer crewmembers on bombers, tankers, fighters, or other airplanes. In time, they may advance to senior management or command positions.

INTEREST CODE

This occupation generally appeals to people whose primary Interest Code is **Realistic. Realistic** jobs:

- Allow you to work with your hands
- Let you see the results of your work
- Involve using machines, tools, and equipment

Pages 8 and 9 explain the Interest Codes

AIRPLANE PILOTS

The military operates one of the largest fleets of specialized airplanes in the world. Supersonic fighters and bombers fly combat missions. Large transports carry troops and equipment. Intelligence gathering airplanes take photographs from high altitudes. Military airplane pilots fly the thousands of jet and propeller airplanes operated by the services.

What They Do

Airplane pilots in the military perform some or all of the following duties:

- Check weather reports to learn about flying conditions

- Develop flight plans showing air routes and schedules

- Contact air traffic controllers to obtain take-off and landing instructions

- Fly airplanes by controlling engines, rudders, elevators, and other controls

- Monitor gauges and dials located on cockpit control panels

- Perform combat maneuvers, take photographs, transport equipment, and patrol areas to carry out flight missions

Physical Demands

Airplane pilots must pass the most demanding physical test of any job in the military. To be accepted for pilot training, applicants must have 20/20 vision and be in top physical condition. They must have very good eye-hand coordination and have extremely quick reaction times to maneuver at high speeds.

Special Requirements

A 4-year college degree is normally required to enter this occupation. Although the military has many women pilots, some specialties involving duty in combat airplanes are open only to men.

Work Environment

Airplane pilots may be stationed at airbases or aboard aircraft carriers anywhere in the world. They fly in all types of weather conditions. Military pilots take off and land on airport runways and aircraft carrier landing decks.

Training Provided

Pilot training is a 2-year program covering 1 year each in initial and advanced training. Initial training includes time spent in flight simulators, classroom training, officer training, and basic flight training. Course content typically includes:

- Aircraft aerodynamics

- Jet and propeller engine operation

- Operation of aircraft navigation systems

- Foul weather flying

- Federal Aviation Administration (FAA) regulations

This is among the most challenging training given by the services; not everyone who attempts this training can meet the strict requirements for completion. Advanced training begins when pilots successfully complete initial training and are awarded their "wings." Advanced training consists of instruction in flying a particular type of aircraft.

Helpful Attributes

Helpful fields of study include physics and aerospace, electrical, or mechanical engineering. Helpful attributes include:

- Strong desire to fly airplanes

- Self-confidence and ability to remain calm in stressful situations

- Determination to complete a very demanding training program

Civilian Counterparts

Civilian airplane pilots who work for passenger airlines and air cargo businesses are called commercial pilots. Other civilian pilots work as flight instructors at local airports, as crop dusters, or as pilots transporting business executives in company planes. Many commercial pilots began their career in the military.

Opportunities

The services have about 16,000 airplane pilots. Each year, they need new pilots due to changes in personnel and the demands of the field. After initial and advanced training, most pilots are assigned to flying squadrons to fly the types of aircraft for which they were trained. In time, pilots train for different aircraft and missions. Eventually, they may advance to senior management or command positions.

INTEREST CODE

This occupation generally appeals to people whose primary Interest Code is *Realistic*. *Realistic* jobs:

- Allow you to work with your hands
- Let you see the results of your work
- Involve using machines, tools, and equipment

Pages 8 and 9 explain the Interest Codes

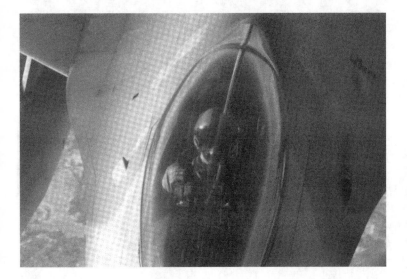

Profile: Lance Hogan

Lieutenant Colonel Lance Hogan knew he wanted to be a fighter pilot from the time he was young. Hearing the stories of his two uncles who had flown fighter planes in World War II and seeing the Thunderbirds flight demonstration team sparked his interest. Lance worked his way through college in Louisiana. When he received his degree, he joined the Air Force.

Lance was first in his flight training class. He chose to specialize in the A-7 Corsair II attack fighter, flying as the on-scene commander for search and rescue operations. His first assignment was to one of the original Flying Tiger squadrons.

Lance really enjoyed the demanding search and rescue missions. He practiced ground attack and coordinating artillery, naval gunfire, air strikes, and other resources required to rescue air crews shot down in enemy territory. During this tour he was promoted to captain.

After a year of special staff training in Washington, DC, Lance went back to flying, this time in the F-4 Phantom II. Lance served a 1-year tour at Taegu Airbase in Korea. As the squadron scheduling officer, he managed all flight training requirements for the squadron. During this tour, he was promoted to major.

His duties at Taegu prepared him for his next assignment at MacDill Air Force Base (AFB), FL. Here, Lance taught pilots who had just earned their wings air-to-ground combat tactics. He also learned to fly the new F-16 fighter and became one of the first instructor pilots for this aircraft.

At MacDill, Lance was selected for very special duty. He and his family moved to Nellis AFB, NV. In an unusual tour, Lance flew 4-1/2 years with the elite Thunderbirds flight demonstration team. Normally, pilots who are selected to join the Thunderbirds stay only 2 years. Lance toured Europe, South America, and almost all 50 states, including Alaska and Hawaii.

Now with Air Force staff at Langley AFB, VA, Lance coordinates all activities of Air Force tactical demonstration aircraft and squadrons worldwide. In his off-duty time, he is completing a master's degree in aerospace science. "I like my job now," he says, "but I am looking forward to flying again." He hopes to command a squadron sometime in the near future.

SAMPLE CAREER PATH

Command Pilot   15–18 years

Command pilots lead a squadron, flight operations group, or command an air facility. They direct flight operations of a major flying unit and advise headquarters commanders on squadron operations. They continue to fly missions to maintain expert flying skills.

Flight Leader   9–11 years

Flight leaders command several airplanes on flying missions, such as air strikes, patrols, or transporting cargo. They manage combat missions, planning target selections and personnel utilization as well as a squadron department, such as maintenance, training, or safety. They also instruct pilots in squadron missions and tactics and evaluate pilots' flying, leadership, and management skills.

Senior Pilot   4 years

Senior pilots plan and fly operational missions, fly as first pilot in large airplanes, and lead flights of two or more aircraft on missions. They also instruct new pilots and explain mission plans and assignments to flight crews.

Pilot

Pilots plan flights, considering weather, fuel, and aircraft loading. They also participate in planning missions and tactics. They may fly missions alone, as part of a group of airplanes, or as copilot in a large airplane.

The years shown represent typical time-in-service before advancement to that level. Actual career advancement depends on individual experience and performance.

HELICOPTER PILOTS

Helicopters can take off from and land on small areas. They can also hover in one spot in the air. The military uses these versatile aircraft to transport troops and cargo, perform search and rescue missions, and provide close combat support for ground troops. Helicopter pilots fly the many helicopters operated by the services.

What They Do

Helicopter pilots in the military perform some or all of the following duties:

- Prepare flight plans showing air routes and schedules

- Fly helicopters by controlling engines, flight controls, and other systems

- Monitor gauges and dials located on cockpit control panels

- Perform combat maneuvers, spot and observe enemy positions, transport troops and equipment, and evacuate wounded troops

- Check weather reports to learn about flying conditions

Physical Demands

Helicopter pilots must pass some of the most demanding physical tests of any job in the military. To be accepted for pilot training, applicants must have excellent vision and be in top physical condition. They must have very good eye-hand-foot coordination and have quick reflexes.

Training Provided

Job training consists of 1 to 2 years of academic and flight instruction. Flight training consists of at least 80 hours of flying time. Training length varies depending on specialty. Course content typically includes:

- Principles of helicopter operation

- Principles of helicopter inspection

- Flying techniques and emergency procedures

- Combat skills and tactics

Special Requirements

A 4-year college degree is normally required to enter this occupation. Some specialties in the Army do not require a 4-year college degree, but are only open to personnel who have been in the service for several years and who are selected for a special pilot training program. Although there are women helicopter pilots, some specialties are open only to men.

Helpful Attributes

Helpful fields of study include physics and aerospace, electrical, or mechanical engineering. Helpful attributes include:

- Strong desire to fly aircraft

- Determination to complete a very demanding training program

- Self-confidence and ability to remain calm under stress

Work Environment

Helicopter pilots are stationed at military bases or aboard aircraft carriers around the world. They fly in all types of weather conditions. Helicopter pilots take off and land from airports, forward landing areas, and ship landing decks.

Civilian Counterparts

Civilian helicopter pilots work for police forces, local commuter services, and private businesses. They also work as crop dusters, fire fighters, traffic spotters, and helicopter flight instructors.

Opportunities

The military has about 6,500 helicopter pilots. The services need new pilots each year due to changes in personnel and the demands of the field. After receiving their pilot rating, helicopter pilots are assigned to flying units. With experience, they may become group leaders or flight instructors. Helicopter pilots may advance to senior management and command positions.

INTEREST CODE

This occupation generally appeals to people whose primary Interest Code is *Realistic*. *Realistic* jobs:

- Allow you to work with your hands
- Let you see the results of your work
- Involve using machines, tools, and equipment

Pages 8 and 9 explain the Interest Codes

SHIP AND SUBMARINE OFFICERS

Ships and submarines are organized by departments, such as engineering, communications, weapons, and supply. Ship and submarine officers work as team members to manage the various departments aboard their vessels.

What They Do

Ship and submarine officers in the military perform some or all of the following duties:

- Command vessels of all sizes at sea or in coastal waters
- Plan and manage the operating departments, under the captain's direction
- Plan and manage training exercises, such as target practice, aircraft operations, damage control drills, and searches for enemy submarines
- Evaluate subordinate personnel and recommend awards and promotions
- Direct search and rescue missions

Special Requirements

A 4-year college degree is normally required to enter this occupation. Although there are women ship officers, some assignments, such as submarine duty, are open only to men.

Helpful Attributes

Helpful fields of study include engineering, oceanography, mathematics, and computer science. Helpful attributes include:

- Ability to organize and direct the work of others
- Interest in sailing and being at sea

Work Environment

Ship and submarine officers work aboard their vessels. Engineering officers are subjected to hot, humid, and noisy environments. Submarine officers work in confined spaces for extended periods.

Physical Demands

Good vision and normal color vision are required for reading color-coded charts and maps.

Training Provided

Job training consists of classroom instruction and practical experience in one of the following departments: air, weapons, operations, communications, engineering, deck, administration, or supply. Training length varies depending on specialty. Course content typically includes:

- Management and organization of ship or submarine operations
- Piloting and navigation of ships
- Interpretation of maritime laws and policies

Further training occurs on the job and through advanced courses.

Civilian Counterparts

Civilian ship officers work for private maritime passenger, freight, and tanker firms. With the exception of duties that are combat related, their duties are similar to those performed by military ship officers. They may also be called ship captains, ship mates, or deck officers.

Opportunities

The services have about 6,000 ship and submarine officers. Each year, they need officers due to changes in personnel and the demands of the field. After job training, officers are assigned to management positions in one of the ship's departments. With experience and demonstrated ability to lead, they assume greater responsibility. Depending on their specialty, ship and submarine officers gain experience in more than one department. Also, they are regularly reassigned to different ships or submarines where they meet and work with new people. Between sea tours, they work and attend training at shore bases. Eventually, ship and submarine officers may be selected to command a vessel.

INTEREST CODE

This occupation generally appeals to people whose primary Interest Code is *Enterprising. Enterprising* jobs:

- Are fast-paced
- Require that you take on a lot of responsibility

Pages 8 and 9 explain the Interest Codes

Profile: James Stoddard

From the time James (Jim) Stoddard was in high school in New York City, he wanted to be a Navy submarine officer, and then he qualified for the Naval Academy. "I felt the discipline at the academy would help me get the most out of my education." Adapting well to academy life, he graduated near the top of his class with a degree in Naval Architecture.

After submarine school in Groton, Connecticut, he went on his first submarine to the Western Pacific. Here, he felt the first thrill of command responsibility as an Officer of the Deck. On watch, he directed the "sailing" and safe operations of his submarine. "The Officer of the Deck is completely trusted by the submarine's captain," Jim says, "I was representing the captain and in charge of the vessel and her crew."

Jim worked hard and advanced rapidly. As a Lieutenant, he was assigned to graduate studies at the Massachusetts Institute of Technology and the Woods Hole Oceanographic Institution. He went on to nuclear power school and tours in several nuclear-powered ballistic missile submarines.

Jim served tours in all the major departments of a submarine. He mastered engineering, weapons, and operations. As he gained experience, he became a master tactician and assisted the Captains of the submarines on which he served. They used their knowledge of the underwater environment to keep their submarine hidden while carrying out missions assigned to their vessel. He was decorated several times for submarine operations and leadership.

During his career Jim and his wife have enjoyed a unique part of Navy life, and a special commitment to each other. Whenever possible, she joined him at the ports his submarines would visit. They spent time together in Australia, England, Germany, and many ports elsewhere in the world.

Today he is the Captain of a nuclear attack submarine. Jim says he has most enjoyed the responsibility of each assignment. "And," he adds, "I have really seen the world."

SAMPLE CAREER PATH

Ship Captain   15–18 years

Ship or submarine captains command the operations of a ship or submarine and its crew. They implement orders by planning exercises and maneuvers to carry out missions. Captains direct daily operations and plan tactics. As part of a naval staff, they direct the planning of fleet operations exercises.

Executive/Staff Officer   9–11 years

Executive/Staff officers are second in command on a ship or submarine. They issue orders and instructions to assist the ship's captain and command the vessel in the captain's absence. They also manage administrative and maintenance activities.

Department Head   4 years

Department heads manage major functional areas on a ship such as engineering, navigation/operations, or combat systems. They plan and coordinate the department's activities and conduct drills to evaluate the department's performance in emergency or combat situations. They also train new officers in seamanship and leadership.

Division Officer

Ship and submarine officers usually begin their careers as division officers on vessels. They command a division of 10 to 50 Sailors, stand watches in a variety of functional areas, and plan work schedules.

The years shown represent typical time-in-service before advancement to that level. Actual career advancement depends on individual experience and performance.

SHIP ENGINEERS

Engines are a ship's main source of power for propulsion, heat, and electricity. Ship engines are massive; some are as large as the power plants that generate electricity for small cities. Ship engineers direct the engineering departments aboard ships and submarines. They are responsible for engine operations, maintenance, and repair. They are also responsible for shipboard heating and power generation.

What They Do

Ship engineers in the military perform some or all of the following duties:

- Direct engine room operations in nuclear or diesel-powered vessels

- Direct crews that inspect and maintain the electrical generators that supply power for lights, weapons, and equipment

- Direct crews that inspect and maintain the heating plants and air conditioning systems

- Direct crews that inspect and maintain ship transmission and propulsion systems

- Direct engine room repairs

Special Requirements

A 4-year college degree is normally required to enter this occupation. Nuclear specialties require a 4-year college degree in nuclear engineering.

Helpful Attributes

Helpful fields of study include civil, mechanical, and electrical engineering. Helpful attributes include:

- Interest in planning and directing the work of others

- Interest in engines and machines

Training Provided

Job training consists of 3 to 12 months of instruction. Training length varies depending on specialty; the time required for nuclear specialties is the longest. Course content typically includes:

- Inspection and maintenance of marine engines, electrical systems, and fuel systems

- Operation and maintenance of power plants and related machinery

Further training occurs on the job and through advanced courses. Nuclear specialties involve extensive training in reactor operations.

Work Environment

Ship engineers work in engine rooms, where the noise levels and temperatures may be high.

Civilian Counterparts

Civilian ship engineers work for shipping lines, transport companies, and some government agencies. They perform duties similar to those performed by military ship engineers. Civilian ship engineers may also be called engine room supervisors, deck engineers or marine engineers.

Opportunities

The services have about 3,000 ship engineers. Each year, they need new ship engineers due to changes in personnel and the demands of the field. After job training, ship engineers work as assistant engineers under the direction of a chief engineer. With experience, they may advance to become chief engineer in charge of an engineering department. Eventually, they may advance to senior management and command positions.

INTEREST CODE

This occupation generally appeals to people whose primary Interest Code is *Enterprising. Enterprising* jobs:

- Are fast-paced

- Require that you take on a lot of responsibility

Pages 8 and 9 explain the Interest Codes

TRANSPORTATION MAINTENANCE MANAGERS

The military's transportation system is made up of many different kinds of carriers, including ships, aircraft, trucks, and buses. Repair and maintenance schedules for each type of vehicle must be carefully planned and managed. Transportation maintenance managers direct personnel who repair and maintain the military's transportation equipment.

What They Do

Transportation maintenance managers in the military perform some or all of the following duties:

- Direct repair shop and garage operations

- Set work schedules for repair shop staff

- Oversee the ordering and use of repair parts, equipment, and supplies

- Check repairs to make sure they are complete and finished on schedule

- Oversee the preparation of maintenance records and reports

- Develop maintenance standards and policies

- Plan and develop training programs for staff

Special Requirements

A 4-year college degree is normally required to enter this occupation.

Helpful Attributes

Helpful fields of study include business administration, transportation management, vehicle and maintenance operations, and mechanical engineering. Helpful attributes include:

- Interest in planning and directing the work of others

- Interest in developing detailed plans

Training Provided

Job training consists of 16 to 22 weeks of classroom instruction. Course content typically includes:

- Management of aircraft or aircraft electronics (avionics) maintenance

- Management of vehicle, railroad, and other equipment maintenance

- Use of management information systems

Work Environment

Transportation maintenance managers work in offices located in maintenance yards, shops, and garages.

Civilian Counterparts

Civilian transportation maintenance managers work in auto, bus, truck, and heavy construction equipment repair garages. They also work for aircraft service companies, aircraft builders, and commercial airline companies. They perform duties similar to those performed by military transportation maintenance managers. They may also be called maintenance superintendents.

Opportunities

The services have close to 5,000 transportation maintenance managers. Each year, they need new maintenance managers due to changes in personnel and the demands of the field. After job training, transportation maintenance managers gain experience managing maintenance personnel. In time, they may become managers of larger maintenance facilities and advance to command positions.

INTEREST CODE

This occupation generally appeals to people whose primary Interest Code is **Enterprising. Enterprising** jobs:

- Are fast-paced

- Require that you take on a lot of responsibility

Pages 8 and 9 explain the Interest Codes

TRANSPORTATION MANAGERS

Each year, the military transports thousands of service men and women and tons of material to bases across the U.S. and overseas. Ships, aircraft, trucks, buses, vans, and trains are all part of the military's transportation system. Transportation managers direct the transport of military personnel and material by air, road, rail, and water.

What They Do

Transportation managers in the military perform some or all of the following duties:

- Determine the fastest and most economical way to transport cargo or personnel

- Direct the packing and crating of cargo

- Direct the loading of freight and passengers

- Schedule shipments to ensure fast and timely deliveries

- Schedule pick-up and delivery of shipments

- Coordinate transfer of cargo between different modes of transportation (rail, air, water, etc.)

- Coordinate with commercials shippers and host country transportation services

- Oversee the handling of special items, such as medicine and explosives

- See that transport forms, records, and reports are prepared correctly

Helpful Attributes

Helpful fields of study include transportation management, supply management, operations research, logistics, and business or public administration. Helpful attributes include:

- Interest in planning and directing the work of others

- Ability to work under tight schedules

Special Requirements

A 4-year college degree is normally required to enter this occupation.

Training Provided

Job training consists of between 8 and 12 weeks of classroom instruction. Training length varies depending on specialty. Course content typically includes:

- Transportation management

- Ways to work with civilian and other military service carriers

- Freight classifications

- Applicable military policies and Federal/local laws

- Handling of special items, such as medicine and explosives

Civilian Counterparts

Civilian transportation managers work for airlines, railroads, bus lines, trucking companies, and shipping firms. They perform duties similar to those performed by military transportation managers. However, civilian transportation managers normally specialize in one area of transportation, such as air, water, truck, or railroad transportation.

Work Environment

Transportation managers work in cargo and passenger terminals and depots.

Opportunities

The services have about 4,000 transportation managers. Each year, they need new managers due to changes in personnel and the demands of the field. After job training, transportation managers gain experience on the job. In time, they may advance to senior management or command positions in cargo transportation operations.

INTEREST CODE

This occupation generally appeals to people whose primary Interest Code is **Enterprising. Enterprising** jobs:

- Are fast-paced
- Require that you take on a lot of responsibility

Pages 8 and 9 explain the Interest Codes

Profile: Douglas Kronchek

Douglas (Doug) Kronchek went to work on an automobile assembly line right after high school. Knowing he would probably be drafted, he chose the Army and enlisted. Doug did so well in aircraft maintenance training, he was encouraged to apply for Officer Candidate School where he earned his commission. He chose the transportation corps because he wanted to stay close to aircraft and maintenance.

Doug spent his first tour in Vietnam, leading a platoon in aircraft maintenance. After that tour he held several more responsible positions in the United States.

At the end of his obligated service, Doug went back to civilian life and attended school full-time on the GI Bill. After 2 years, the Army offered him the chance to return to active duty. He and his wife thought it over. Remembering the variety and challenge of Army life, they decided to return.

Doug spent a year in Vietnam, then a long tour in Okinawa where his family joined him. He then returned to the States where he completed his bachelor's degree with full funding from the Army and the GI Bill, and his master's degree in transportation management with partial funding from the Army.

A high point in his career was a 2-year tour as the Army port and air terminal expert with the Navy. Doug arranged the transportation to move people and supplies to and from the U.S. scientific research stations in Antarctica. He says, "I worked with private and government transportation agencies and officials from the United States, Australia, and New Zealand."

Doug has spent the past several years at the Pentagon in Washington, DC, as chief logistician for the Pacific. He is the expert on all Army transportation and supply activity in the Pacific.

Just selected for his next assignment, Colonel Doug Kronchek will assume command of an Army transportation movement control center. "It's going to be fun," he says. "It's a new challenge in a new area for me. My command will control movement of Army personnel, equipment, and supplies through the transportation network to destinations around the world."

SAMPLE CAREER PATH

Transportation Director — 15–18 years

Transportation Directors command transportation operations or direct operations at a transportation center. These commands can range from truck or boat transportation battalions to air transportation terminals. Transportation Directors also advise senior base and area commanders on transportation matters. They also direct inspection and repair programs for the transportation activities they command.

Transportation Staff Officer — 9–11 years

Senior transportation officers coordinate with other military services to transport supplies from air, sea, or land bases to troops in the field. They also develop long-range plans for use of transportation equipment and personnel. They evaluate new transportation procedures and equipment for military applicability. Transportation Officers advise combat and operational commanders on transportation matters. They also teach transportation courses

Senior Transportation Officer — 4 years

Senior transportation officers inspect transportation, maintenance, or operations facilities. They also command companies of trucks or other transportation vehicles. They plan missions and operations to support base and field operations. Senior transportation officers also evaluate the performance of junior transportation officers and senior enlisted personnel.

Transportation Officer

Transportation officers are assigned to truck, air, boat, port (harbor), or terminal units. They direct enlisted personnel in operating and maintaining transportation equipment, and schedule equipment use. They also personnel assignments and train them in transportation procedures. Transportation officers are responsible for preparing reports showing the use and costs of operations.

The years shown represent typical time-in-service before advancement to that level. Actual career advancement depends on individual experience and performance.

Glossary

Active Duty – Continuous duty on a daily basis. Comparable to "full-time" as used in reference to a civilian job.

Allowances – Money, other than basic pay, to compensate in certain specified situations for expenses such as meals, rent, clothing, and travel. Also, compensation is given for maintaining proficiency in specific skill areas such as flying or parachuting.

Artillery – Large cannons or missile launchers used in combat.

ASVAB – Armed Services Vocational Aptitude Battery. A test that provides students with academic and vocational aptitude scores to assist them in career exploration and decision-making. ASVAB scores are used by the military services to determine enlistment eligibility and to assign occupational specialties.

Base – A locality or installation on which a military force relies for supplies or from where it initiates operations.

Basic Pay – The amount of pay a military member receives, as determined by pay grade and length of service. Basic pay does not include other benefits such as allowances and bonuses.

Basic Training – A rigorous orientation to the military, lasting from six to ten weeks, which provides a transition from civilian to military life.

Civilian – Anyone not on active duty in the military.

Commissary – A store on a military base that sells groceries and other items at a substantial discount to military personnel.

Commissioned Officer – A member of the military holding the rank of second lieutenant or ensign or above. This role in the military is similar to that of a manager or executive.

DEP – Delayed Entry Program. A military program that allows an applicant to delay entry into active duty for up to one year, for such things as finishing school, etc.

Drill – To train or exercise in military operations.

Duty – Assigned task or occupation.

Enlisted Member – Military personnel below the rank of warrant or commissioned officers. This role is similar to that of a company employee or supervisor.

Enlistee – A service member, not a warrant or commissioned officer, who has been accepted by the military and has taken the Oath of Enlistment.

Enlistment Agreement/Enlistment Contract – A legal contract between the military and an enlistment applicant, which contains information such as enlistment date, term of enlistment, and other options such as a training program guarantee or a cash bonus.

GI Bill Benefits – A program of education benefits for individuals entering the military. This program enables service persons to set aside money to be used later for educational purposes.

Inactive Reserve Duty – Affiliation with the military in a non-training, non-paying status after completing minimum obligation of active duty service.

Infantry – Units of men trained, armed, and equipped to fight on foot.

Job Specialty – A specific job or occupation in one of the five services.

MEPS – Military Entrance Processing Stations, which are located around the country. The enlistment process occurs at each of these stations.

NCO – Non-commissioned Officer. An enlisted member in pay grades E-4 or higher.

Obligation – The period of time one agrees to serve on active duty, in the reserve, or a combination of both .

OCS – Officer Candidate School. Program for college graduates with no prior military training who wish to become military officers. Also, qualified enlisted members who wish to become officers may attend OCS. After successful completion, candidates are commissioned as military officers.

OTS (OTG) – Officer Training School (Group). See OCS, Officer Candidate School.

Officer – See commissioned officer.

Pay Grade – A level of employment, as designated by the military. There are 9 enlisted pay grades and 10 officer pay grades through which personnel can progress during their career. Pay grade and length of service determine a service member's pay.

Quarters – Living accommodations or housing.

Recruit – See enlistee.

Regular Military Compensation – Total value of basic pay, allowances, and tax savings, which represents the amount of pay a civilian worker would need to earn to receive the same take home "pay" as a service member.

Reserves – The Reserves are those people in the military who are not presently on full-time, active duty. In a national emergency, reservists can be called up immediately to serve on active duty because they are highly trained by the services and drill regularly. During peacetime, they perform functions in support of the active duty forces in our country's defense, such as installation and repair of communications equipment. Reservists are also entitled to some of the employment benefits available to active military personnel.

ROTC – Reserve Officers' Training Corps. Training given to undergraduate college students who plan to become military officers. Often they receive scholarships for tuition, books, fees, uniforms, and a monthly allowance.

Service Classifier – A military information specialist who helps applicants select a military occupational field.

Service Obligation – The amount of time an enlisted member agrees to serve in the military, as stated in the enlistment agreement.

Station – A place of assigned duty.

Tour of Duty – A period of obligated service. Also used to describe a type of duty tour, such as a "Mediterranean tour."

Indexes

Title Index

This index is an alphabetical listing of occupational titles that represent military occupations described in *Military Careers*. The page number listed next to each title indicates where the occupation is described. The titles in capital letters and bold print are the main titles of the 140 military occupations described in the book. The remainder of the titles are alternate names for these occupations or specialties within them. The alternate titles were drawn from several sources including: (1) *Standard Occupational Classification* (SOC) occupations, (2) *Dictionary of Occupational Titles* occupations; (3) titles found in civilian career information resources,

such as the *Occupational Outlook Handbook* and computerized career information delivery systems (CIDS); and (4) commonly used job titles.

This index is useful if you know the name of an occupation and want to find out whether it is available in the military. For any title listed in the index, you can read the description of what the occupation is like in the military by turning to the page number listed next to it. If you do not find the exact title you are interested in, try to find a similar title under which the same occupation might be listed.

M

N

O

Interest Code Index

This index lists the 140 military occupations described in this publication sorted by interest code (Realistic, Investigative, Artistic, Social, Enterprising, and Conventional). Within each interest code group, the occupations are sorted alphabetically. If you have taken an interest inventory, you may use your results to search for military occupations that may interest you. To find out more about interest codes, refer to pages 4 and 9 of this book.

- **Realistic:** Activities that allow you to work with your hand and involve using machines, tools, and equipment.

- **Investigative:** Activities that involve learning about a ne subject area or allow you to use your knowledge to sol problems or create things or ideas.

- **Artistic:** Activities that allow you to write, paint, play a mus cal instrument, or use your imagination to do original wor

- **Social:** Activities that allow you to use your skills to intera effectively with others and involve working with and helpin others.

- **Enterprising:** Activities that allow you to take a leadershi role or speak in front of groups, such as those that requi that you take on a lot of responsibility.

- **Conventional:** Activities that allow you to use organizationa clerical, and arithmetic skills and require attention to deta or accuracy.

REALISTIC

INVESTIGATIVE

ARTISTIC

SOCIAL

ENTERPRISING

CONVENTIONAL

SOC Code Index (by Occupation)

This index lists civilian counterparts to the 140 military occupations described in this book. The organization of this index is similar to the organization of the military occupations in the Table of Contents. Enlisted occupations are listed first, followed by officer occupations. Below each military occupation, the counterpart civilian occupations are listed according to their *Standard Occupational Classification* (SOC) codes.

The SOC Code Index is useful when you want to find civilian counterparts to the military occupations described in this guide. Knowledge of how military training and employment relates to civilian employment may be helpful in career planning. SOC codes may also be used to help locate additional information in other resources about civilian occupations.

ENGINEERING, SCIENCE, AND TECHNICAL OCCUPATIONS

HEALTH CARE OCCUPATIONS

Military Officer Occupations

COMBAT SPECIALTY OCCUPATIONS

ENGINEERING, SCIENCE, AND TECHNICAL OCCUPATIONS

DOT Code Index (by Occupation)

This index lists civilian counterparts to the 140 military occupations described in this book. The organization of this index is similar to the organization of the military occupations in the Table of Contents. Enlisted occupations are listed first, followed by officer occupations. Below each military occupation, the counterpart civilian occupations are listed according to their *Dictionary of Occupational Titles* (DOT) codes.

The DOT Code Index is useful when you want to find civilian counterparts to the military occupations described in this guide. Knowledge of how military training and employment relates to civilian employment may be helpful in career planning. DOT codes may also be used to help locate additional information in other publications about any civilian counterpart occupation (for example, the *Dictionary of Occupational Titles* and *Occupational Outlook Handbook*).

Military Enlisted Occupations

ADMINISTRATIVE OCCUPATIONS

ADMINISTRATIVE SUPPORT SPECIALISTS 56

129.107-026	PASTORAL ASSISTANT
201.362-010	LEGAL SECRETARY
201.362-030	SECRETARY
203.362-010	CLERK-TYPIST
209.362-026	PERSONNEL CLERK
209.562-010	CLERK, GENERAL
219.362-010	ADMINISTRATIVE CLERK

FINANCE AND ACCOUNTING SPECIALISTS 58

209.362-026	PERSONNEL CLERK
210.382-010	AUDIT CLERK
210.382-014	BOOKKEEPER
215.137-014	SUPERVISOR, PAYROLL
215.382-014	PAYROLL CLERK
216.382-062	STATISTICAL CLERK
216.482-010	ACCOUNTING CLERK
219.362-010	ADMINISTRATIVE CLERK
222.387-062	STOREKEEPER
290.477-014	SALES CLERK

FLIGHT OPERATIONS SPECIALISTS 59

215.362-010	CREW SCHEDULER
248.387-010	FLIGHT OPERATIONS SPECIALIST
921.683-050	INDUSTRIAL-TRUCK OPERATOR

LEGAL SPECIALISTS AND COURT REPORTERS 60

119.267-026	PARALEGAL
201.362-010	LEGAL SECRETARY
202.362-010	SHORTHAND REPORTER
219.362-010	ADMINISTRATIVE CLERK

PREVENTIVE MAINTENANCE ANALYSTS 61

213.362-010	COMPUTER OPERATOR
213.382-010	COMPUTER PERIPHERAL EQUIPMENT OPERATOR
221.362-010	AIRCRAFT-LOG CLERK
221.367-038	MAINTENANCE DATA ANALYST
221.367-066	SCHEDULER, MAINTENANCE

SALES AND STOCK SPECIALISTS 62

222.387-058	STOCK CLERK
290.477-014	SALES CLERK

COMBAT SPECIALTY OCCUPATIONS

ARMORED ASSAULT VEHICLE CREW MEMBERS 66

378.363-010	ARMOR RECONNAISSANCE SPECIALIST
378.367-030	RECONNAISSANCE CREWMEMBER
378.683-010	AMPHIBIAN CREWMEMBER
378.683-014	POWERED BRIDGE SPECIALIST

ARTILLERY AND MISSILE CREW MEMBERS 68

222.137-018	MAGAZINE SUPERVISOR
378.367-010	ARTILLERY OR NAVAL GUNFIRE OBSERVER
378.367-014	FIELD ARTILLERY OPERATIONS SPECIALIST
378.682-010	REDEYE GUNNER
378.684-018	FIELD ARTILLERY CREWMEMBER
378.684-030	LIGHT AIR DEFENSE ARTILLERY CREWMEMBER
632.261-018	ORDNANCE ARTIFICER

INFANTRY 70

199.384-010	DECONTAMINATOR
378.363-010	ARMOR RECONNAISSANCE SPECIALIST
378.367-030	RECONNAISSANCE CREWMEMBER
378.464-010	ANTITANK ASSAULT GUNNER
378.684-014	COMBAT RIFLE CREWMEMBER
378.684-022	INFANTRY INDIRECT FIRE CREWMEMBER
378.684-026	INFANTRY WEAPONS CREWMEMBER

SPECIAL FORCES 72

378.367-030	RECONNAISSANCE CREWMEMBER
378.464-010	ANTITANK ASSAULT GUNNER
378.684-014	COMBAT RIFLE CREWMEMBER
379.384-010	SCUBA DIVER
899.261-010	DIVER

CONSTRUCTION OCCUPATIONS

BUILDING ELECTRICIANS 76

824.261-010	ELECTRICIAN

193.262-034	RADIOTELEPHONE OPERATOR
193.362-014	RADIO-INTELLIGENCE OPERATOR
203.582-018	CRYPTOGRAPHIC-MACHINE OPERATOR
203.582-050	TELEGRAPHIC-TYPEWRITER OPERATOR
213.362-010	COMPUTER OPERATOR
235.662-010	COMMAND AND CONTROL SPECIALIST
822.261-022	STATION INSTALLER-AND-REPAIRER
822.281-010	AUTOMATIC-EQUIPMENT TECHNICIAN
822.281-018	MAINTENANCE MECHANIC, TELEPHONE
823.261-018	RADIO MECHANIC
823.261-026	AVIONICS TECHNICIAN
828.261-022	ELECTRONICS MECHANIC

030.162-010	COMPUTER PROGRAMMER
030.167-014	SYSTEMS ANALYST
031.132-010	SUPERVISOR, NETWORK CONTROL OPERATORS
031.262-014	NETWORK CONTROL OPERATOR
032.132-010	USER SUPPORT ANALYST SUPERVISOR
032.262-010	USER SUPPORT ANALYST
039.162-014	DATA BASE DESIGN ANALYST
039.264-010	MICROCOMPUTER SUPPORT SPECIALIST
193.362-014	RADIO-INTELLIGENCE OPERATOR
203.582-054	DATA ENTRY CLERK
213.362-010	COMPUTER OPERATOR
213.382-010	COMPUTER PERIPHERAL EQUIPMENT OPERATOR
235.662-010	COMMAND AND CONTROL SPECIALIST
828.261-022	ELECTRONICS MECHANIC

079.367-018	MEDICAL-SERVICE TECHNICIAN
143.062-022	CAMERA OPERATOR
143.062-030	PHOTOGRAPHER, STILL
168.264-014	SAFETY INSPECTOR
168.267-062	INVESTIGATOR
379.384-010	SCUBA DIVER
806.264-010	HULL INSPECTOR
806.381-046	SHIPFITTER
899.261-010	DIVER

029.261-014	POLLUTION-CONTROL TECHNICIAN
079.161-010	INDUSTRIAL HYGIENIST
168.267-042	FOOD AND DRUG INSPECTOR
168.267-086	HAZARDOUS WASTE MANAGEMENT SPECIALIST
199.167-010	RADIATION MONITOR
389.684-010	EXTERMINATOR

018.261-022	MOSAICIST
029.167-010	AERIAL-PHOTOGRAPH INTERPRETER
059.267-010	INTELLIGENCE SPECIALIST
059.267-014	INTELLIGENCE SPECIALIST
193.362-014	RADIO-INTELLIGENCE OPERATOR
193.382-010	ELECTRONIC INTELLIGENCE OPERATIONS SPECIALIST
199.267-014	CRYPTANALYST
203.582-018	CRYPTOGRAPHIC-MACHINE OPERATOR

213.362-010	COMPUTER OPERATOR
249.387-014	INTELLIGENCE CLERK
375.167-042	SPECIAL AGENT
378.267-010	COUNTERINTELLIGENCE AGENT
378.382-010	AIRBORNE SENSOR SPECIALIST
378.382-018	UNATTENDED-GROUND-SENSOR SPECIALIST

025.062-010	METEOROLOGIST
025.267-014	WEATHER OBSERVER

011.261-018	NONDESTRUCTIVE TESTER
199.361-010	RADIOGRAPHER
819.281-018	WELD INSPECTOR

222.367-038	MAGAZINE KEEPER
632.261-010	AIRCRAFT-ARMAMENT MECHANIC
632.261-014	FIRE-CONTROL MECHANIC
632.261-018	ORDNANCE ARTIFICER
828.261-022	ELECTRONICS MECHANIC

193.382-010	ELECTRONIC INTELLIGENCE OPERATIONS SPECIALIST
196.167-014	NAVIGATOR
235.662-010	COMMAND AND CONTROL SPECIALIST
823.261-026	AVIONICS TECHNICIAN
828.261-022	ELECTRONICS MECHANIC

828.261-022	ELECTRONICS MECHANIC

005.281-010	DRAFTER, CIVIL
018.167-034	SURVEYOR ASSISTANT, INSTRUMENTS
018.167-046	SURVEYOR, MARINE
018.261-010	DRAFTER, CARTOGRAPHIC
018.261-022	MOSAICIST
018.261-026	PHOTOGRAMMETRIST
029.167-010	AERIAL-PHOTOGRAPH INTERPRETER

193.382-010	ELECTRONIC INTELLIGENCE OPERATIONS SPECIALIST

HEALTH CARE OCCUPATIONS

078.362-022	ELECTROENCEPHALOGRAPHIC TECHNOLOGIST
078.362-030	CARDIOPULMONARY TECHNOLOGIST
079.374-010	EMERGENCY MEDICAL TECHNICIAN

620.381-014	MECHANIC, ENDLESS TRACK VEHICLE
625.281-010	DIESEL MECHANIC
638.261-030	MACHINE REPAIRER, MAINTENANCE
638.281-010	FIRE-FIGHTING-EQUIPMENT SPECIALIST
638.281-014	MAINTENANCE MECHANIC
807.381-010	AUTOMOBILE-BODY REPAIRER
825.281-022	ELECTRICIAN, AUTOMOBILE

HEATING AND COOLING MECHANICS 186

620.281-010	AIR-CONDITIONING MECHANIC
623.281-034	MAINTENANCE MECHANIC, ENGINE
637.261-014	HEATING-AND-AIR-CONDITIONING INSTALLER-SERVICER
637.261-026	REFRIGERATION MECHANIC
862.381-030	PLUMBER

MARINE ENGINE MECHANICS 188

197.130-010	MARINE ENGINEER
620.261-022	CONSTRUCTION EQUIPMENT MECHANIC
623.271-034	MAINTENANCE MECHANIC, ENGINE
623.281-026	MACHINIST, MARINE ENGINE
623.281-034	MAINTENANCE MECHANIC, ENGINE
623.281-038	MOTORBOAT MECHANIC
625.281-010	DIESEL MECHANIC
625.281-018	ENGINE REPAIRER, SERVICE
631.261-014	POWERHOUSE MECHANIC
950.382-026	STATIONARY ENGINEER

POWERHOUSE MECHANICS 190

625.281-026	GAS-ENGINE REPAIRER
631.261-014	POWERHOUSE MECHANIC
639.281-010	AVIATION SUPPORT EQUIPMENT REPAIRER
805.361-010	BOILER HOUSE MECHANIC
824.261-010	ELECTRICIAN
825.281-014	ELECTRICIAN
950.382-010	BOILER OPERATOR

Military Officer Occupations

COMBAT SPECIALTY OCCUPATIONS

ARMORED ASSAULT VEHICLE OFFICERS 234

| None | None |

ARTILLERY AND MISSILE OFFICERS 236

019.061-022	ORDNANCE ENGINEER
189.167-038	SUPERINTENDENT, AMMUNITION STORAGE
632.131-010	ARTILLERY-MAINTENANCE SUPERVISOR
806.261-038	INSPECTOR, MISSILE
828.161-010	SUPERVISOR, ELECTRONICS SYSTEMS MAINTENANCE

COMBAT MISSION SUPPORT OFFICERS 238

| 184.117-050 | MANAGER, OPERATIONS |

INFANTRY OFFICERS 240

| 378.137-010 | INFANTRY UNIT LEADER |

SPECIAL FORCES OFFICERS 242

196.263-014	AIRPLANE PILOT, COMMERCIAL
196.263-038	HELICOPTER PILOT
375.167-030	LAUNCH COMMANDER, HARBOR POLICE

ENGINEERING, SCIENCE, AND TECHNICAL OCCUPATIONS

AEROSPACE ENGINEERS 245

002.061-010	AERODYNAMICIST
002.061-014	AERONAUTICAL ENGINEER
002.061-018	AERONAUTICAL TEST ENGINEER
002.061-026	AERONAUTICAL-RESEARCH ENGINEER
007.061-014	MECHANICAL ENGINEER
019.167-014	PROJECT ENGINEER

CIVIL ENGINEERS 246

003.167-018	ELECTRICAL ENGINEER, POWER SYSTEM
005.061-014	CIVIL ENGINEER
182.167-026	SUPERINTENDENT, CONSTRUCTION
184.161-014	SUPERINTENDENT, WATER-AND-SEWER SYSTEMS
188.117-030	COMMISSIONER, PUBLIC WORKS

COMMUNICATIONS MANAGERS 248

184.117-082	SUPERINTENDENT, COMMUNICATIONS
184.167-062	MANAGER, COMMUNICATIONS STATION
184.167-230	SUPERVISOR OF COMMUNICATIONS
193.167-018	SUPERINTENDENT, RADIO COMMUNICATIONS
193.262-022	RADIO OFFICER
822.131-010	CENTRAL-OFFICE-REPAIRER SUPERVISOR
823.131-010	COMMUNICATIONS ELECTRICIAN SUPERVISOR
823.131-018	SUPERVISOR, AVIONICS SHOP
828.161-010	SUPERVISOR, ELECTRONICS SYSTEMS MAINTENANCE

COMPUTER SYSTEMS OFFICERS 250

030.167-010	CHIEF, COMPUTER PROGRAMMER
030.167-014	SYSTEMS ANALYST
033.162-014	DATA RECOVERY PLANNER
033.167-010	COMPUTER SYSTEMS HARDWARE ANALYST
169.167-030	MANAGER, DATA PROCESSING
213.132-010	SUPERVISOR, COMPUTER OPERATIONS

ELECTRICAL AND ELECTRONICS ENGINEERS 251

003.061-030	ELECTRONICS ENGINEER
003.061-034	ELECTRONICS-DESIGN ENGINEER
710.131-014	SUPERVISOR, INSTRUMENT MAINTENANCE
823.131-010	COMMUNICATIONS ELECTRICIAN SUPERVISOR
828.161-010	SUPERVISOR, ELECTRONICS SYSTEMS MAINTENANCE

ENVIRONMENTAL HEALTH AND SAFETY OFFICERS 252

005.061-030	SANITARY ENGINEER
012.061-014	SAFETY ENGINEER
012.167-034	INDUSTRIAL-HEALTH ENGINEER
012.167-054	QUALITY CONTROL ENGINEER
015.021-010	HEALTH PHYSICIST
019.061-010	BIOMEDICAL ENGINEER

EXECUTIVE, ADMINISTRATIVE, AND MANAGERIAL OCCUPATIONS

DOT Code Index (by DOT Number)

This index lists civilian counterparts to the 140 military occupations described in this book. The civilian occupations listed here are in numerical order by their *Dictionary of Occupational Titles* (DOT) codes. The DOT, published by the U.S. Department of Labor, defines and classifies over 12,000 civilian occupations found in the U.S. labor force.

The page number listed for each DOT code and title indicates the location of that military occupational description in the Military Occupations section. This index is useful when you know a DOT code and want to find out whether it has a military counterpart. The index is also useful as a general reference list of civilian occupations that have military counterparts described in the Military Occupations section.

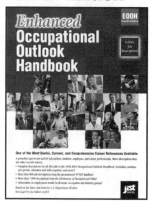

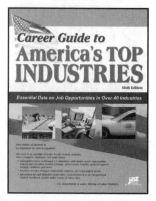

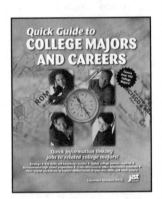

Federal Resume Guidebook, Third Edition

Kathryn Kraemer Troutman

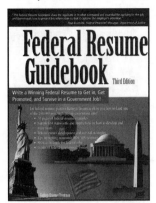

Step-by-step guidance and samples for creating a resume specifically for applying for jobs with the federal government in a format that federal personnel specialists actually prefer.

Writing federal resumes and applying for U.S. government jobs require vastly different approaches than those used to land private-sector jobs. This book provides insider information; paper and electronic resume examples; sample Knowledge, Skills, and Abilities (KSA) statements; and job hunting tips.

ISBN 1-56370-925-2 / Order Code LP-J9252 **$21.95**

Guide to America's Federal Jobs, Second Edition

Compiled from Various Federal Resources by JIST Editors

Each year, about 300,000 jobs open up with America's largest employer: the federal government. But finding out about these jobs is not a simple process. With thousands of job openings spread over hundreds of federal agencies, departments, and locations, there are opportunities for nearly every person in all major occupations.

Navigate vacancy announcements and application requirements, Internet sources of job leads, descriptions of major agencies and departments, current information about salaries and benefits, and guidelines for creating a federal resume.

ISBN 1-56370-526-5 / Order Code LP-J5265 / **$18.95**

FBI Careers

Thomas H. Ackerman

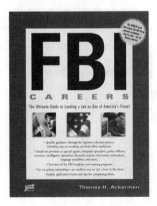

No other book gives so much specific information about what it takes to land a job with the FBI. For example, most books focus on special agent jobs, yet more than half of the FBI's workforce is made up of support personnel from chemists to fingerprint specialists to foreign language specialists.

Get step-by-step advice for getting through the complicated application process, exactly what to expect in the testing and interviewing phases, details on numerous positions, an overview of the FBI Academy and training programs, and tips on getting student internships.

ISBN 1-56370-890-6 / Order Code LP-J8906 / **$18.95**

Best Career and Education Web Sites,
Fourth Edition
Rachel Singer Gordon and Anne Wolfinger

This book lists and reviews the 340 best sites on the Internet for information on careers, college, training, and job search. Explore career alternatives; find thousands of job openings across North America—and the world; put your online resume into the hands of hiring managers; prepare for interviews by researching potential employers; explore a career in the military, or transition from the military to a civilian career; choose the right college, technical school, or other training program, and apply online; find out about financial aid options; and much more.

ISBN 1-56370-960-0 / Order Code LP-J9600 / **$12.95**

Getting the Job You Really Want, Fourth Edition
Michael Farr

The most widely used workbook on self-directed career planning and job search at schools, colleges, and employment programs in North America!

Offers new information on using the Internet and other technology effectively in the job search. Lots of interactive worksheets and commonsense advice guide readers step-by-step through the process of getting the job they really want.

The techniques presented have helped millions of people find better jobs in less time.

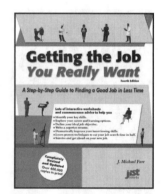

ISBN 1-56370-803-5 / Order Code LP-J8035 / **$12.95**

Your Career and Life Plan Portfolio, Second Edition
Editors at JIST

This new edition takes you through the process of self-assessment, education and career planning, and portfolio development. The pullout pages help you explore and document your skills and values; review and organize your accomplishments, experiences, and abilities; set a career direction; and much more.

ISBN 1-56370-907-4 / Order Code LP-J9074 / **$9.95**

JIST Ordering Information

JIST specializes in publishing the very best results-oriented career and self-directed job search material. Since 1981 we have been a leading publisher in career assessment devices, books, videos, and software. We continue to strive to make our materials the best there are, so that people can stay abreast of what's happening in the labor market, and so they can clarify and articulate their skills and experiences for themselves as well as for prospective employers. **Our products are widely available through your local bookstores, wholesalers, and distributors.**

The World Wide Web

For more occupational or book information, get online and see our Web site at **www.jist.com**. Advance information about new products, services, and training events is continually updated.

Quantity Discounts Available!

Quantity discounts are available for businesses, schools, and other organizations.

The JIST Guarantee

We want you to be happy with everything you buy from JIST. If you aren't satisfied with a product, return it to us within 30 days of purchase along with the reason for the return. Please include a copy of the packing list or invoice to guarantee quick credit to your order.

How to Order

For your convenience, the last page of this book contains an order form.

Consumer Order Line:
Call toll free 1-800-648-JIST.
Please have your credit card (VISA, MC, or AMEX) information ready!

Mail your order to:
JIST Publishing, Inc.
8902 Otis Avenue
Indianapolis, IN 46216-1033

Fax your order:
Toll free 1-800-JIST-FAX

Order online:
www.jist.com

JIST Order and Catalog Request Form

Purchase Order #: _____ (Required by some organizations)

Billing Information

Organization Name: _____
Accounting Contact: _____
Street Address: _____
_____
_____

City, State, ZIP: _____
Phone Number: ( ) _____

Phone: 1-800-648-JIST
Fax: 1-800-JIST-FAX
World Wide Web Address:
www.jist.com

Shipping Information with Street Address (If Different from Above)

Organization Name: _____
Contact: _____
Street Address: (We *cannot* ship to P.O. boxes) _____
_____

City, State, ZIP: _____
Phone Number: ( ) _____

Credit Card Purchases:
VISA____ MC____ AMEX____
Card Number: _____
Exp. Date: _____
Name As on Card: _____
Signature: _____

Quantity	Order Code	Product Title	Unit Price	Total
	——	**Free JIST Catalog**	**Free**	——

jist Publishing
8902 Otis Avenue
Indianapolis, IN 46216

Shipping Fees

In the continental U.S. add 7% of subtotal:
- Minimum amount charged = $5.00
- FREE shipping on any prepaid orders over $50.00

Above pricing is for regular ground shipment only. For rush or special delivery, call JIST Customer Service at 1-800-648-JIST for the correct shipping fee.

Outside the continental U.S. call JIST Customer Service at 1-800-648-JIST for an estimate of these fees.

Payment in U.S. funds only!

Subtotal	
+Shipping (See left)	
+6% Sales Tax Indiana Residents	
TOTAL	

JIST thanks you for your ord